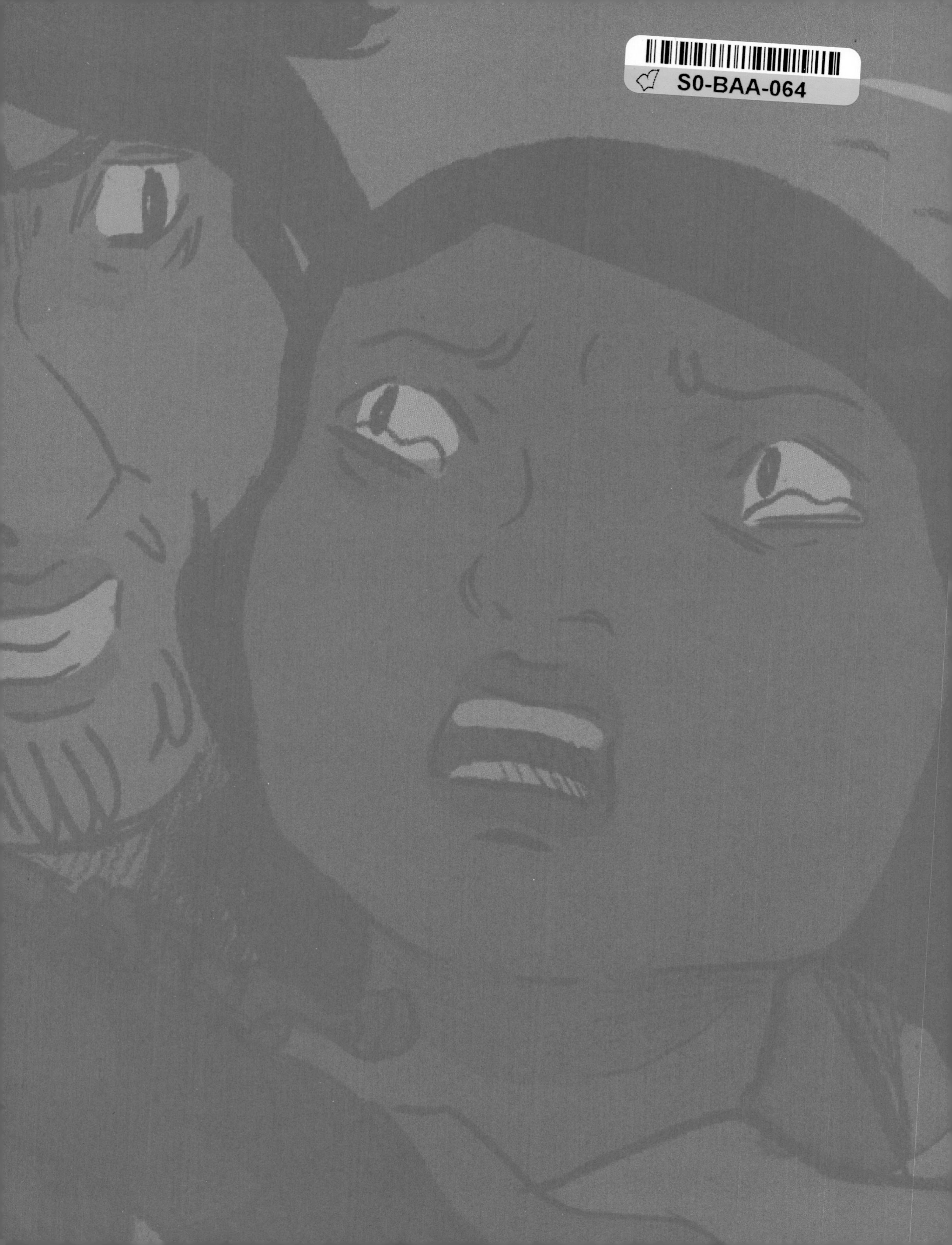

Phoolan Devi
REBEL QUEEN

This book was inspired by the autobiographical book *Moi, Phoolan Devi, reine des bandits* by Phoolan Devi and Marie-Thérèse Cuny with the collaboration of Paul Rambali
© Editions Fixot, 1996 and Editions Robert Laffont, S.A., 2013.
(U.S. edition: *I, Phoolan Devi*; Little Brown and Company, 1996).
ISBN 978-1-68112-251-9
© 2018 Casterman
© 2020 NBM for the English translation
Library of Congress Control Number: 2019958016
Translation by Montana Kane
Lettering by Ortho
First Publication April 2020
Printed in Turkey

This graphic novel is also available as an e-book

Claire Fauvel

Phoolan Devi

Rebel Queen

nbm
GRAPHIC NOVELS

Who is Phoolan Devi?

This is the incredible story of a poor, low caste girl turned bandit, and then a bandit turned Member of Parliament. Before talking about her, I must first tell you about my father. He's not a bandit; his thing is music and writing. He has never been produced or published, and yet he writes great stuff, like *Bandits, Con Artists and Terrorists*. In that book, he makes a chronological list of all the famous outlaws in history, from Robin Hood to Mesrine, from Billy the Kid to Bonnie and Clyde and Germany's Red Army Faction. And that is how a few years ago I came to discover, tucked in between two mythical bandits, one Phoolan Devi. She's Indian and her story has the power of a tale that is both terrible and modern, in which a vengeful princess battles a bunch of horrible demons.

Later, I found out that the princess, who's not actually a princess, wrote an autobiography titled *I, Phoolan Devi* (U.S. edition: Little Brown and Company). "Wrote" is not the right word; "dictated" is more appropriate, for the young woman was illiterate, and it was thanks to the diligence and hard work of her publisher that her words were put to paper for the first time. Over the course of more than four hundred pages, she tells of the contempt and humiliation she was forced to endure ever since she was a child, which led her down the path of revolt. The book is like a kick to the stomach out of which you don't emerge unscathed. That is the tale I wanted to recreate in the graphic novel format, without trying to distinguish truth from fiction and reality from myth, and without claiming to provide a historical testimony. I simply used her own words, because they are of unparalleled sincerity, at times horribly violent and at other times imbued with the naiveté of childhood. Her life cannot be reduced to the umpteenth tale of a woman who was raped and takes up arms to exact revenge on her aggressors; above all else, Phoolan was a little girl endowed with an innate sense of justice who wouldn't accept to be humiliated and exploited in the name of tradition.

She went from being a virtual slave to a rebel, a pariah, and ultimately a bandit. Her transformation wasn't unique, but in keeping with a historical tradition associated with the region she grew up in. In the Chambal Valley of northern India, stories glamorizing the feats of the dacoits, Indian bandits that both terrified and fascinated the population, have been passed down for generations. The extreme poverty of the rural communities is what gave birth to the dacoits. The region's geographical location, at the crossroads of three states, made it easy for them to avoid lawsuits by simply changing jurisdictions. Lastly, the ravines, rocky formation that recall the Grand Canyon in the U.S., provided the perfect terrain in which to hide out.

Phoolan was the spiritual descendant of a great number of outlaws that came before her, such as Rani Lakshmi Bai, a heroine of India's First War of Independence, who, in the second half of the 19th century, headed up an army of ten thousand men to fight the English; or Paan Singh Tomar, the prizewinning athlete from the 50s who went underground when the Indian government refused to give him back land that had been stolen from him. There is no shortage of tales starring bloodthirsty killers or modern-day Robin Hoods in the region, and yet Phoolan Devi's story stands apart. Was it because of her feisty, generous nature and her young age that all of India took a passionate interest in her life and that the poor and the disenfranchised adopted her as a sister? Or was it because more than anything else, her life story is a reflection of the tragic condition of women and of the lower castes in today's India? For we can't avoid talking about those castes. Indeed, it is difficult to tell the story of Phoolan Devi's life without addressing the conflict between the Mallahs and the Thakurs, a constant reality that pursued her throughout her life.

Hinduism's founding texts divide Indian society into four categories: at the very top of the social ladder are the Brahmins (priests), followed by the Kshatriyas (warriors) and the Vaishyas (merchants); at the bottom of the pyramid come the Shudras (servants). These four main groups are then subdivided into more than a thousand different communities. Lastly, the untouchables, or Dalits, are excluded from the system and doomed to the lowest, filthiest occupations. Indian law theoretically prohibits any discrimination based on caste, but in the reality of day-to-day life, inequalities persist. Phooloan belongs to the Mallah community, meaning farmers and fishermen (the Shudra caste), some of whom work for Thakurs (of the Kshatriya caste), who sometimes use the advantage of their higher social rank to exploit them.

The fight Phoolan wages in this book is therefore two-pronged: it is both against the religious system of the castes, and against the power of the patriarchy that still dictates the terms of men-women rapport in rural India.

Phoolan Devi's story is about all of that and more. Like Durga, her favorite goddess, Phoolan embodies strength, courage and tenacity. In turn naïve and violent, she is India itself, in all its contradictions and excess. In short, the woman you are about to meet is a rebel—a genuine rebel, the real deal… enjoy the ride!

Claire F.

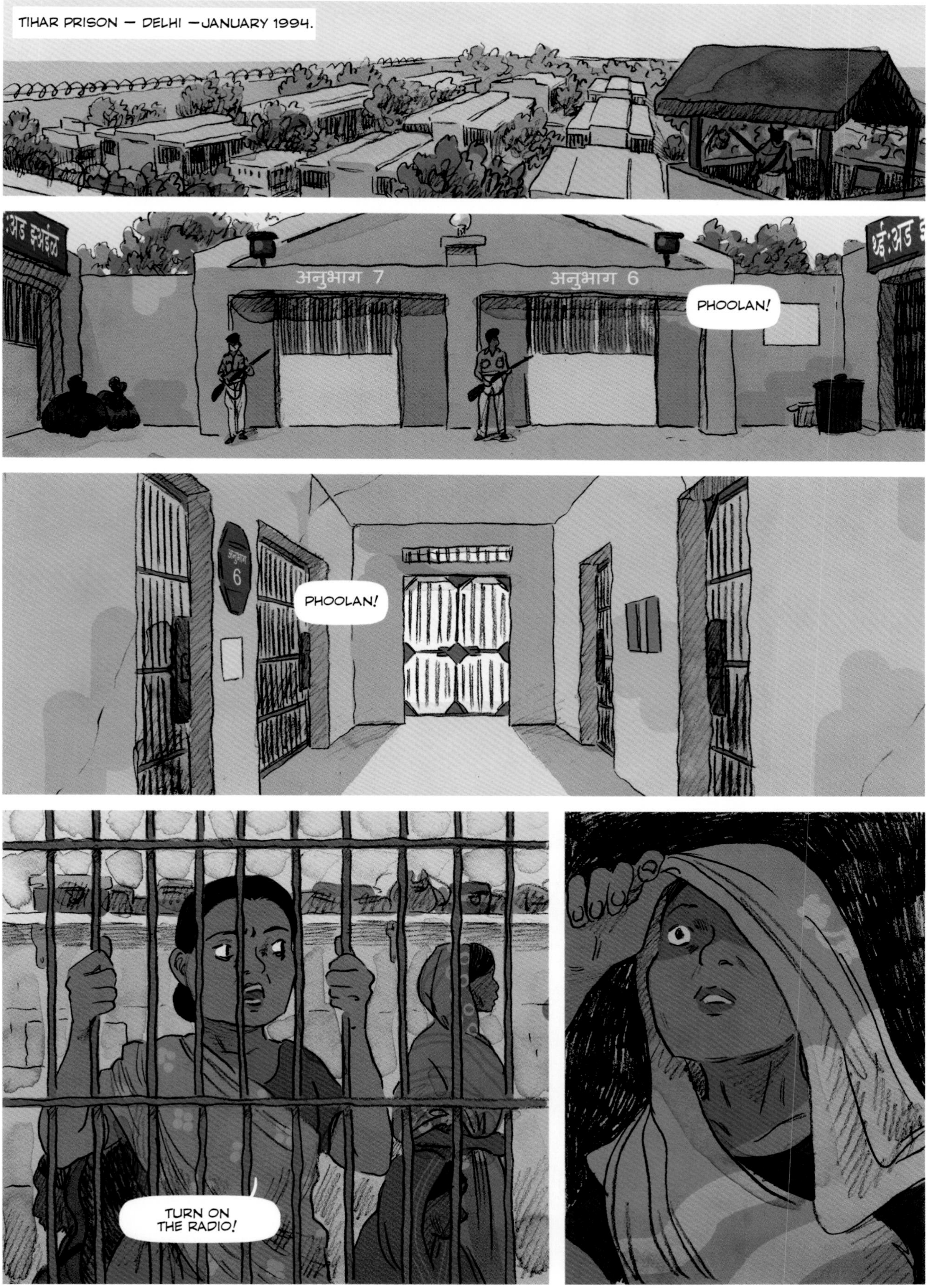
TIHAR PRISON — DELHI —JANUARY 1994.
अनुभाग 7
अनुभाग 6
PHOOLAN!
अनुभाग 6
PHOOLAN!
TURN ON THE RADIO!

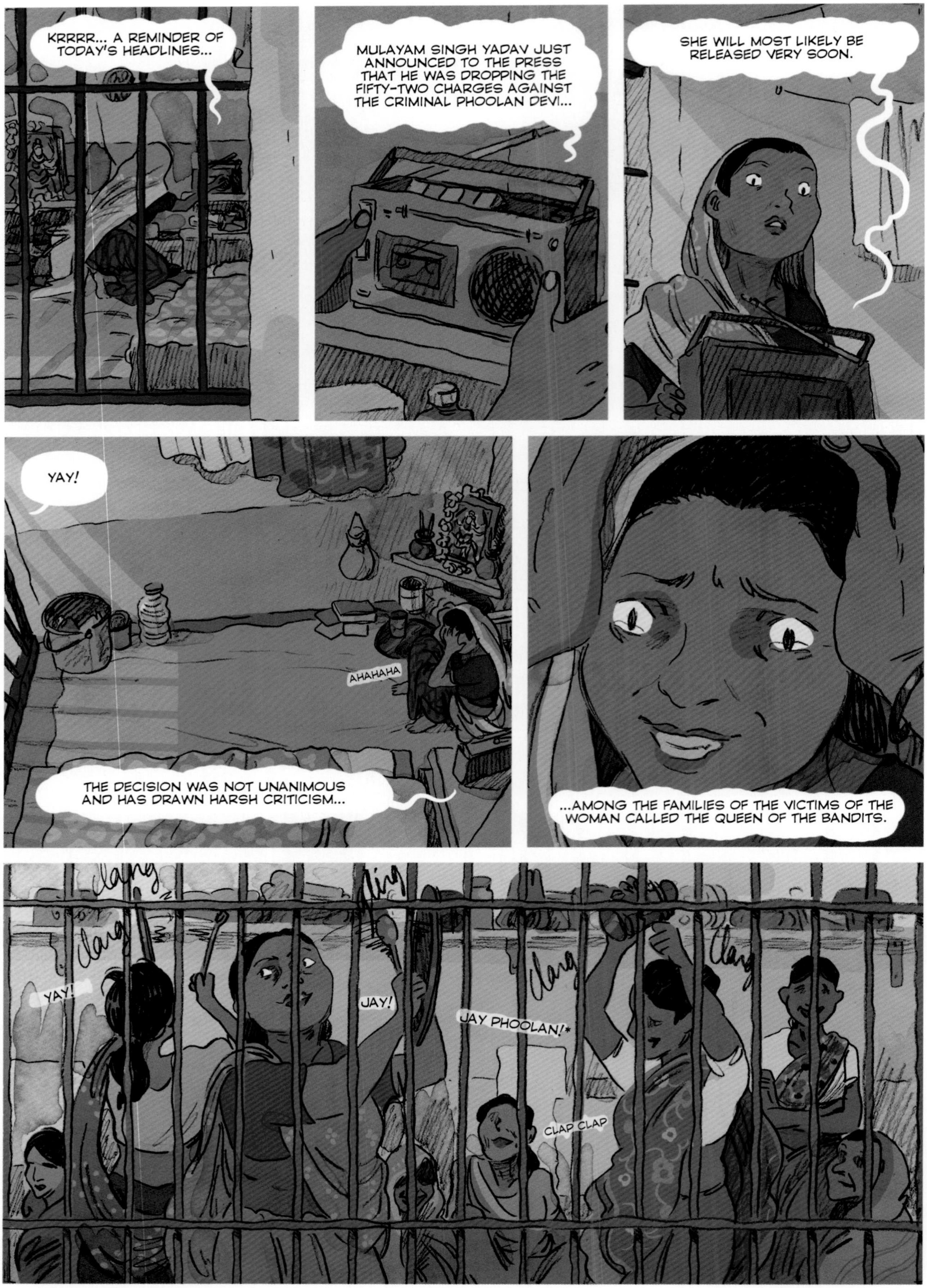
KRRRR... A REMINDER OF TODAY'S HEADLINES...
MULAYAM SINGH YADAV JUST ANNOUNCED TO THE PRESS THAT HE WAS DROPPING THE FIFTY-TWO CHARGES AGAINST THE CRIMINAL PHOOLAN DEVI...
SHE WILL MOST LIKELY BE RELEASED VERY SOON.
YAY!
AHAHAHA
THE DECISION WAS NOT UNANIMOUS AND HAS DRAWN HARSH CRITICISM...
...AMONG THE FAMILIES OF THE VICTIMS OF THE WOMAN CALLED THE QUEEN OF THE BANDITS.
clang
ding
clang
YAY!
JAY!
JAY PHOOLAN!*
clang
clang
CLAP CLAP

*VICTORY, GLORY TO PHOOLAN.

THE NEXT DAY.

NAMASTE,* PHOOLAN.

I'M SURE YOU'VE ALREADY HEARD, BUT I WANTED TO TELL YOU IN PERSON.

THE UTTAR PRADESH HAS DROPPED ALL CHARGES AGAINST YOU. YOU'LL BE FREE, SOON!

THANK YOU, MRS. BEDI.

"FREE." I ALLOWED THAT WORD TO ENTER MY MIND FOR THE FIRST TIME IN YEARS.

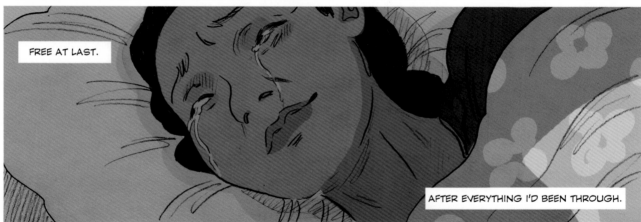
FREE AT LAST.

AFTER EVERYTHING I'D BEEN THROUGH.

*GOOD DAY.

TWENTY YEARS EARLIER — GURHA KA PURWA — UTTAR PRADESH.

I WAS AROUND NINE. NOBODY KNEW MY EXACT DATE OF BIRTH.

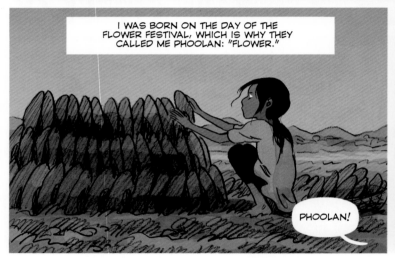

I WAS BORN ON THE DAY OF THE FLOWER FESTIVAL, WHICH IS WHY THEY CALLED ME PHOOLAN: "FLOWER."

PHOOLAN!

HURRY, IT'S DINNER TIME!

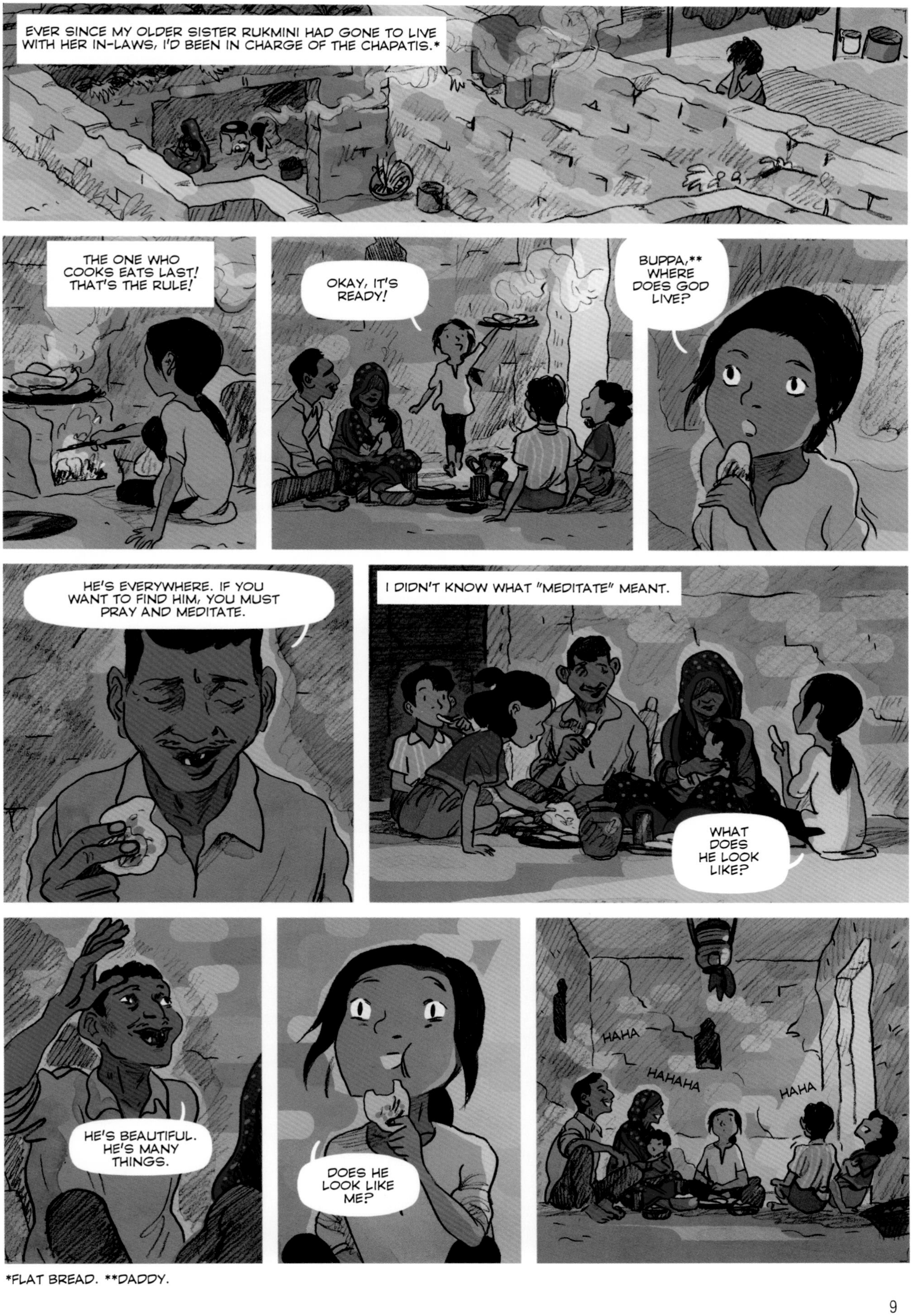
EVER SINCE MY OLDER SISTER RUKMINI HAD GONE TO LIVE WITH HER IN-LAWS, I'D BEEN IN CHARGE OF THE CHAPATIS.*
THE ONE WHO COOKS EATS LAST! THAT'S THE RULE!
OKAY, IT'S READY!
BUPPA,** WHERE DOES GOD LIVE?
HE'S EVERYWHERE. IF YOU WANT TO FIND HIM, YOU MUST PRAY AND MEDITATE.
I DIDN'T KNOW WHAT "MEDITATE" MEANT.
WHAT DOES HE LOOK LIKE?
HE'S BEAUTIFUL. HE'S MANY THINGS.
DOES HE LOOK LIKE ME?
HAHA
HAHAHA
HAHA

*FLAT BREAD. **DADDY.

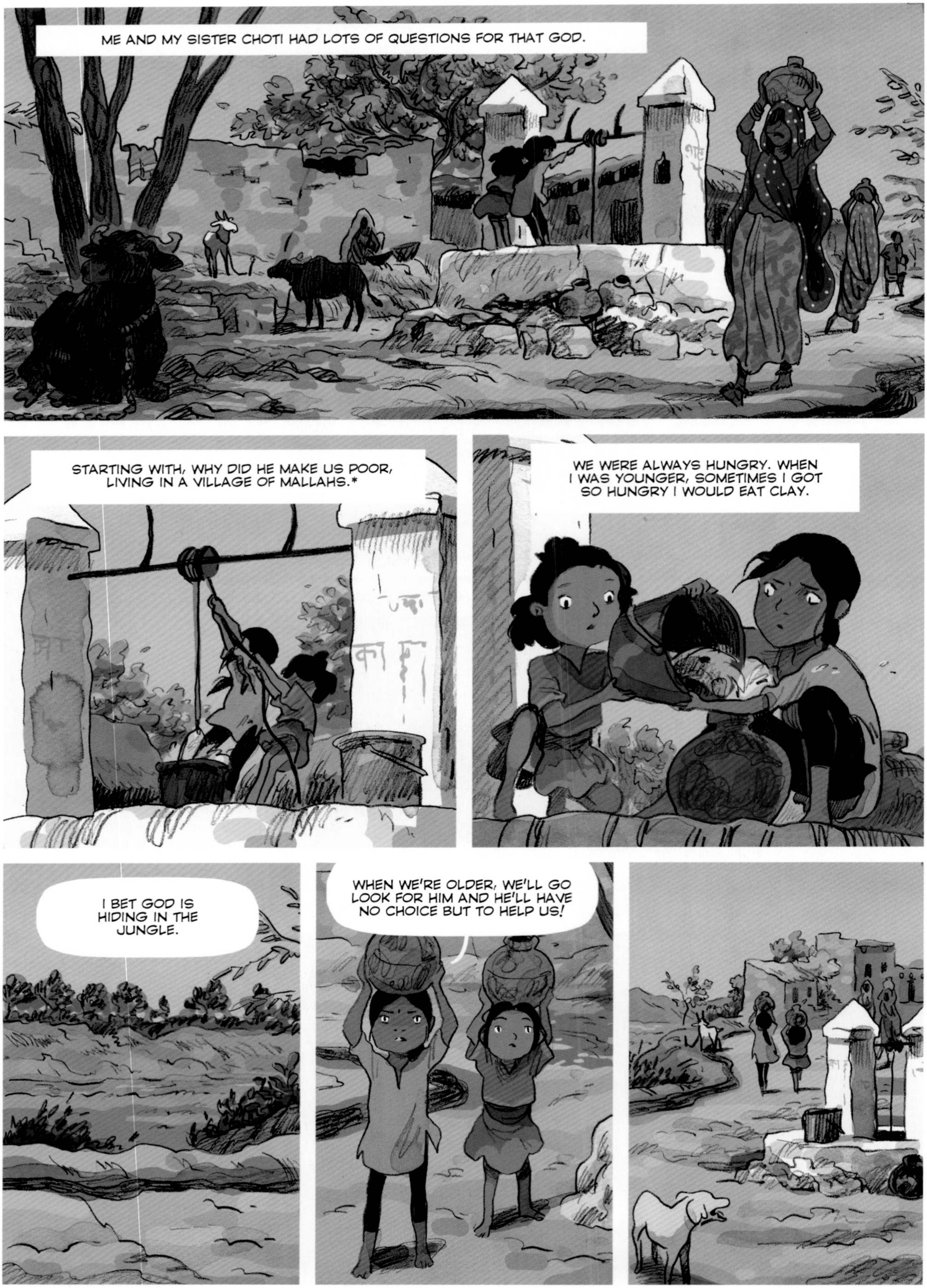
ME AND MY SISTER CHOTI HAD LOTS OF QUESTIONS FOR THAT GOD.
STARTING WITH, WHY DID HE MAKE US POOR, LIVING IN A VILLAGE OF MALLAHS.*
WE WERE ALWAYS HUNGRY. WHEN I WAS YOUNGER, SOMETIMES I GOT SO HUNGRY I WOULD EAT CLAY.
I BET GOD IS HIDING IN THE JUNGLE.
WHEN WE'RE OLDER, WE'LL GO LOOK FOR HIM AND HE'LL HAVE NO CHOICE BUT TO HELP US!

*MALLAHS BELONG TO THE SHUDRA CASTE (FARMERS AND SERVANTS), THE LOWEST OF ALL.

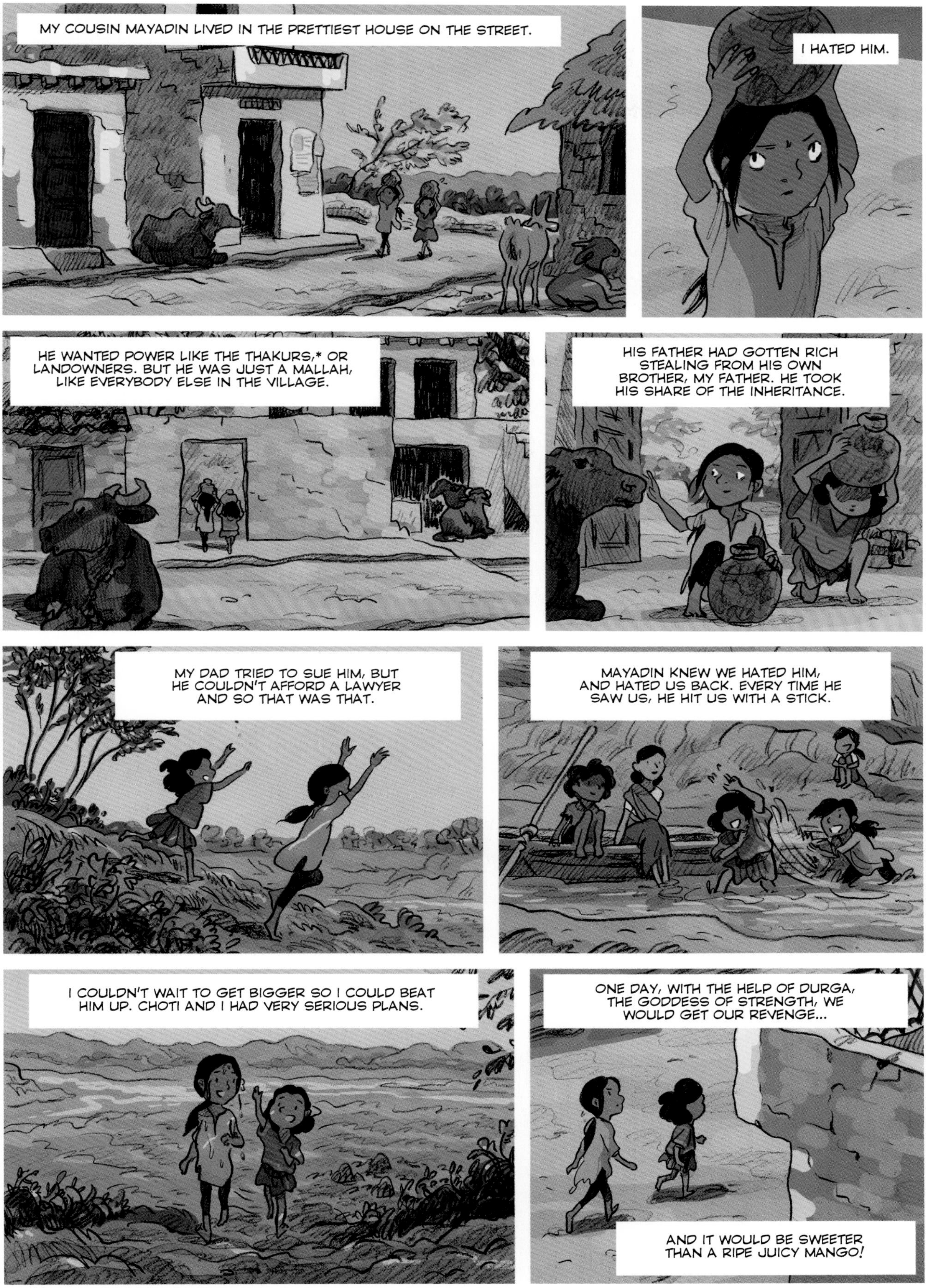
MY COUSIN MAYADIN LIVED IN THE PRETTIEST HOUSE ON THE STREET.
I HATED HIM.
HE WANTED POWER LIKE THE THAKURS,* OR LANDOWNERS. BUT HE WAS JUST A MALLAH, LIKE EVERYBODY ELSE IN THE VILLAGE.
HIS FATHER HAD GOTTEN RICH STEALING FROM HIS OWN BROTHER, MY FATHER. HE TOOK HIS SHARE OF THE INHERITANCE.
MY DAD TRIED TO SUE HIM, BUT HE COULDN'T AFFORD A LAWYER AND SO THAT WAS THAT.
MAYADIN KNEW WE HATED HIM, AND HATED US BACK. EVERY TIME HE SAW US, HE HIT US WITH A STICK.
I COULDN'T WAIT TO GET BIGGER SO I COULD BEAT HIM UP. CHOTI AND I HAD VERY SERIOUS PLANS.
ONE DAY, WITH THE HELP OF DURGA, THE GODDESS OF STRENGTH, WE WOULD GET OUR REVENGE...
AND IT WOULD BE SWEETER THAN A RIPE JUICY MANGO!

*THAKURS BELONG TO THE KSHATRIYA CASTE (RULERS, WARRIORS), ONE OF THE HIGHEST.

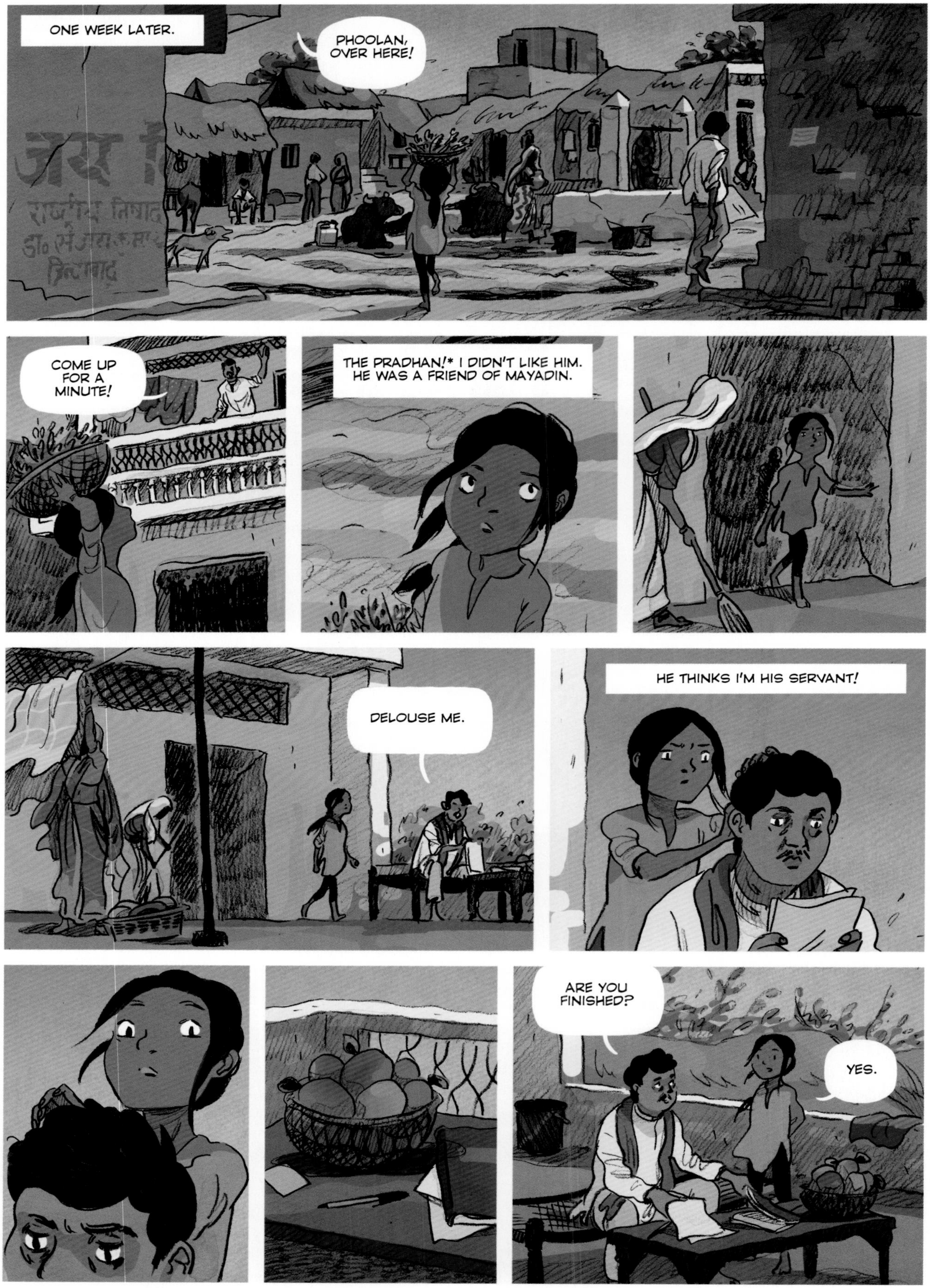
ONE WEEK LATER.
PHOOLAN, OVER HERE!
COME UP FOR A MINUTE!
THE PRADHAN!* I DIDN'T LIKE HIM. HE WAS A FRIEND OF MAYADIN.
DELOUSE ME.
HE THINKS I'M HIS SERVANT!
ARE YOU FINISHED?
YES.

*CHIEF OF THE FEDERATION OF VILLAGES.

SAY, COULD I HAVE A MANGO?

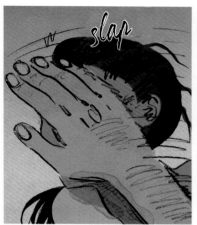

slap

HOW DARE YOU?

TODAY IT'S A MANGO, TOMORROW IT'LL BE SOMETHING ELSE!

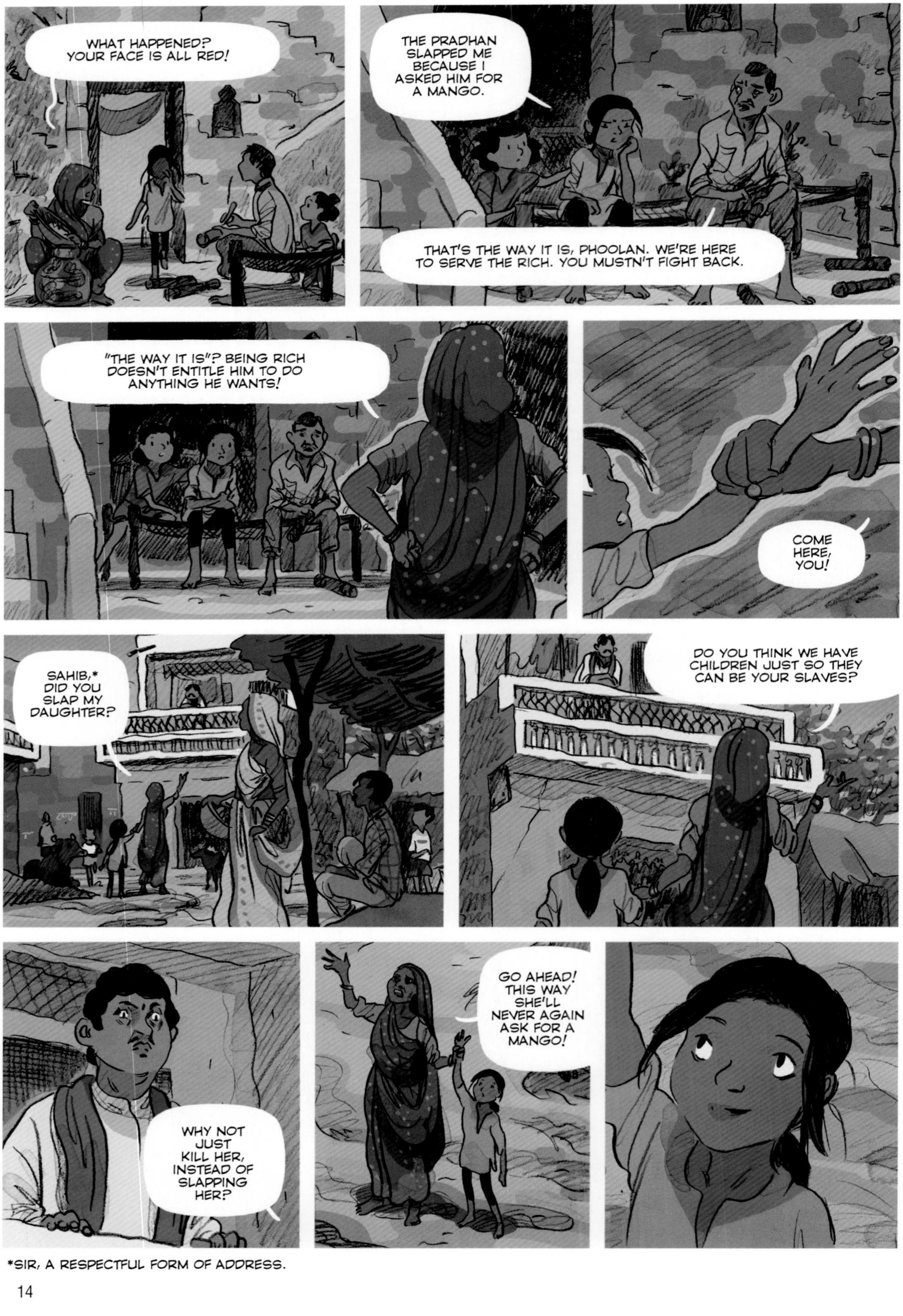
WHAT HAPPENED? YOUR FACE IS ALL RED!
THE PRADHAN SLAPPED ME BECAUSE I ASKED HIM FOR A MANGO.
THAT'S THE WAY IT IS, PHOOLAN. WE'RE HERE TO SERVE THE RICH. YOU MUSTN'T FIGHT BACK.
"THE WAY IT IS"? BEING RICH DOESN'T ENTITLE HIM TO DO ANYTHING HE WANTS!
COME HERE, YOU!
SAHIB,* DID YOU SLAP MY DAUGHTER?
DO YOU THINK WE HAVE CHILDREN JUST SO THEY CAN BE YOUR SLAVES?
WHY NOT JUST KILL HER, INSTEAD OF SLAPPING HER?
GO AHEAD! THIS WAY SHE'LL NEVER AGAIN ASK FOR A MANGO!

*SIR, A RESPECTFUL FORM OF ADDRESS.

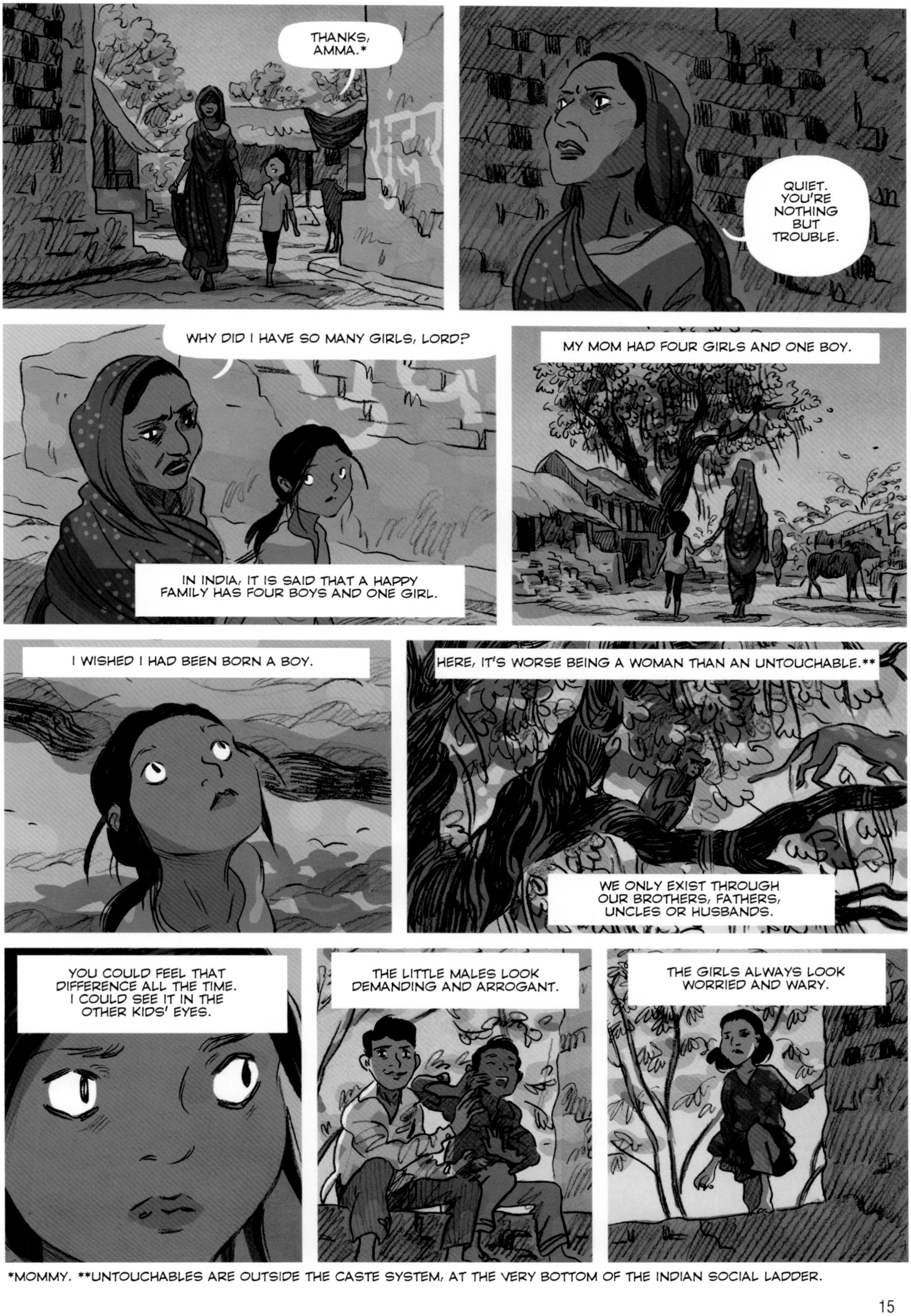
THANKS, AMMA.*
QUIET. YOU'RE NOTHING BUT TROUBLE.
WHY DID I HAVE SO MANY GIRLS, LORD?
IN INDIA, IT IS SAID THAT A HAPPY FAMILY HAS FOUR BOYS AND ONE GIRL.
MY MOM HAD FOUR GIRLS AND ONE BOY.
I WISHED I HAD BEEN BORN A BOY.
HERE, IT'S WORSE BEING A WOMAN THAN AN UNTOUCHABLE.**
WE ONLY EXIST THROUGH OUR BROTHERS, FATHERS, UNCLES OR HUSBANDS.
YOU COULD FEEL THAT DIFFERENCE ALL THE TIME. I COULD SEE IT IN THE OTHER KIDS' EYES.
THE LITTLE MALES LOOK DEMANDING AND ARROGANT.
THE GIRLS ALWAYS LOOK WORRIED AND WARY.

*MOMMY. **UNTOUCHABLES ARE OUTSIDE THE CASTE SYSTEM, AT THE VERY BOTTOM OF THE INDIAN SOCIAL LADDER.

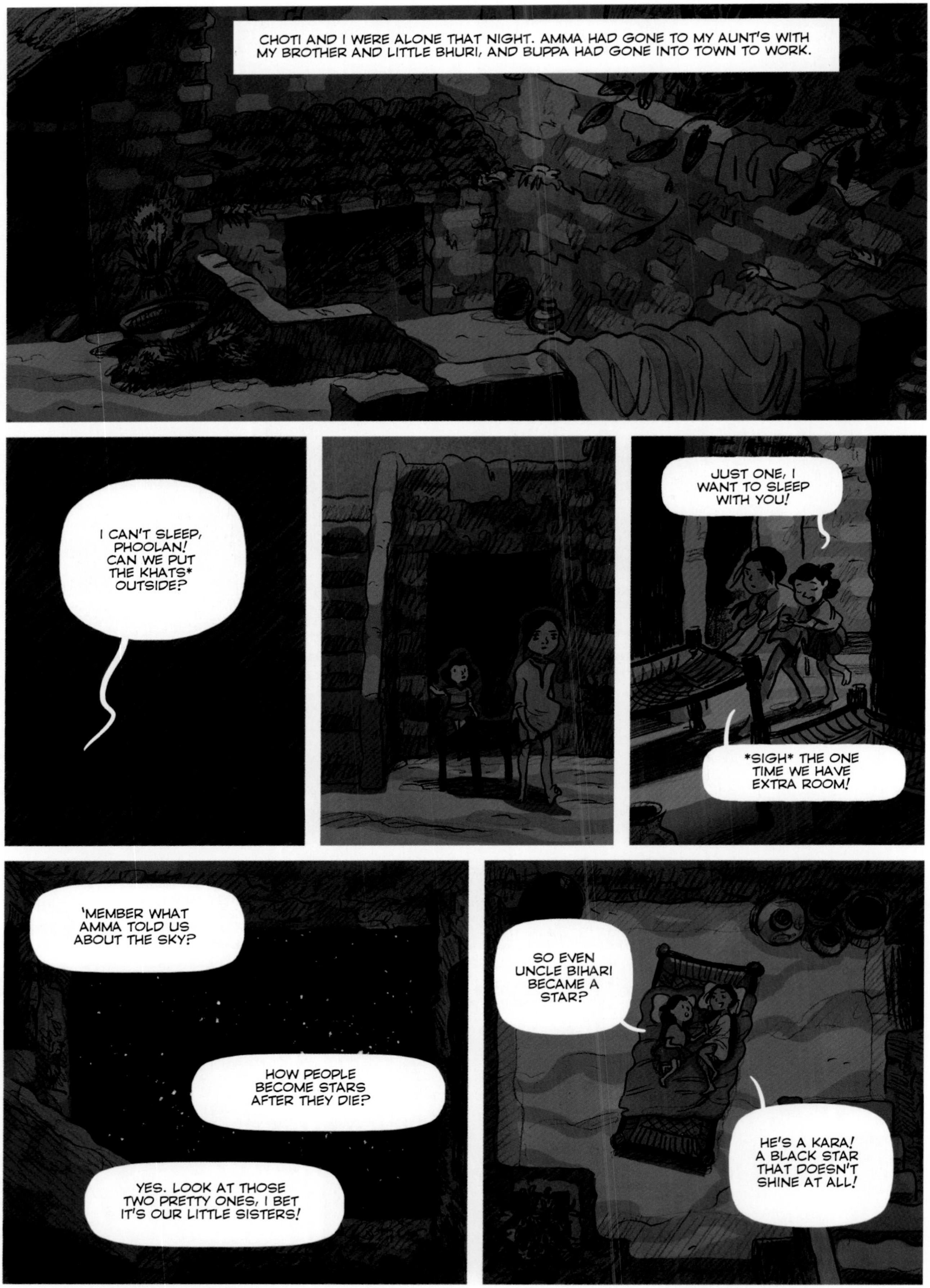
CHOTI AND I WERE ALONE THAT NIGHT. AMMA HAD GONE TO MY AUNT'S WITH MY BROTHER AND LITTLE BHURI, AND BUPPA HAD GONE INTO TOWN TO WORK.
I CAN'T SLEEP, PHOOLAN! CAN WE PUT THE KHATS* OUTSIDE?
JUST ONE, I WANT TO SLEEP WITH YOU!
SIGH THE ONE TIME WE HAVE EXTRA ROOM!
'MEMBER WHAT AMMA TOLD US ABOUT THE SKY?
HOW PEOPLE BECOME STARS AFTER THEY DIE?
YES. LOOK AT THOSE TWO PRETTY ONES, I BET IT'S OUR LITTLE SISTERS!
SO EVEN UNCLE BIHARI BECAME A STAR?
HE'S A KARA! A BLACK STAR THAT DOESN'T SHINE AT ALL!

*A BED OF WOVEN ROPE.

I OFTEN HAD A HARD TIME FALLING ASLEEP AT NIGHT.

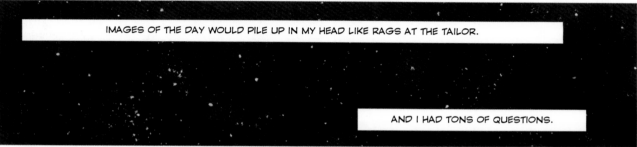

IMAGES OF THE DAY WOULD PILE UP IN MY HEAD LIKE RAGS AT THE TAILOR.

AND I HAD TONS OF QUESTIONS.

WHAT WAS THE WORLD LIKE OUTSIDE MY VILLAGE? HOW FAR DID IT GO?

DID IT END WHERE THE RED SUN SETS EVERY NIGHT ON THE BANKS OF THE YAMUNA?

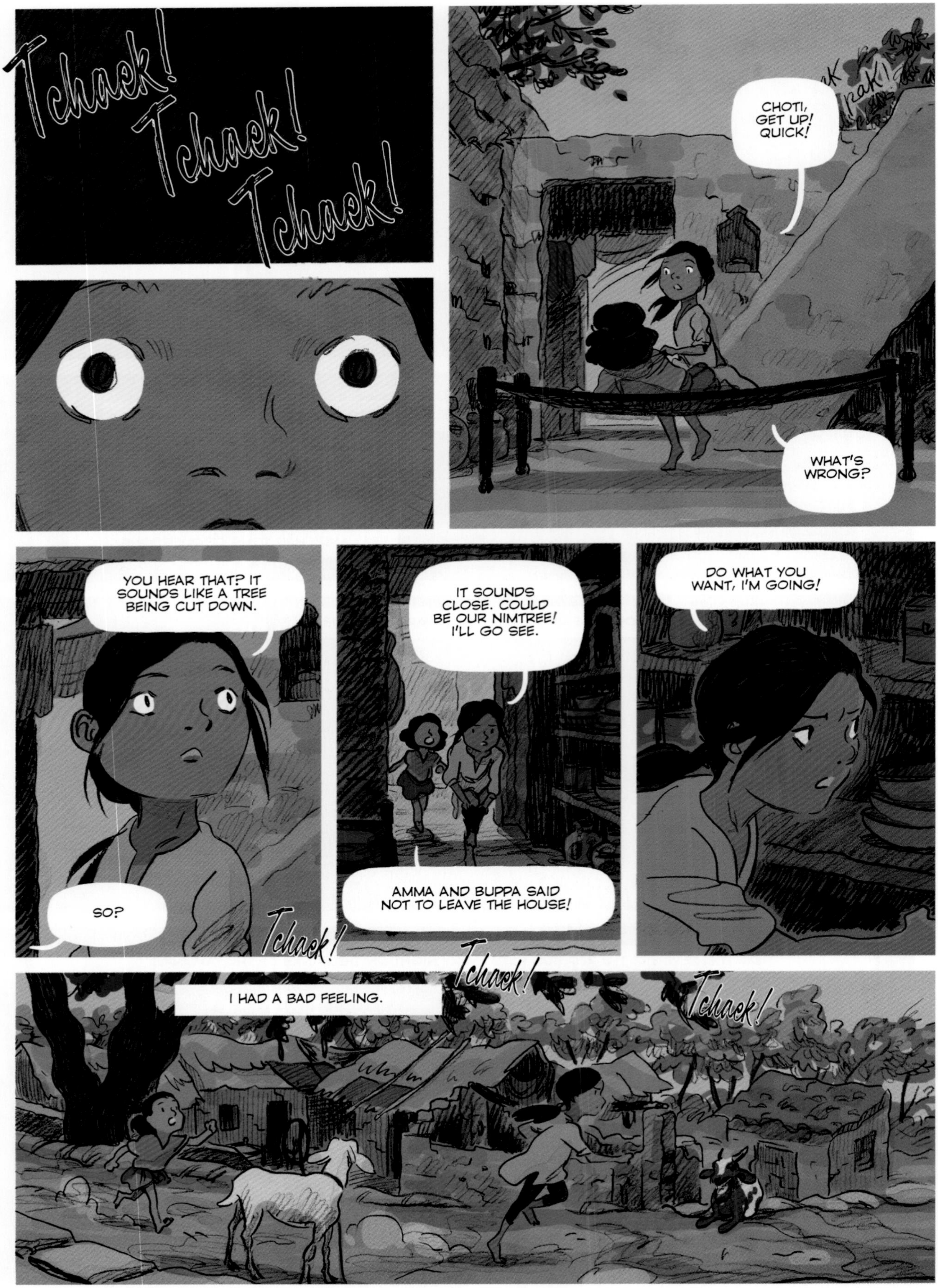
Tchack! Tchack! Tchack!
CHOTI, GET UP! QUICK!
WHAT'S WRONG?
YOU HEAR THAT? IT SOUNDS LIKE A TREE BEING CUT DOWN.
SO?
IT SOUNDS CLOSE. COULD BE OUR NIMTREE! I'LL GO SEE.
AMMA AND BUPPA SAID NOT TO LEAVE THE HOUSE!
DO WHAT YOU WANT, I'M GOING!
Tchack!
Tchack!
I HAD A BAD FEELING.
Tchack!

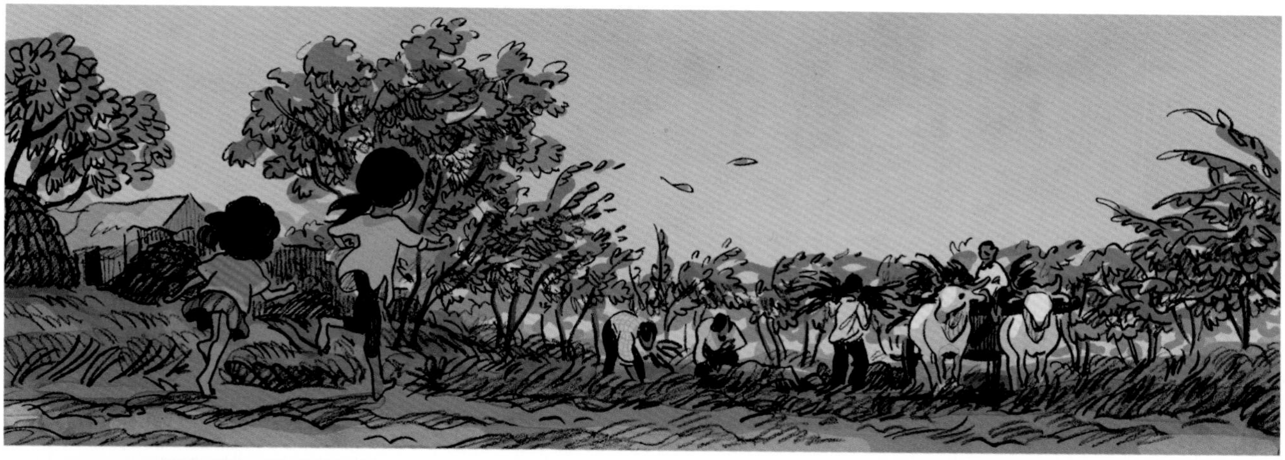

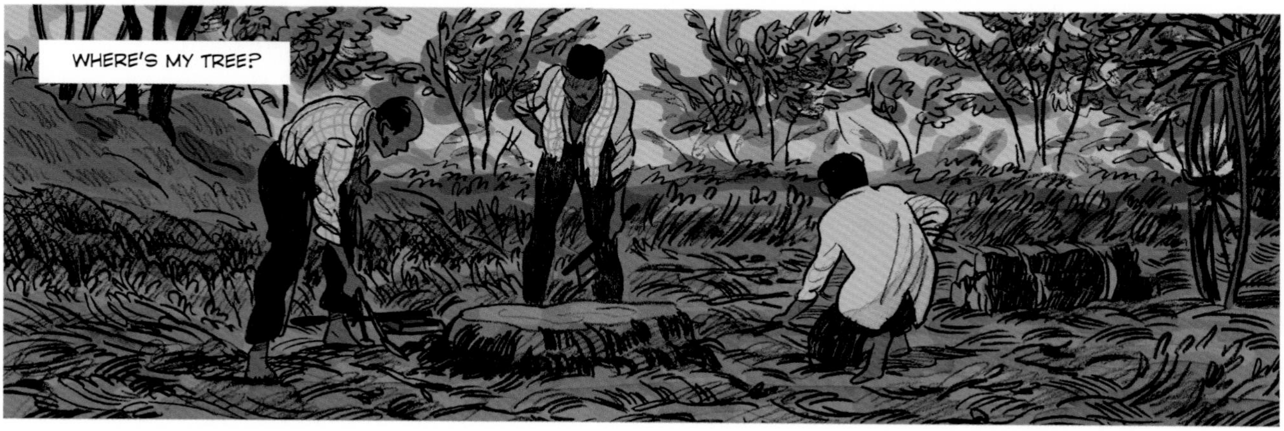
WHERE'S MY TREE?

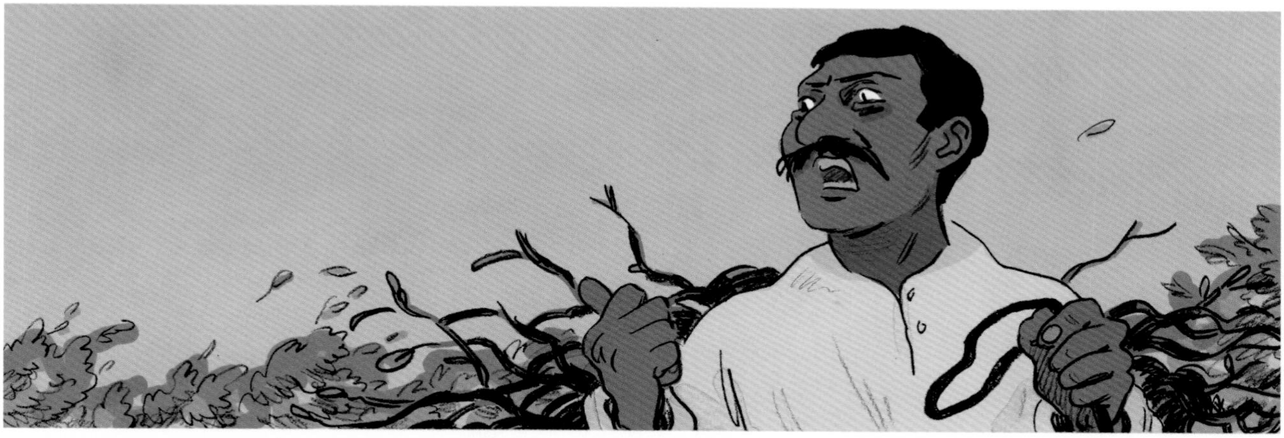

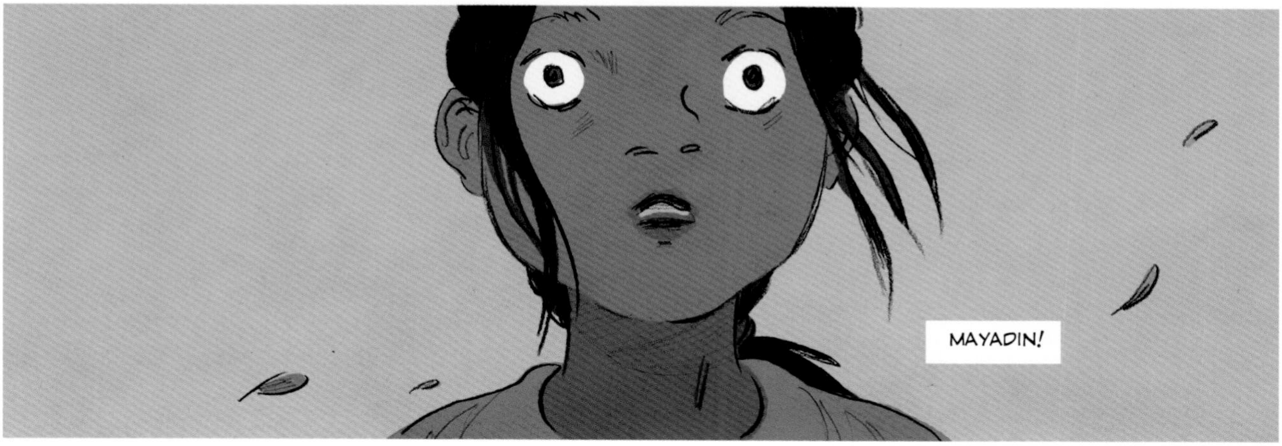
MAYADIN!

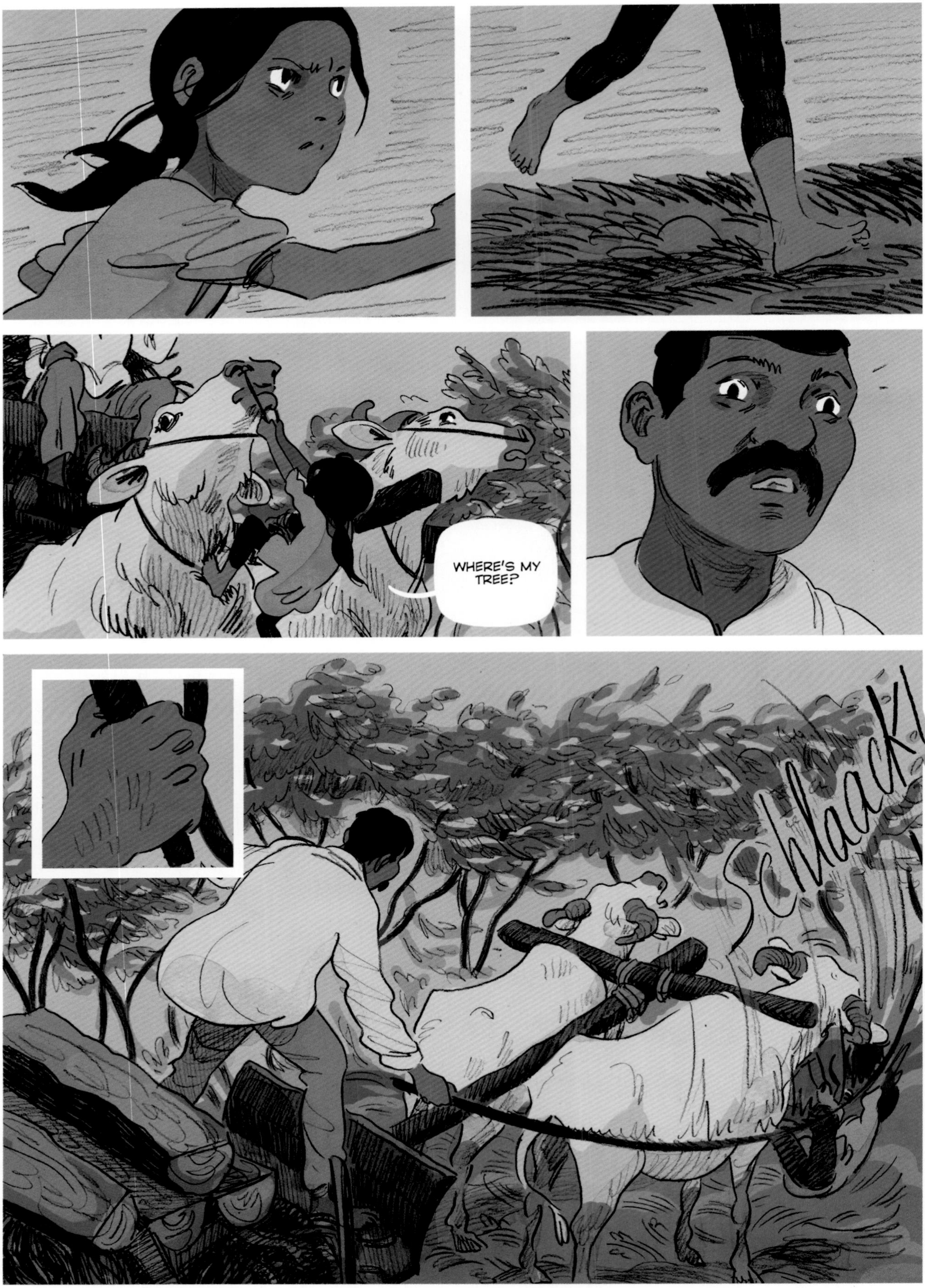
WHERE'S MY TREE?
Schlaack!

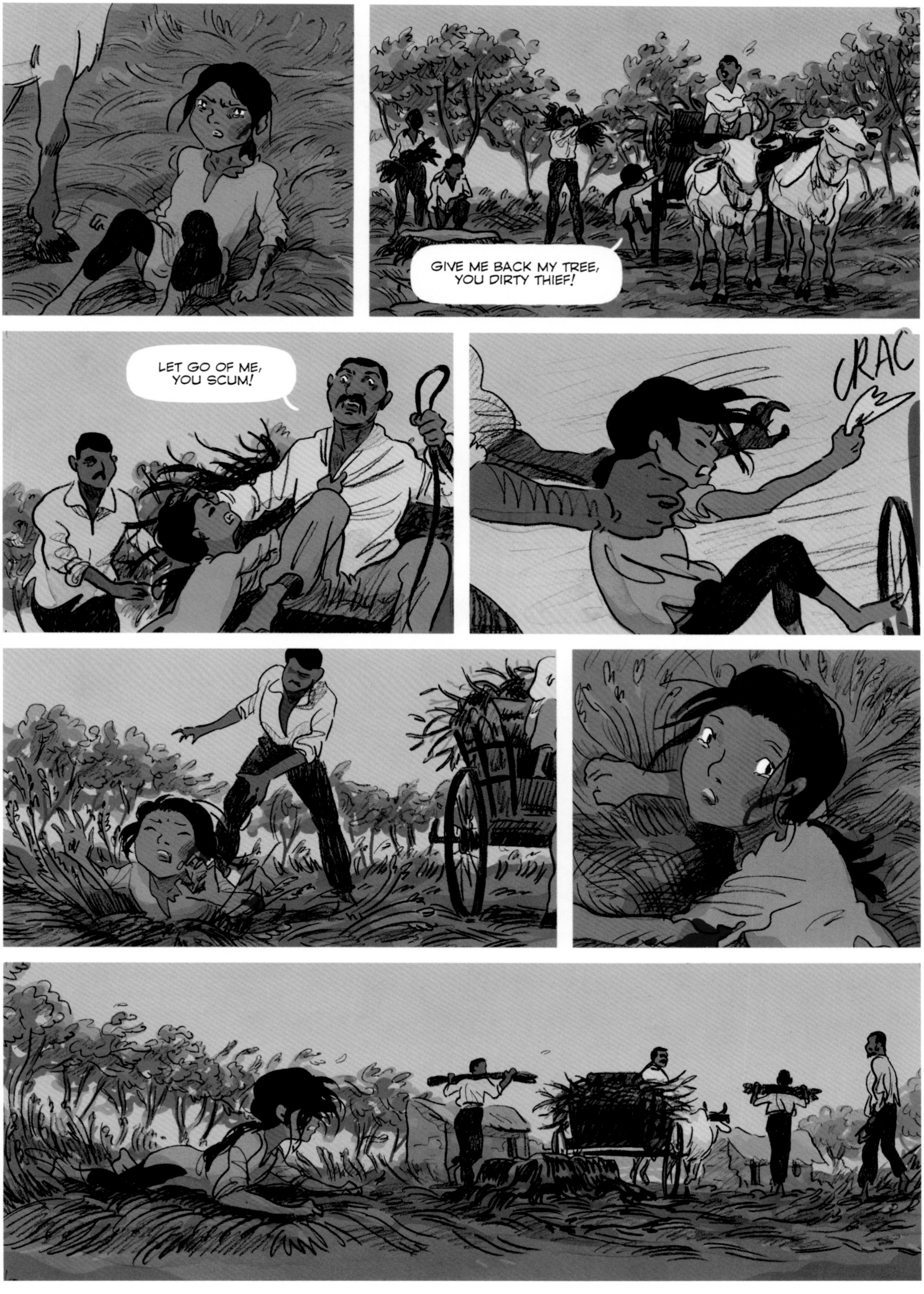
GIVE ME BACK MY TREE, YOU DIRTY THIEF!
LET GO OF ME, YOU SCUM!
CRAC

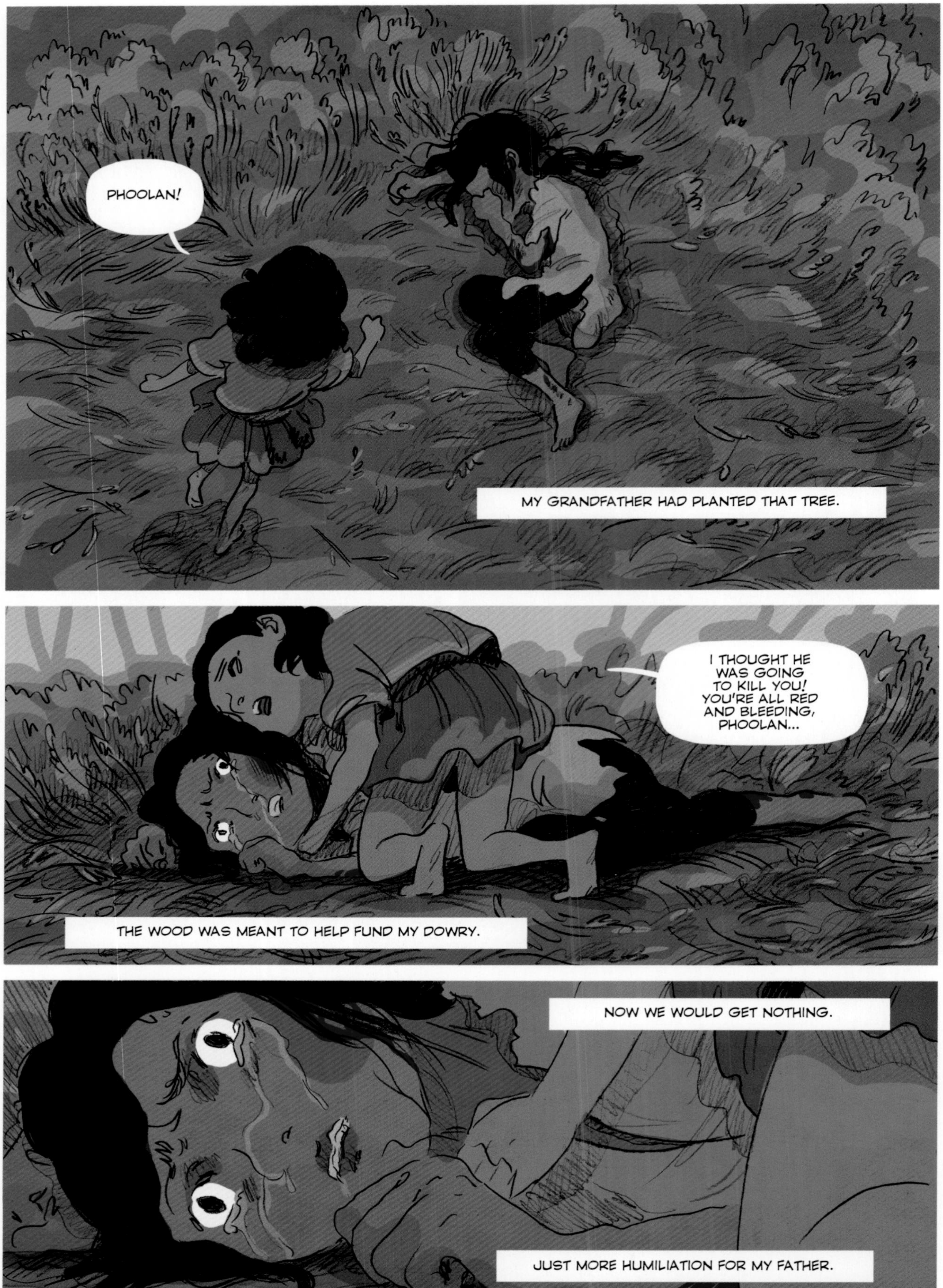
PHOOLAN!
MY GRANDFATHER HAD PLANTED THAT TREE.
I THOUGHT HE WAS GOING TO KILL YOU! YOU'RE ALL RED AND BLEEDING, PHOOLAN...
THE WOOD WAS MEANT TO HELP FUND MY DOWRY.
NOW WE WOULD GET NOTHING.
JUST MORE HUMILIATION FOR MY FATHER.

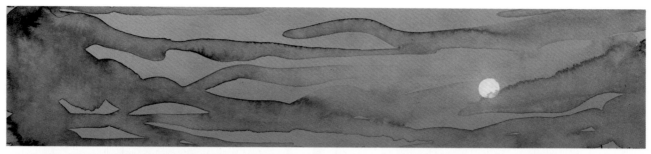

I'LL GO FILE A COMPLAINT TOMORROW.

IT'S POINTLESS. WE HAVE NO PROOF.

SHUT UP! YOU NEVER FIGHT BACK!

EVEN PHOOLAN HAS MORE BACKBONE!

PLEASE HELP US, GOD.

ENOUGH WITH THE GOD TALK!

WHERE IS HE, HUH?

IS HE GOING TO PAY FOR YOUR WEDDING? ASK HIM!

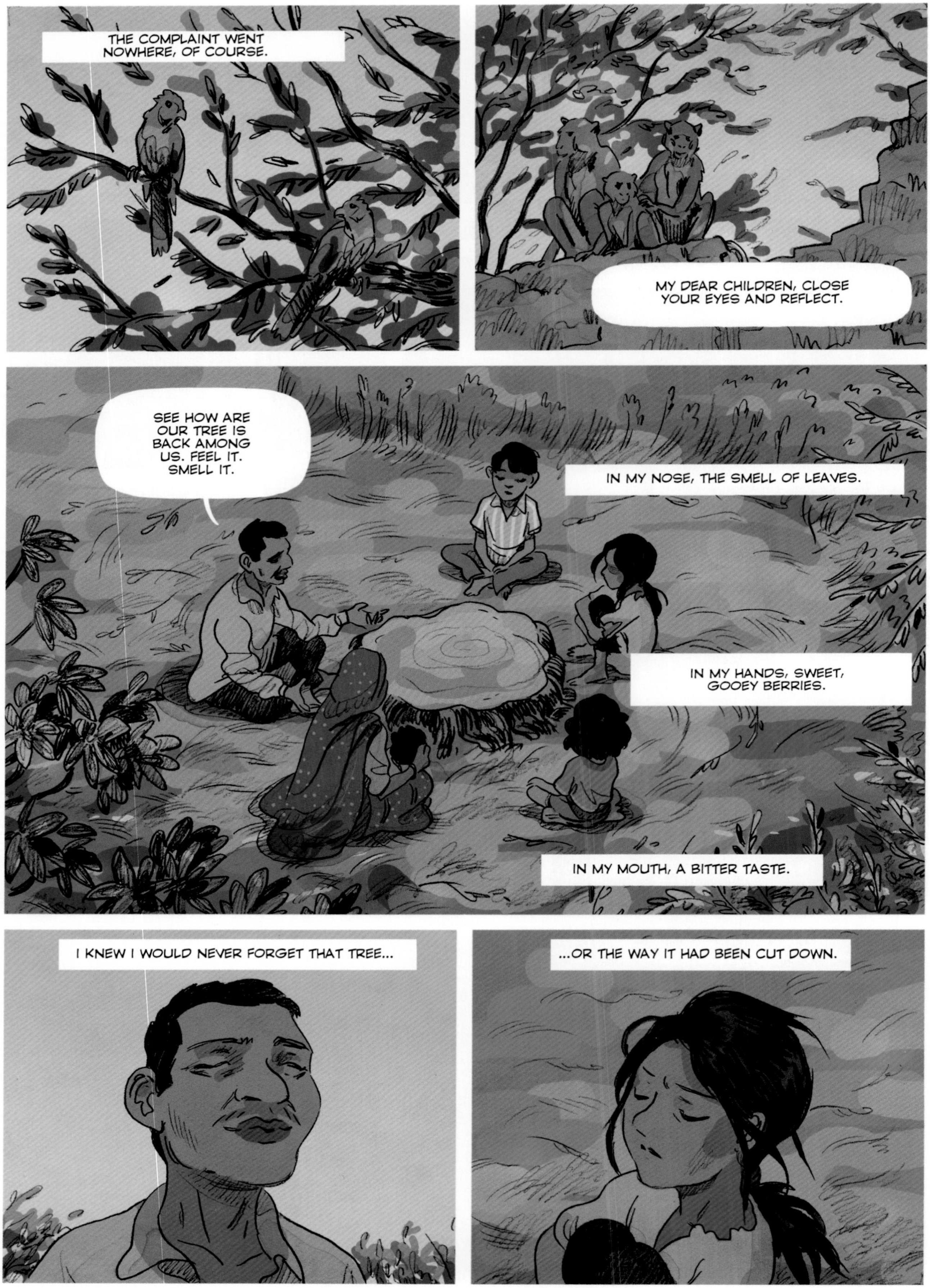
THE COMPLAINT WENT NOWHERE, OF COURSE.
MY DEAR CHILDREN, CLOSE YOUR EYES AND REFLECT.
SEE HOW ARE OUR TREE IS BACK AMONG US. FEEL IT. SMELL IT.
IN MY NOSE, THE SMELL OF LEAVES.
IN MY HANDS, SWEET, GOOEY BERRIES.
IN MY MOUTH, A BITTER TASTE.
I KNEW I WOULD NEVER FORGET THAT TREE...
...OR THE WAY IT HAD BEEN CUT DOWN.

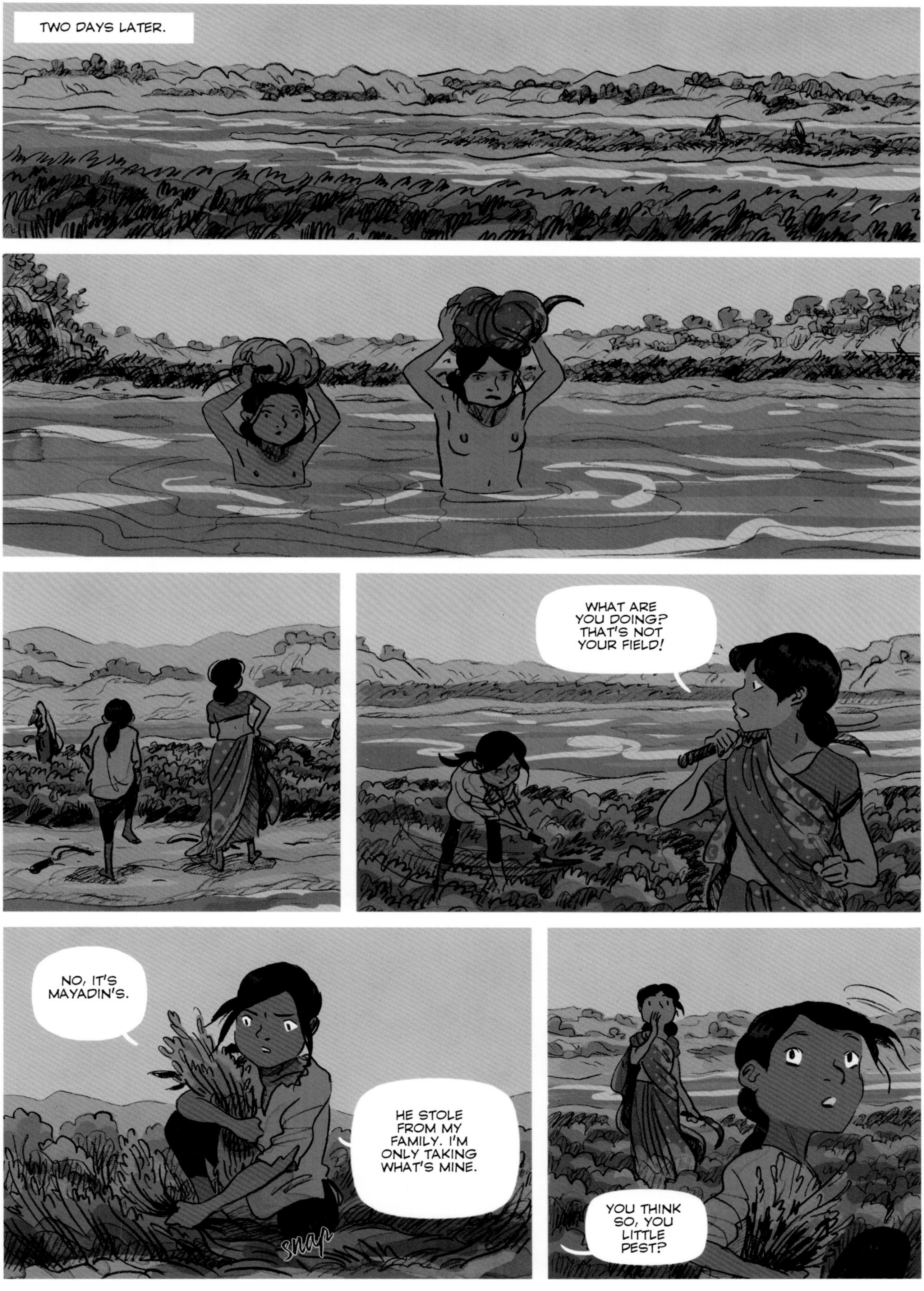
TWO DAYS LATER.
WHAT ARE YOU DOING? THAT'S NOT YOUR FIELD!
NO, IT'S MAYADIN'S.
HE STOLE FROM MY FAMILY. I'M ONLY TAKING WHAT'S MINE.
snap
YOU THINK SO, YOU LITTLE PEST?

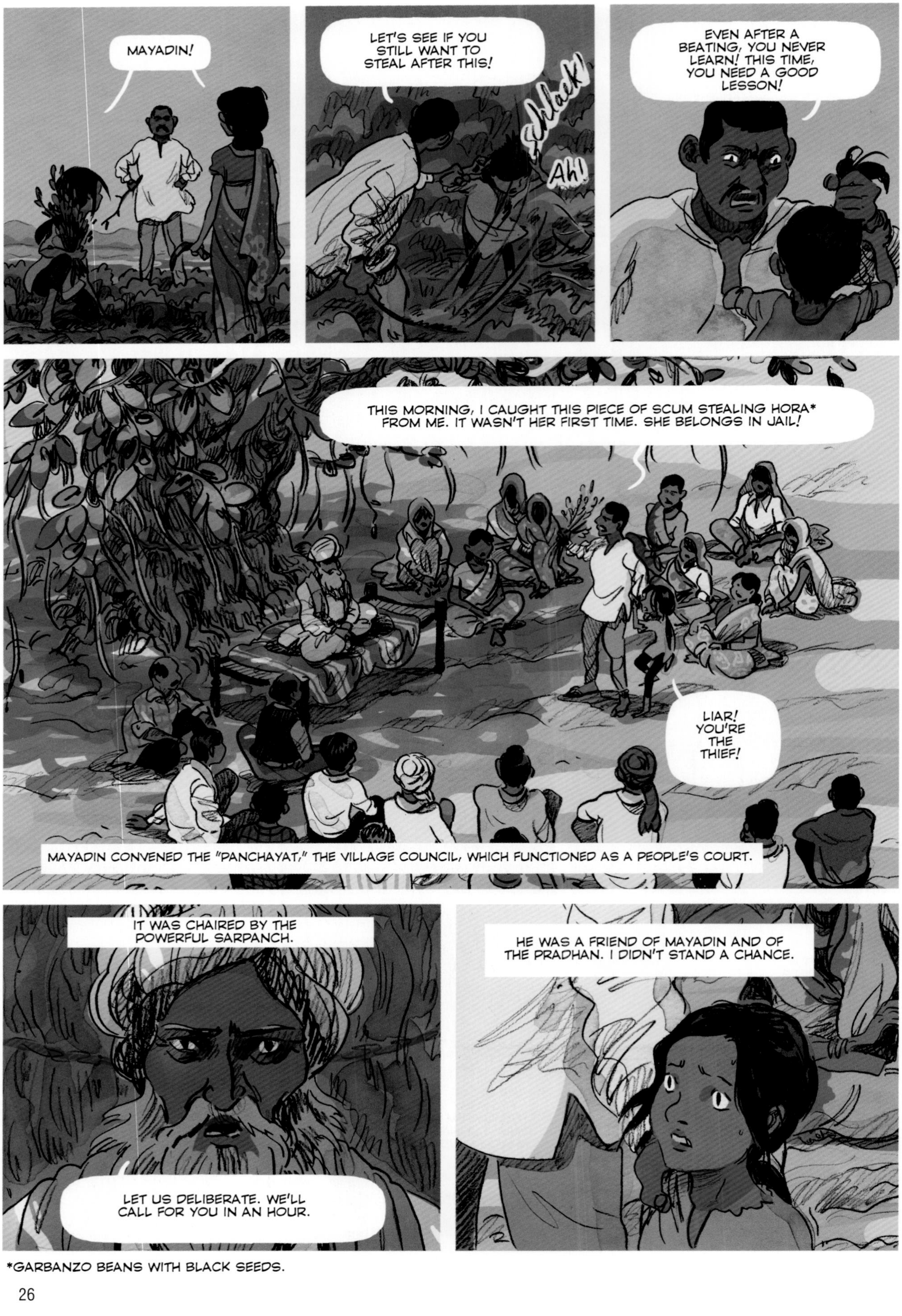
MAYADIN!
LET'S SEE IF YOU STILL WANT TO STEAL AFTER THIS!
SHLACK!
AH!
EVEN AFTER A BEATING, YOU NEVER LEARN! THIS TIME, YOU NEED A GOOD LESSON!
THIS MORNING, I CAUGHT THIS PIECE OF SCUM STEALING HORA* FROM ME. IT WASN'T HER FIRST TIME. SHE BELONGS IN JAIL!
LIAR! YOU'RE THE THIEF!
MAYADIN CONVENED THE "PANCHAYAT," THE VILLAGE COUNCIL, WHICH FUNCTIONED AS A PEOPLE'S COURT.
IT WAS CHAIRED BY THE POWERFUL SARPANCH.
LET US DELIBERATE. WE'LL CALL FOR YOU IN AN HOUR.
HE WAS A FRIEND OF MAYADIN AND OF THE PRADHAN. I DIDN'T STAND A CHANCE.

*GARBANZO BEANS WITH BLACK SEEDS.

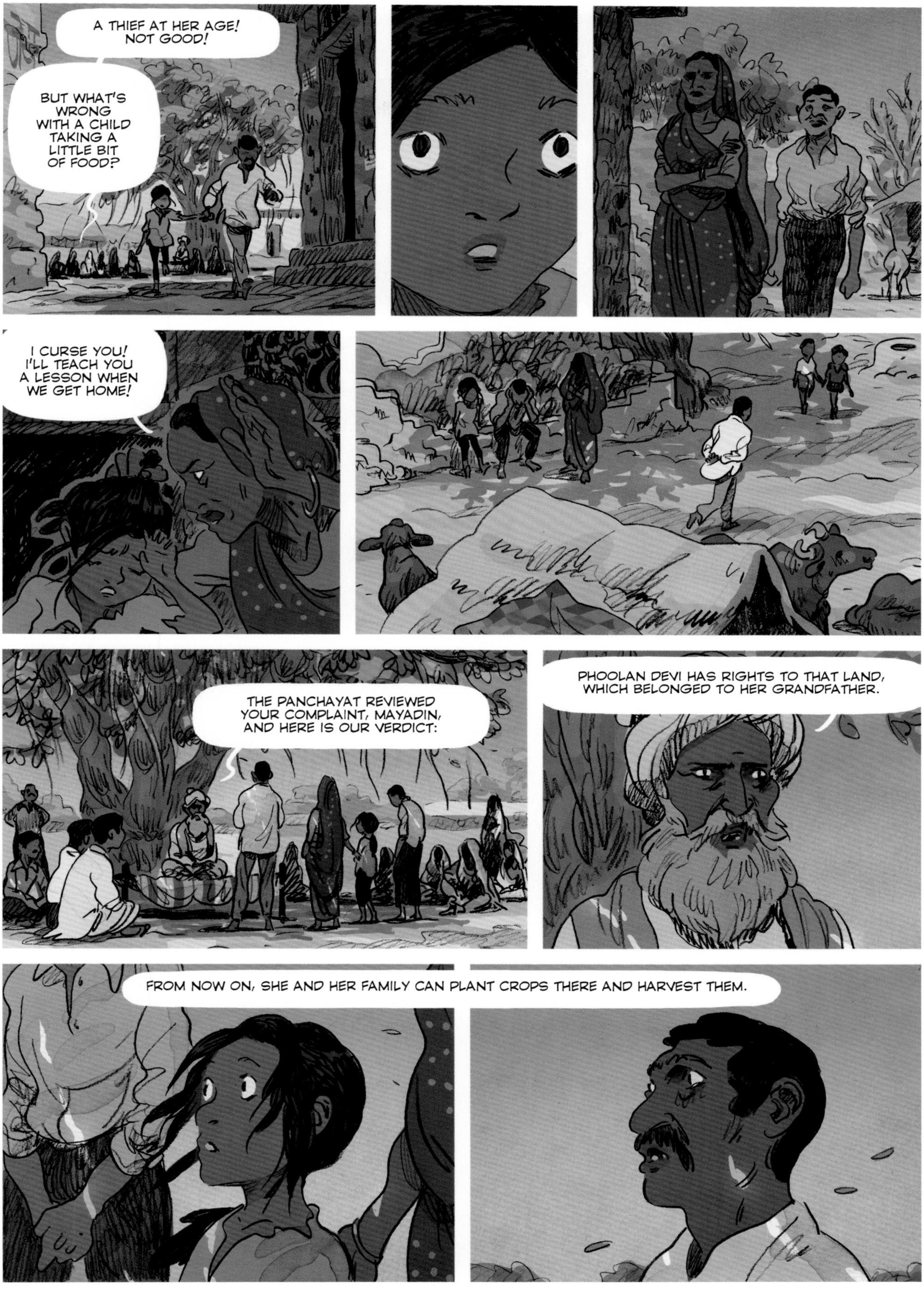
A THIEF AT HER AGE! NOT GOOD!
BUT WHAT'S WRONG WITH A CHILD TAKING A LITTLE BIT OF FOOD?
I CURSE YOU! I'LL TEACH YOU A LESSON WHEN WE GET HOME!
THE PANCHAYAT REVIEWED YOUR COMPLAINT, MAYADIN, AND HERE IS OUR VERDICT:
PHOOLAN DEVI HAS RIGHTS TO THAT LAND, WHICH BELONGED TO HER GRANDFATHER.
FROM NOW ON, SHE AND HER FAMILY CAN PLANT CROPS THERE AND HARVEST THEM.

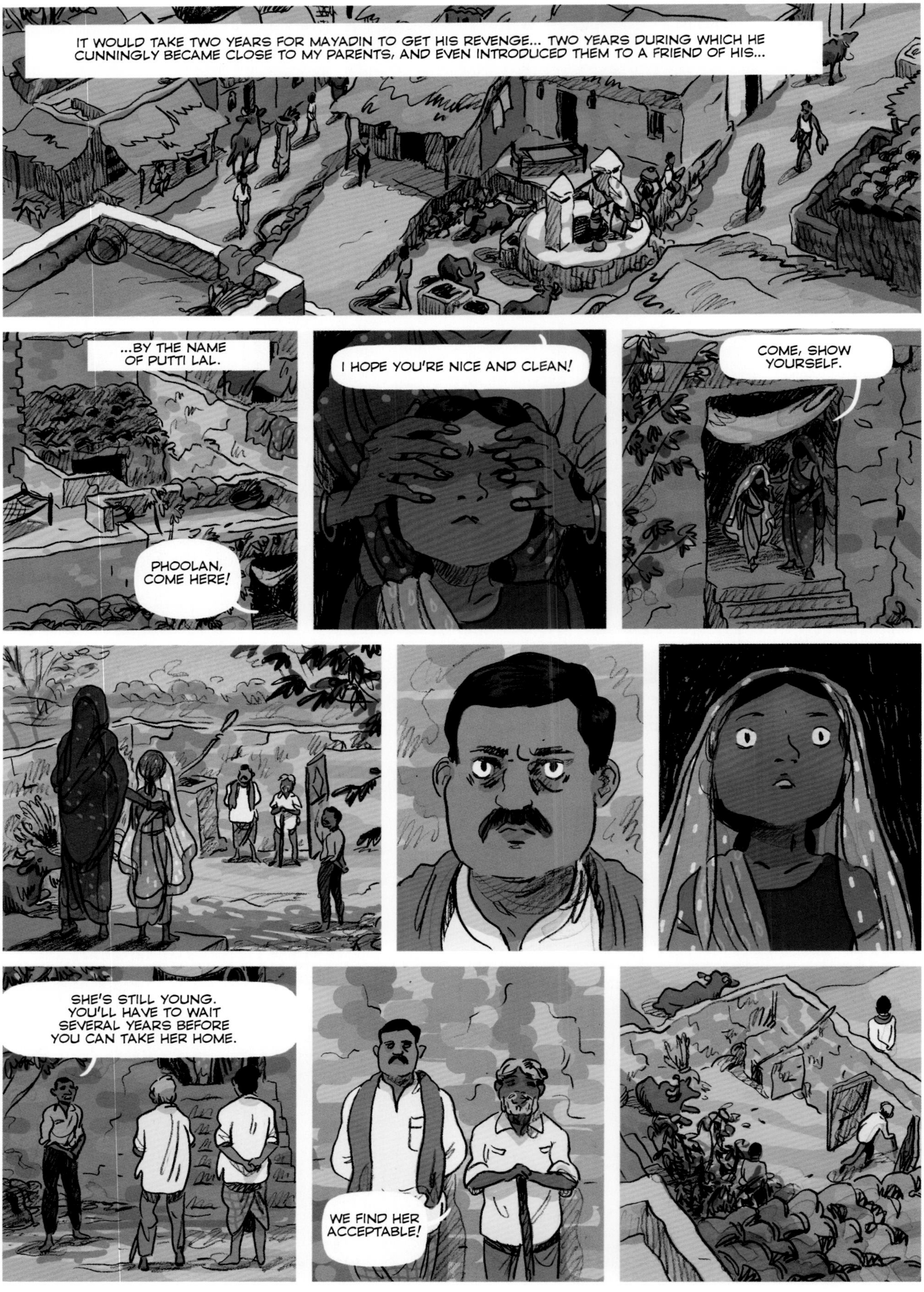
IT WOULD TAKE TWO YEARS FOR MAYADIN TO GET HIS REVENGE... TWO YEARS DURING WHICH HE CUNNINGLY BECAME CLOSE TO MY PARENTS, AND EVEN INTRODUCED THEM TO A FRIEND OF HIS...
...BY THE NAME OF PUTTI LAL.
PHOOLAN, COME HERE!
I HOPE YOU'RE NICE AND CLEAN!
COME, SHOW YOURSELF.
SHE'S STILL YOUNG. YOU'LL HAVE TO WAIT SEVERAL YEARS BEFORE YOU CAN TAKE HER HOME.
WE FIND HER ACCEPTABLE!

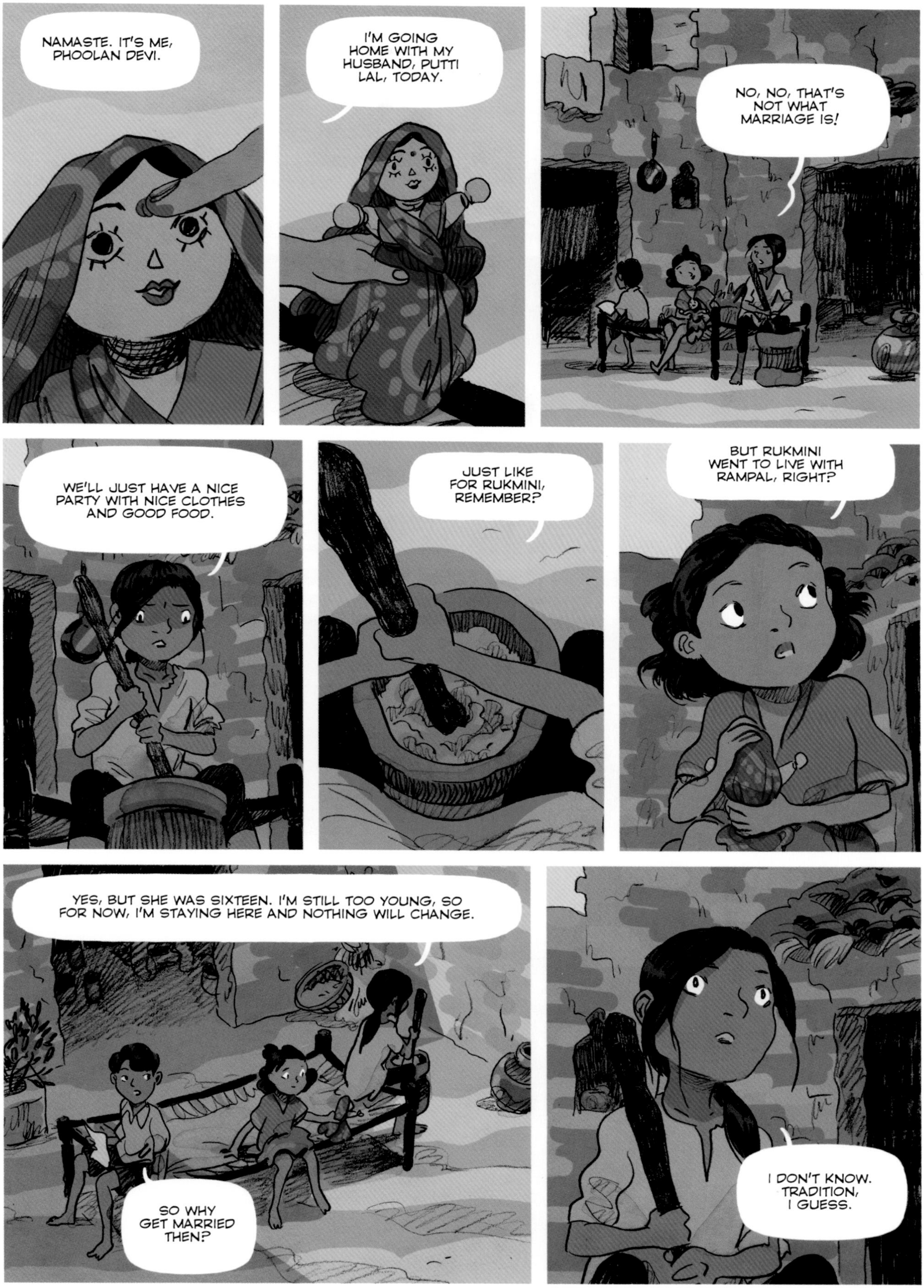
NAMASTE. IT'S ME, PHOOLAN DEVI.
I'M GOING HOME WITH MY HUSBAND, PUTTI LAL, TODAY.
NO, NO, THAT'S NOT WHAT MARRIAGE IS!
WE'LL JUST HAVE A NICE PARTY WITH NICE CLOTHES AND GOOD FOOD.
JUST LIKE FOR RUKMINI, REMEMBER?
BUT RUKMINI WENT TO LIVE WITH RAMPAL, RIGHT?
YES, BUT SHE WAS SIXTEEN. I'M STILL TOO YOUNG, SO FOR NOW, I'M STAYING HERE AND NOTHING WILL CHANGE.
SO WHY GET MARRIED THEN?
I DON'T KNOW. TRADITION, I GUESS.

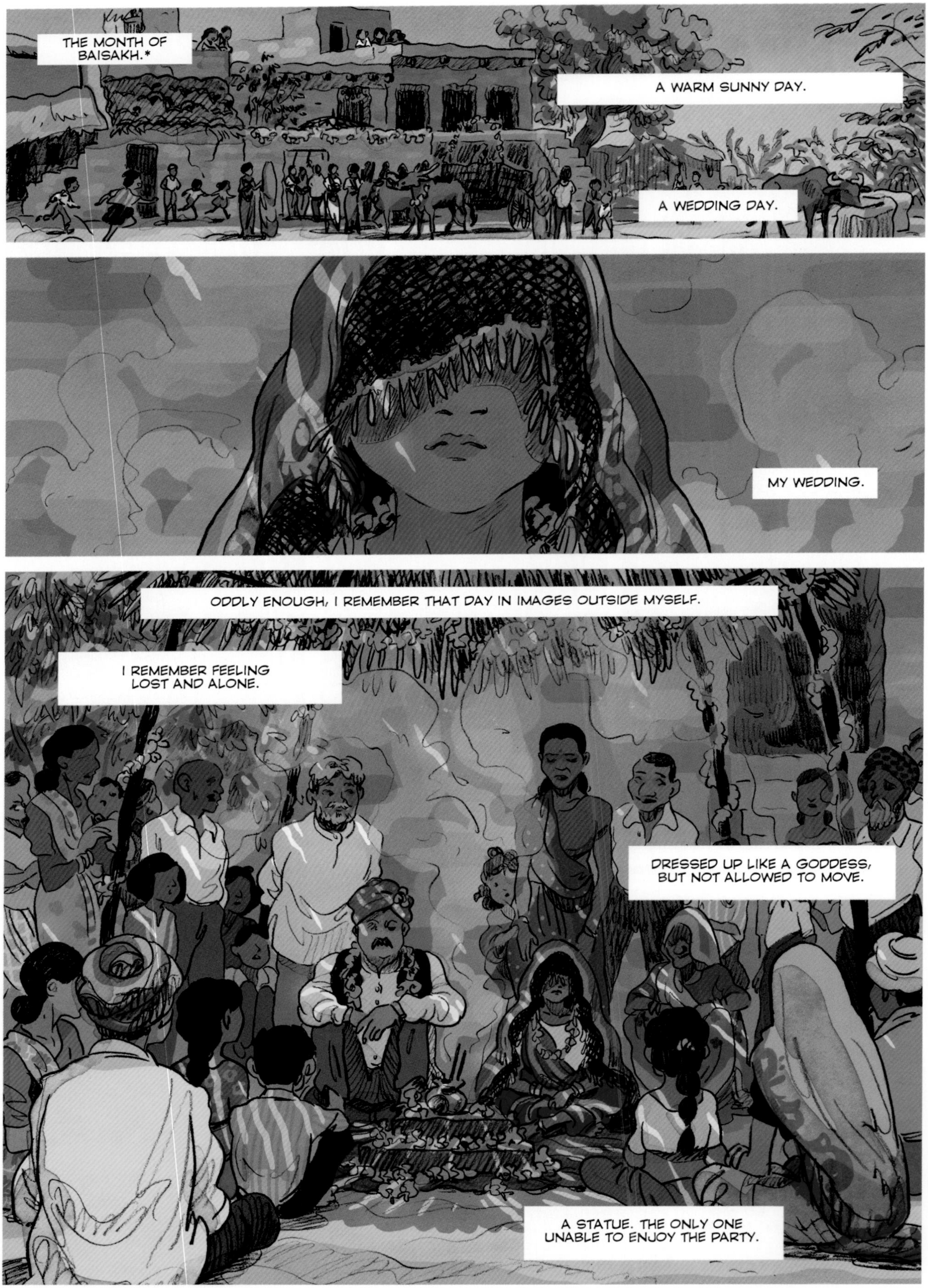
THE MONTH OF BAISAKH.*
A WARM SUNNY DAY.
A WEDDING DAY.
MY WEDDING.
ODDLY ENOUGH, I REMEMBER THAT DAY IN IMAGES OUTSIDE MYSELF.
I REMEMBER FEELING LOST AND ALONE.
DRESSED UP LIKE A GODDESS, BUT NOT ALLOWED TO MOVE.
A STATUE. THE ONLY ONE UNABLE TO ENJOY THE PARTY.

*APRIL/MAY IN THE BENGALI CALENDAR.

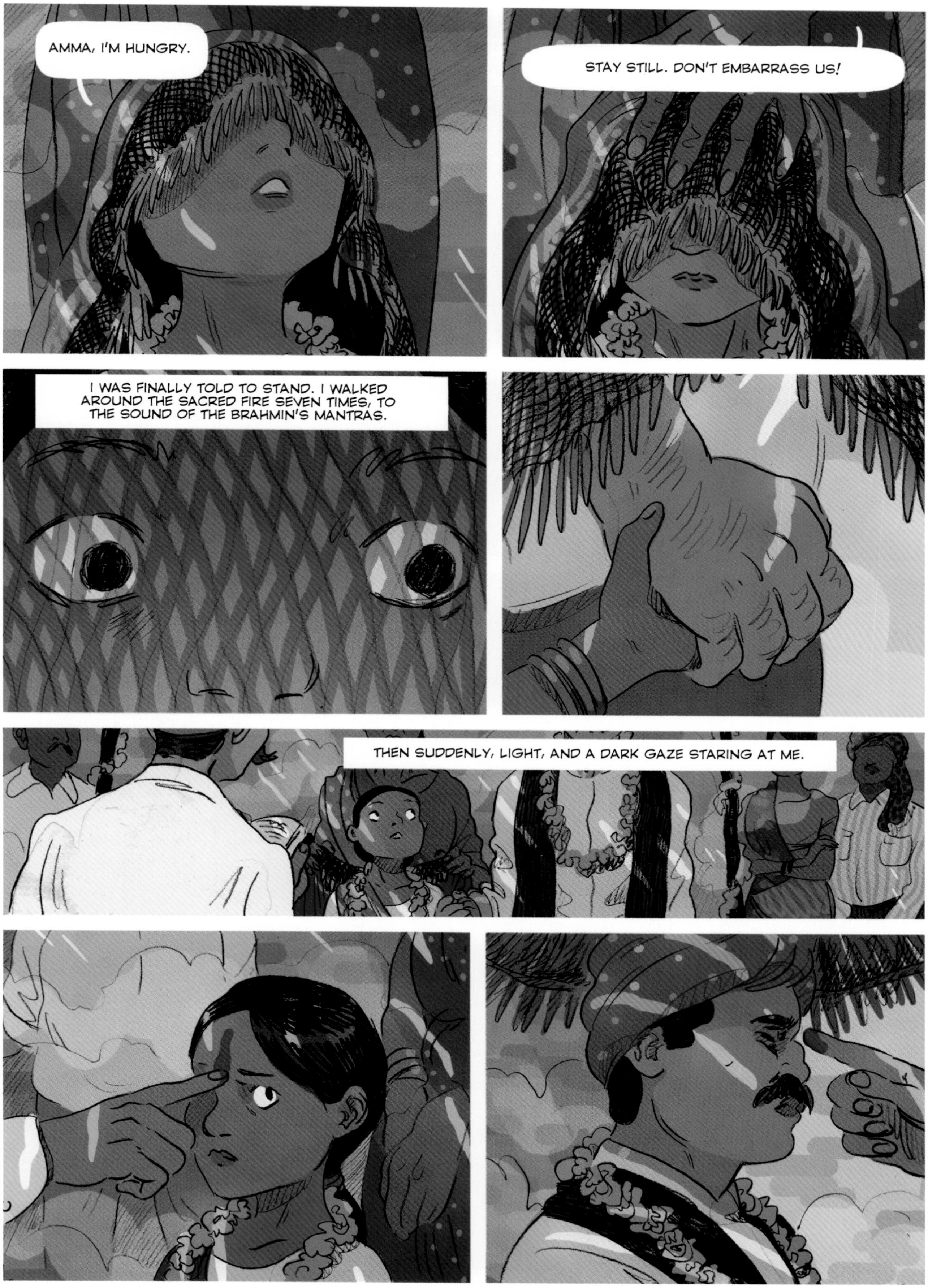
AMMA, I'M HUNGRY.
STAY STILL. DON'T EMBARRASS US!
I WAS FINALLY TOLD TO STAND. I WALKED AROUND THE SACRED FIRE SEVEN TIMES, TO THE SOUND OF THE BRAHMIN'S MANTRAS.
THEN SUDDENLY, LIGHT, AND A DARK GAZE STARING AT ME.

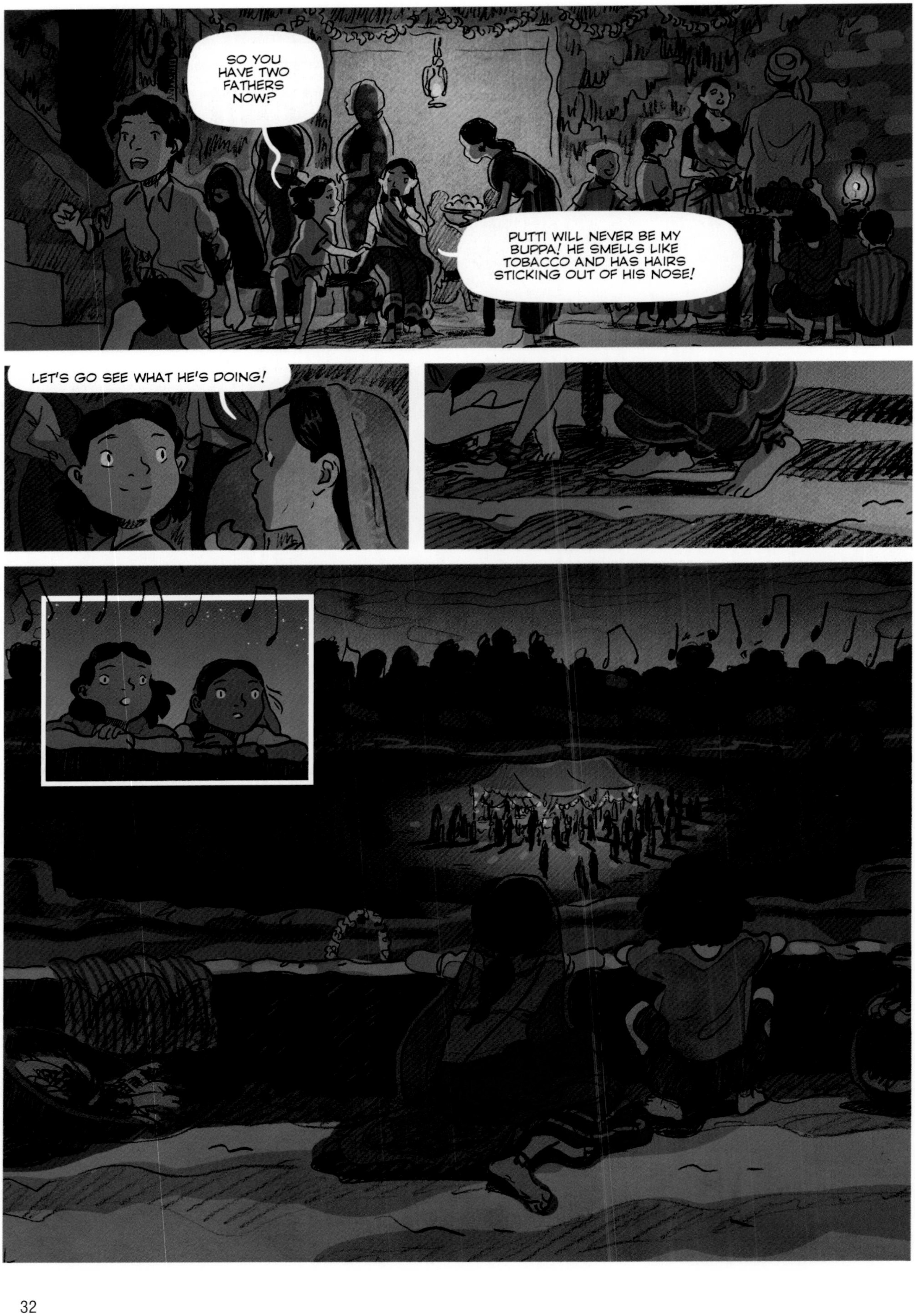
SO YOU HAVE TWO FATHERS NOW?
PUTTI WILL NEVER BE MY BUPPA! HE SMELLS LIKE TOBACCO AND HAS HAIRS STICKING OUT OF HIS NOSE!
LET'S GO SEE WHAT HE'S DOING!

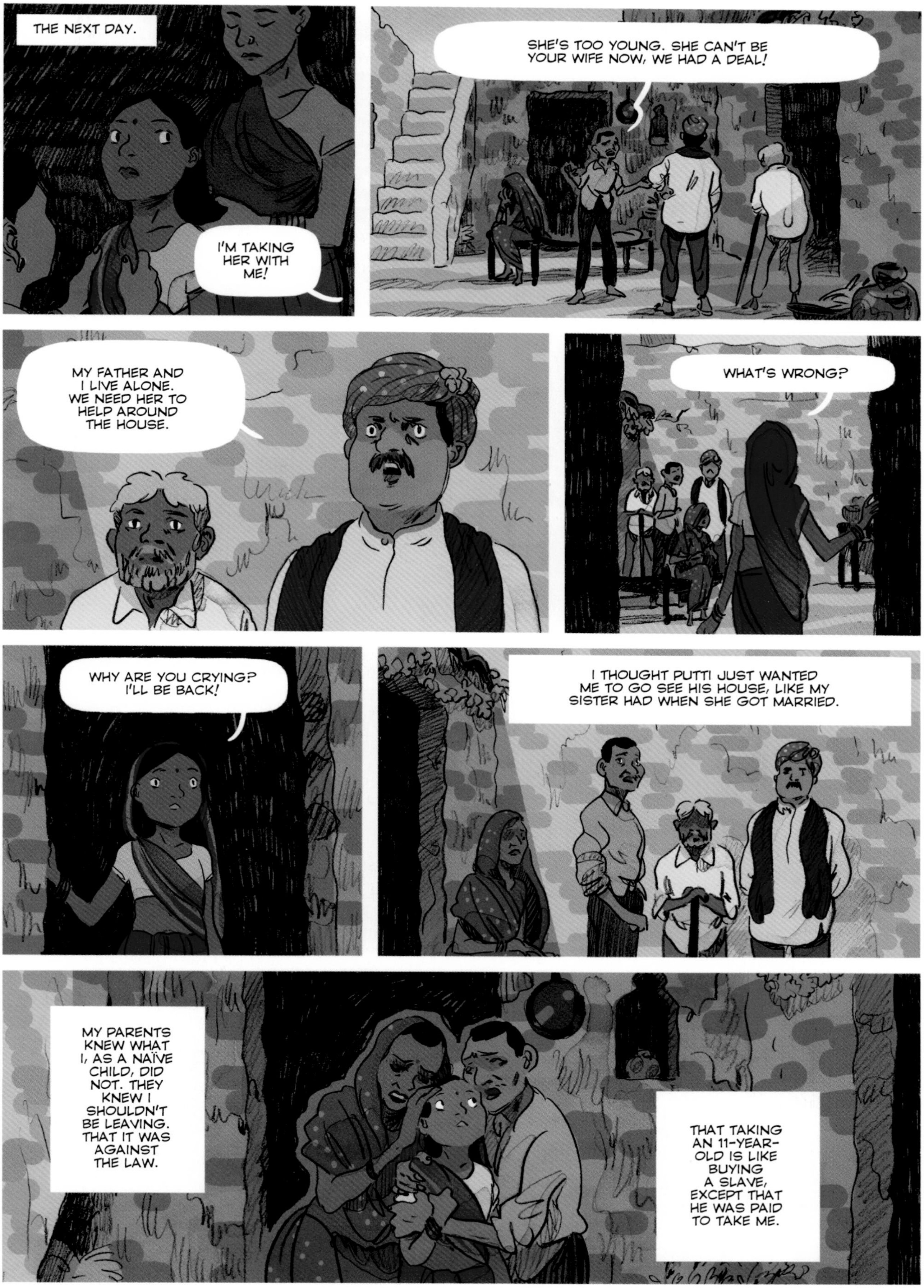
THE NEXT DAY.
I'M TAKING HER WITH ME!
SHE'S TOO YOUNG. SHE CAN'T BE YOUR WIFE NOW, WE HAD A DEAL!
MY FATHER AND I LIVE ALONE. WE NEED HER TO HELP AROUND THE HOUSE.
WHAT'S WRONG?
WHY ARE YOU CRYING? I'LL BE BACK!
I THOUGHT PUTTI JUST WANTED ME TO GO SEE HIS HOUSE, LIKE MY SISTER HAD WHEN SHE GOT MARRIED.
MY PARENTS KNEW WHAT I, AS A NAÏVE CHILD, DID NOT. THEY KNEW I SHOULDN'T BE LEAVING. THAT IT WAS AGAINST THE LAW.
THAT TAKING AN 11-YEAR-OLD IS LIKE BUYING A SLAVE, EXCEPT THAT HE WAS PAID TO TAKE ME.

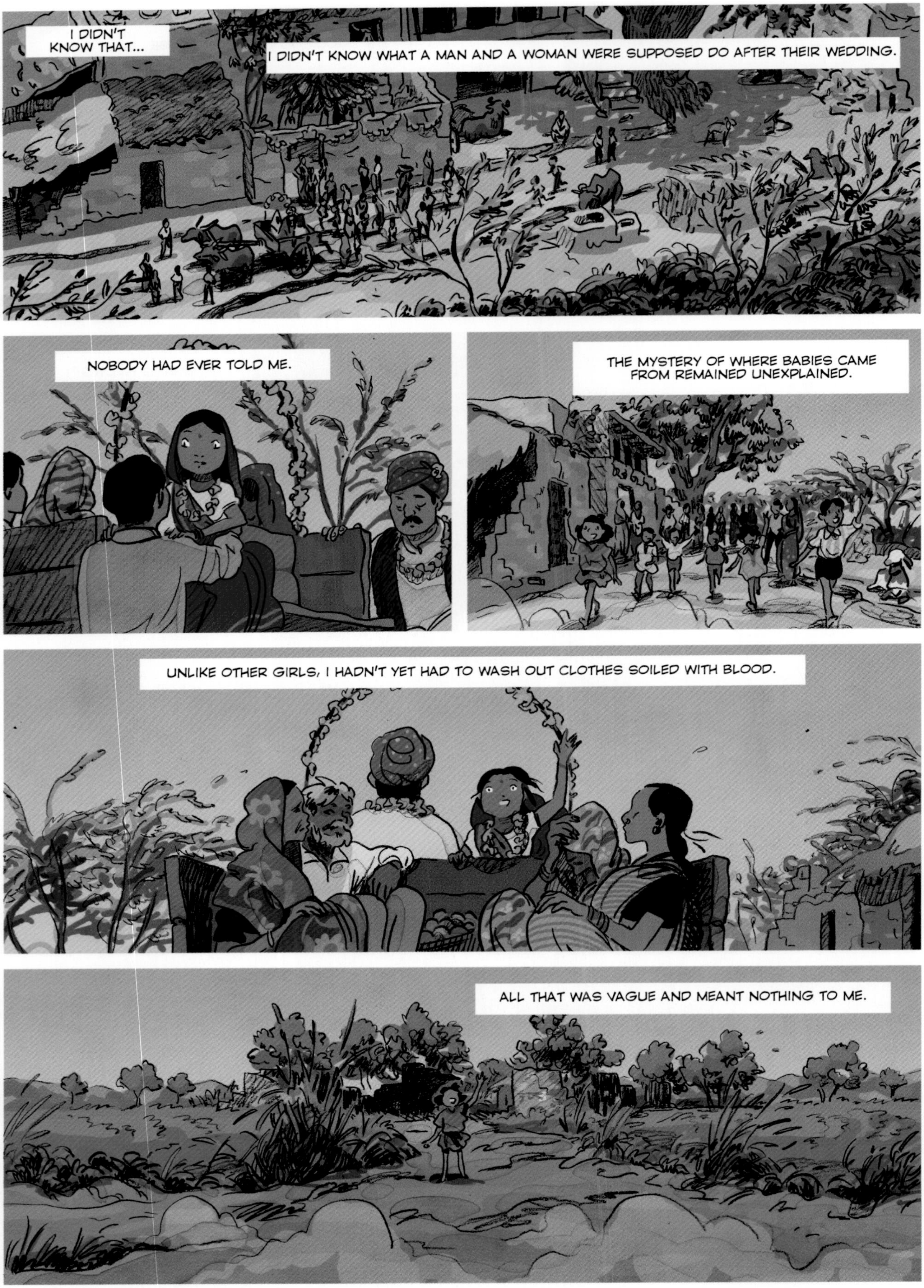
I DIDN'T KNOW THAT...
I DIDN'T KNOW WHAT A MAN AND A WOMAN WERE SUPPOSED DO AFTER THEIR WEDDING.
NOBODY HAD EVER TOLD ME.
THE MYSTERY OF WHERE BABIES CAME FROM REMAINED UNEXPLAINED.
UNLIKE OTHER GIRLS, I HADN'T YET HAD TO WASH OUT CLOTHES SOILED WITH BLOOD.
ALL THAT WAS VAGUE AND MEANT NOTHING TO ME.

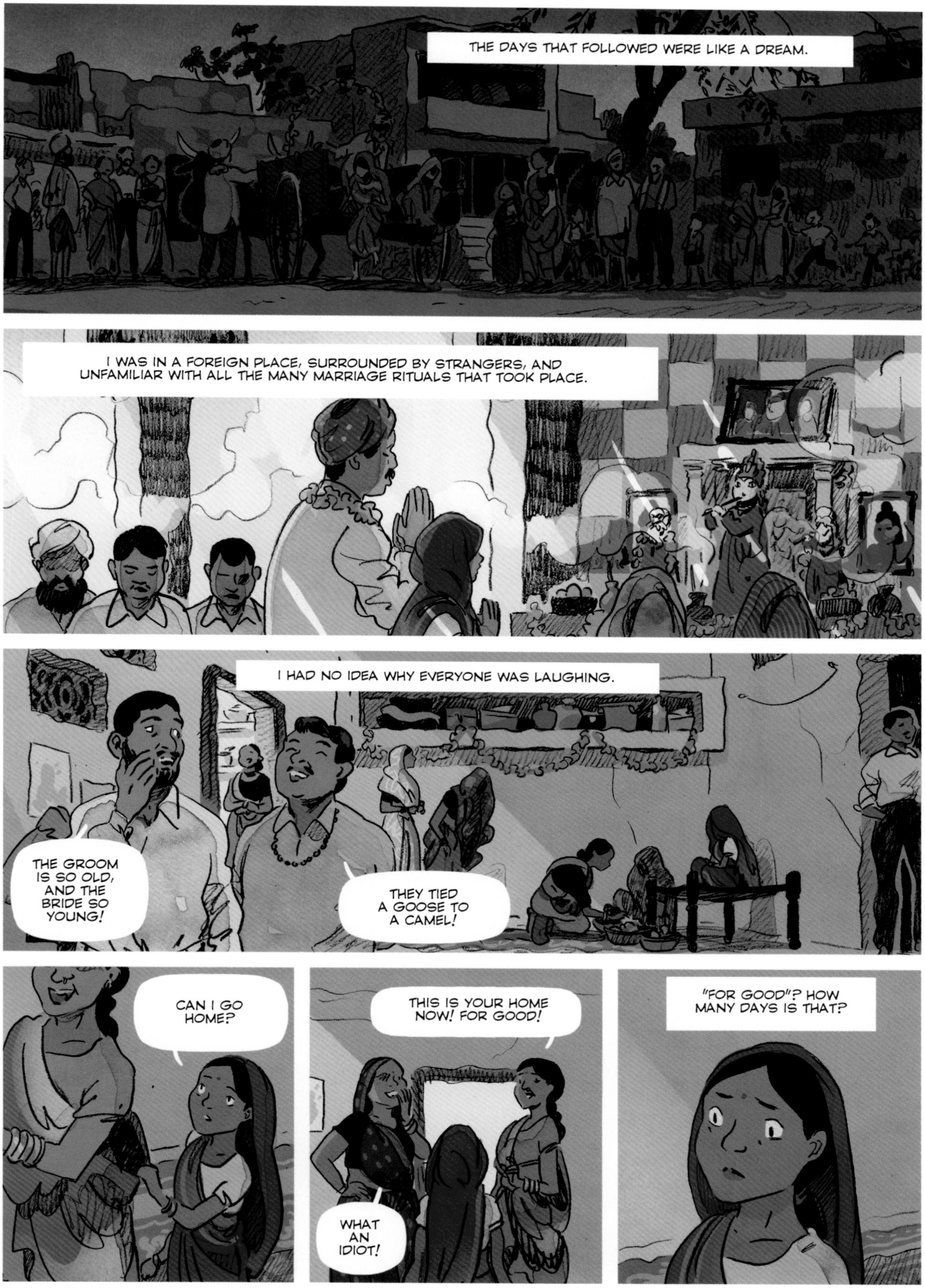
THE DAYS THAT FOLLOWED WERE LIKE A DREAM.
I WAS IN A FOREIGN PLACE, SURROUNDED BY STRANGERS, AND UNFAMILIAR WITH ALL THE MANY MARRIAGE RITUALS THAT TOOK PLACE.
I HAD NO IDEA WHY EVERYONE WAS LAUGHING.
THE GROOM IS SO OLD, AND THE BRIDE SO YOUNG!
THEY TIED A GOOSE TO A CAMEL!
CAN I GO HOME?
THIS IS YOUR HOME NOW! FOR GOOD!
WHAT AN IDIOT!
"FOR GOOD"? HOW MANY DAYS IS THAT?

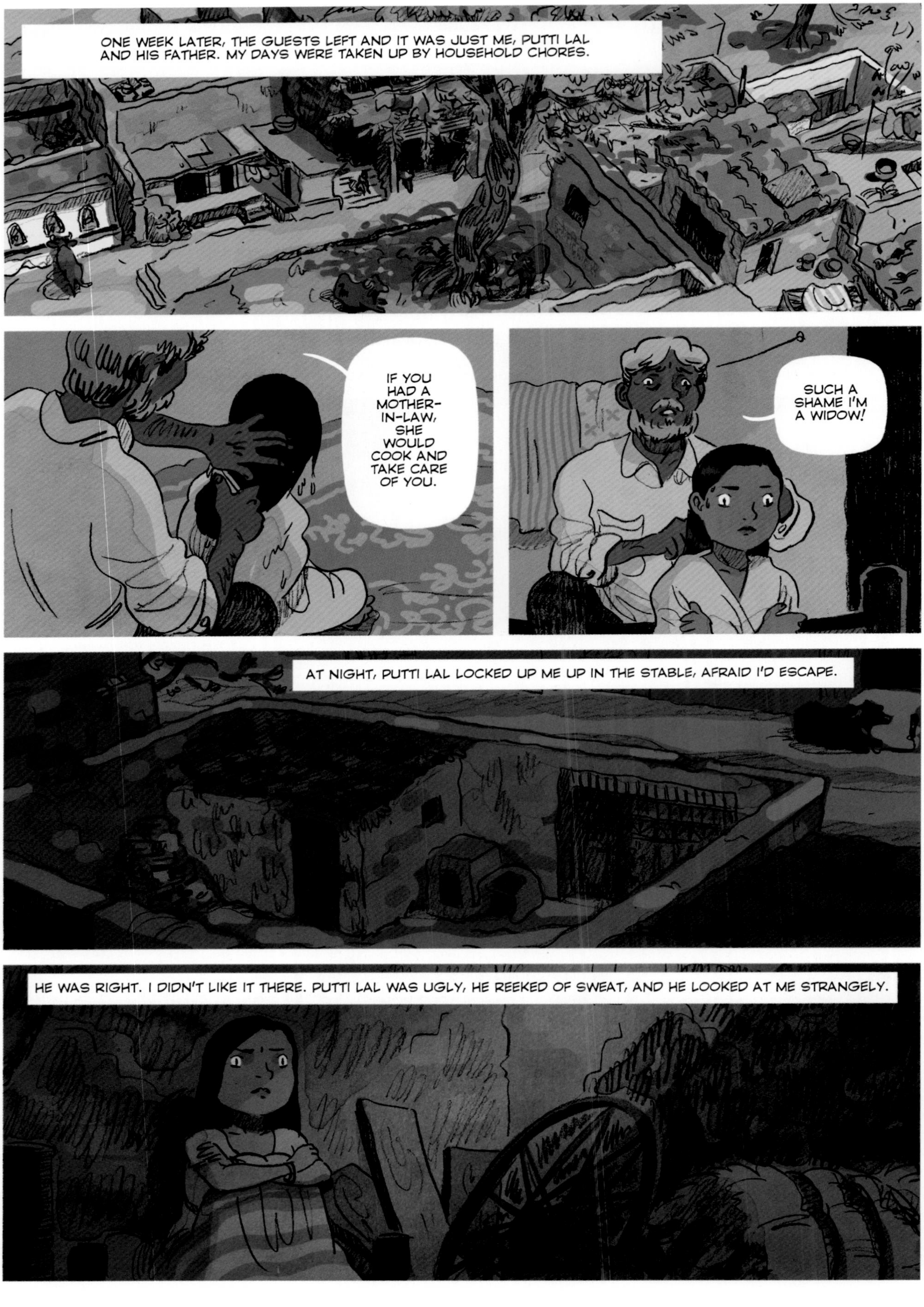
ONE WEEK LATER, THE GUESTS LEFT AND IT WAS JUST ME, PUTTI LAL AND HIS FATHER. MY DAYS WERE TAKEN UP BY HOUSEHOLD CHORES.
IF YOU HAD A MOTHER-IN-LAW, SHE WOULD COOK AND TAKE CARE OF YOU.
SUCH A SHAME I'M A WIDOW!
AT NIGHT, PUTTI LAL LOCKED UP ME UP IN THE STABLE, AFRAID I'D ESCAPE.
HE WAS RIGHT. I DIDN'T LIKE IT THERE. PUTTI LAL WAS UGLY, HE REEKED OF SWEAT, AND HE LOOKED AT ME STRANGELY.

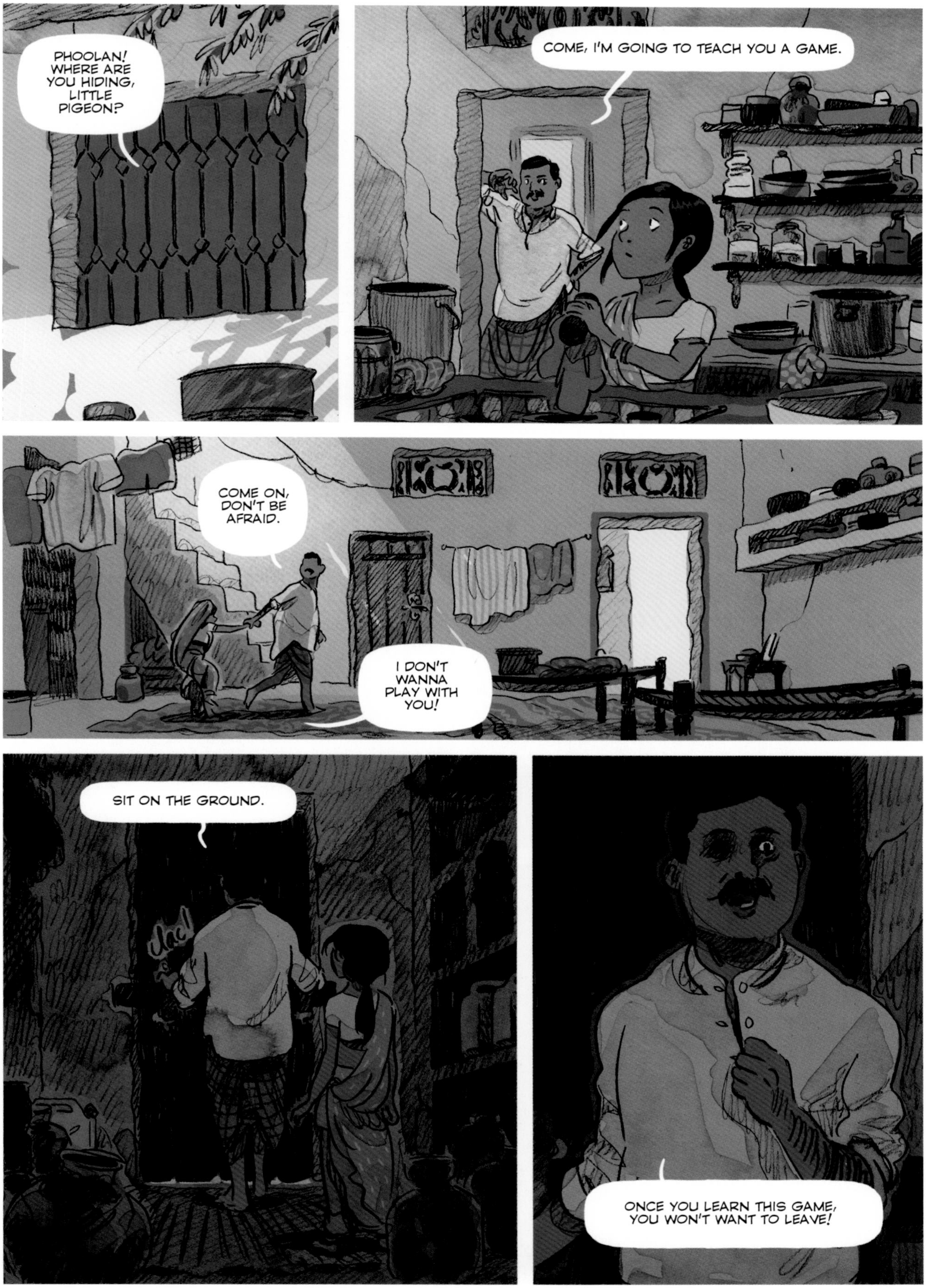
PHOOLAN! WHERE ARE YOU HIDING, LITTLE PIGEON?
COME, I'M GOING TO TEACH YOU A GAME.
COME ON, DON'T BE AFRAID.
I DON'T WANNA PLAY WITH YOU!
SIT ON THE GROUND.
ONCE YOU LEARN THIS GAME, YOU WON'T WANT TO LEAVE!

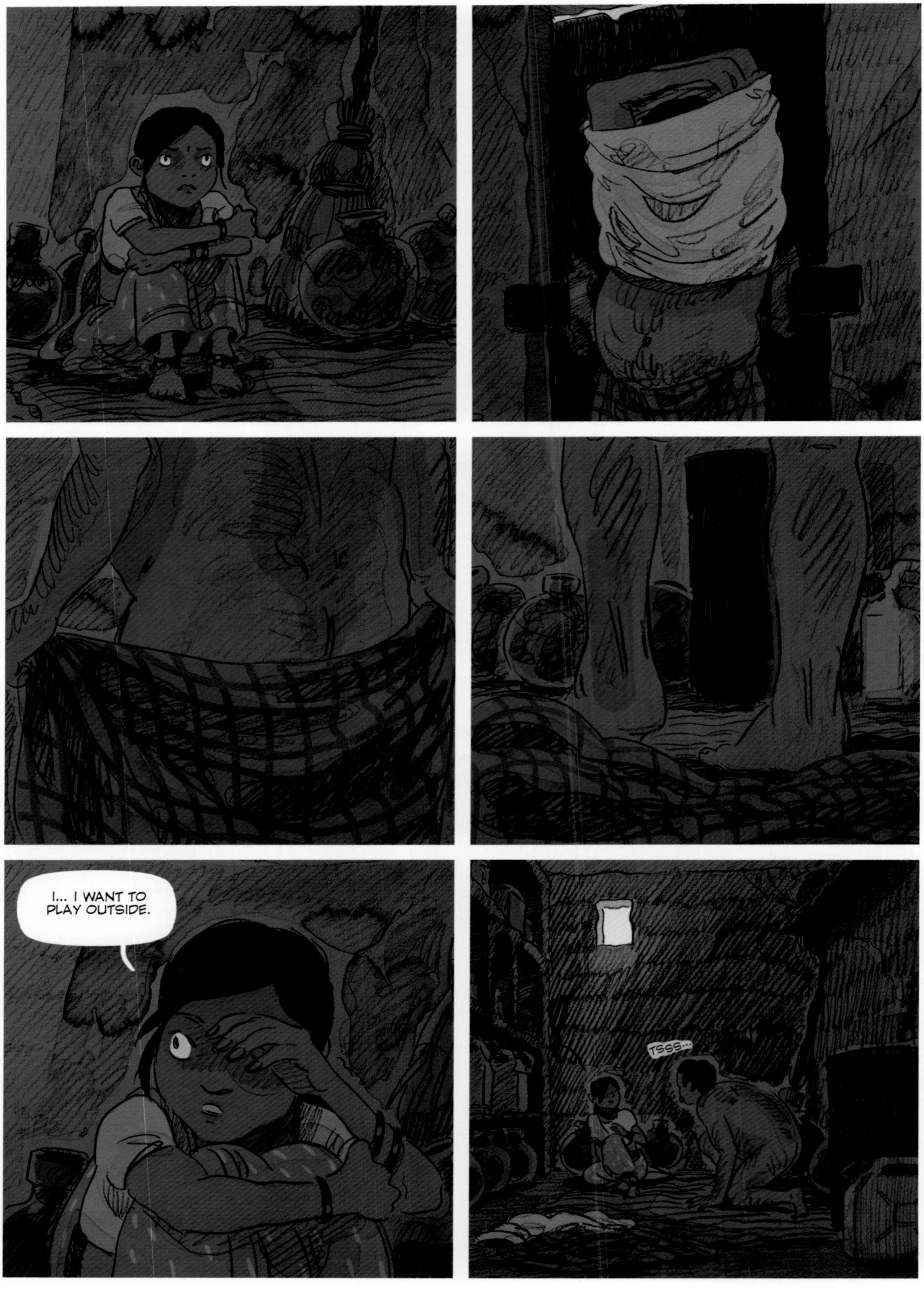
I... I WANT TO PLAY OUTSIDE.
TSSS...

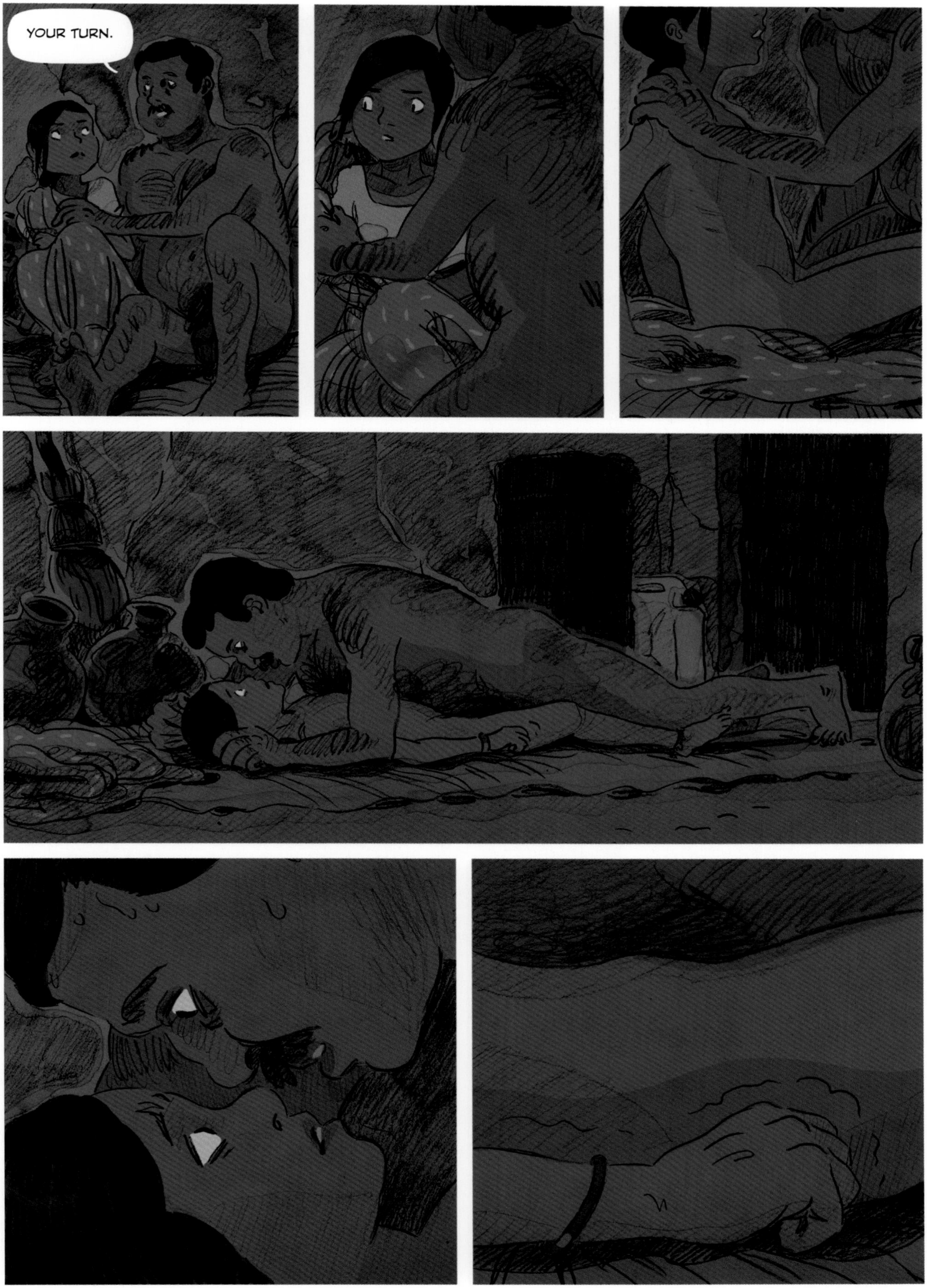
YOUR TURN.

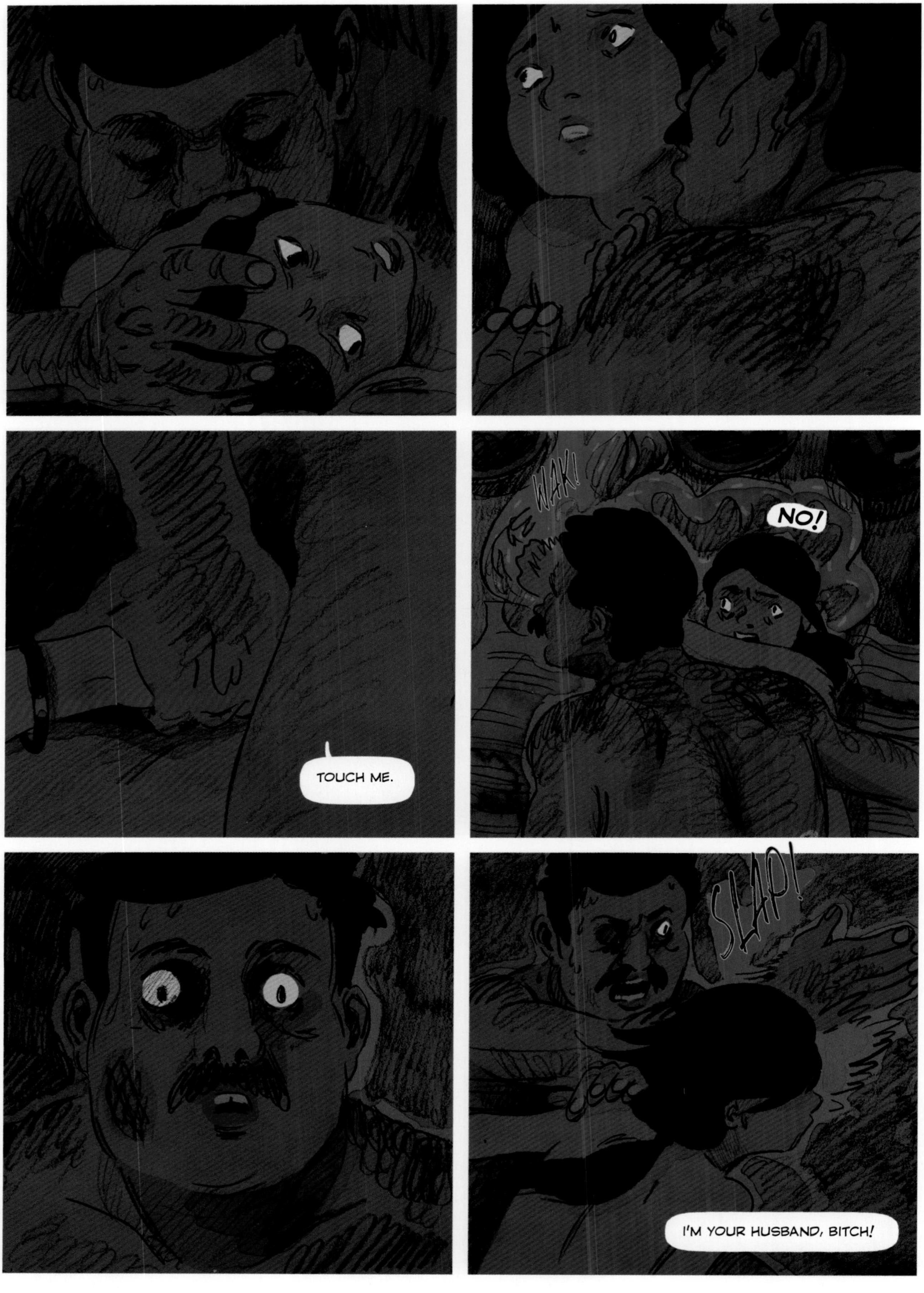
TOUCH ME.
WAK!
NO!
SLAP!
I'M YOUR HUSBAND, BITCH!

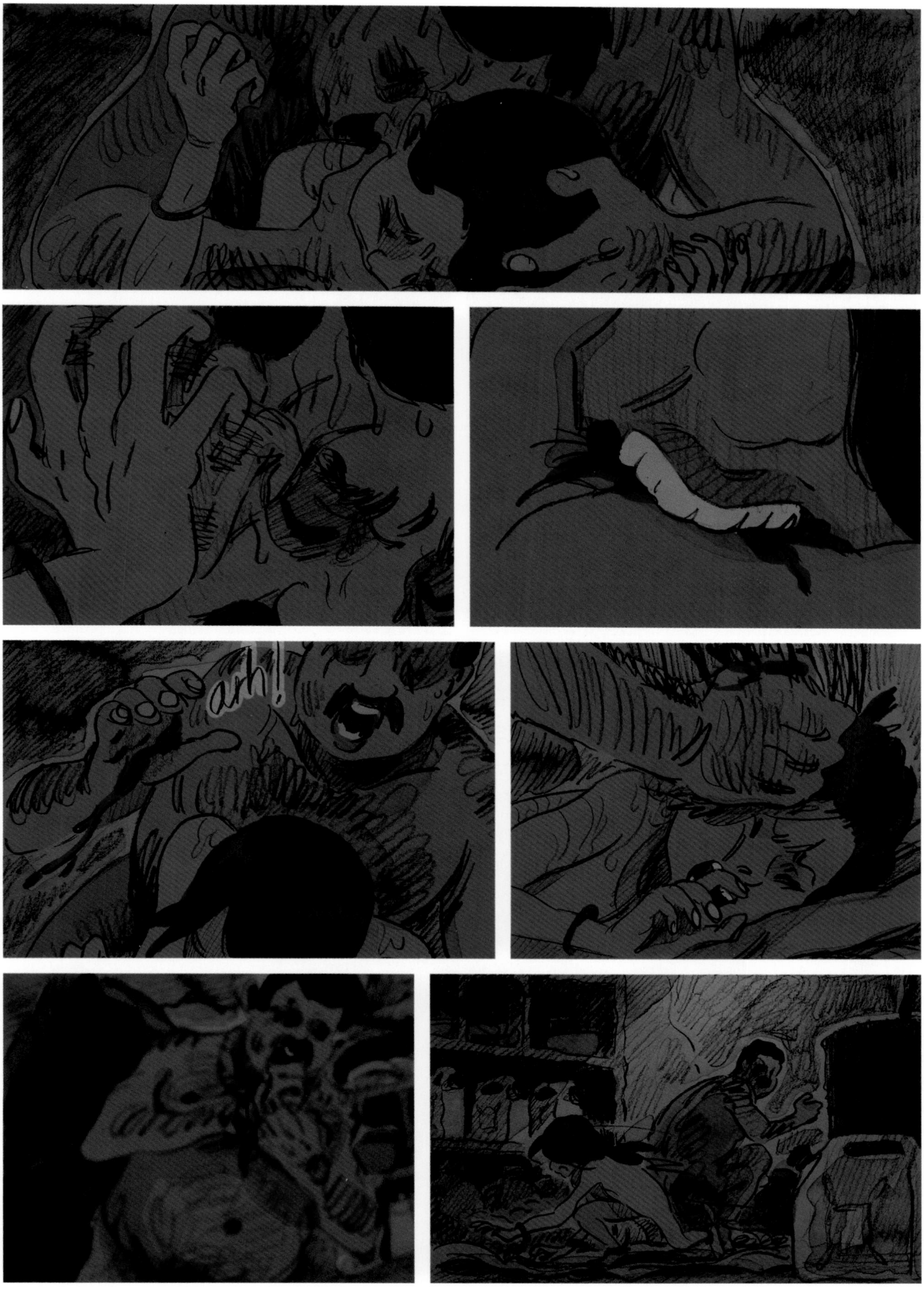
arh!

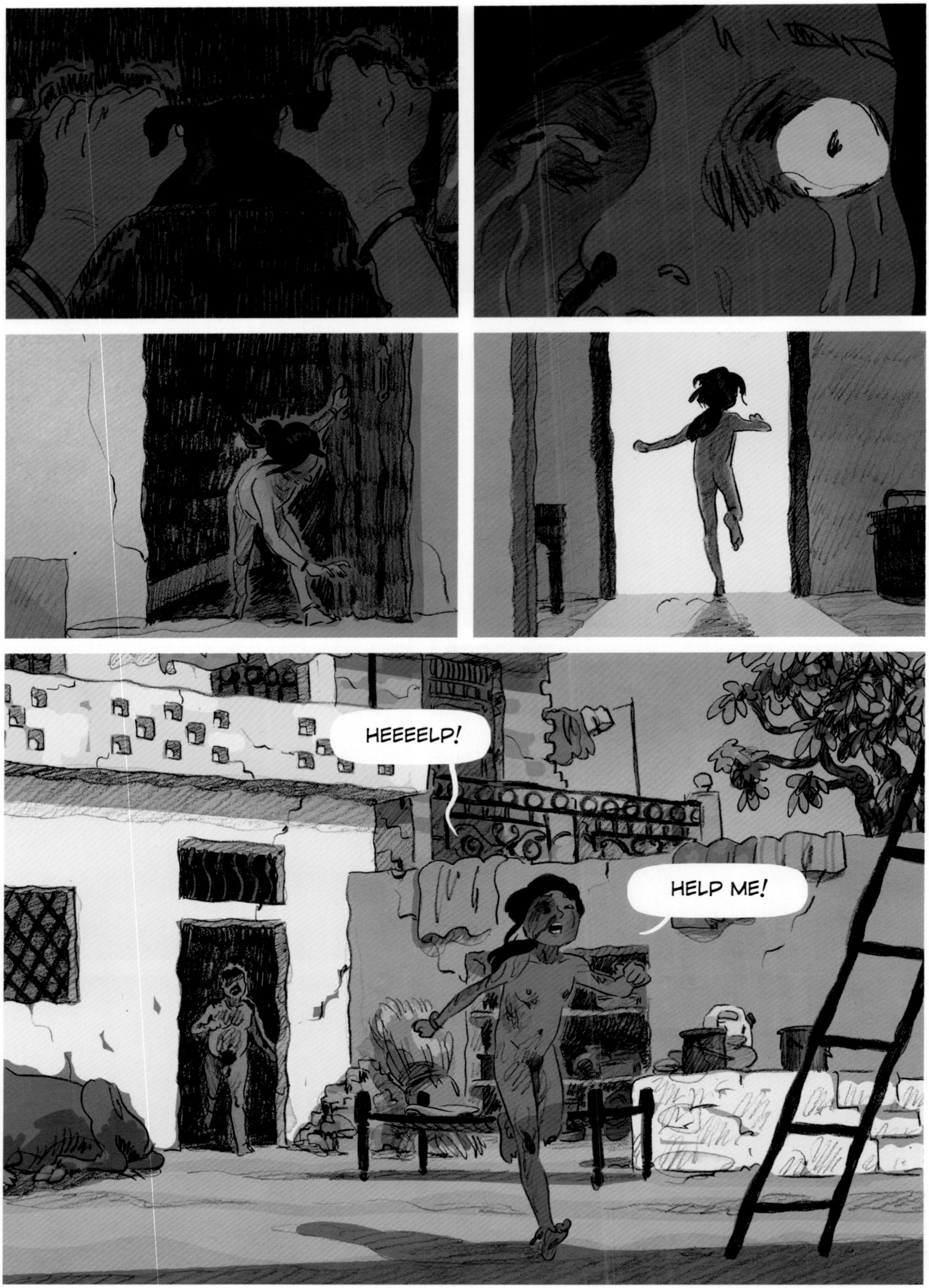
HEEEELP!
HELP ME!

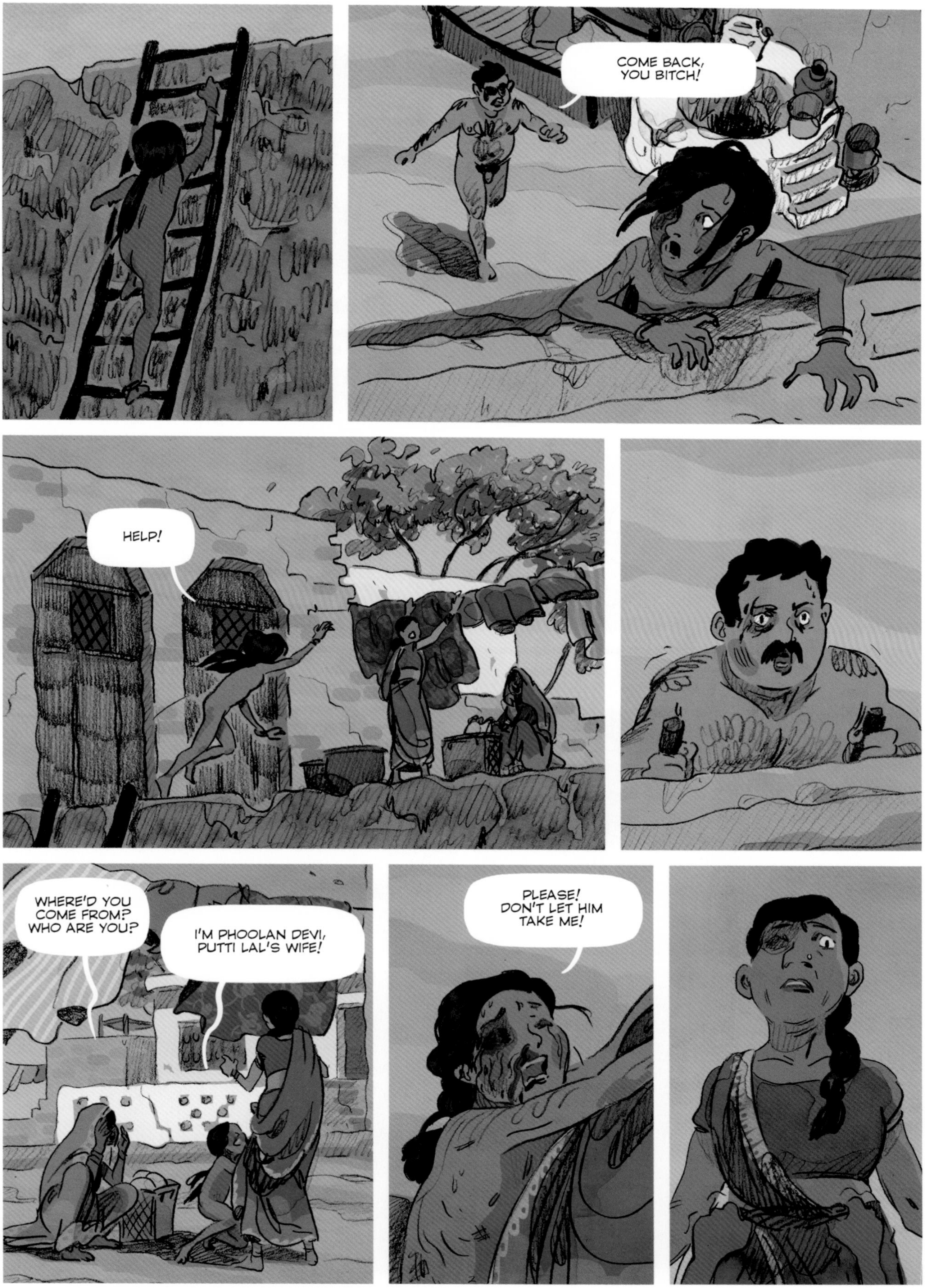
COME BACK, YOU BITCH!
HELP!
WHERE'D YOU COME FROM? WHO ARE YOU?
I'M PHOOLAN DEVI, PUTTI LAL'S WIFE!
PLEASE! DON'T LET HIM TAKE ME!

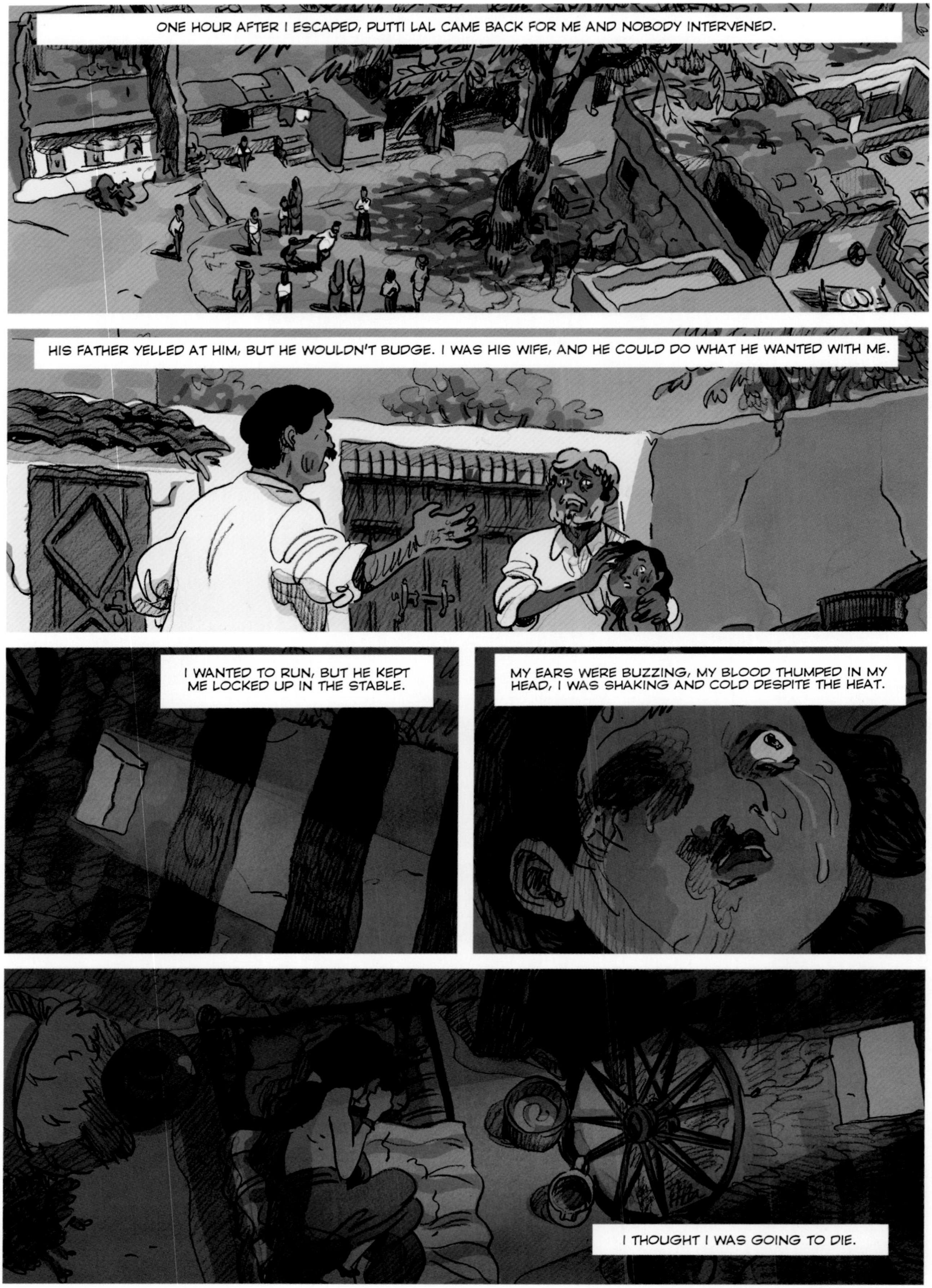
ONE HOUR AFTER I ESCAPED, PUTTI LAL CAME BACK FOR ME AND NOBODY INTERVENED.
HIS FATHER YELLED AT HIM, BUT HE WOULDN'T BUDGE. I WAS HIS WIFE, AND HE COULD DO WHAT HE WANTED WITH ME.
I WANTED TO RUN, BUT HE KEPT ME LOCKED UP IN THE STABLE.
MY EARS WERE BUZZING, MY BLOOD THUMPED IN MY HEAD, I WAS SHAKING AND COLD DESPITE THE HEAT.
I THOUGHT I WAS GOING TO DIE.

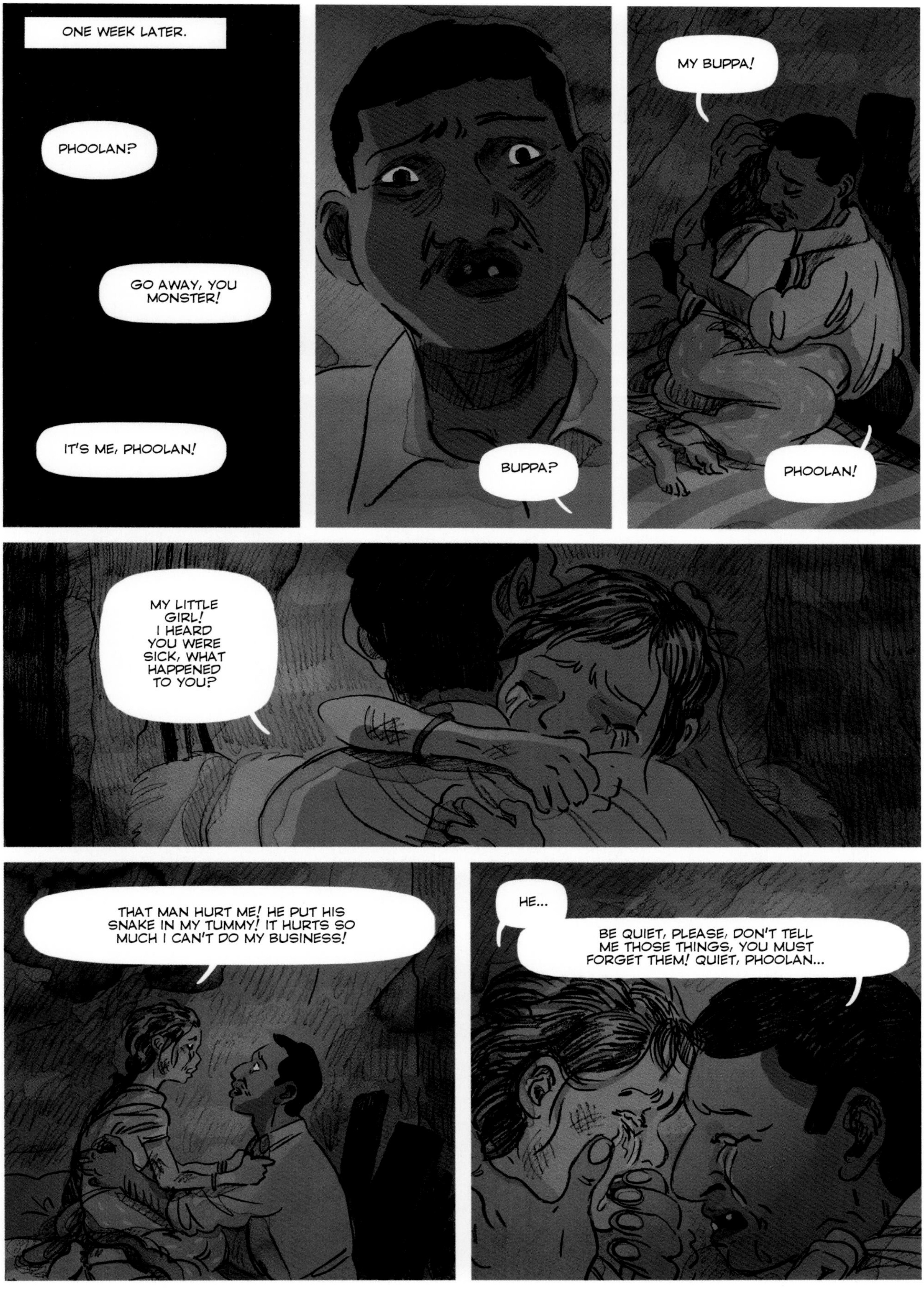
ONE WEEK LATER.
PHOOLAN?
GO AWAY, YOU MONSTER!
IT'S ME, PHOOLAN!
BUPPA?
MY BUPPA!
PHOOLAN!
MY LITTLE GIRL! I HEARD YOU WERE SICK, WHAT HAPPENED TO YOU?
THAT MAN HURT ME! HE PUT HIS SNAKE IN MY TUMMY! IT HURTS SO MUCH I CAN'T DO MY BUSINESS!
HE...
BE QUIET, PLEASE, DON'T TELL ME THOSE THINGS, YOU MUST FORGET THEM! QUIET, PHOOLAN...

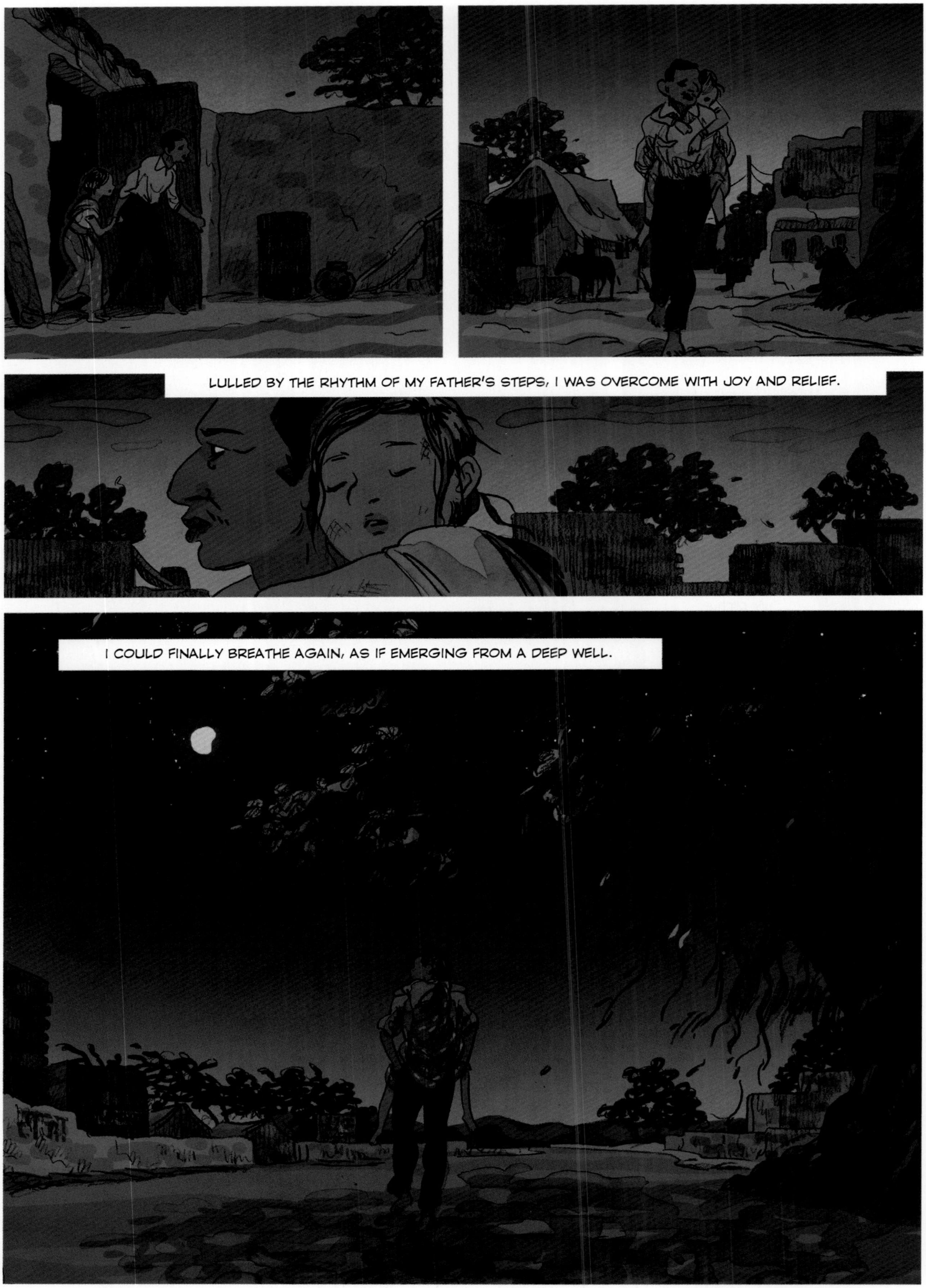
LULLED BY THE RHYTHM OF MY FATHER'S STEPS, I WAS OVERCOME WITH JOY AND RELIEF.
I COULD FINALLY BREATHE AGAIN, AS IF EMERGING FROM A DEEP WELL.

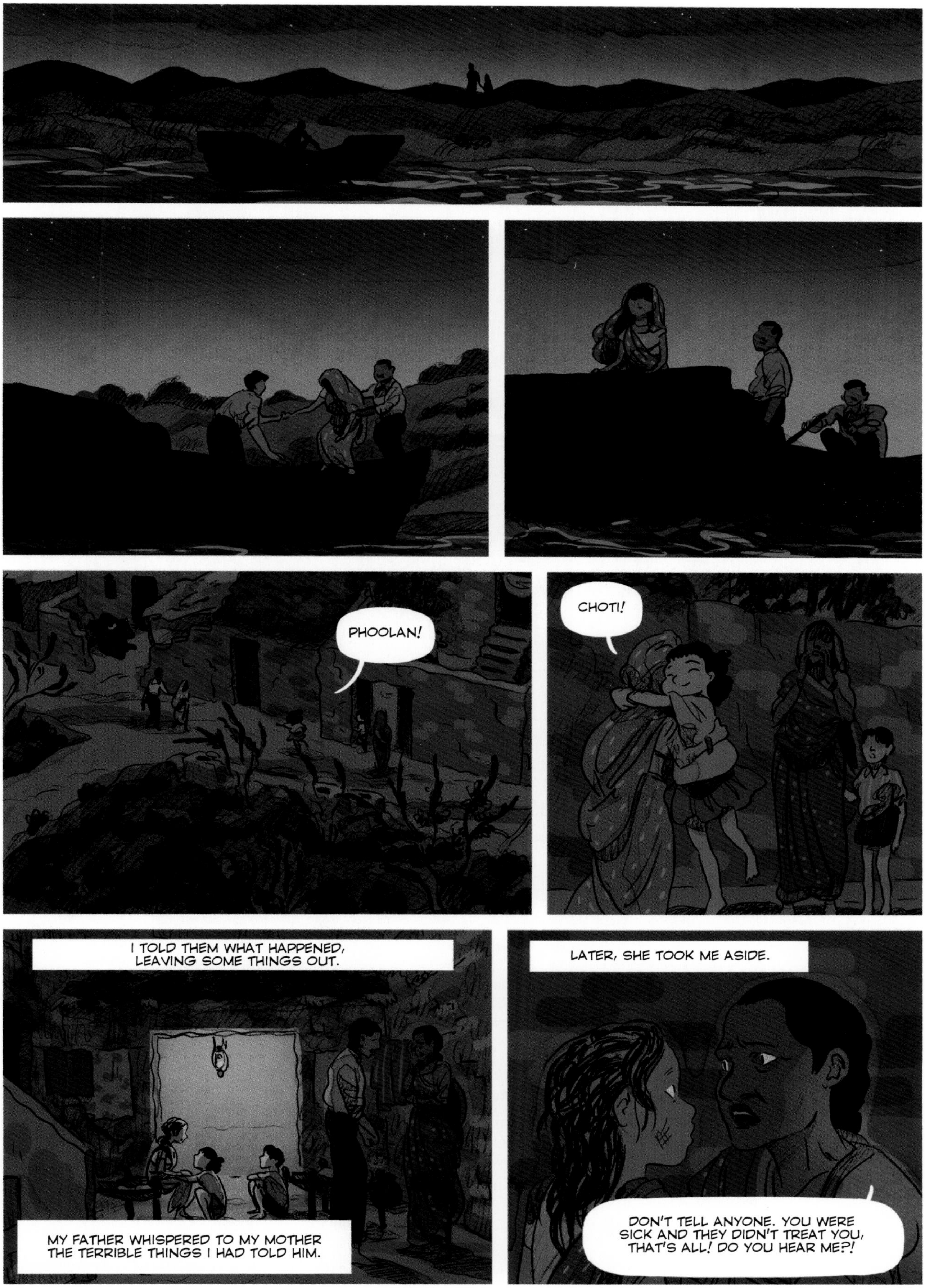
PHOOLAN!
CHOTI!
I TOLD THEM WHAT HAPPENED, LEAVING SOME THINGS OUT.
MY FATHER WHISPERED TO MY MOTHER THE TERRIBLE THINGS I HAD TOLD HIM.
LATER, SHE TOOK ME ASIDE.
DON'T TELL ANYONE. YOU WERE SICK AND THEY DIDN'T TREAT YOU, THAT'S ALL! DO YOU HEAR ME?!

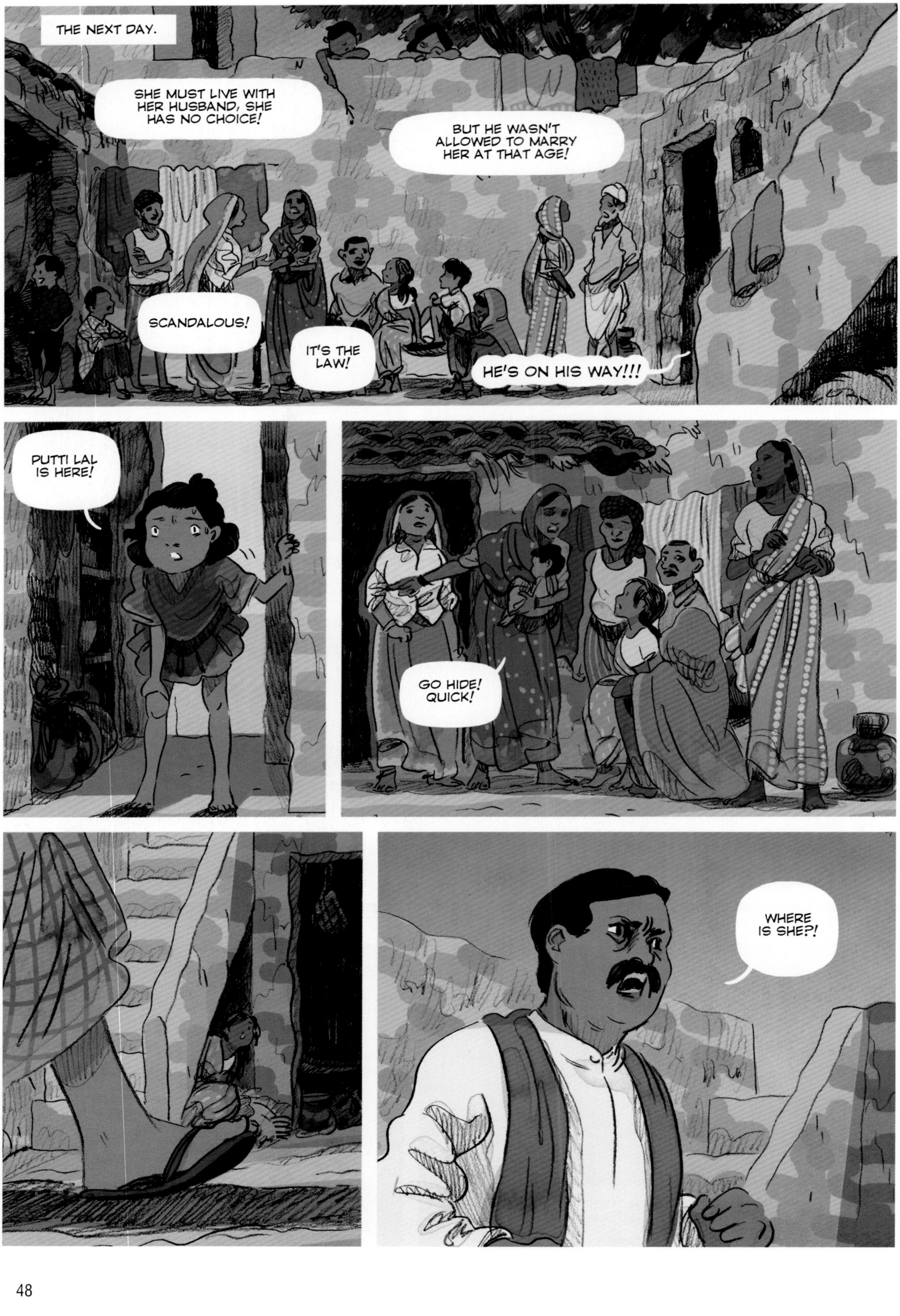
THE NEXT DAY.
SHE MUST LIVE WITH HER HUSBAND, SHE HAS NO CHOICE!
BUT HE WASN'T ALLOWED TO MARRY HER AT THAT AGE!
SCANDALOUS!
IT'S THE LAW!
HE'S ON HIS WAY!!!
PUTTI LAL IS HERE!
GO HIDE! QUICK!
WHERE IS SHE?!

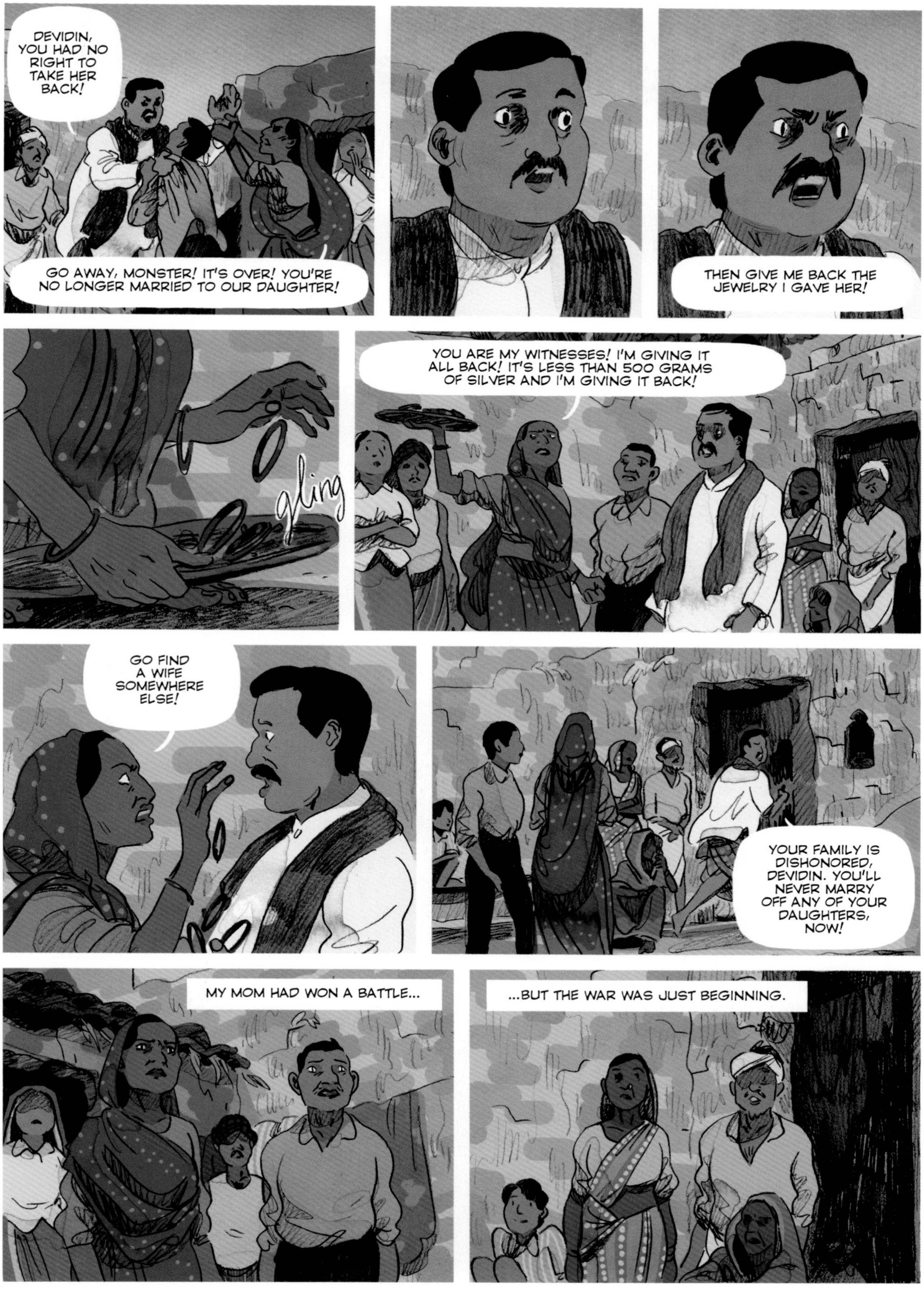
DEVIDIN, YOU HAD NO RIGHT TO TAKE HER BACK!
GO AWAY, MONSTER! IT'S OVER! YOU'RE NO LONGER MARRIED TO OUR DAUGHTER!
THEN GIVE ME BACK THE JEWELRY I GAVE HER!
gling
YOU ARE MY WITNESSES! I'M GIVING IT ALL BACK! IT'S LESS THAN 500 GRAMS OF SILVER AND I'M GIVING IT BACK!
GO FIND A WIFE SOMEWHERE ELSE!
YOUR FAMILY IS DISHONORED, DEVIDIN. YOU'LL NEVER MARRY OFF ANY OF YOUR DAUGHTERS, NOW!
MY MOM HAD WON A BATTLE...
...BUT THE WAR WAS JUST BEGINNING.

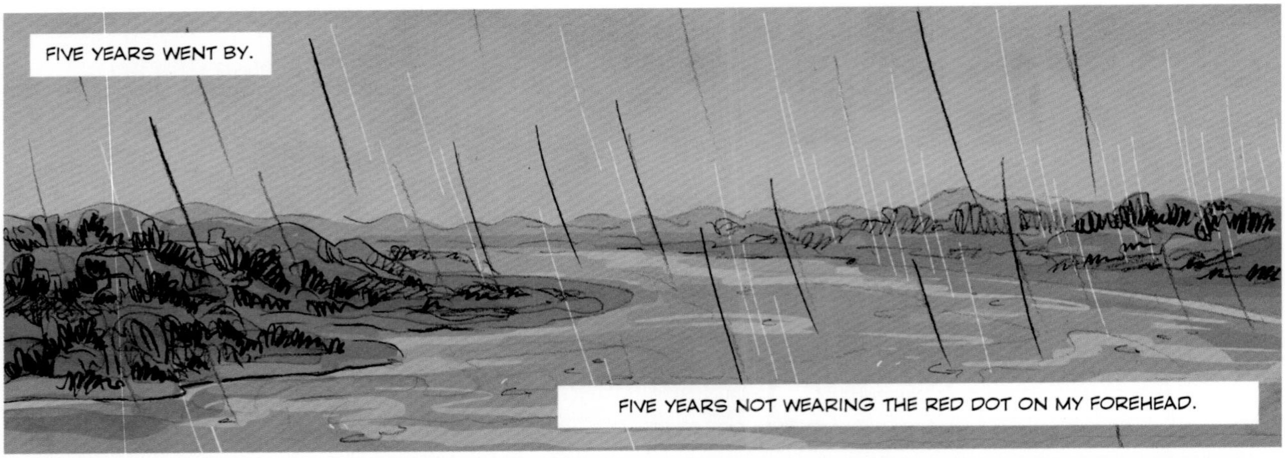
FIVE YEARS WENT BY.
FIVE YEARS NOT WEARING THE RED DOT ON MY FOREHEAD.

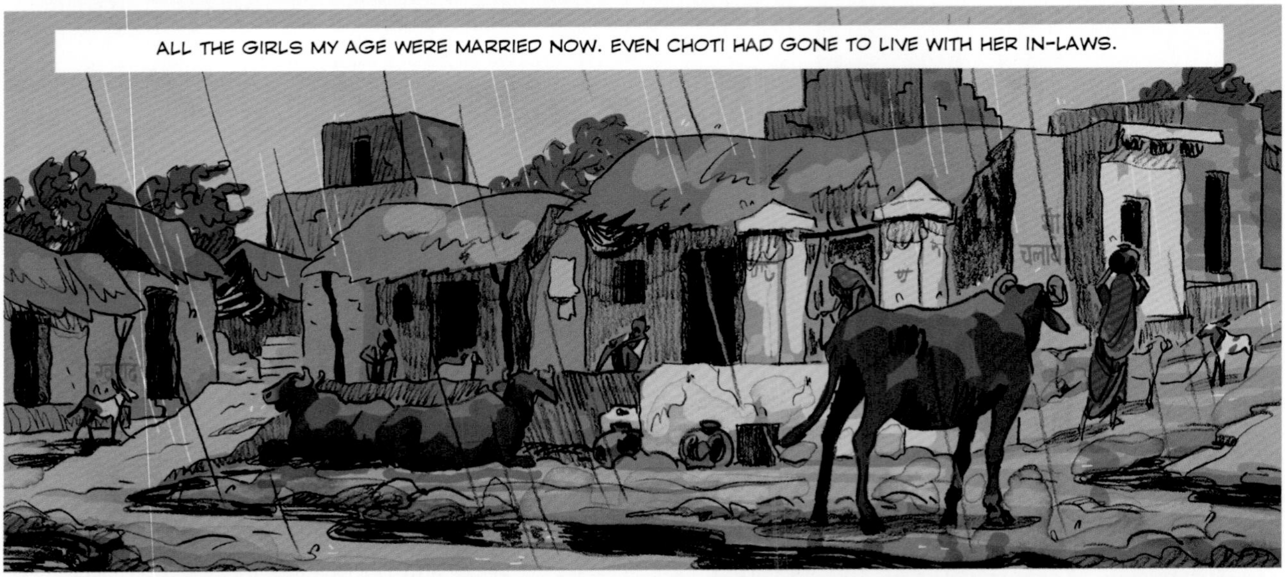
ALL THE GIRLS MY AGE WERE MARRIED NOW. EVEN CHOTI HAD GONE TO LIVE WITH HER IN-LAWS.

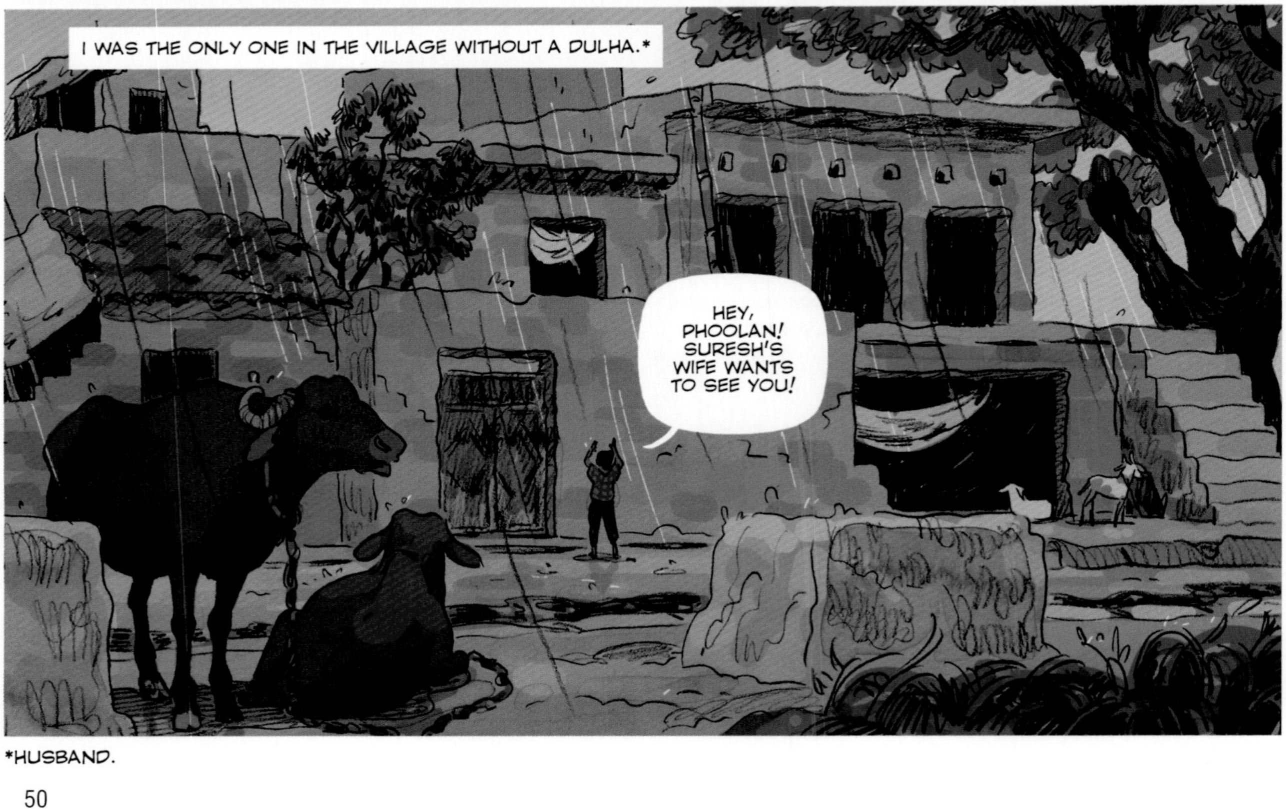
I WAS THE ONLY ONE IN THE VILLAGE WITHOUT A DULHA.*
HEY, PHOOLAN! SURESH'S WIFE WANTS TO SEE YOU!

*HUSBAND.

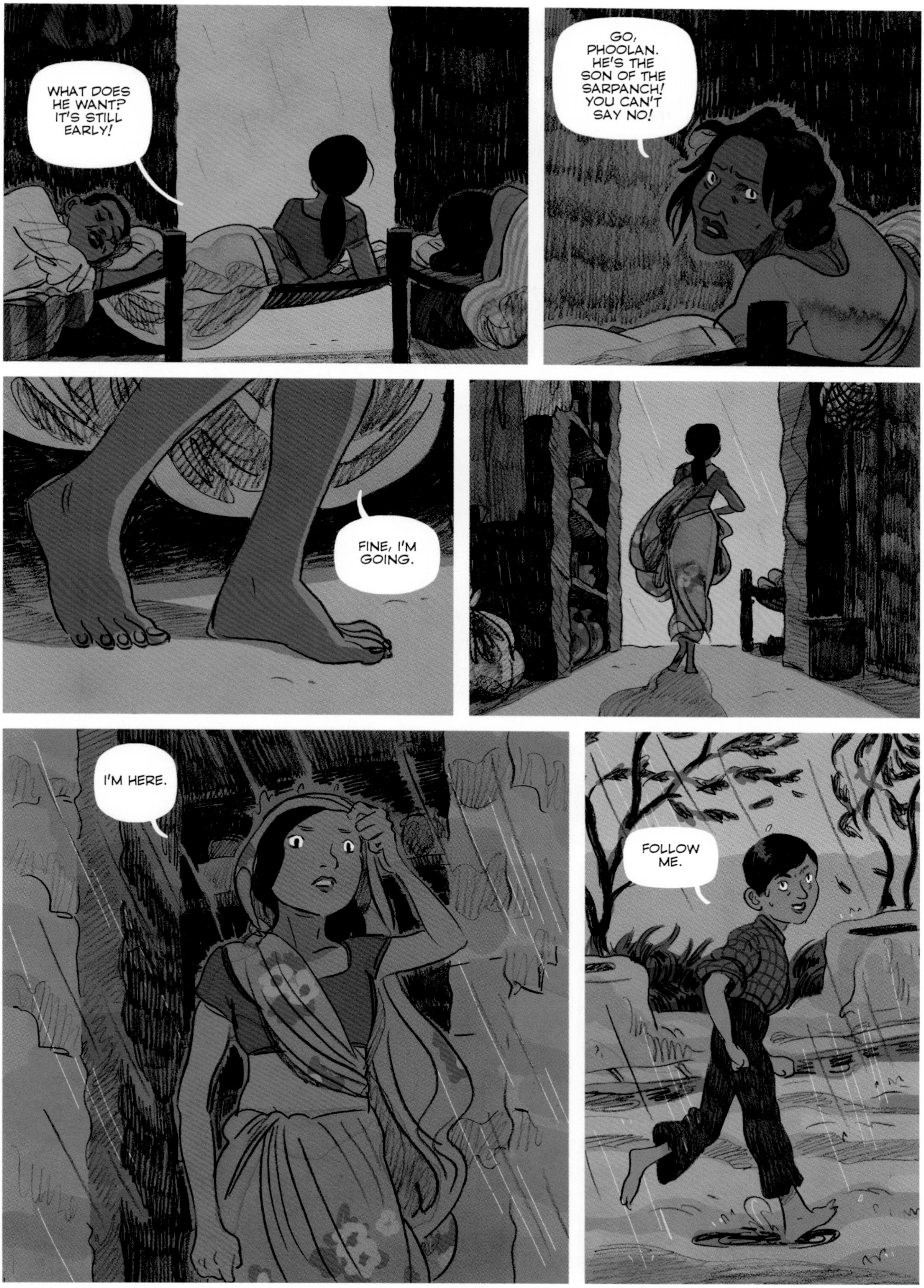
WHAT DOES HE WANT? IT'S STILL EARLY!
GO, PHOOLAN. HE'S THE SON OF THE SARPANCH! YOU CAN'T SAY NO!
FINE, I'M GOING.
I'M HERE.
FOLLOW ME.

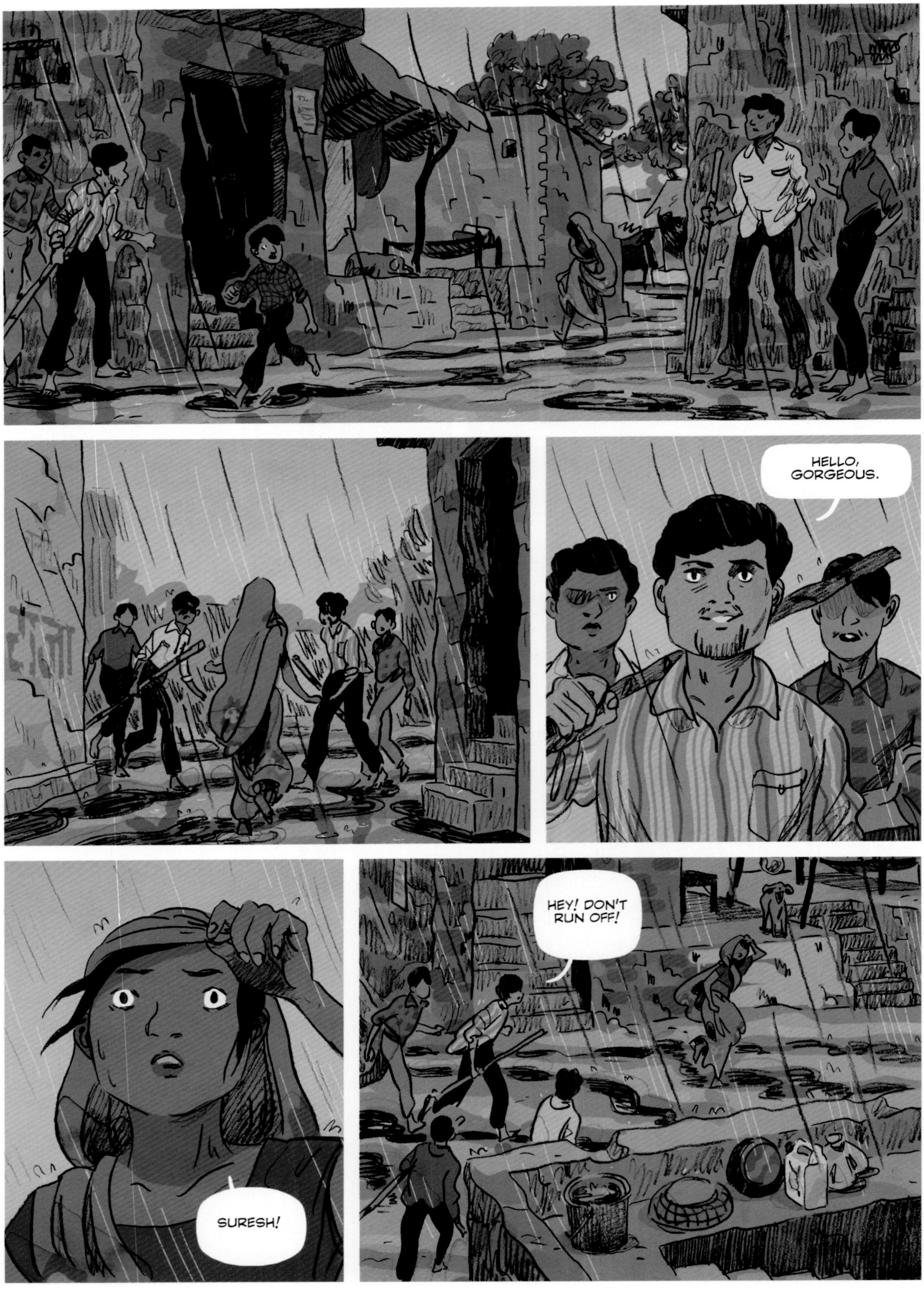
HELLO, GORGEOUS.
SURESH!
HEY! DON'T RUN OFF!

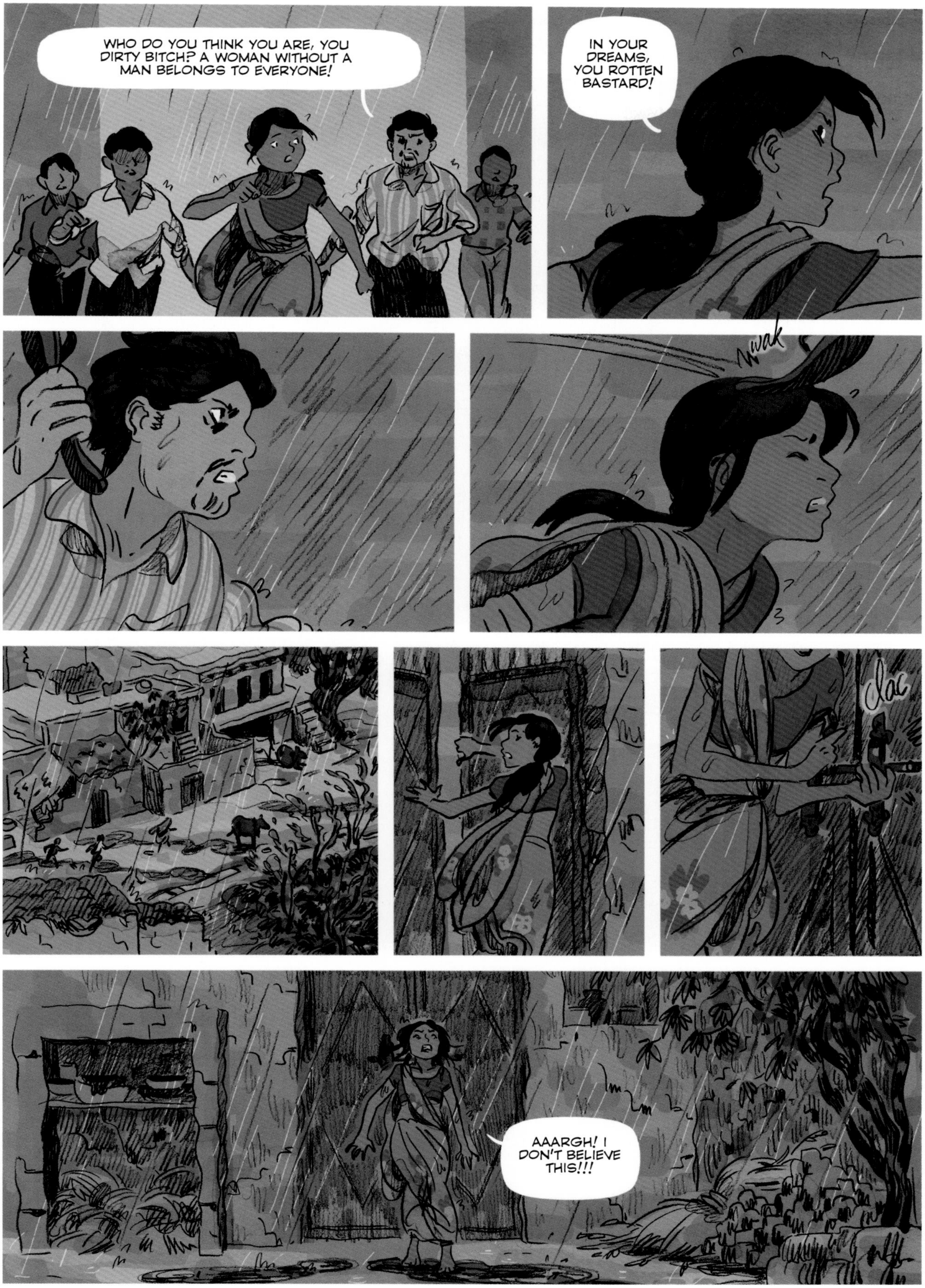
WHO DO YOU THINK YOU ARE, YOU DIRTY BITCH? A WOMAN WITHOUT A MAN BELONGS TO EVERYONE!
IN YOUR DREAMS, YOU ROTTEN BASTARD!
wak
clac
AAARGH! I DON'T BELIEVE THIS!!!

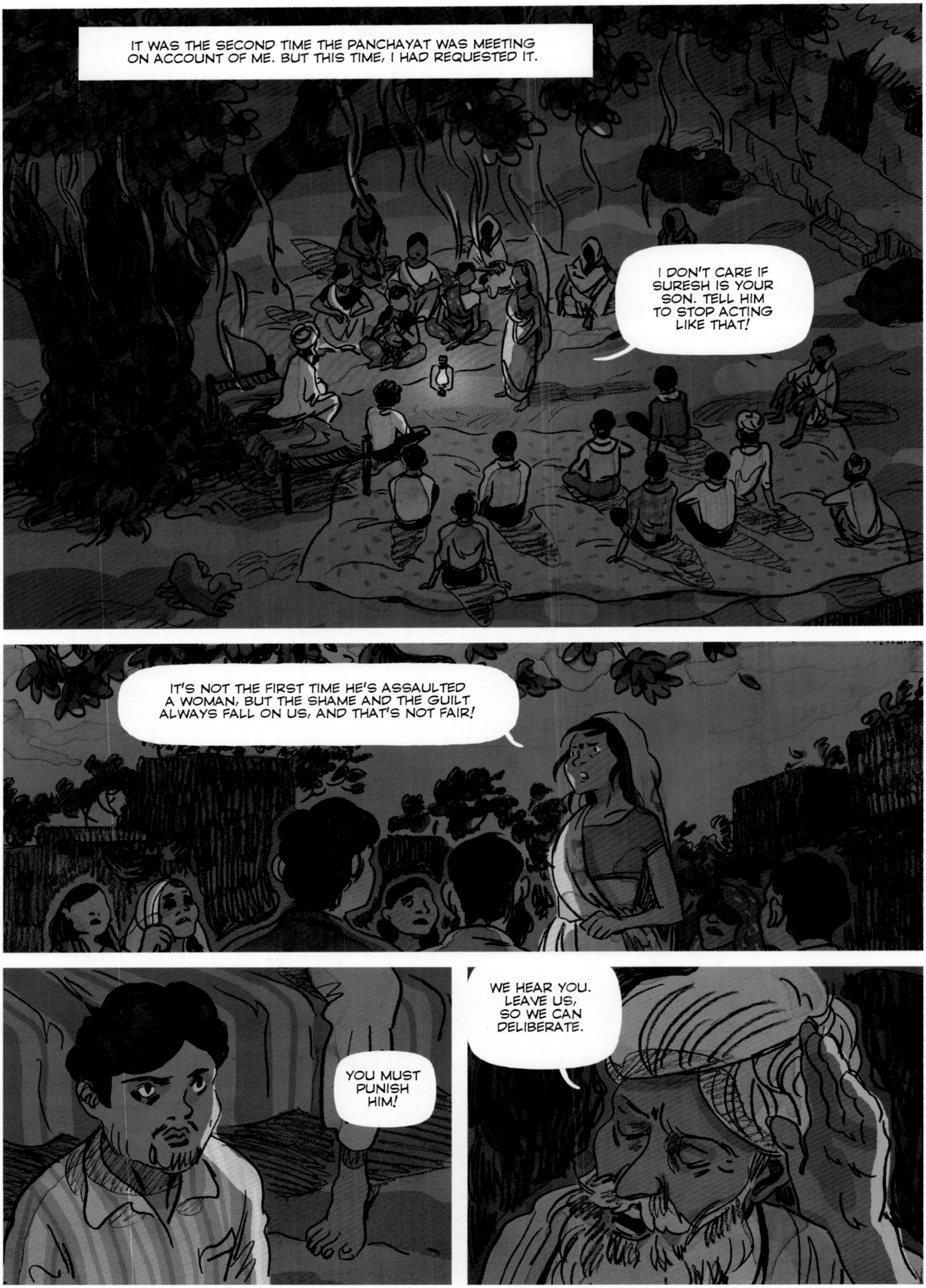
IT WAS THE SECOND TIME THE PANCHAYAT WAS MEETING ON ACCOUNT OF ME. BUT THIS TIME, I HAD REQUESTED IT.
I DON'T CARE IF SURESH IS YOUR SON. TELL HIM TO STOP ACTING LIKE THAT!
IT'S NOT THE FIRST TIME HE'S ASSAULTED A WOMAN, BUT THE SHAME AND THE GUILT ALWAYS FALL ON US, AND THAT'S NOT FAIR!
YOU MUST PUNISH HIM!
WE HEAR YOU. LEAVE US, SO WE CAN DELIBERATE.

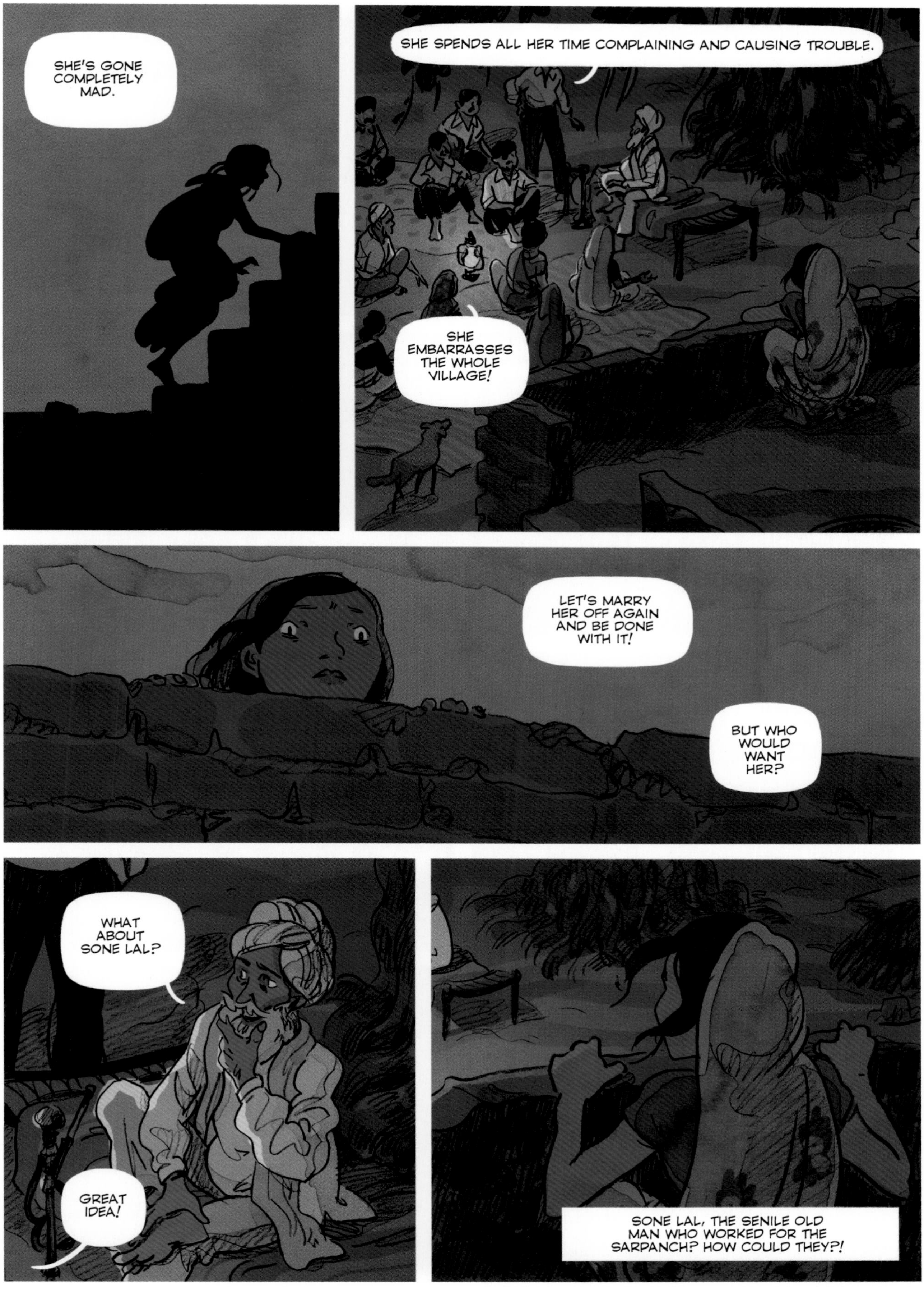
SHE'S GONE COMPLETELY MAD.
SHE SPENDS ALL HER TIME COMPLAINING AND CAUSING TROUBLE.
SHE EMBARRASSES THE WHOLE VILLAGE!
LET'S MARRY HER OFF AGAIN AND BE DONE WITH IT!
BUT WHO WOULD WANT HER?
WHAT ABOUT SONE LAL?
GREAT IDEA!
SONE LAL, THE SENILE OLD MAN WHO WORKED FOR THE SARPANCH? HOW COULD THEY?!

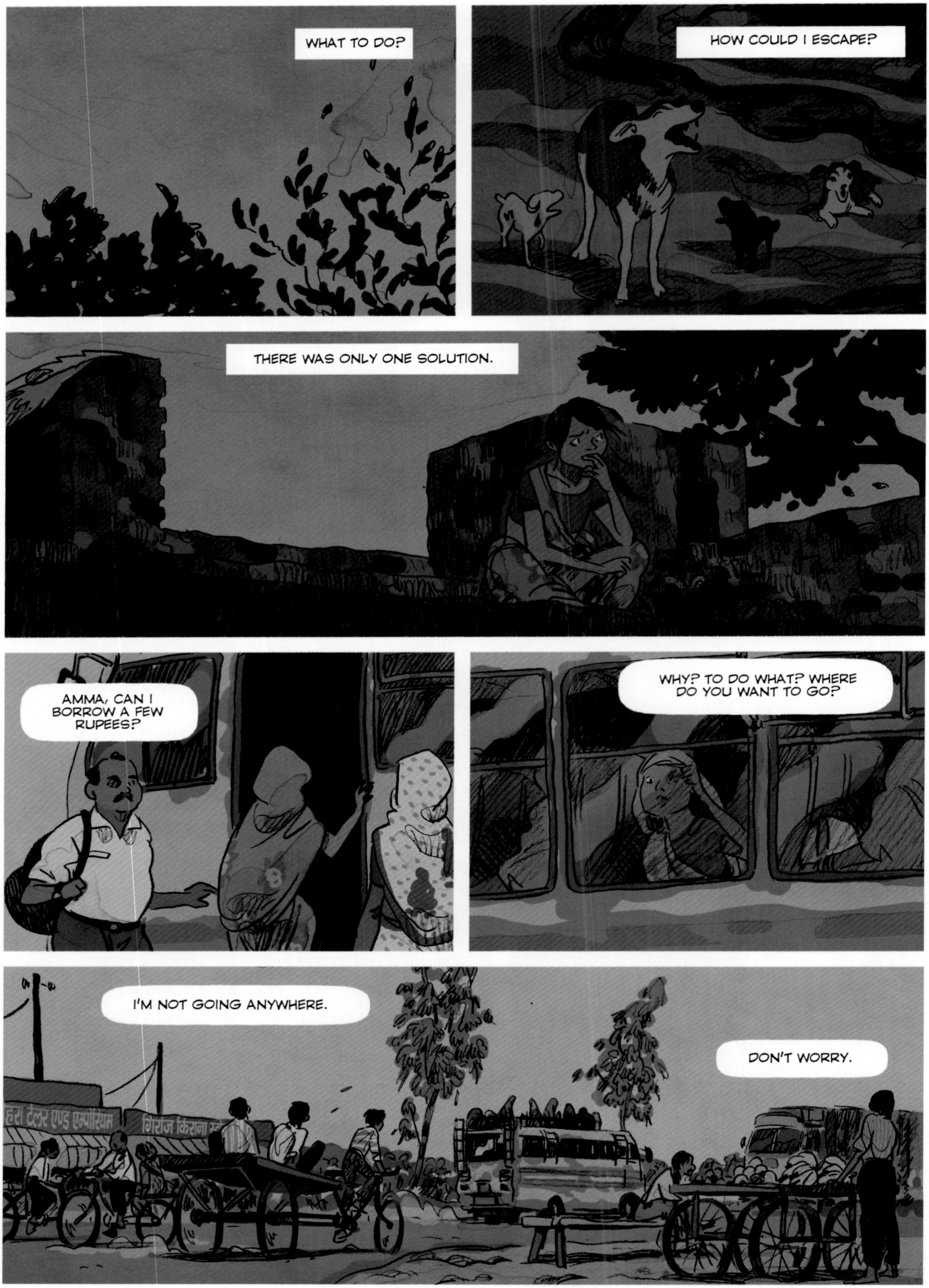
WHAT TO DO?
HOW COULD I ESCAPE?
THERE WAS ONLY ONE SOLUTION.
AMMA, CAN I BORROW A FEW RUPEES?
WHY? TO DO WHAT? WHERE DO YOU WANT TO GO?
I'M NOT GOING ANYWHERE.
DON'T WORRY.

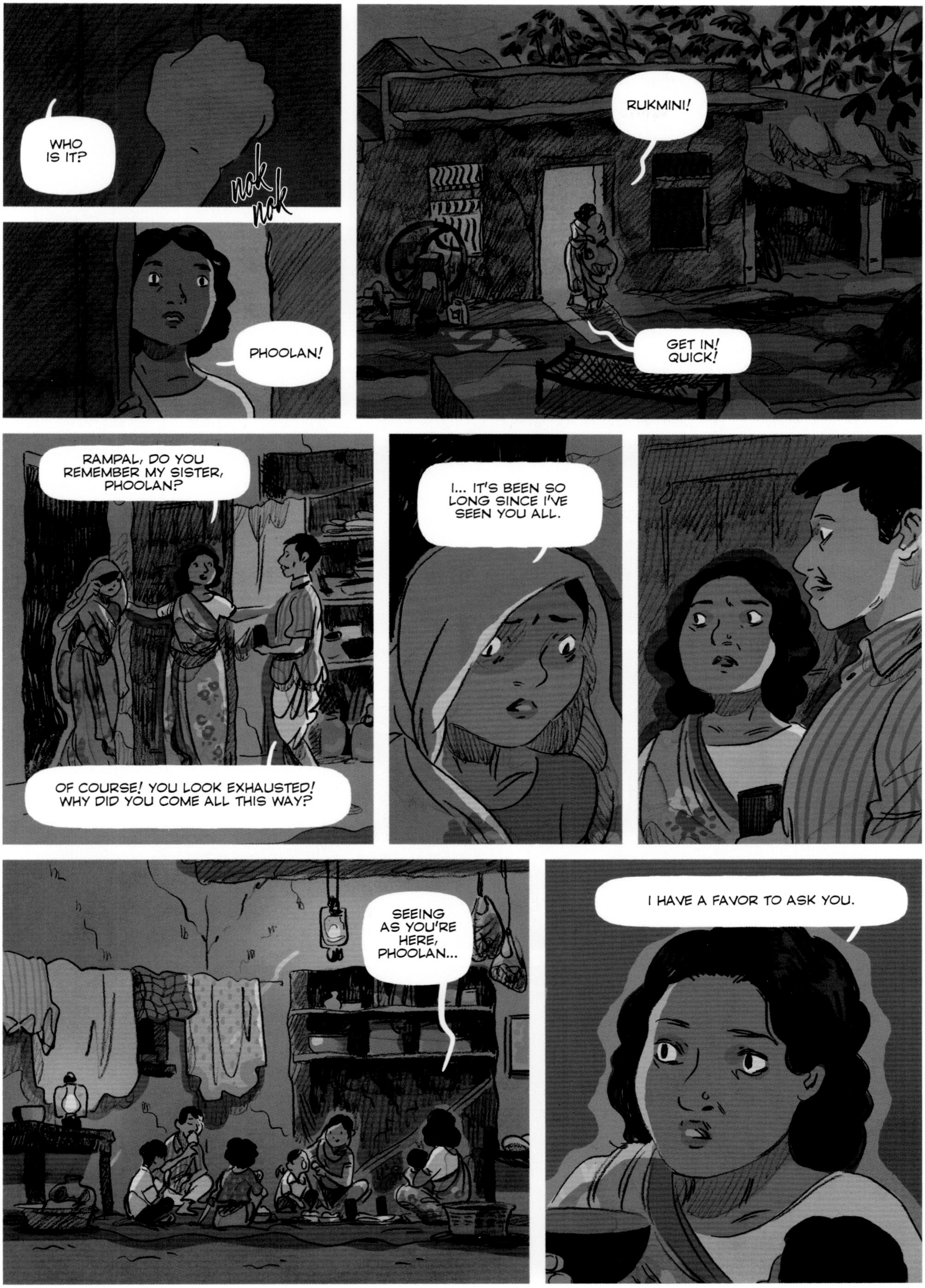
WHO IS IT?
NOK NOK
PHOOLAN!
RUKMINI!
GET IN! QUICK!
RAMPAL, DO YOU REMEMBER MY SISTER, PHOOLAN?
OF COURSE! YOU LOOK EXHAUSTED! WHY DID YOU COME ALL THIS WAY?
I... IT'S BEEN SO LONG SINCE I'VE SEEN YOU ALL.
SEEING AS YOU'RE HERE, PHOOLAN...
I HAVE A FAVOR TO ASK YOU.

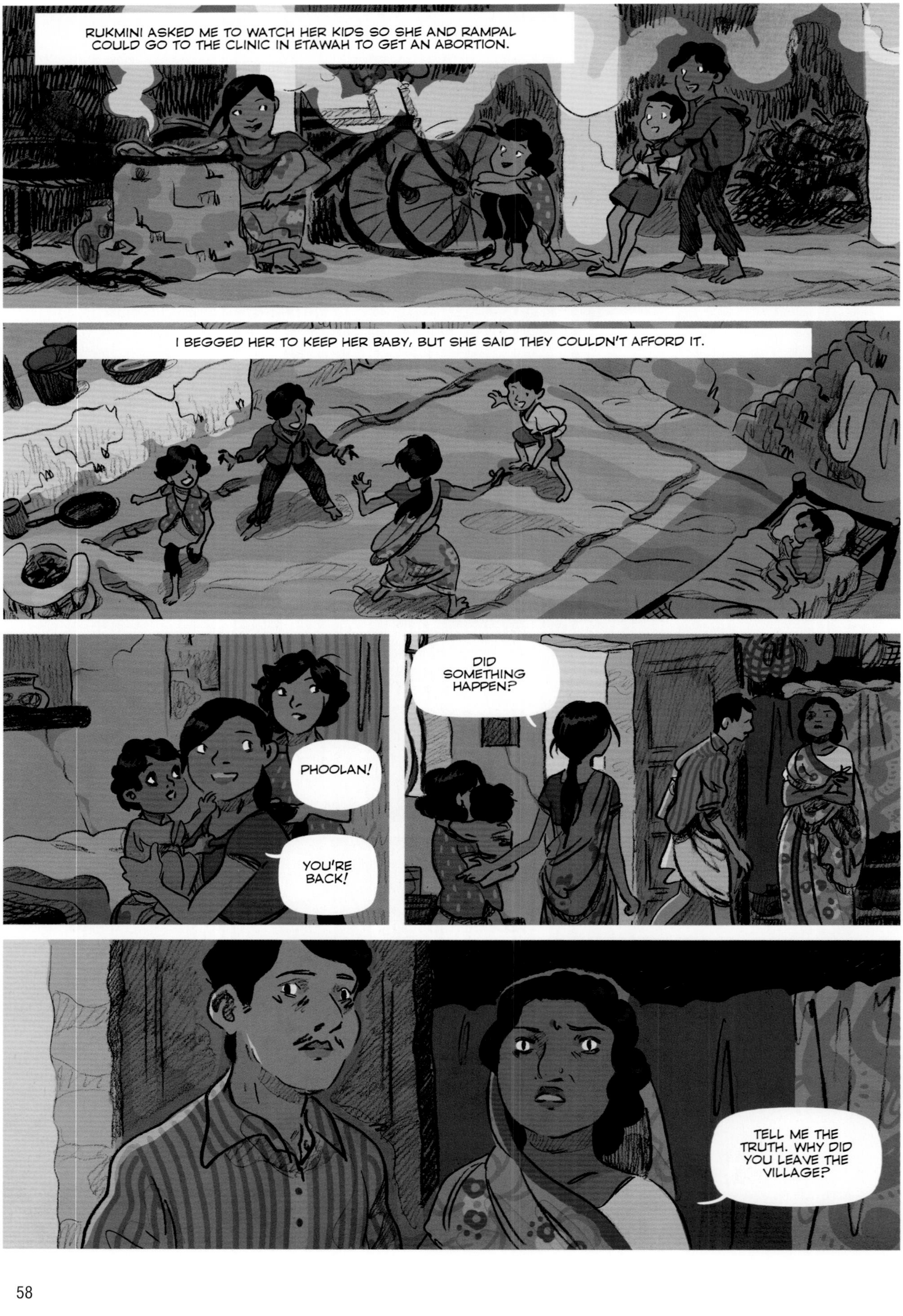
RUKMINI ASKED ME TO WATCH HER KIDS SO SHE AND RAMPAL COULD GO TO THE CLINIC IN ETAWAH TO GET AN ABORTION.
I BEGGED HER TO KEEP HER BABY, BUT SHE SAID THEY COULDN'T AFFORD IT.
PHOOLAN!
YOU'RE BACK!
DID SOMETHING HAPPEN?
TELL ME THE TRUTH. WHY DID YOU LEAVE THE VILLAGE?

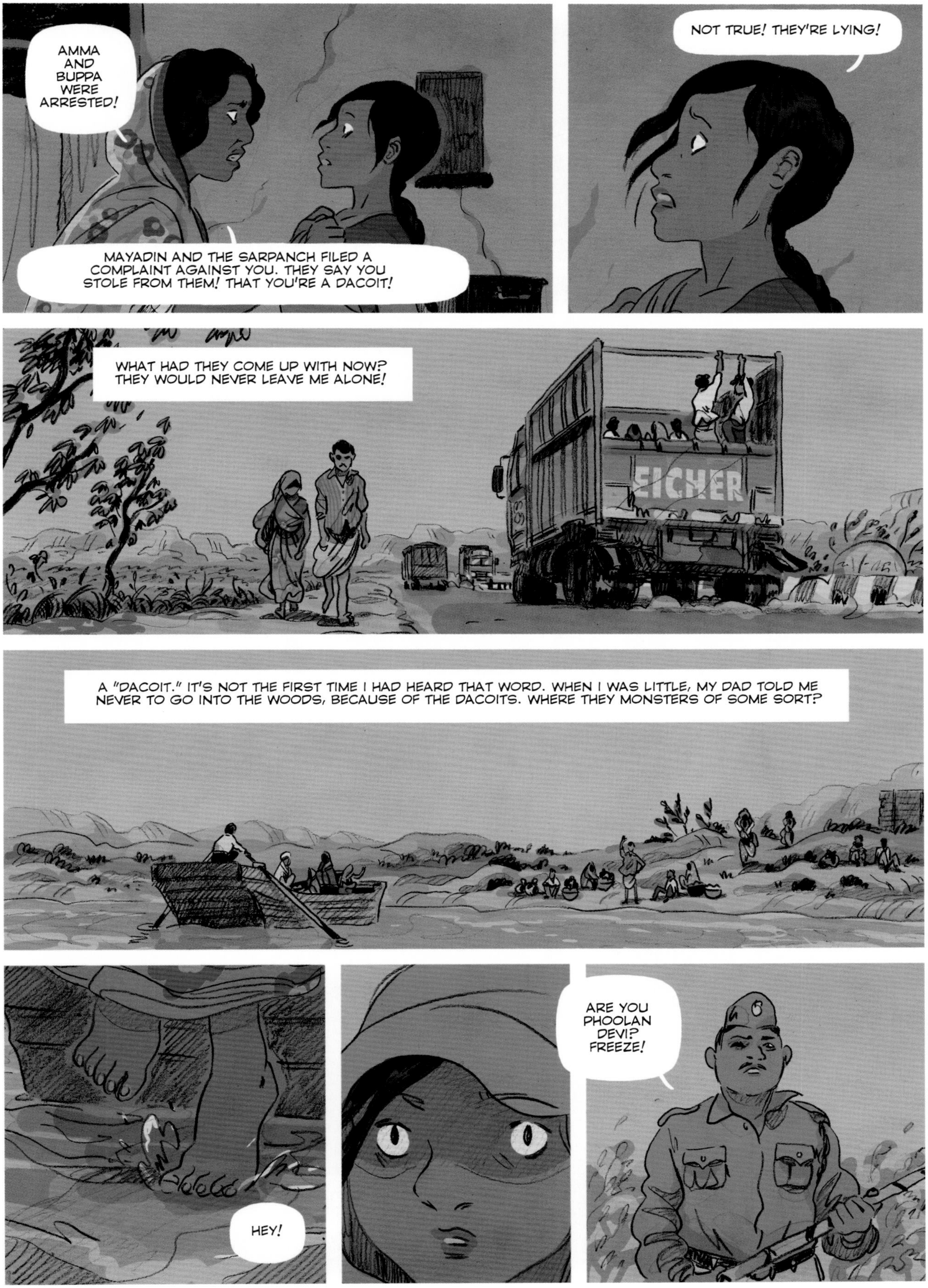
AMMA AND BUPPA WERE ARRESTED!
MAYADIN AND THE SARPANCH FILED A COMPLAINT AGAINST YOU. THEY SAY YOU STOLE FROM THEM! THAT YOU'RE A DACOIT!
NOT TRUE! THEY'RE LYING!
WHAT HAD THEY COME UP WITH NOW? THEY WOULD NEVER LEAVE ME ALONE!
EICHER
A "DACOIT." IT'S NOT THE FIRST TIME I HAD HEARD THAT WORD. WHEN I WAS LITTLE, MY DAD TOLD ME NEVER TO GO INTO THE WOODS, BECAUSE OF THE DACOITS. WHERE THEY MONSTERS OF SOME SORT?
HEY!
ARE YOU PHOOLAN DEVI? FREEZE!

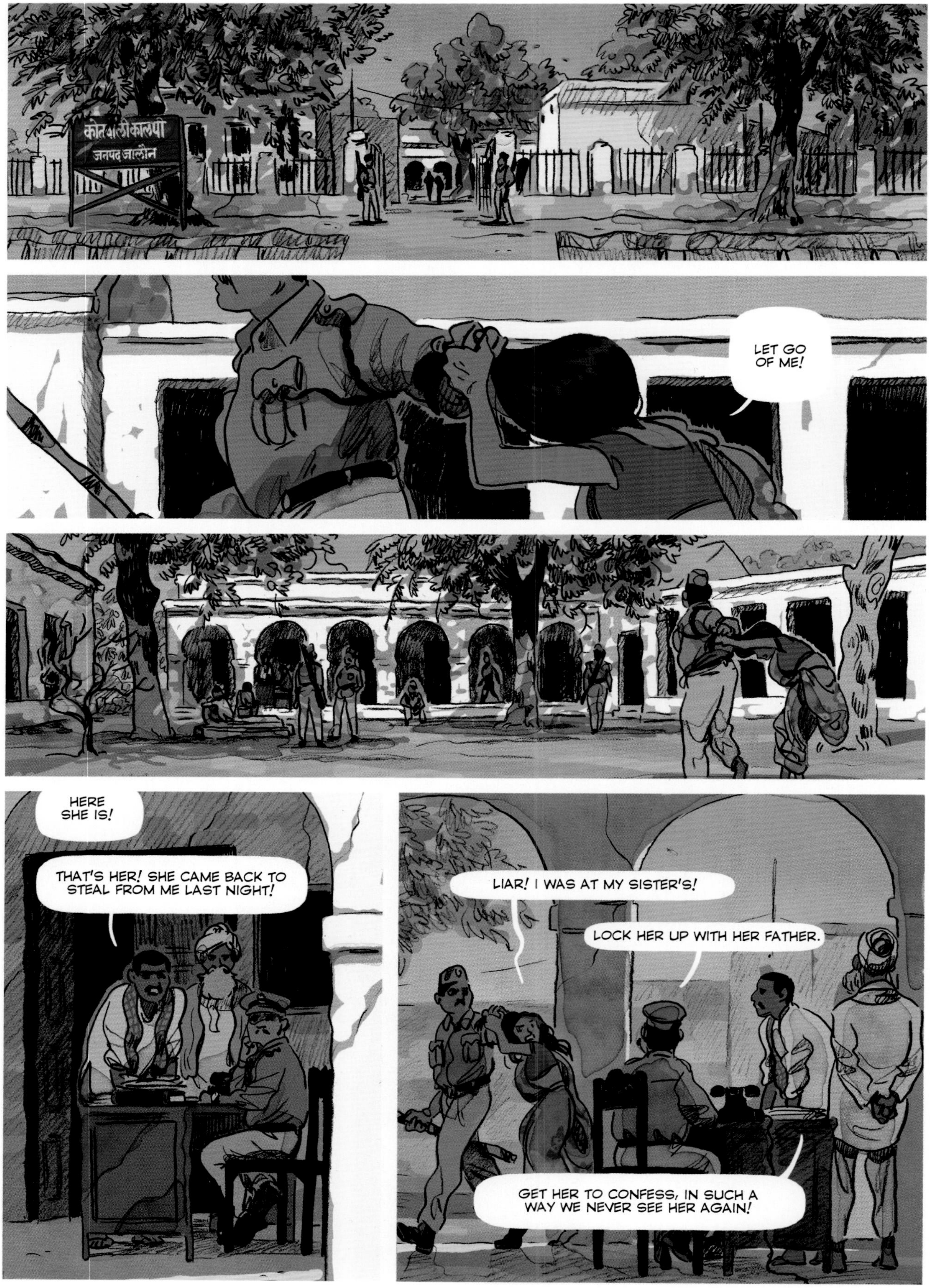
कोतवालीकालपी
जनपद जालौन
LET GO OF ME!
HERE SHE IS!
THAT'S HER! SHE CAME BACK TO STEAL FROM ME LAST NIGHT!
LIAR! I WAS AT MY SISTER'S!
LOCK HER UP WITH HER FATHER.
GET HER TO CONFESS, IN SUCH A WAY WE NEVER SEE HER AGAIN!

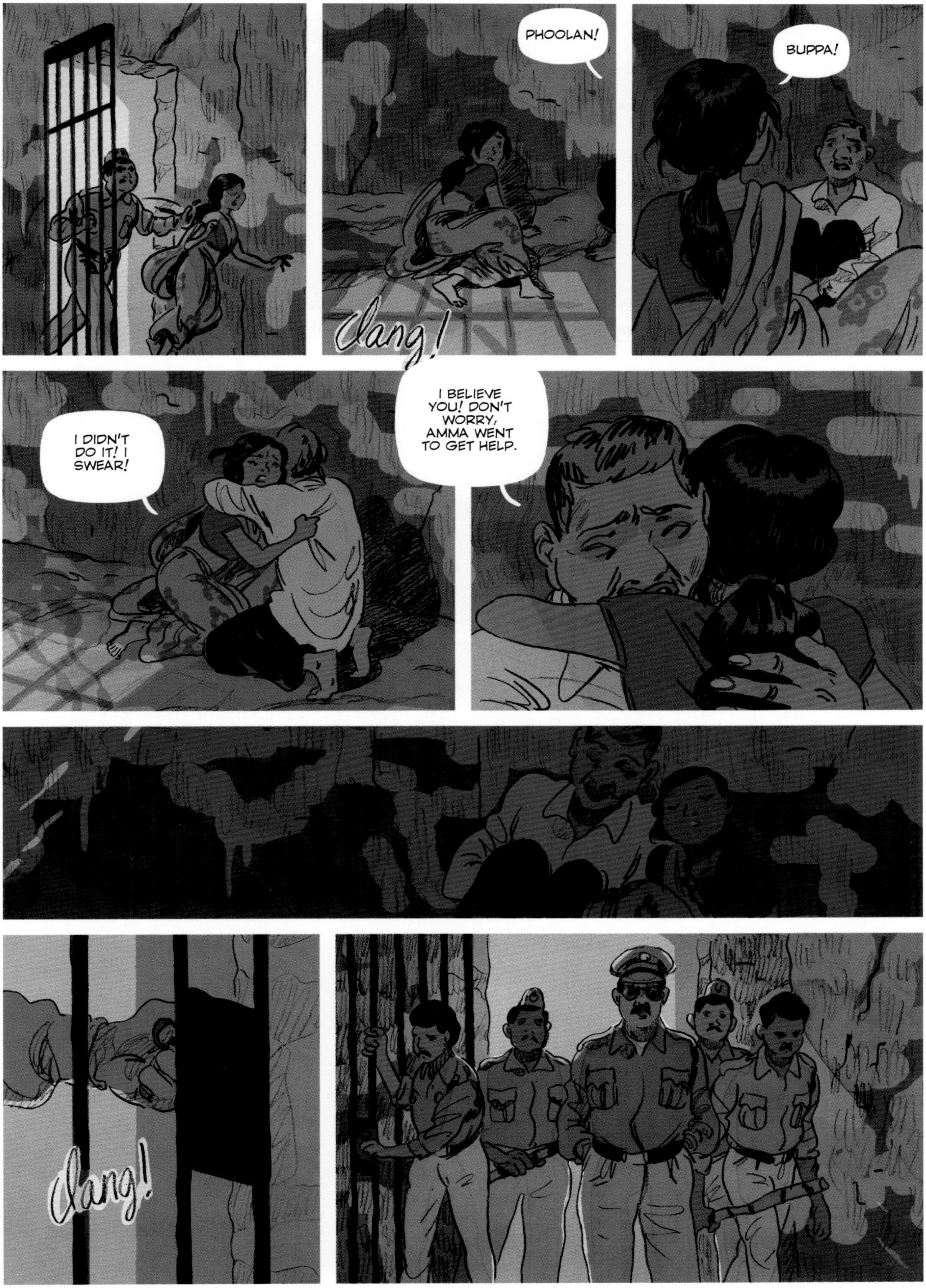
PHOOLAN!
clang!
BUPPA!
I DIDN'T DO IT! I SWEAR!
I BELIEVE YOU! DON'T WORRY, AMMA WENT TO GET HELP.
clang!

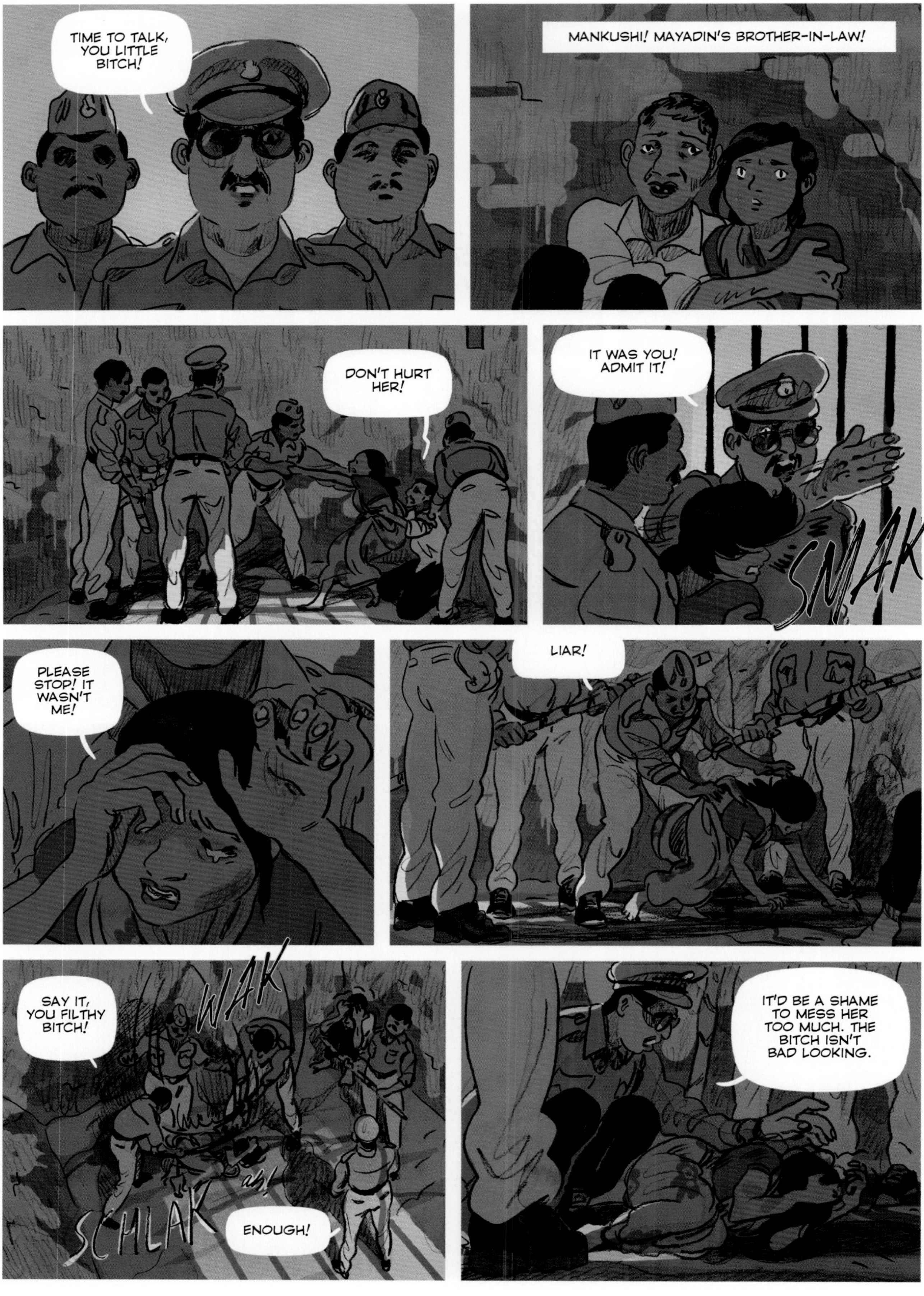
TIME TO TALK, YOU LITTLE BITCH!
MANKUSHI! MAYADIN'S BROTHER-IN-LAW!
DON'T HURT HER!
IT WAS YOU! ADMIT IT!
SMAK
PLEASE STOP! IT WASN'T ME!
LIAR!
SAY IT, YOU FILTHY BITCH!
WAK
SCHLAK
ah!
ENOUGH!
IT'D BE A SHAME TO MESS HER TOO MUCH. THE BITCH ISN'T BAD LOOKING.

YOU SURE IT WASN'T YOU? SHALL WE KEEP GOING?

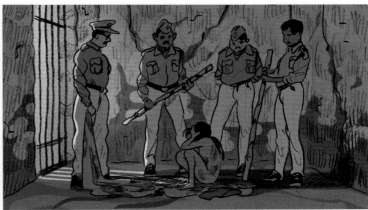

I... I DID IT. LEAVE ME ALONE.

TAKE THAT WHORE AWAY AND PUNISH HER!

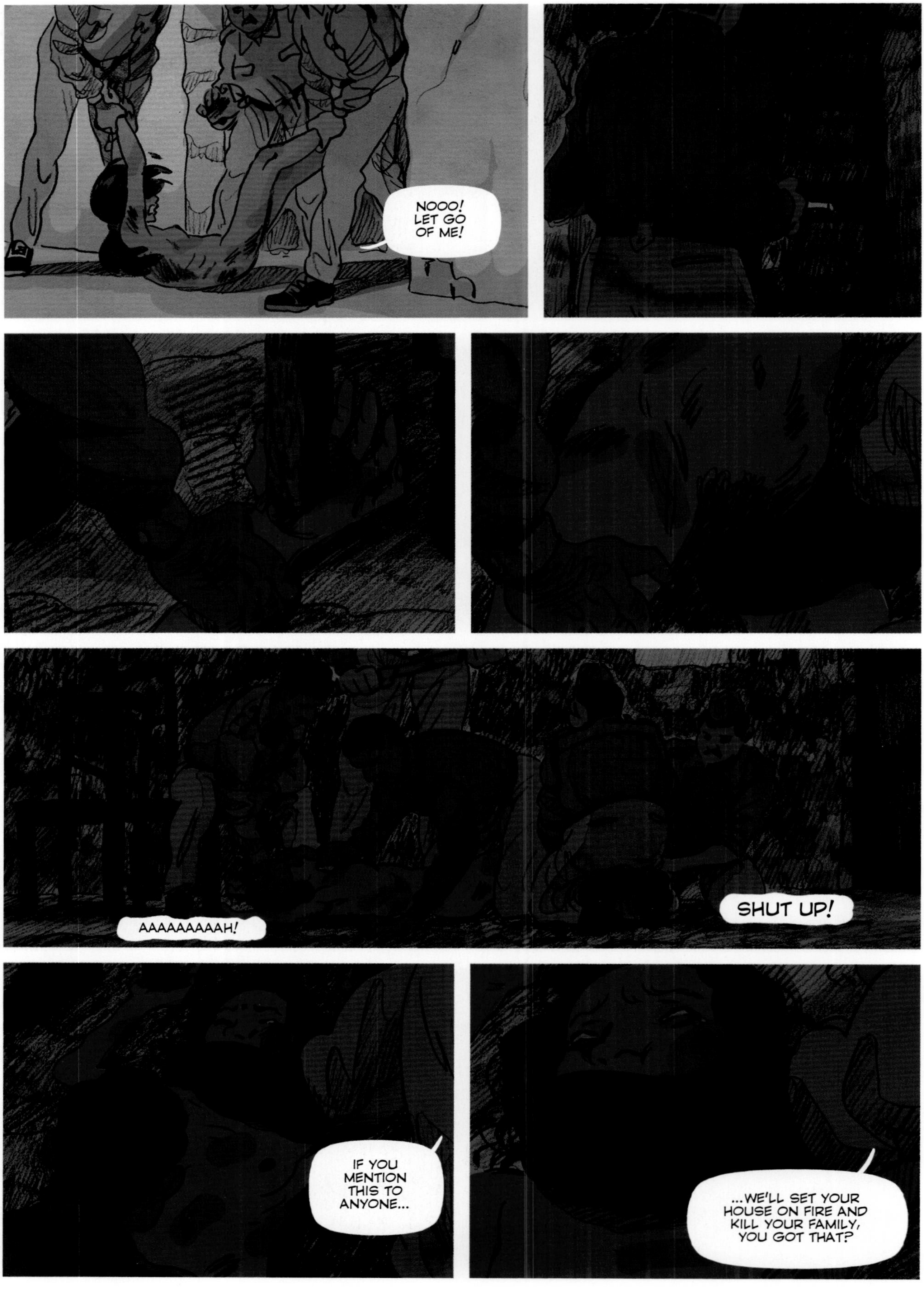
NOOO! LET GO OF ME!
AAAAAAAAAH!
SHUT UP!
IF YOU MENTION THIS TO ANYONE...
...WE'LL SET YOUR HOUSE ON FIRE AND KILL YOUR FAMILY, YOU GOT THAT?

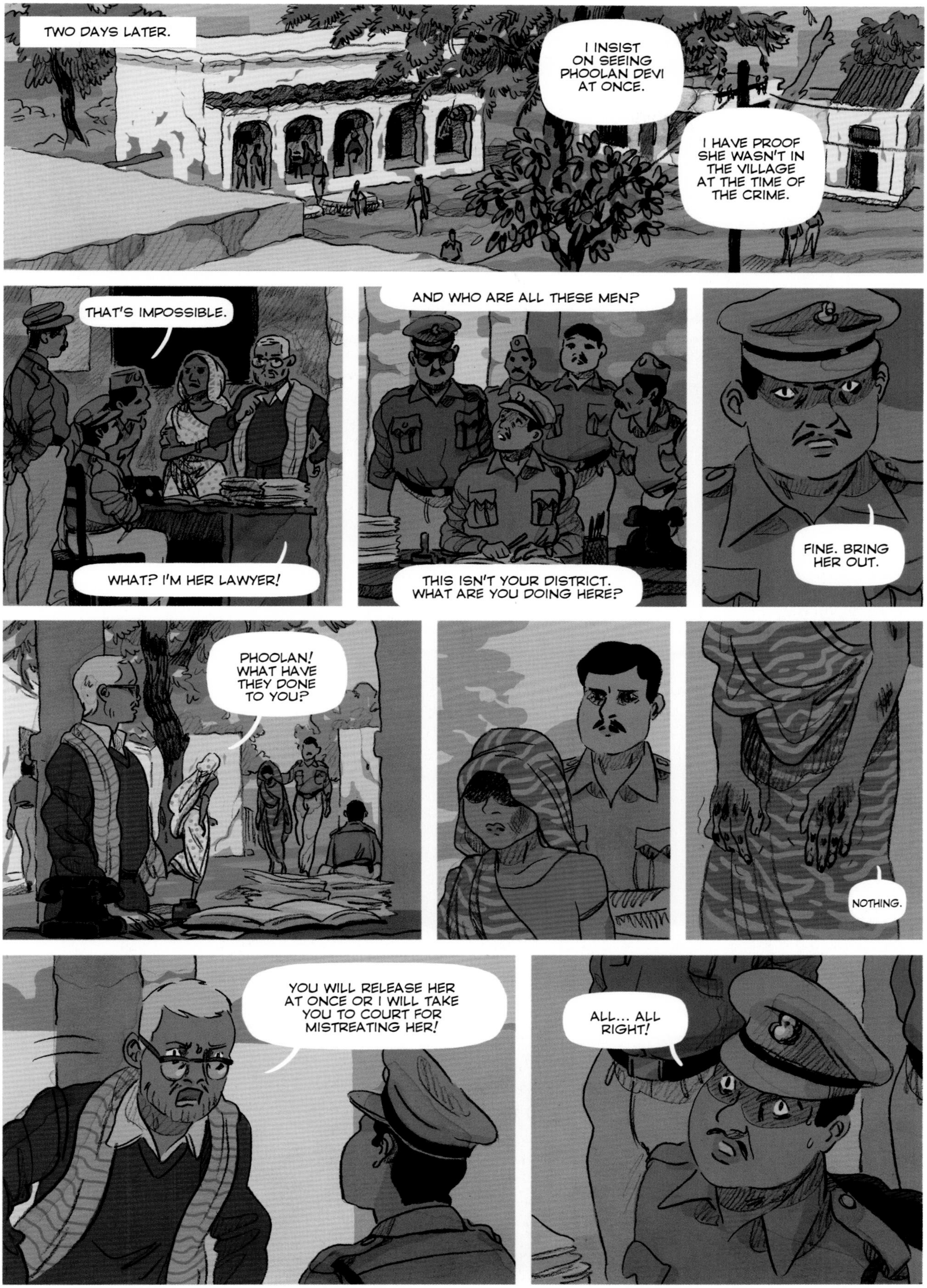
TWO DAYS LATER.
I INSIST ON SEEING PHOOLAN DEVI AT ONCE.
I HAVE PROOF SHE WASN'T IN THE VILLAGE AT THE TIME OF THE CRIME.
THAT'S IMPOSSIBLE.
WHAT? I'M HER LAWYER!
AND WHO ARE ALL THESE MEN?
THIS ISN'T YOUR DISTRICT. WHAT ARE YOU DOING HERE?
FINE. BRING HER OUT.
PHOOLAN! WHAT HAVE THEY DONE TO YOU?
NOTHING.
YOU WILL RELEASE HER AT ONCE OR I WILL TAKE YOU TO COURT FOR MISTREATING HER!
ALL... ALL RIGHT!

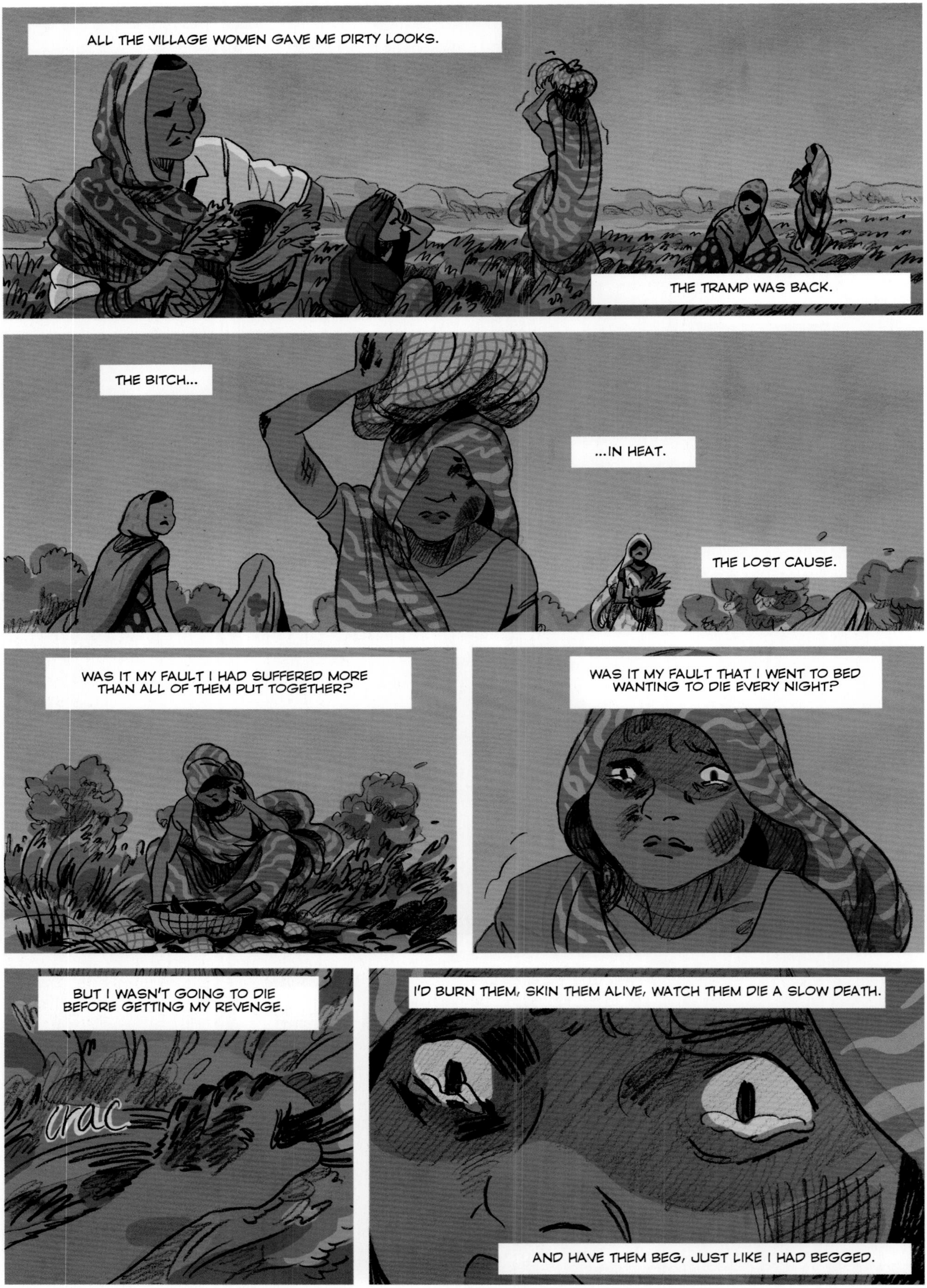
ALL THE VILLAGE WOMEN GAVE ME DIRTY LOOKS.
THE TRAMP WAS BACK.
THE BITCH...
...IN HEAT.
THE LOST CAUSE.
WAS IT MY FAULT I HAD SUFFERED MORE THAN ALL OF THEM PUT TOGETHER?
WAS IT MY FAULT THAT I WENT TO BED WANTING TO DIE EVERY NIGHT?
BUT I WASN'T GOING TO DIE BEFORE GETTING MY REVENGE.
CRAC
I'D BURN THEM, SKIN THEM ALIVE, WATCH THEM DIE A SLOW DEATH.
AND HAVE THEM BEG, JUST LIKE I HAD BEGGED.

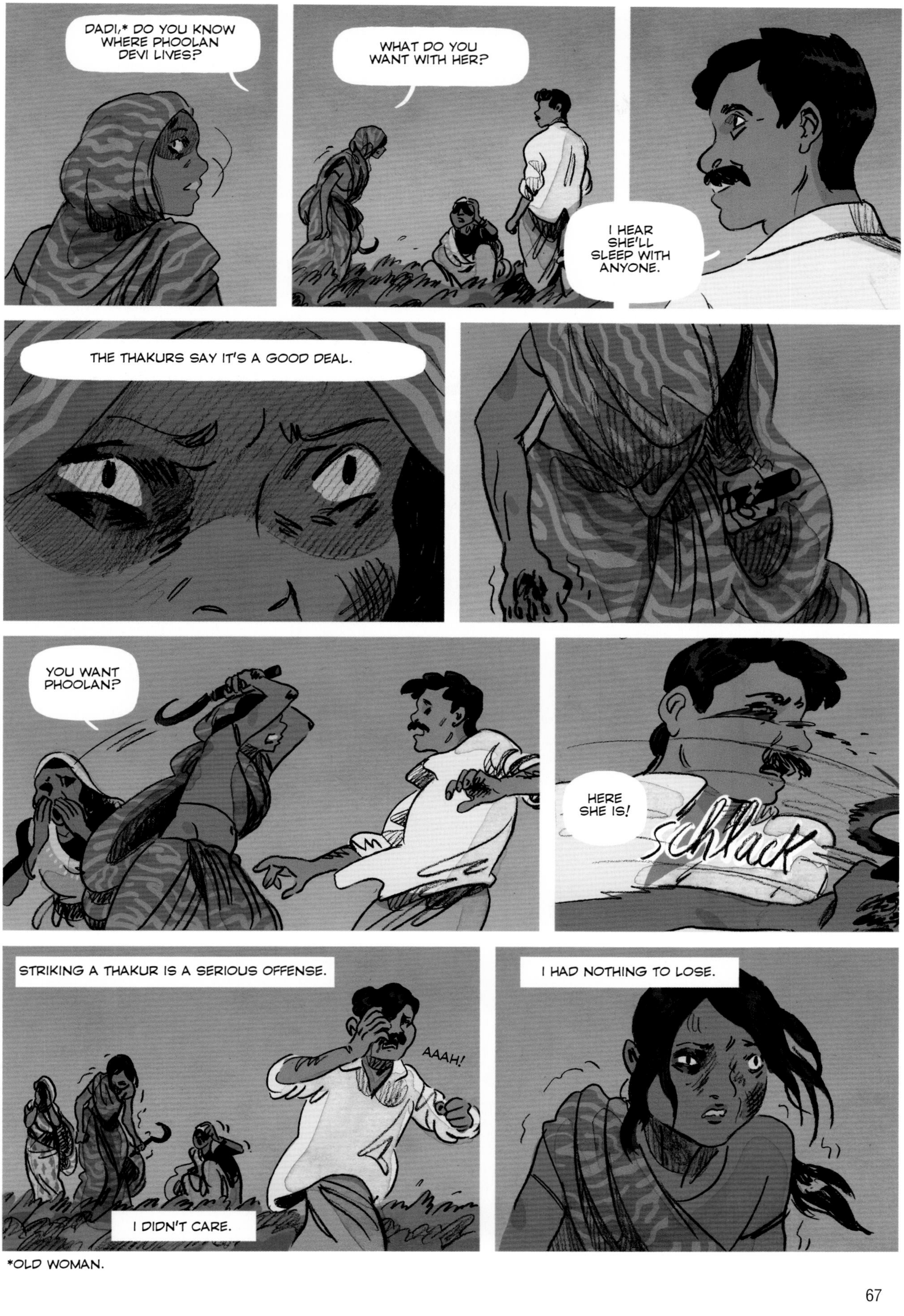
DADI,* DO YOU KNOW WHERE PHOOLAN DEVI LIVES?
WHAT DO YOU WANT WITH HER?
I HEAR SHE'LL SLEEP WITH ANYONE.
THE THAKURS SAY IT'S A GOOD DEAL.
YOU WANT PHOOLAN?
HERE SHE IS!
SCHLACK
STRIKING A THAKUR IS A SERIOUS OFFENSE.
AAAH!
I DIDN'T CARE.
I HAD NOTHING TO LOSE.

*OLD WOMAN.

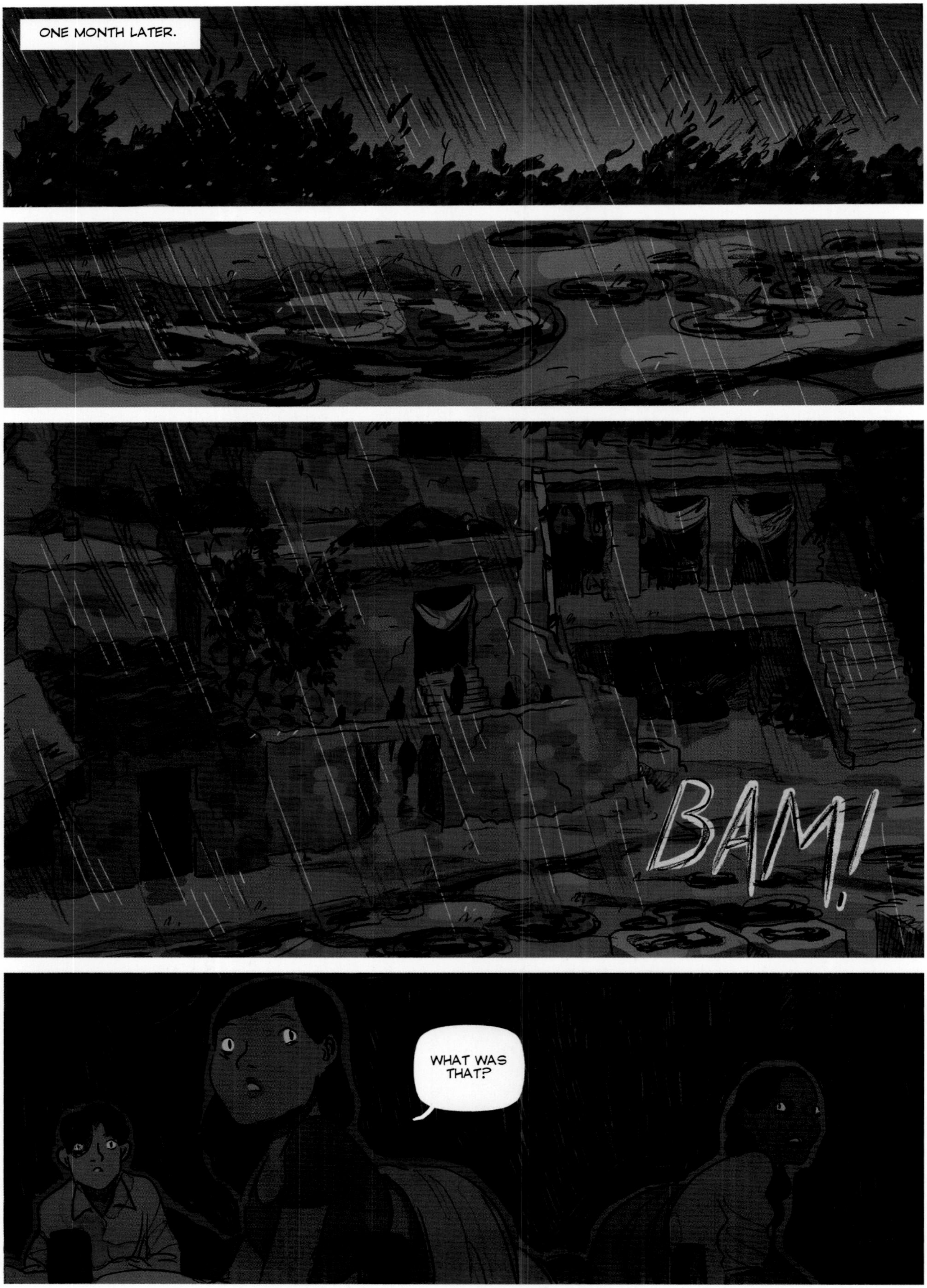
ONE MONTH LATER.
BAM!
WHAT WAS THAT?

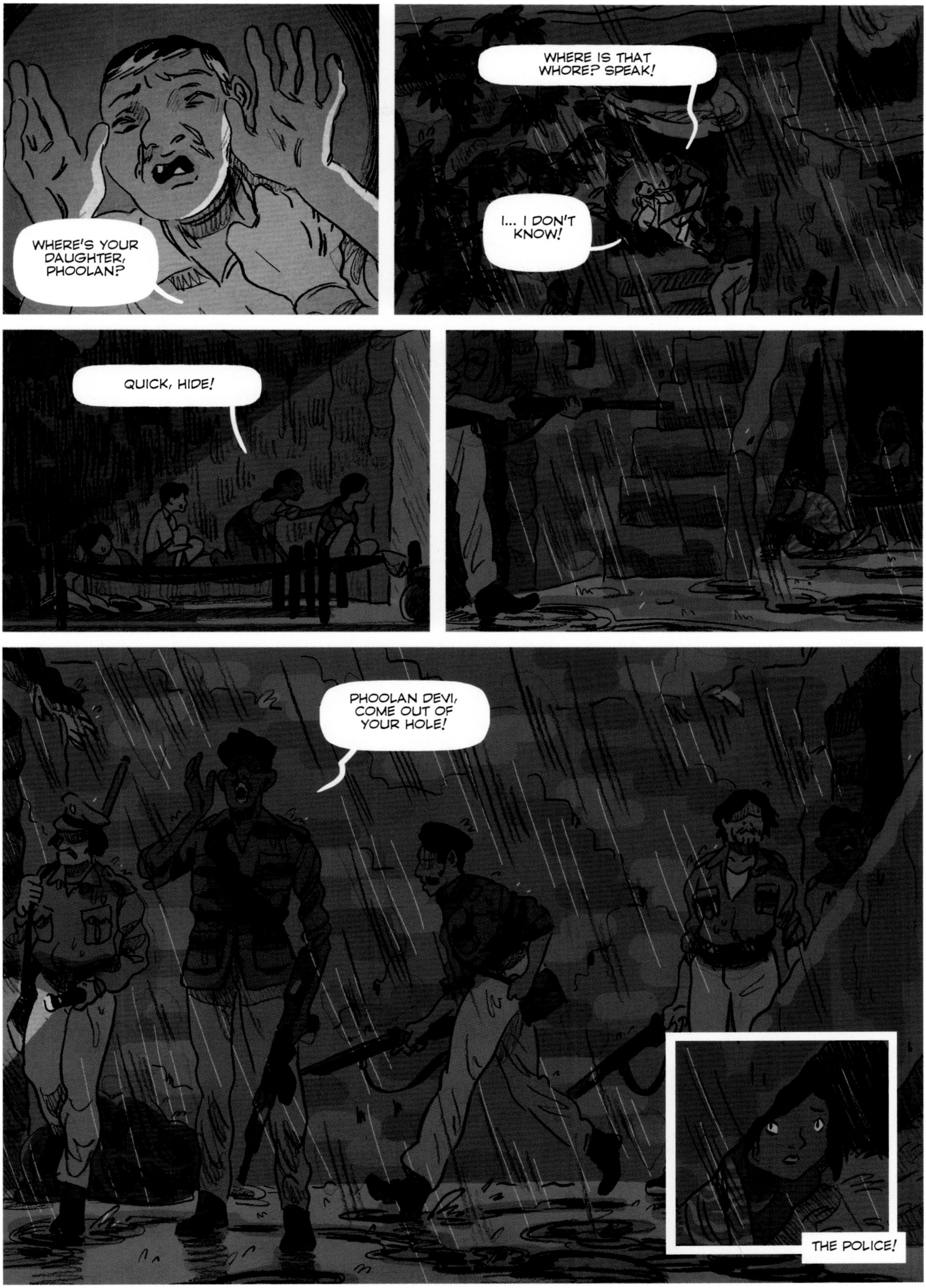
WHERE'S YOUR DAUGHTER, PHOOLAN?
WHERE IS THAT WHORE? SPEAK!
I... I DON'T KNOW!
QUICK, HIDE!
PHOOLAN DEVI, COME OUT OF YOUR HOLE!
THE POLICE!

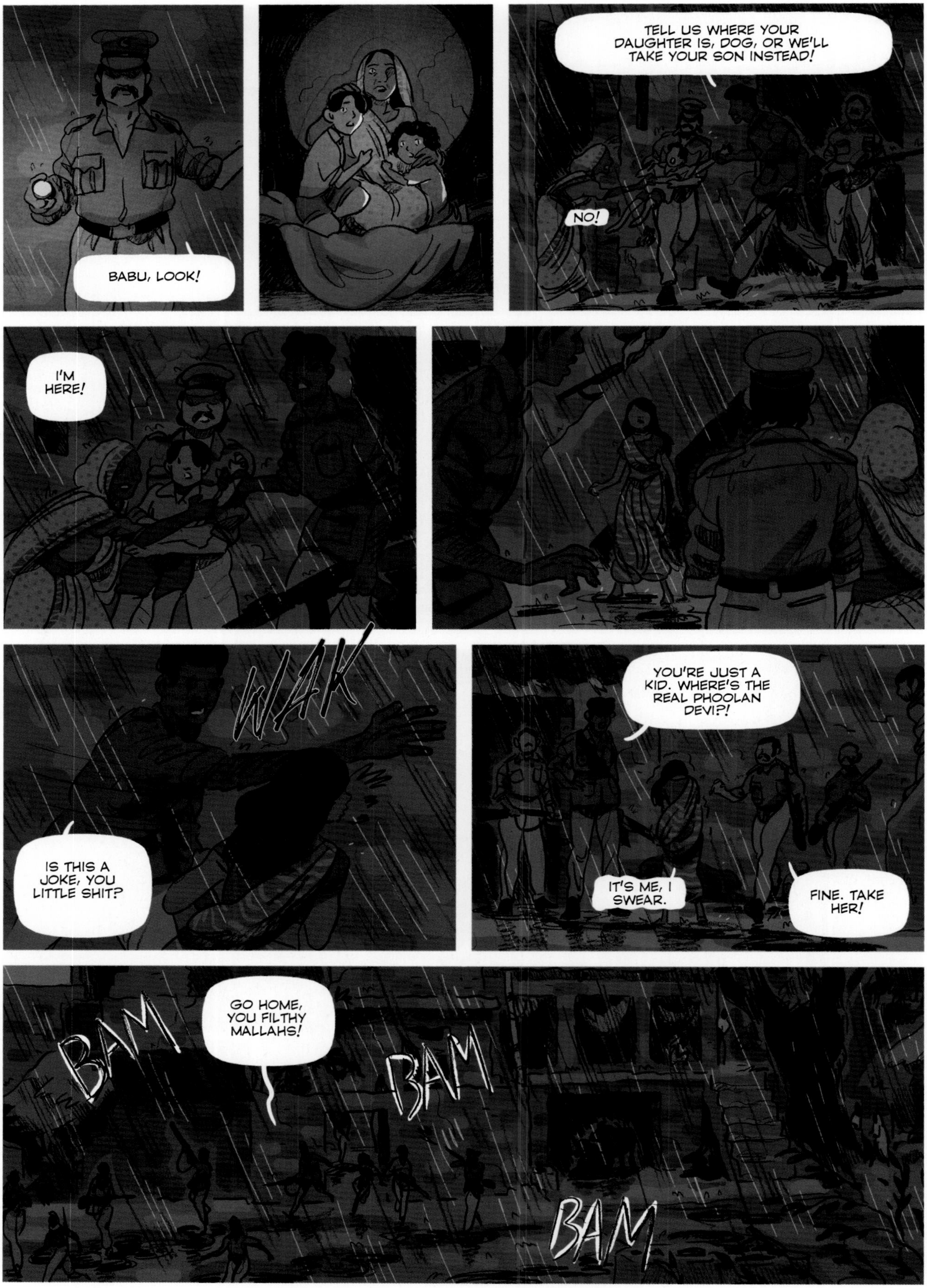
BABU, LOOK!
TELL US WHERE YOUR DAUGHTER IS, DOG, OR WE'LL TAKE YOUR SON INSTEAD!
NO!
I'M HERE!
WAK
IS THIS A JOKE, YOU LITTLE SHIT?
YOU'RE JUST A KID. WHERE'S THE REAL PHOOLAN DEVI?!
IT'S ME, I SWEAR.
FINE. TAKE HER!
BAM
GO HOME, YOU FILTHY MALLAHS!
BAM
BAM

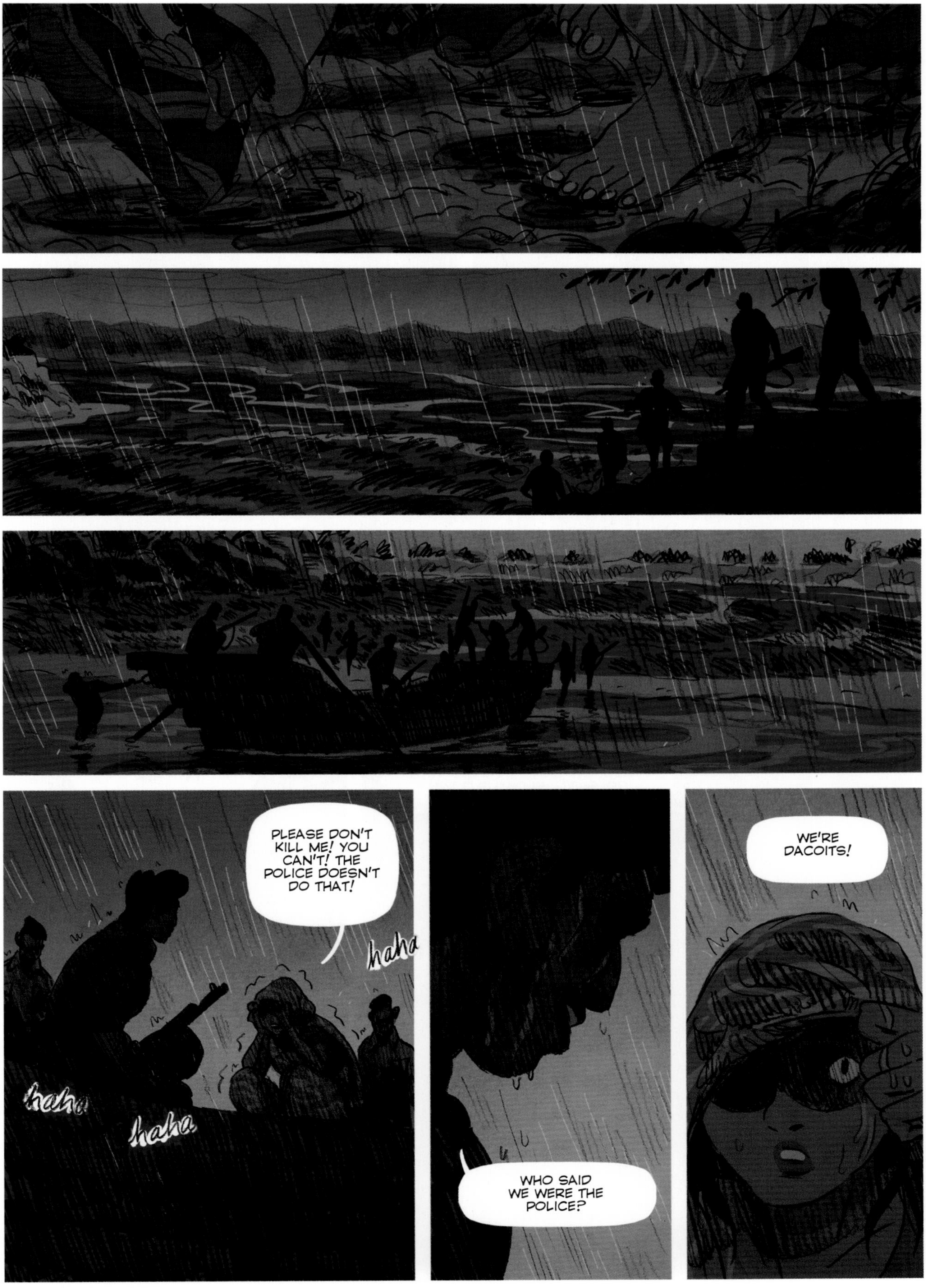
PLEASE DON'T KILL ME! YOU CAN'T! THE POLICE DOESN'T DO THAT!
haha
haha
haha
WHO SAID WE WERE THE POLICE?
WE'RE DACOITS!

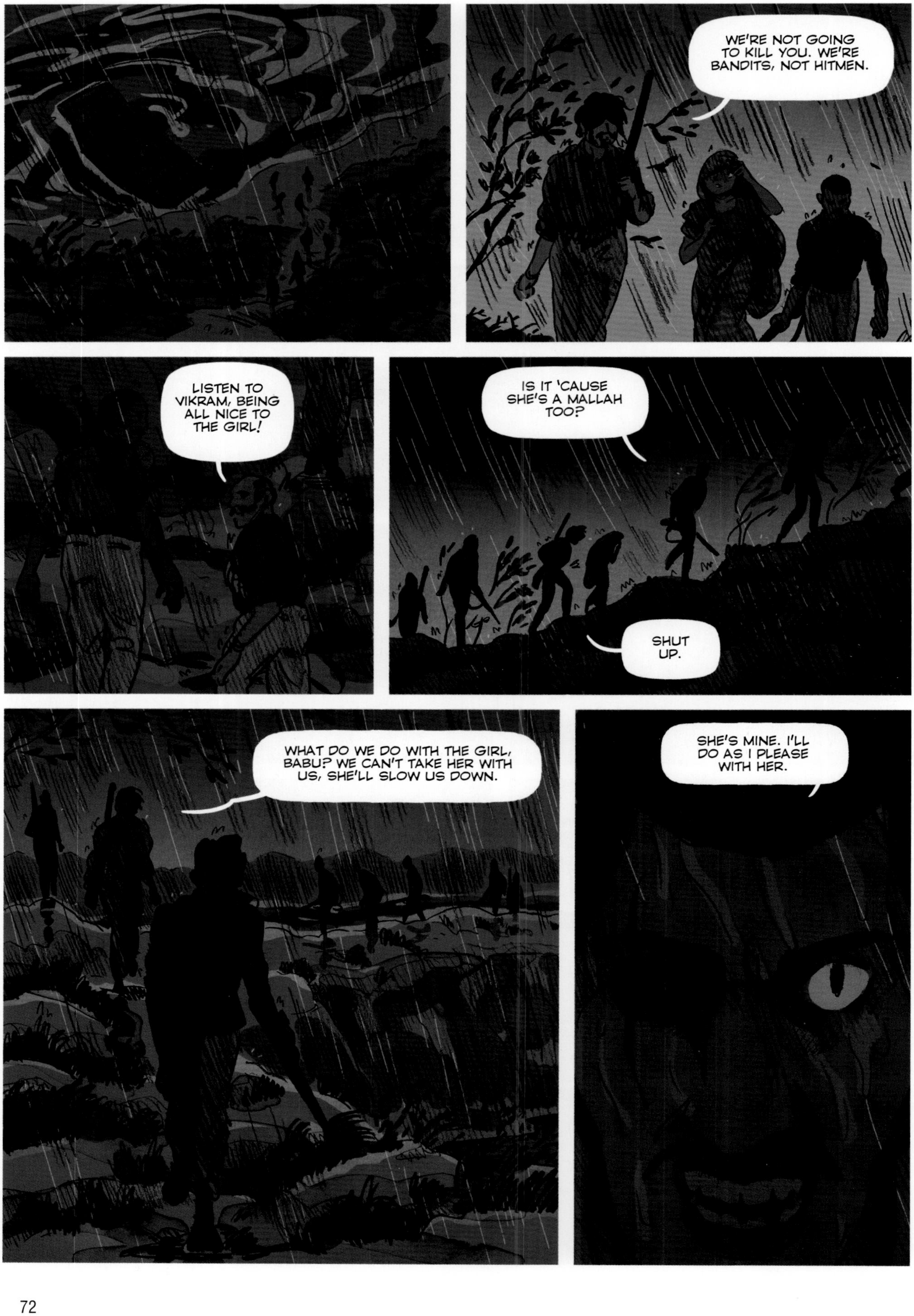
WE'RE NOT GOING TO KILL YOU. WE'RE BANDITS, NOT HITMEN.
LISTEN TO VIKRAM, BEING ALL NICE TO THE GIRL!
IS IT 'CAUSE SHE'S A MALLAH TOO?
SHUT UP.
WHAT DO WE DO WITH THE GIRL, BABU? WE CAN'T TAKE HER WITH US, SHE'LL SLOW US DOWN.
SHE'S MINE. I'LL DO AS I PLEASE WITH HER.

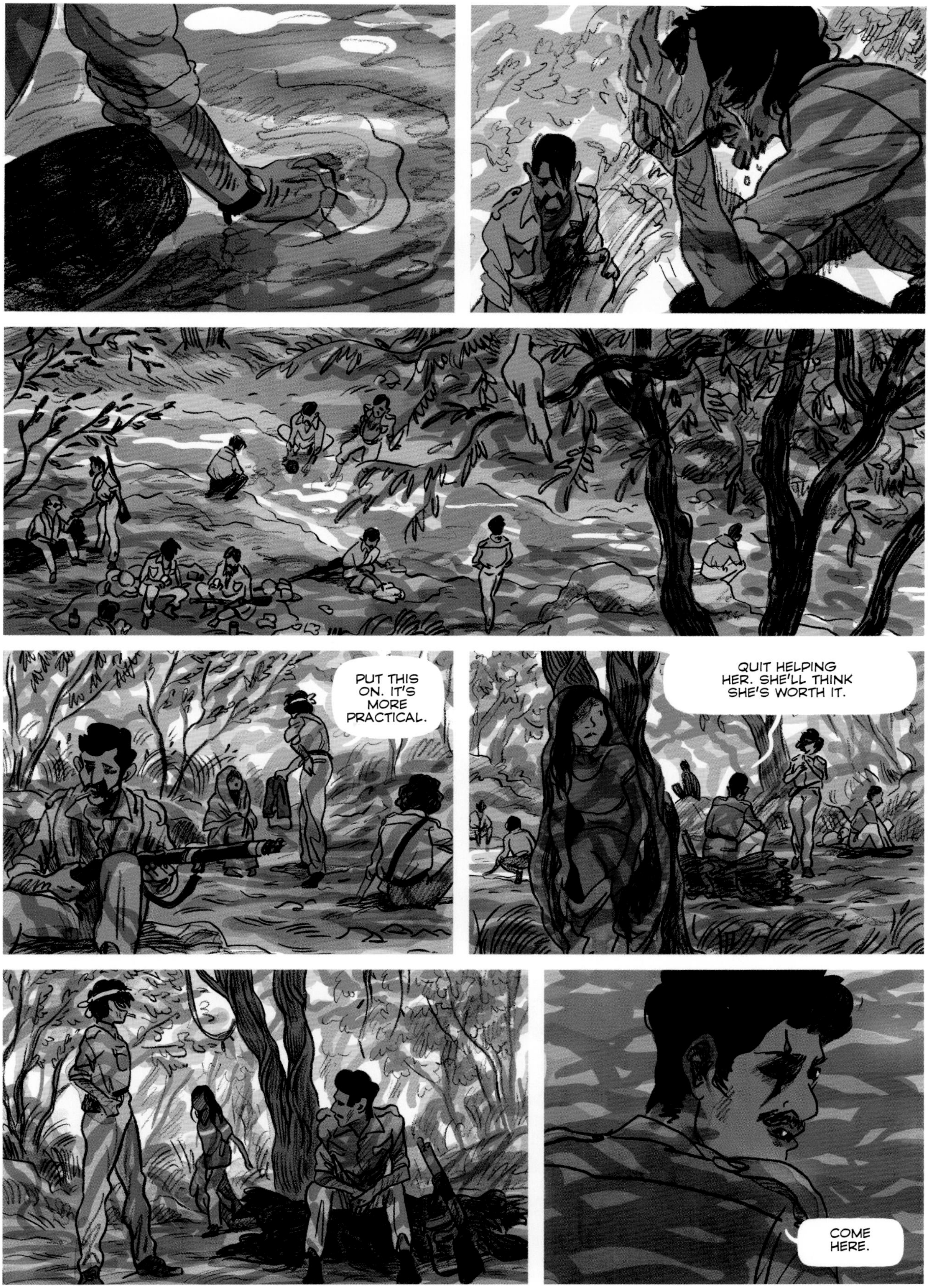
PUT THIS ON. IT'S MORE PRACTICAL.
QUIT HELPING HER. SHE'LL THINK SHE'S WORTH IT.
COME HERE.

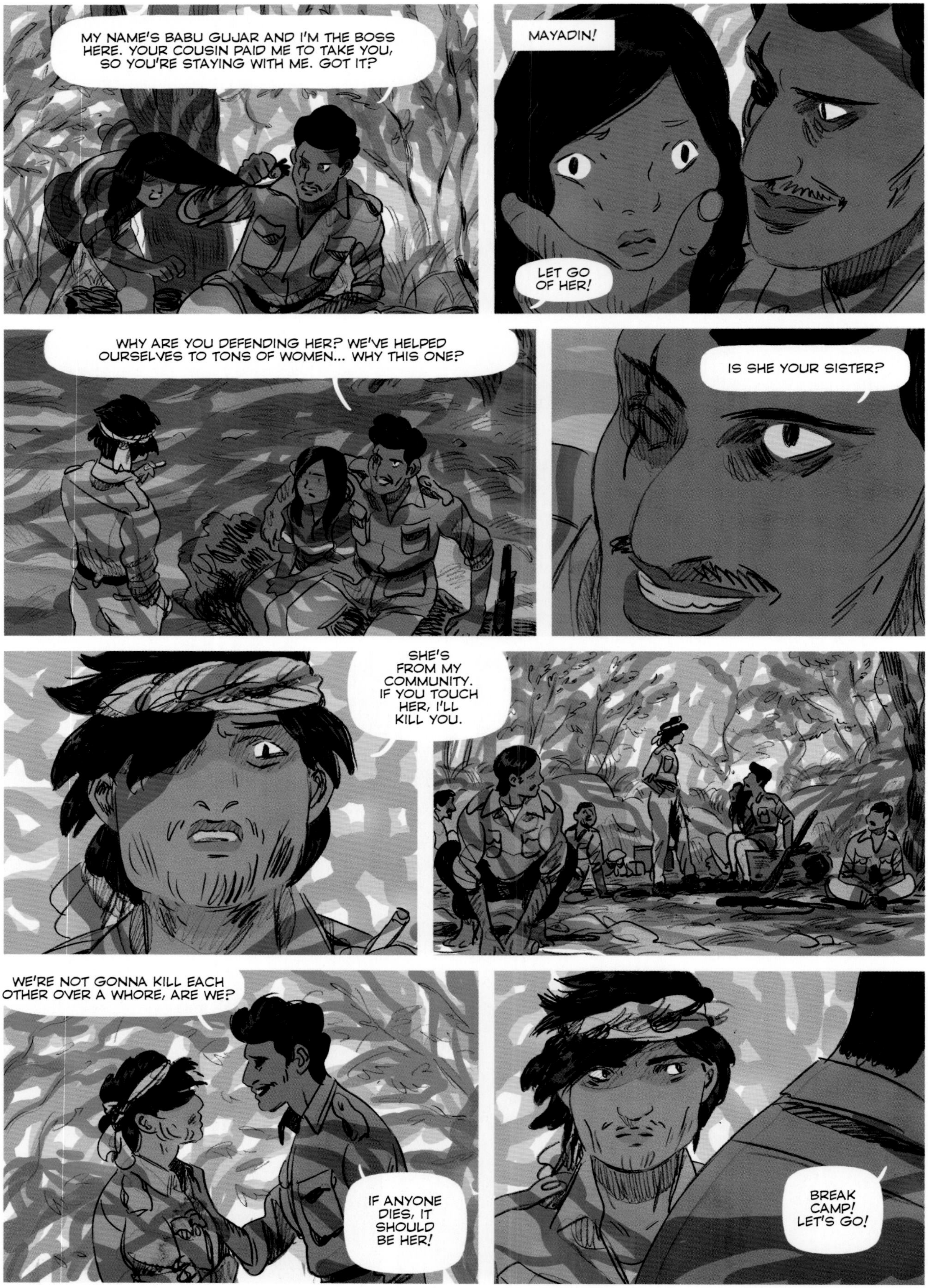

MY NAME'S BABU GUJAR AND I'M THE BOSS HERE. YOUR COUSIN PAID ME TO TAKE YOU, SO YOU'RE STAYING WITH ME. GOT IT?
MAYADIN!
LET GO OF HER!
WHY ARE YOU DEFENDING HER? WE'VE HELPED OURSELVES TO TONS OF WOMEN... WHY THIS ONE?
IS SHE YOUR SISTER?
SHE'S FROM MY COMMUNITY. IF YOU TOUCH HER, I'LL KILL YOU.
WE'RE NOT GONNA KILL EACH OTHER OVER A WHORE, ARE WE?
IF ANYONE DIES, IT SHOULD BE HER!
BREAK CAMP! LET'S GO!

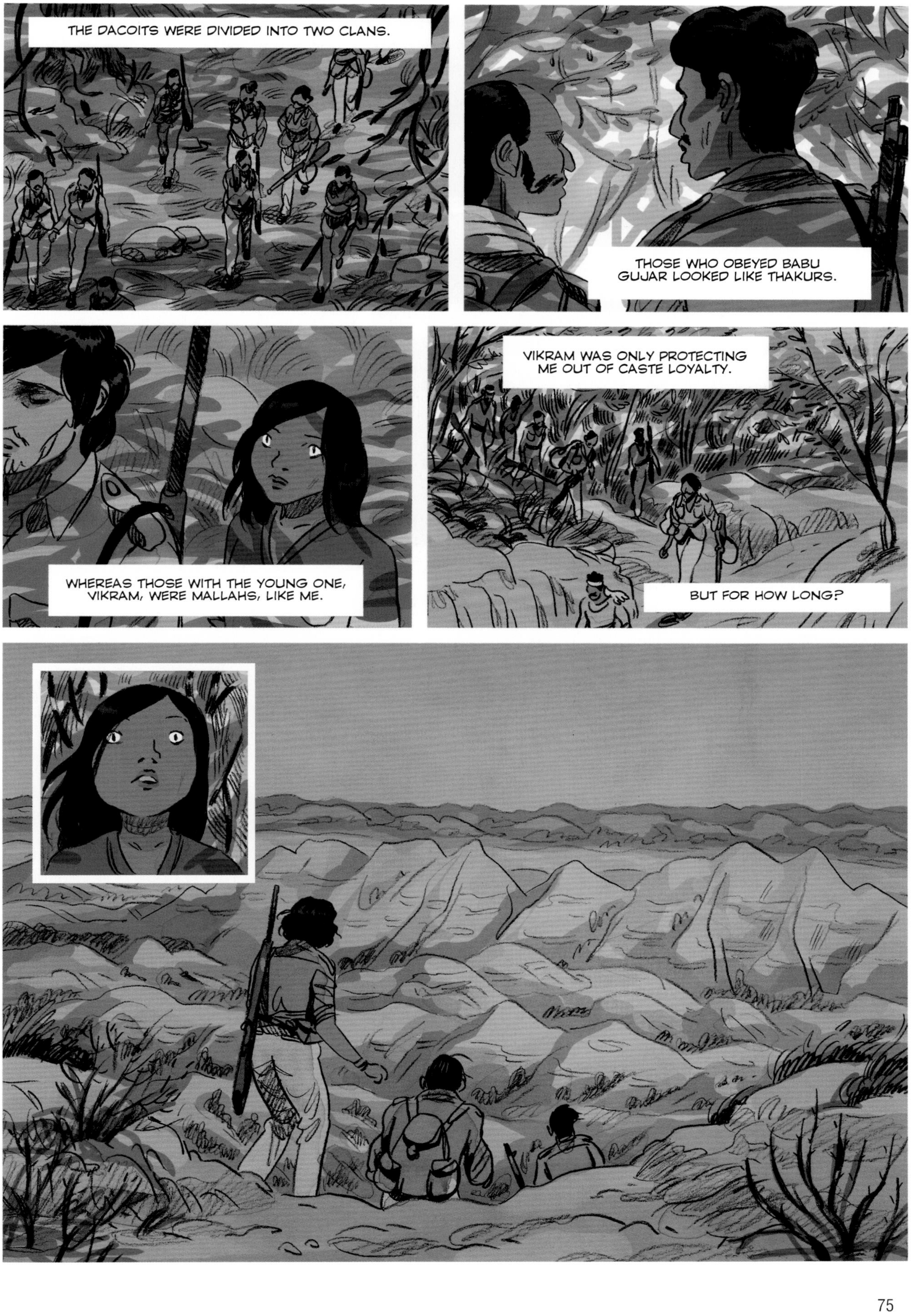
THE DACOITS WERE DIVIDED INTO TWO CLANS.
THOSE WHO OBEYED BABU GUJAR LOOKED LIKE THAKURS.
WHEREAS THOSE WITH THE YOUNG ONE, VIKRAM, WERE MALLAHS, LIKE ME.
VIKRAM WAS ONLY PROTECTING ME OUT OF CASTE LOYALTY.
BUT FOR HOW LONG?

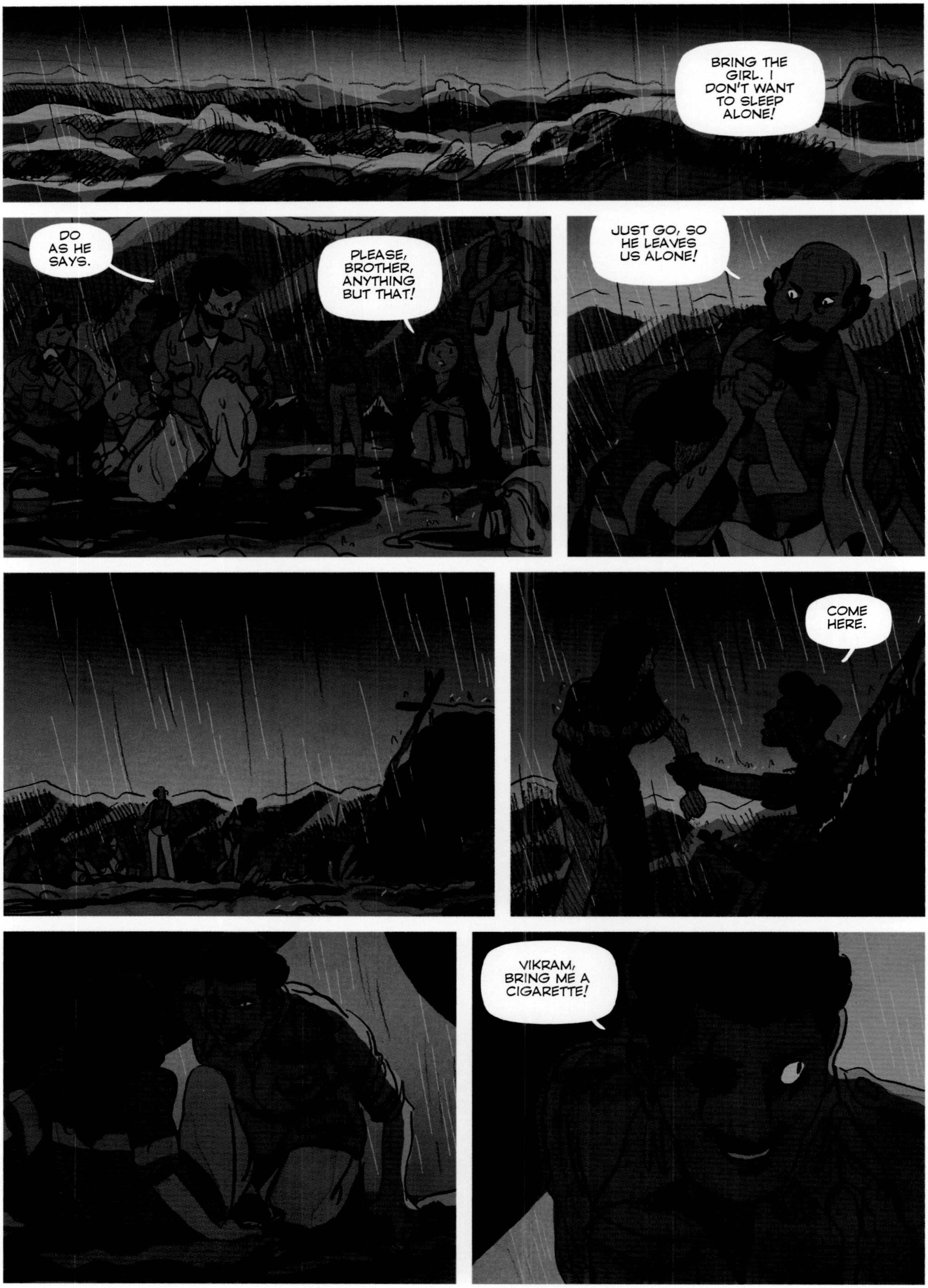
BRING THE GIRL. I DON'T WANT TO SLEEP ALONE!
DO AS HE SAYS.
PLEASE, BROTHER, ANYTHING BUT THAT!
JUST GO, SO HE LEAVES US ALONE!
COME HERE.
VIKRAM, BRING ME A CIGARETTE!

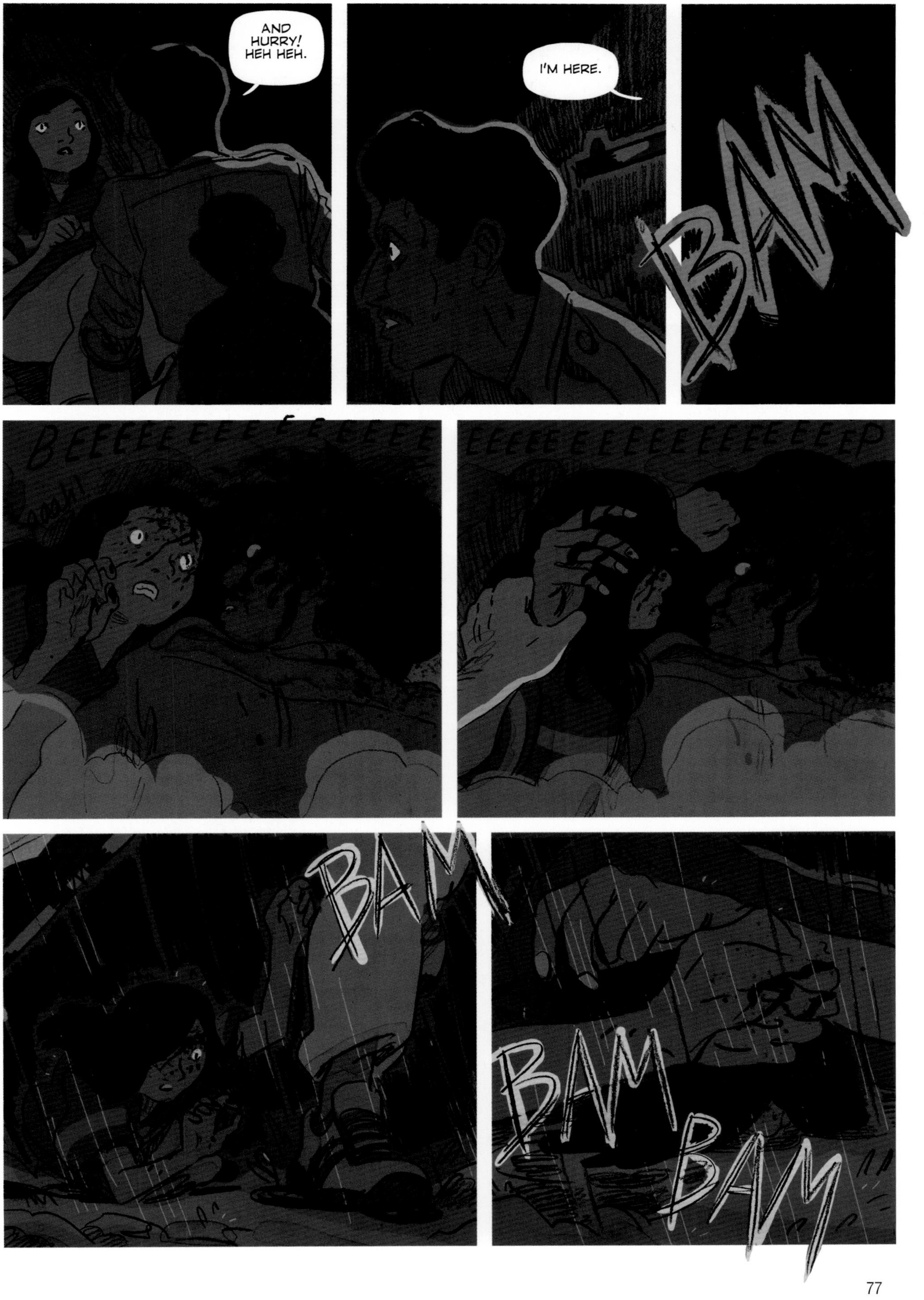
AND HURRY! HEH HEH.
I'M HERE.
BAM
BEEEEEEEEEEEE
EEEEEEEEEEEEEEEEEP
BAM
BAM
BAM

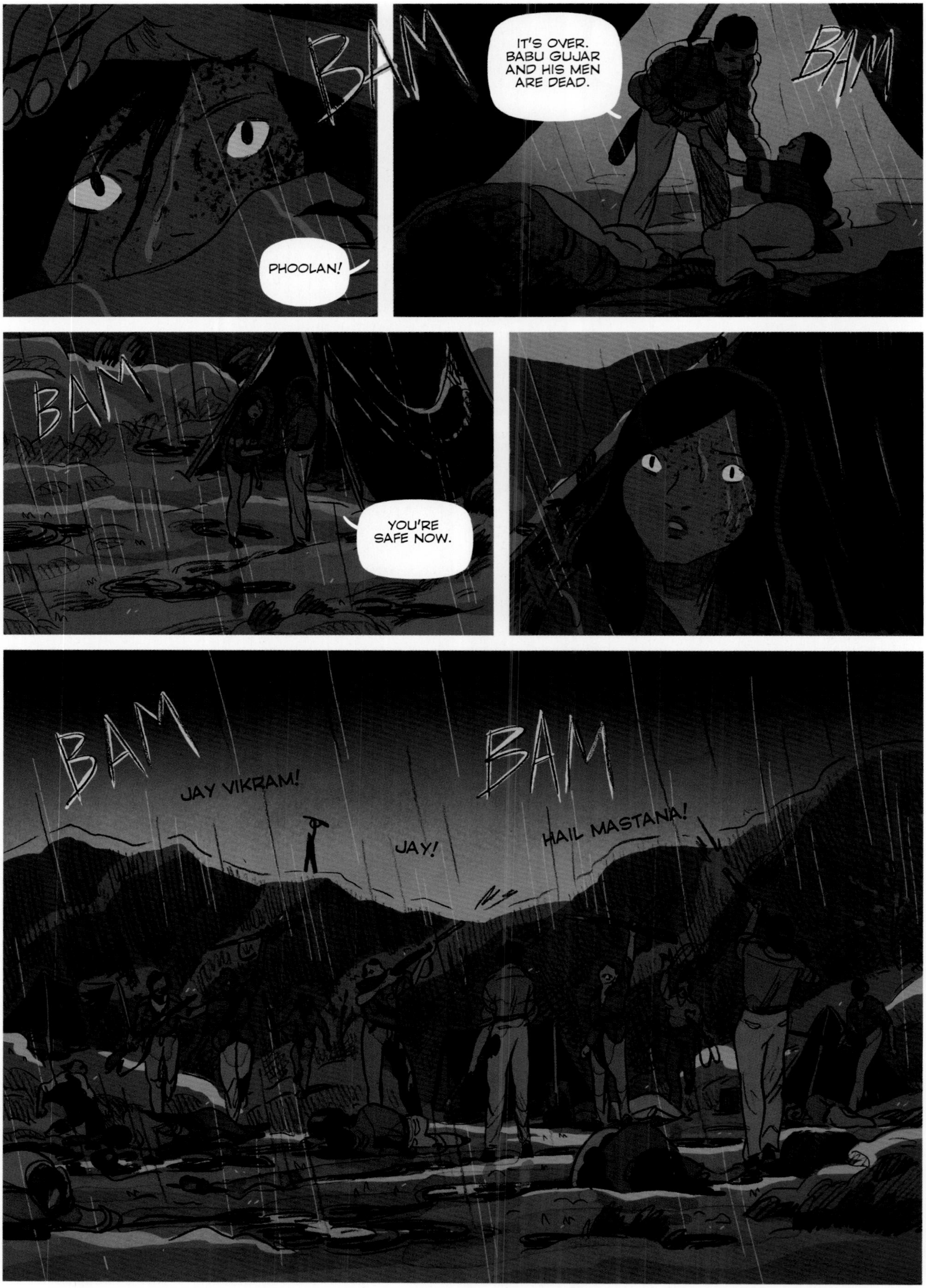
BAM
PHOOLAN!
IT'S OVER. BABU GUJAR AND HIS MEN ARE DEAD.
BAM
BAM
YOU'RE SAFE NOW.
BAM
BAM
JAY VIKRAM!
JAY!
HAIL MASTANA!

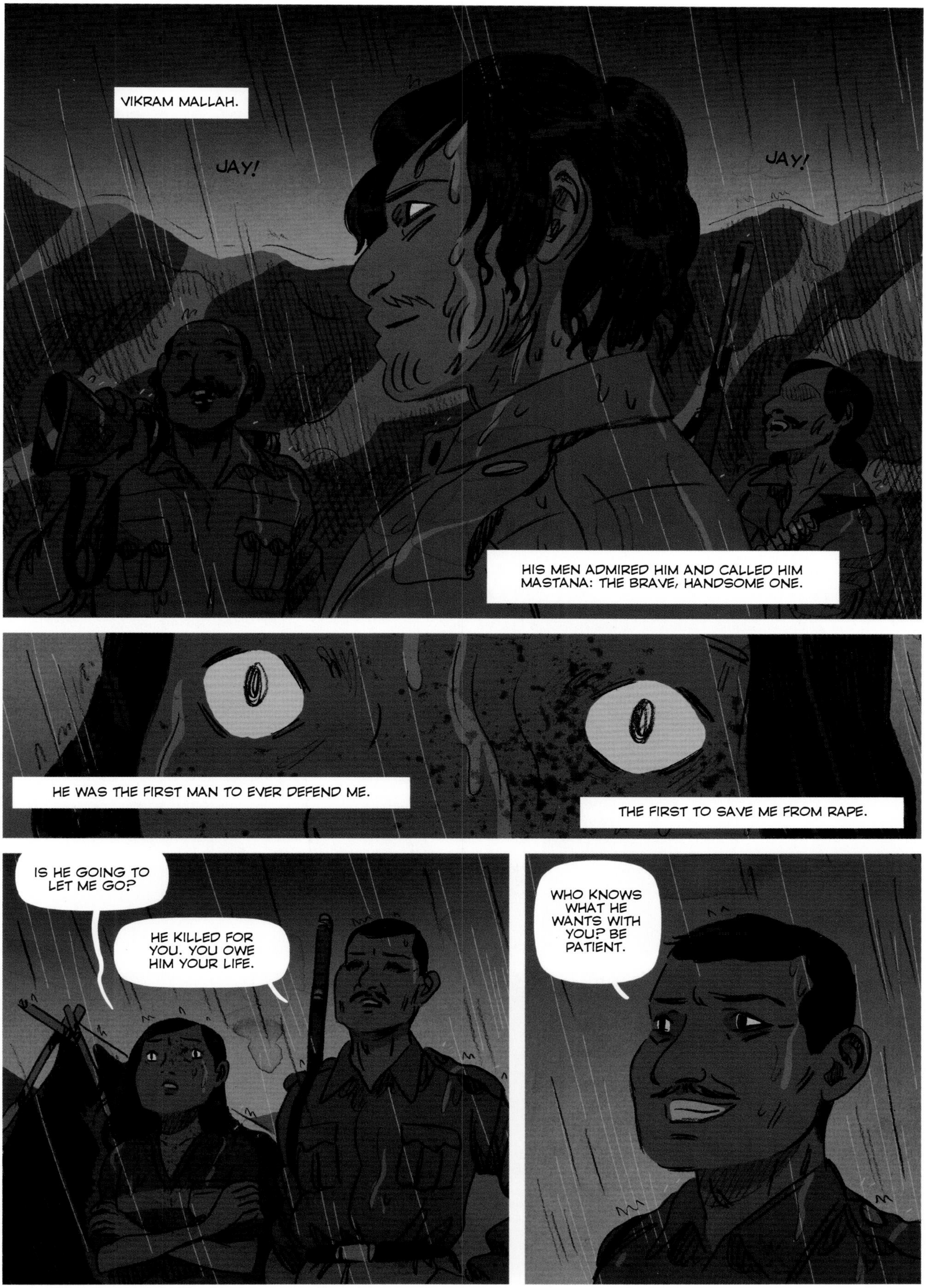

VIKRAM MALLAH.
JAY!
JAY!
HIS MEN ADMIRED HIM AND CALLED HIM MASTANA: THE BRAVE, HANDSOME ONE.
HE WAS THE FIRST MAN TO EVER DEFEND ME.
THE FIRST TO SAVE ME FROM RAPE.
IS HE GOING TO LET ME GO?
HE KILLED FOR YOU. YOU OWE HIM YOUR LIFE.
WHO KNOWS WHAT HE WANTS WITH YOU? BE PATIENT.

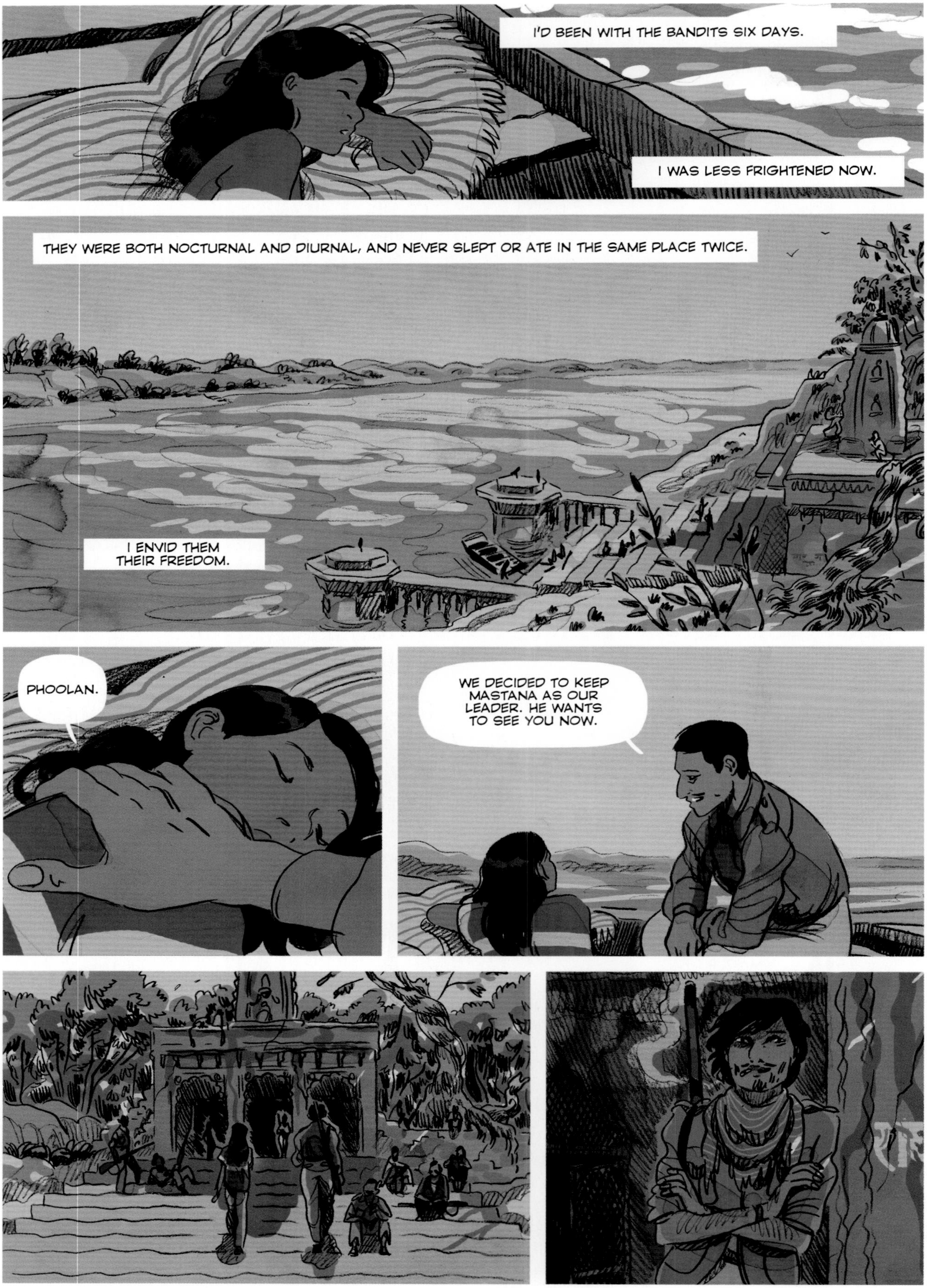
I'D BEEN WITH THE BANDITS SIX DAYS.
I WAS LESS FRIGHTENED NOW.
THEY WERE BOTH NOCTURNAL AND DIURNAL, AND NEVER SLEPT OR ATE IN THE SAME PLACE TWICE.
I ENVID THEM THEIR FREEDOM.
PHOOLAN.
WE DECIDED TO KEEP MASTANA AS OUR LEADER. HE WANTS TO SEE YOU NOW.

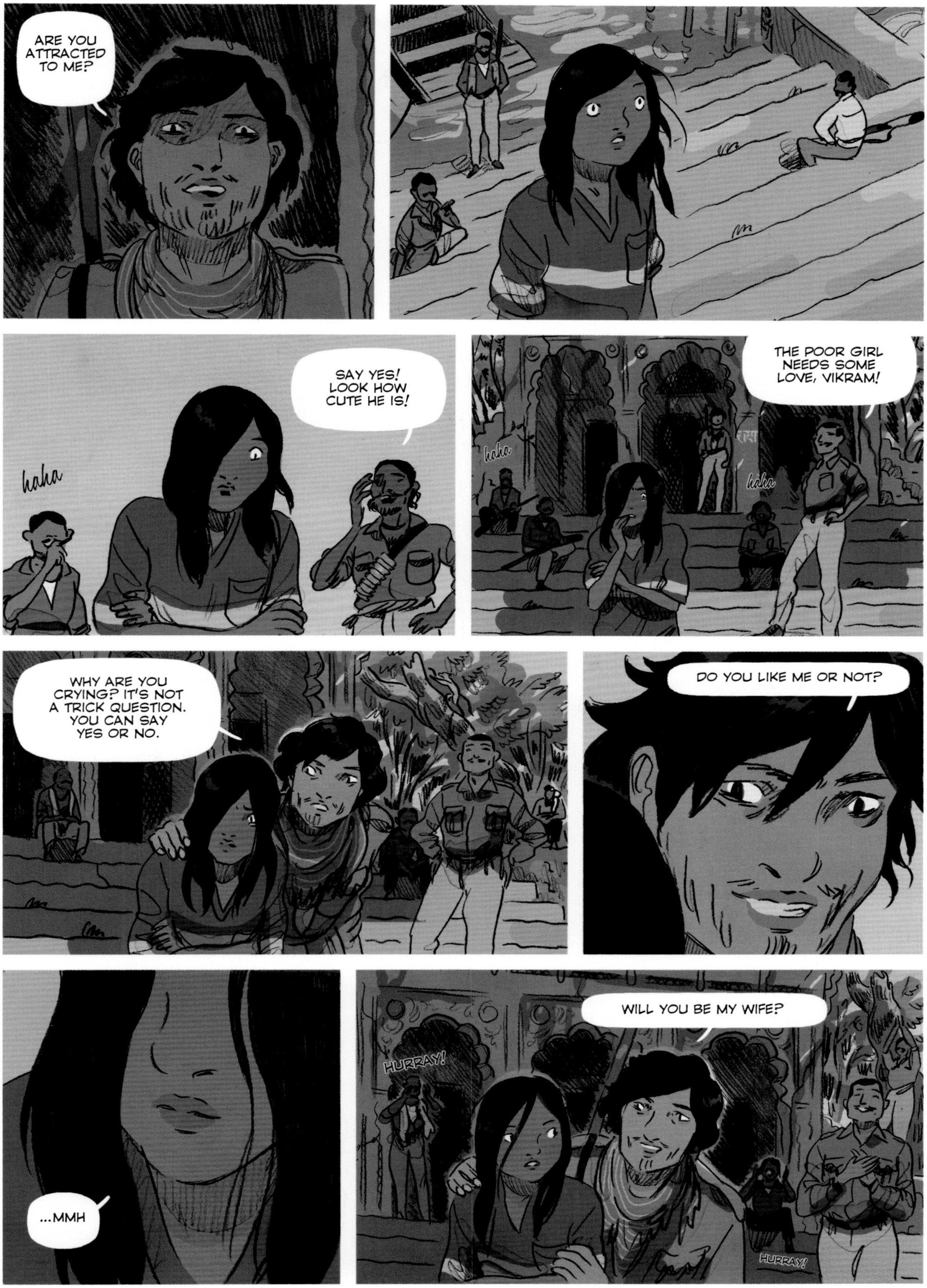
ARE YOU ATTRACTED TO ME?
haha
SAY YES! LOOK HOW CUTE HE IS!
haha
haha
THE POOR GIRL NEEDS SOME LOVE, VIKRAM!
WHY ARE YOU CRYING? IT'S NOT A TRICK QUESTION. YOU CAN SAY YES OR NO.
DO YOU LIKE ME OR NOT?
...MMH
WILL YOU BE MY WIFE?
HURRAY!
HURRAY!

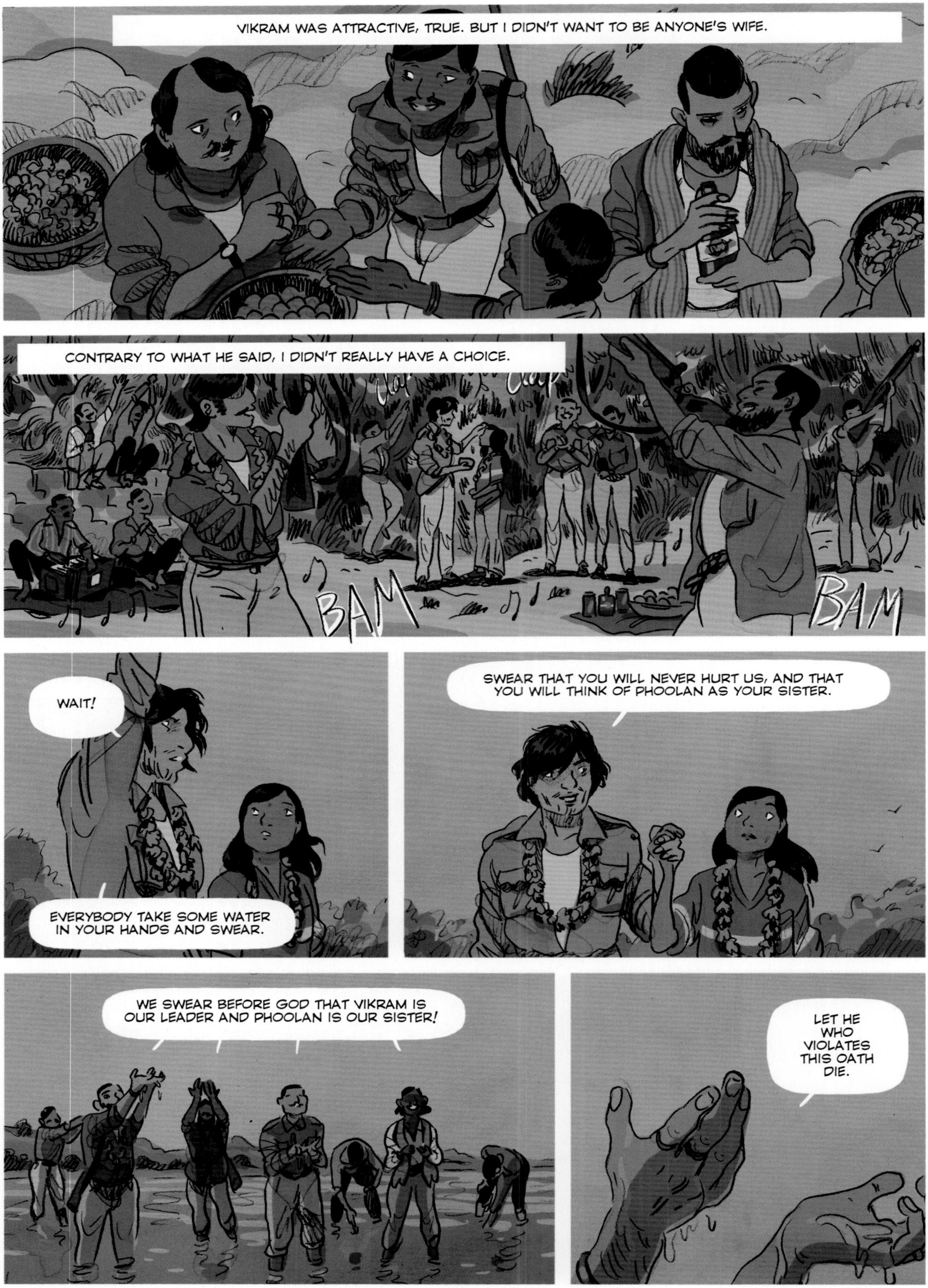
VIKRAM WAS ATTRACTIVE, TRUE. BUT I DIDN'T WANT TO BE ANYONE'S WIFE.
CONTRARY TO WHAT HE SAID, I DIDN'T REALLY HAVE A CHOICE.
BAM
BAM
WAIT!
EVERYBODY TAKE SOME WATER IN YOUR HANDS AND SWEAR.
SWEAR THAT YOU WILL NEVER HURT US, AND THAT YOU WILL THINK OF PHOOLAN AS YOUR SISTER.
WE SWEAR BEFORE GOD THAT VIKRAM IS OUR LEADER AND PHOOLAN IS OUR SISTER!
LET HE WHO VIOLATES THIS OATH DIE.

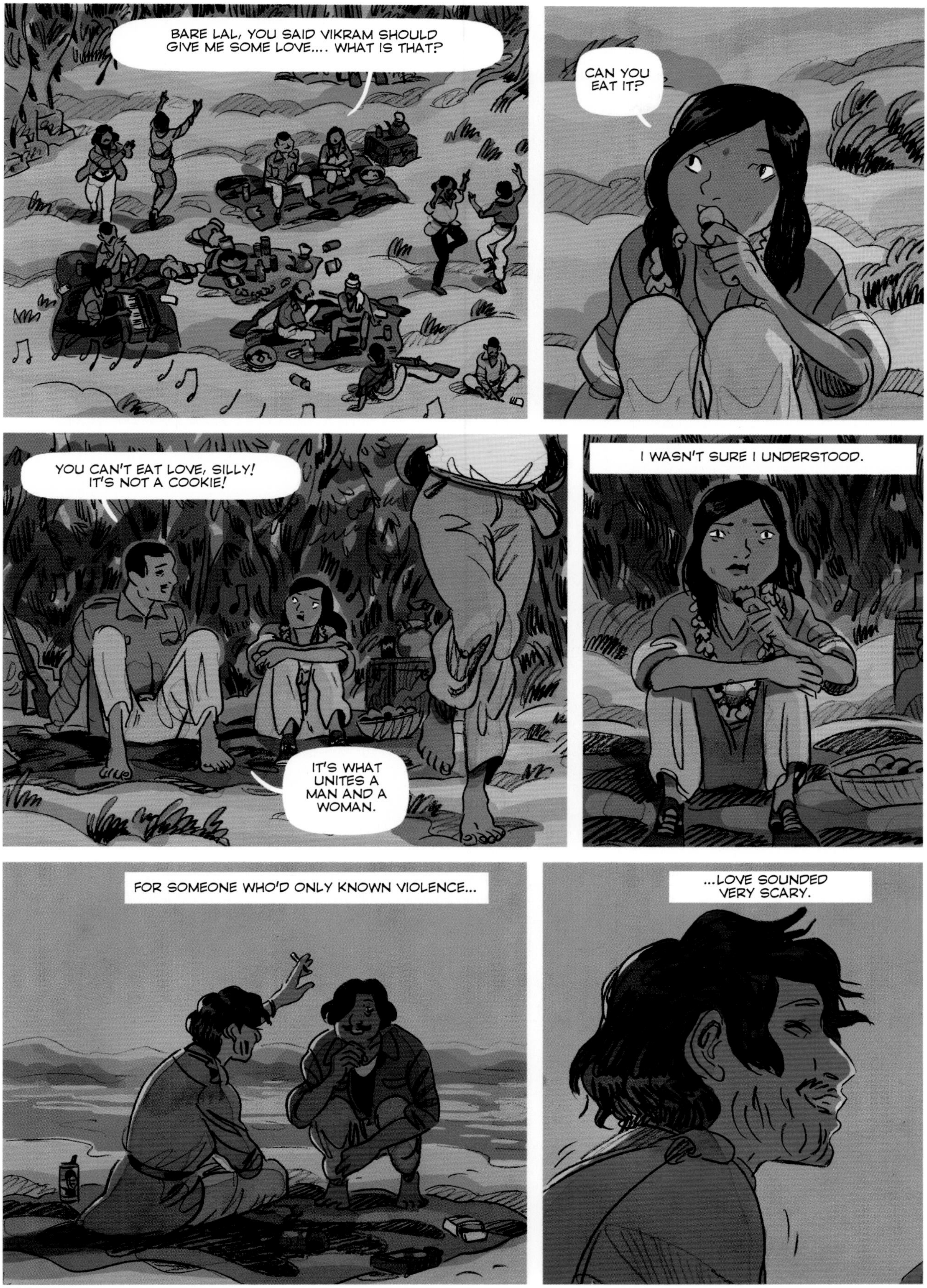

BARE LAL, YOU SAID VIKRAM SHOULD GIVE ME SOME LOVE.... WHAT IS THAT?
CAN YOU EAT IT?
YOU CAN'T EAT LOVE, SILLY! IT'S NOT A COOKIE!
IT'S WHAT UNITES A MAN AND A WOMAN.
I WASN'T SURE I UNDERSTOOD.
FOR SOMEONE WHO'D ONLY KNOWN VIOLENCE...
...LOVE SOUNDED VERY SCARY.

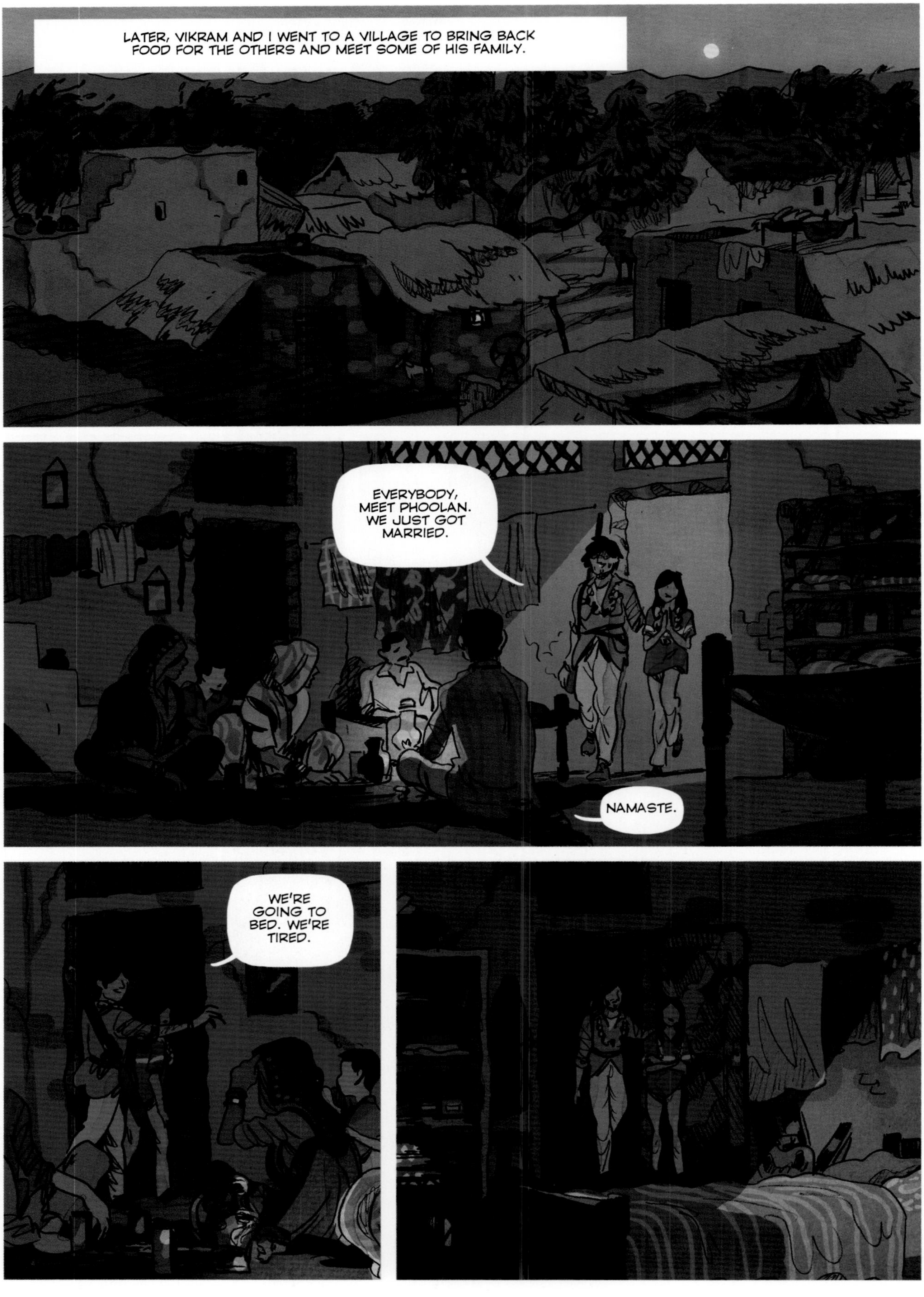
LATER, VIKRAM AND I WENT TO A VILLAGE TO BRING BACK FOOD FOR THE OTHERS AND MEET SOME OF HIS FAMILY.
EVERYBODY, MEET PHOOLAN. WE JUST GOT MARRIED.
NAMASTE.
WE'RE GOING TO BED. WE'RE TIRED.

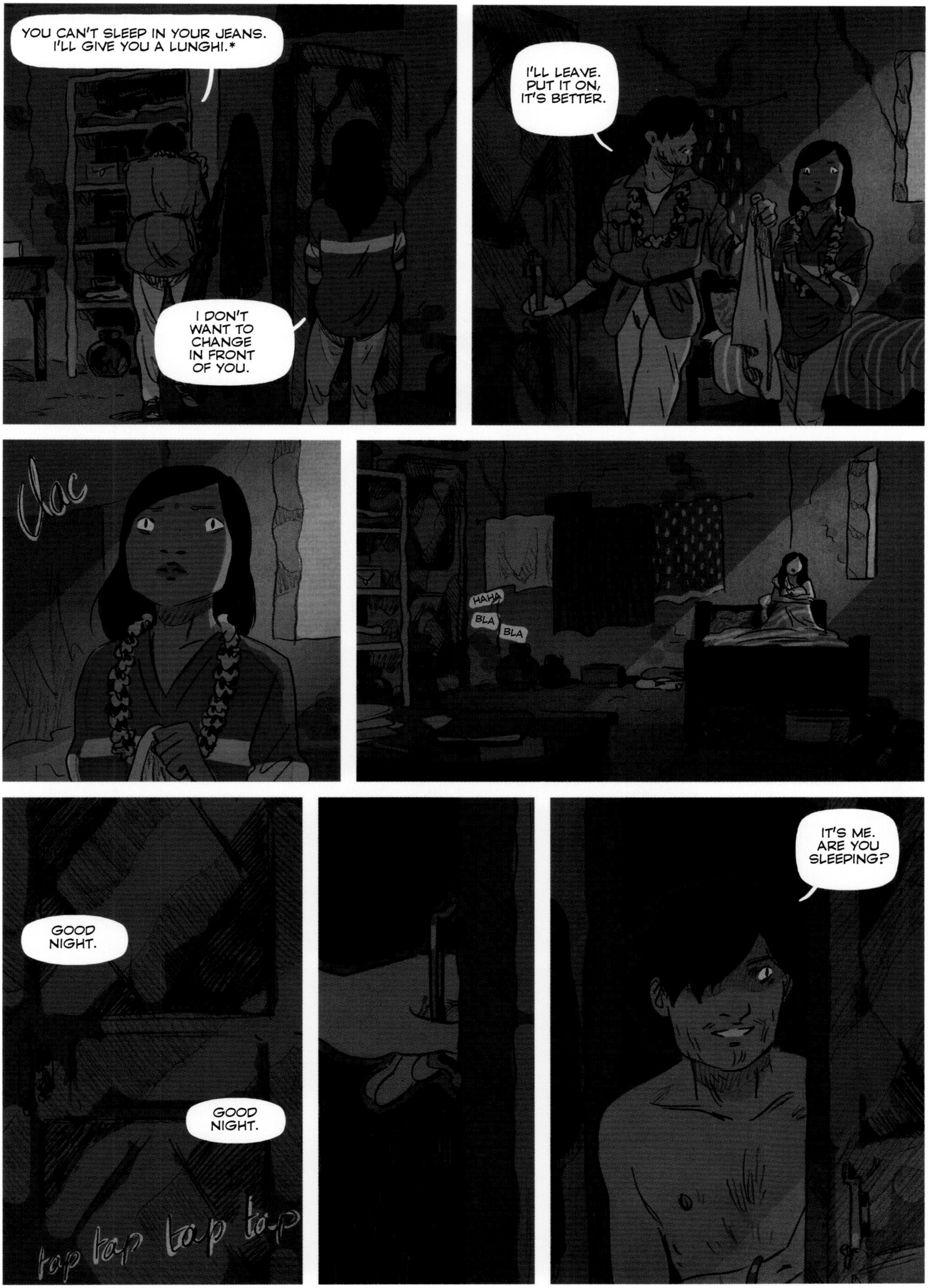
YOU CAN'T SLEEP IN YOUR JEANS. I'LL GIVE YOU A LUNGHI.*
I DON'T WANT TO CHANGE IN FRONT OF YOU.
I'LL LEAVE. PUT IT ON, IT'S BETTER.
Clac
HAHA
BLA
BLA
GOOD NIGHT.
GOOD NIGHT.
tap tap tap tap
IT'S ME. ARE YOU SLEEPING?

*A FABRIC MEN WRAP AROUND THEIR LEGS.

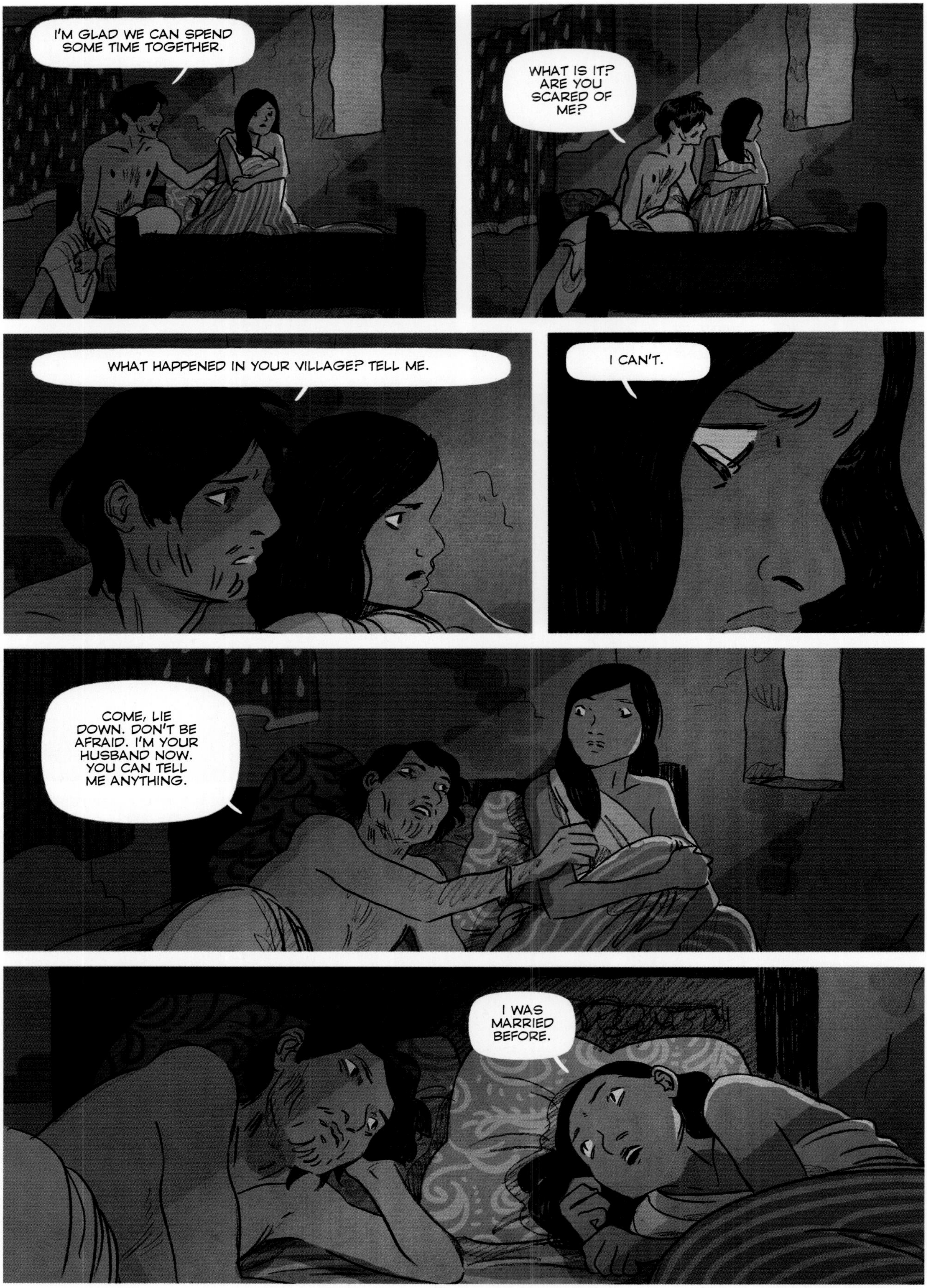
I'M GLAD WE CAN SPEND SOME TIME TOGETHER.
WHAT IS IT? ARE YOU SCARED OF ME?
WHAT HAPPENED IN YOUR VILLAGE? TELL ME.
I CAN'T.
COME, LIE DOWN. DON'T BE AFRAID. I'M YOUR HUSBAND NOW. YOU CAN TELL ME ANYTHING.
I WAS MARRIED BEFORE.

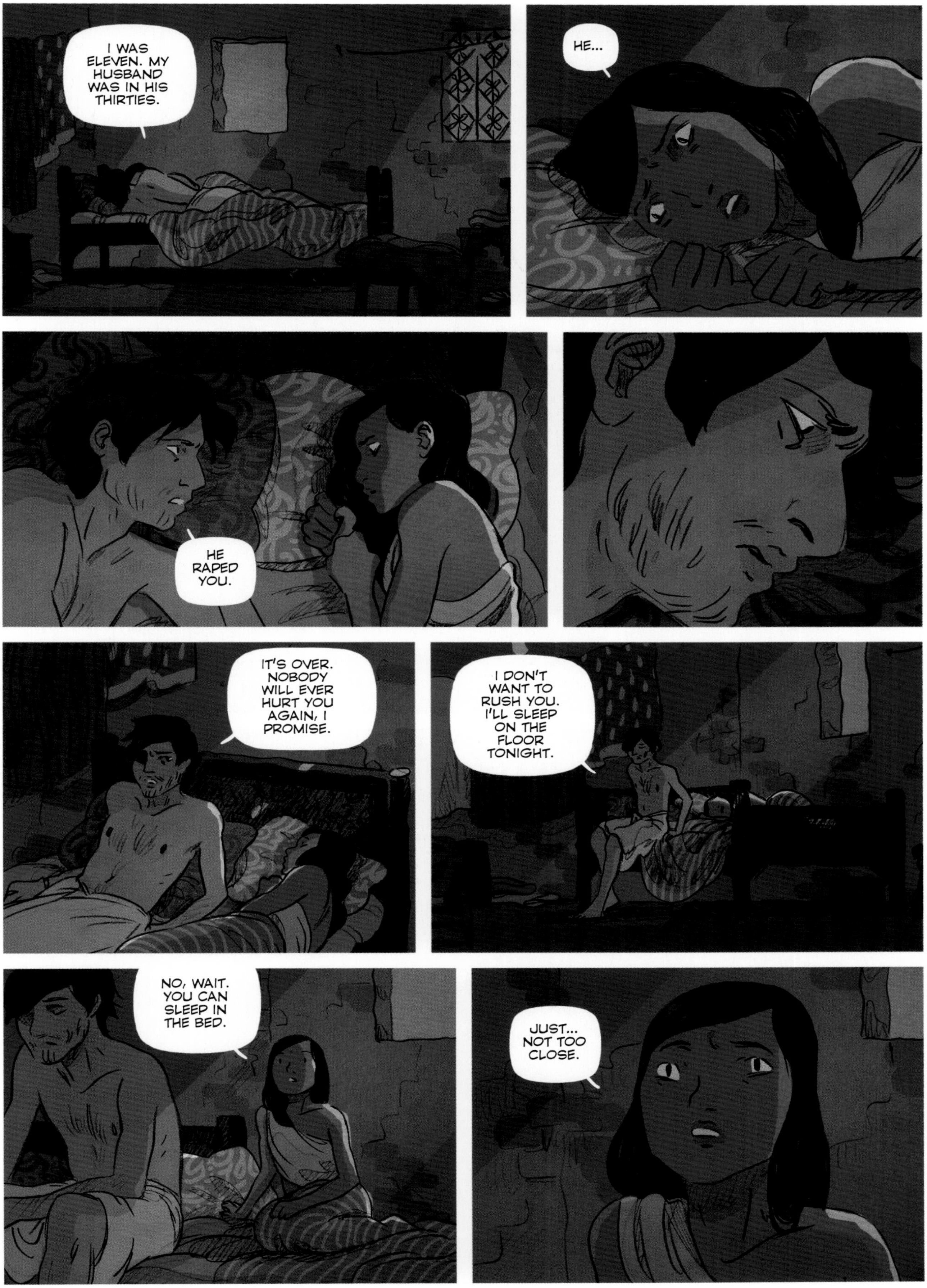
I WAS ELEVEN. MY HUSBAND WAS IN HIS THIRTIES.
HE...
HE RAPED YOU.
IT'S OVER. NOBODY WILL EVER HURT YOU AGAIN, I PROMISE.
I DON'T WANT TO RUSH YOU. I'LL SLEEP ON THE FLOOR TONIGHT.
NO, WAIT. YOU CAN SLEEP IN THE BED.
JUST... NOT TOO CLOSE.

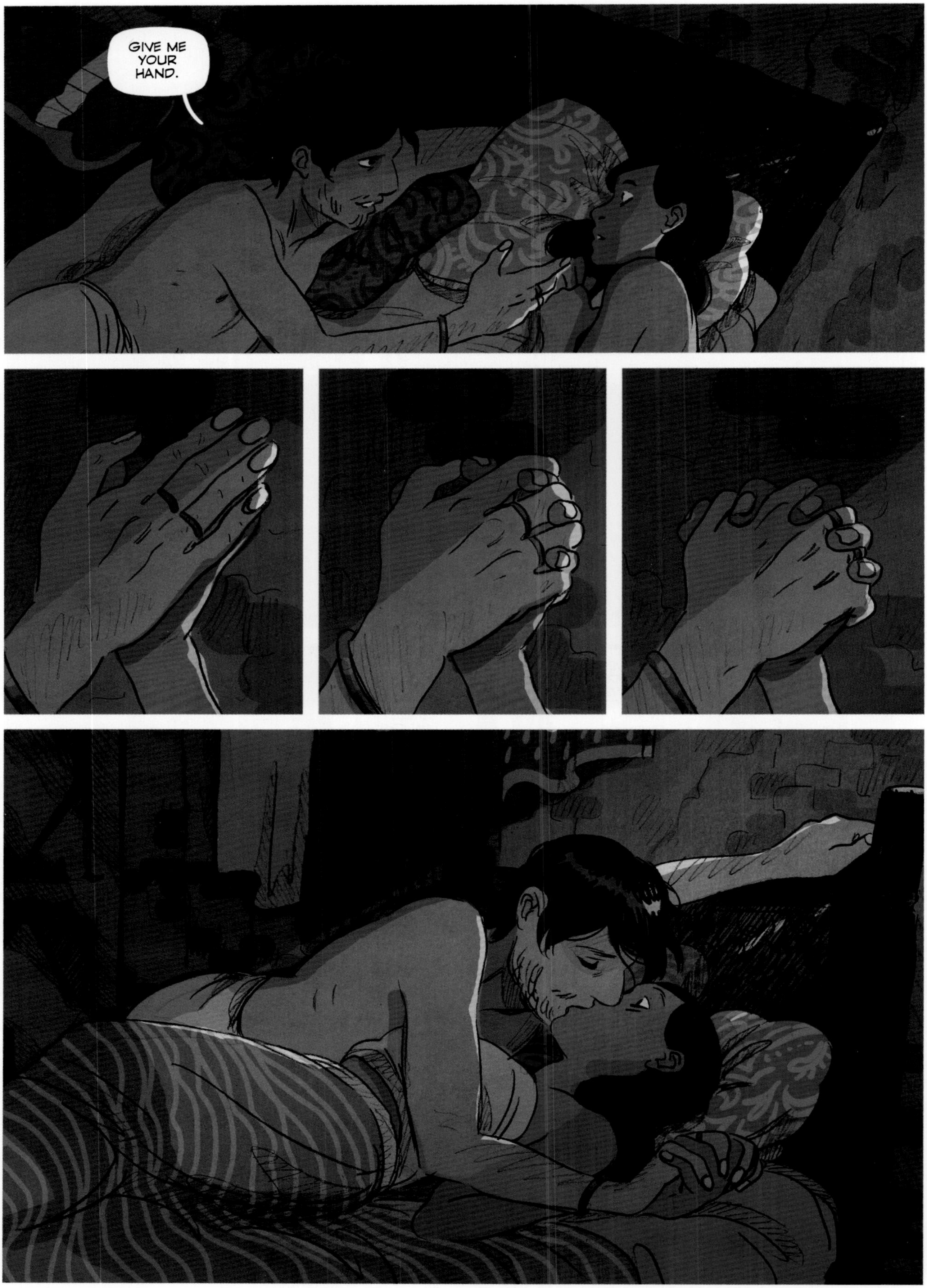
GIVE ME YOUR HAND.

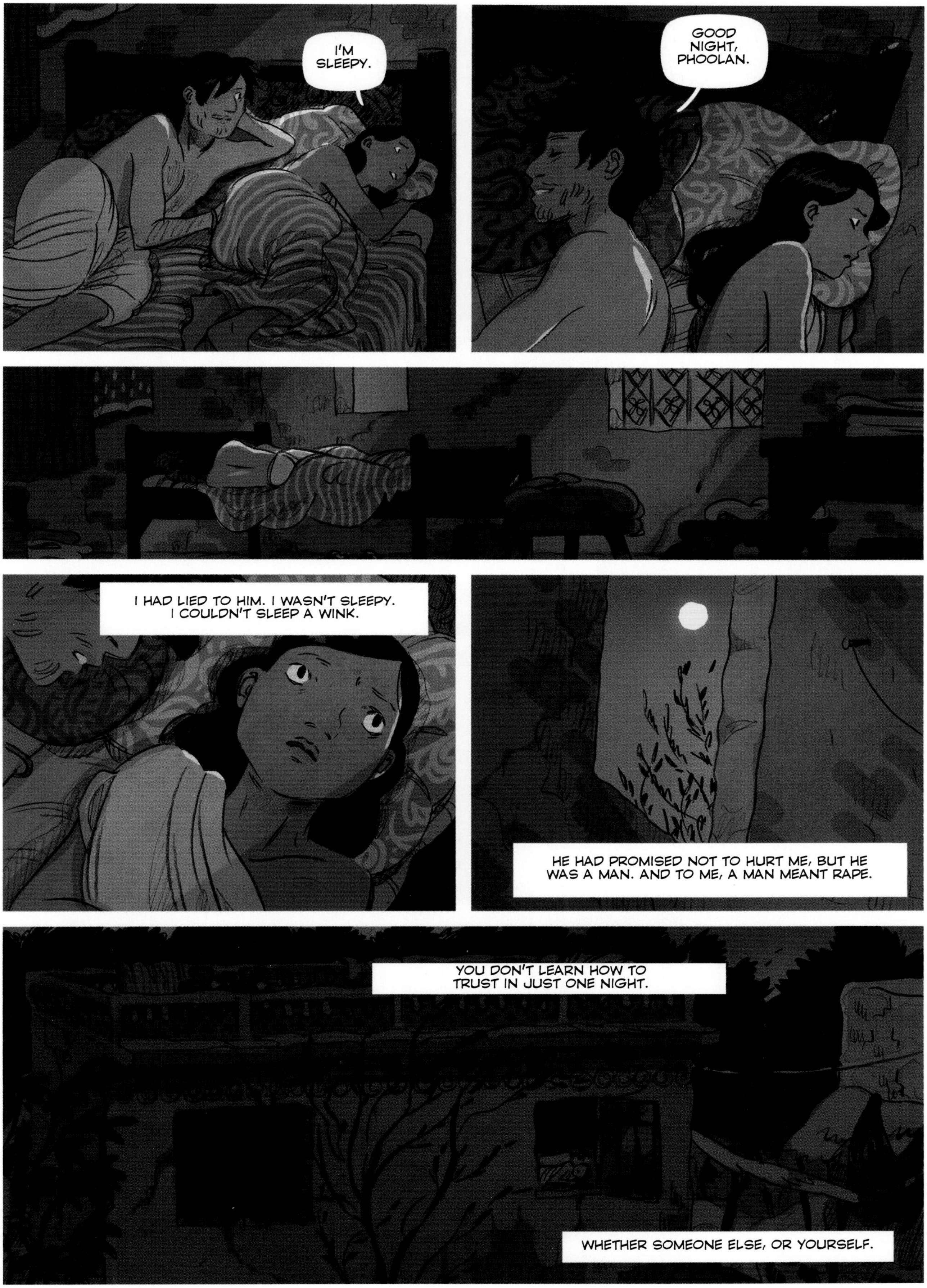
I'M SLEEPY.
GOOD NIGHT, PHOOLAN.
I HAD LIED TO HIM. I WASN'T SLEEPY. I COULDN'T SLEEP A WINK.
HE HAD PROMISED NOT TO HURT ME, BUT HE WAS A MAN. AND TO ME, A MAN MEANT RAPE.
YOU DON'T LEARN HOW TO TRUST IN JUST ONE NIGHT.
WHETHER SOMEONE ELSE, OR YOURSELF.

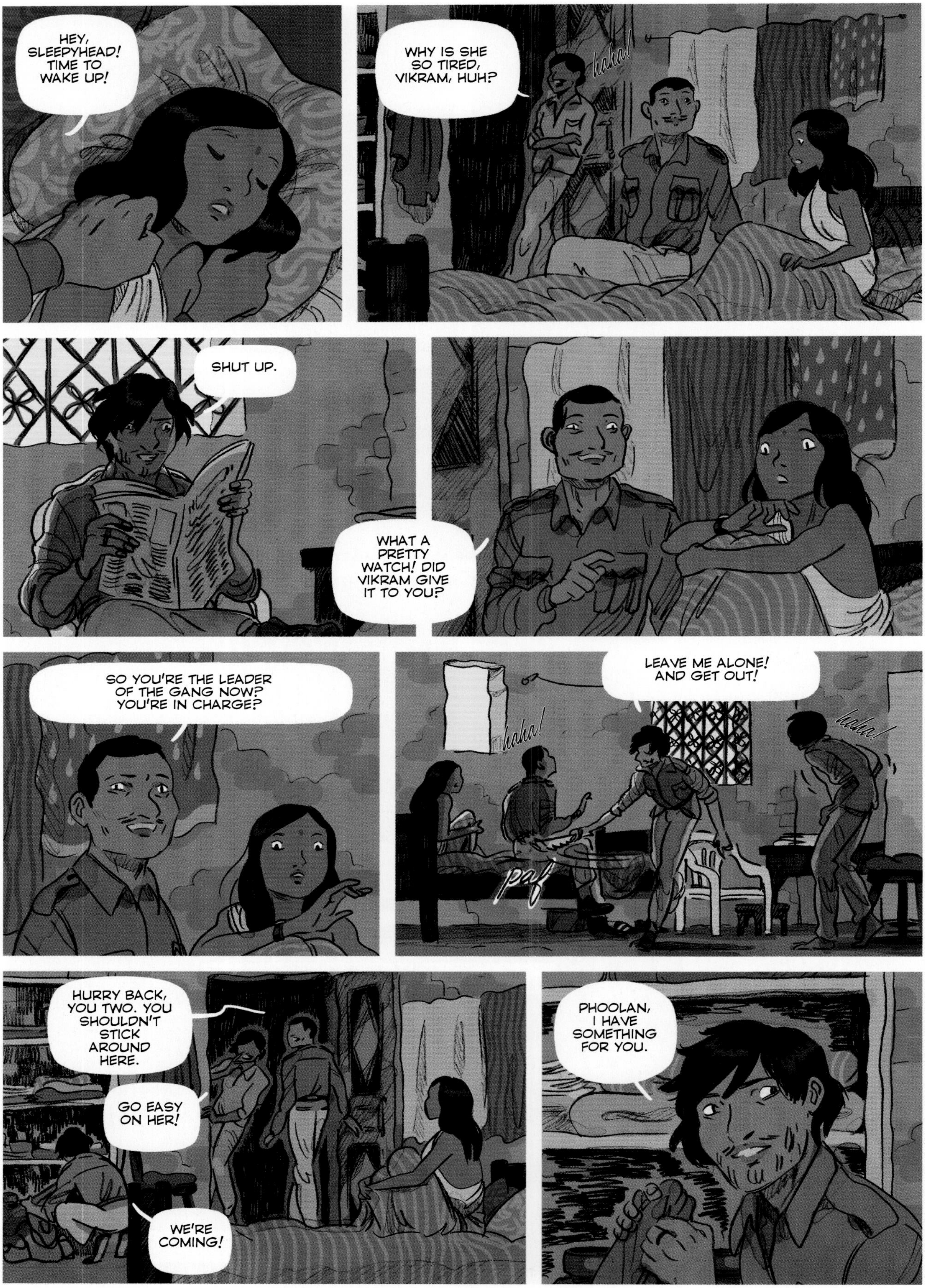
HEY, SLEEPYHEAD! TIME TO WAKE UP!
WHY IS SHE SO TIRED, VIKRAM, HUH?
haha!
SHUT UP.
WHAT A PRETTY WATCH! DID VIKRAM GIVE IT TO YOU?
SO YOU'RE THE LEADER OF THE GANG NOW? YOU'RE IN CHARGE?
LEAVE ME ALONE! AND GET OUT!
haha!
haha!
paf
HURRY BACK, YOU TWO. YOU SHOULDN'T STICK AROUND HERE.
GO EASY ON HER!
WE'RE COMING!
PHOOLAN, I HAVE SOMETHING FOR YOU.

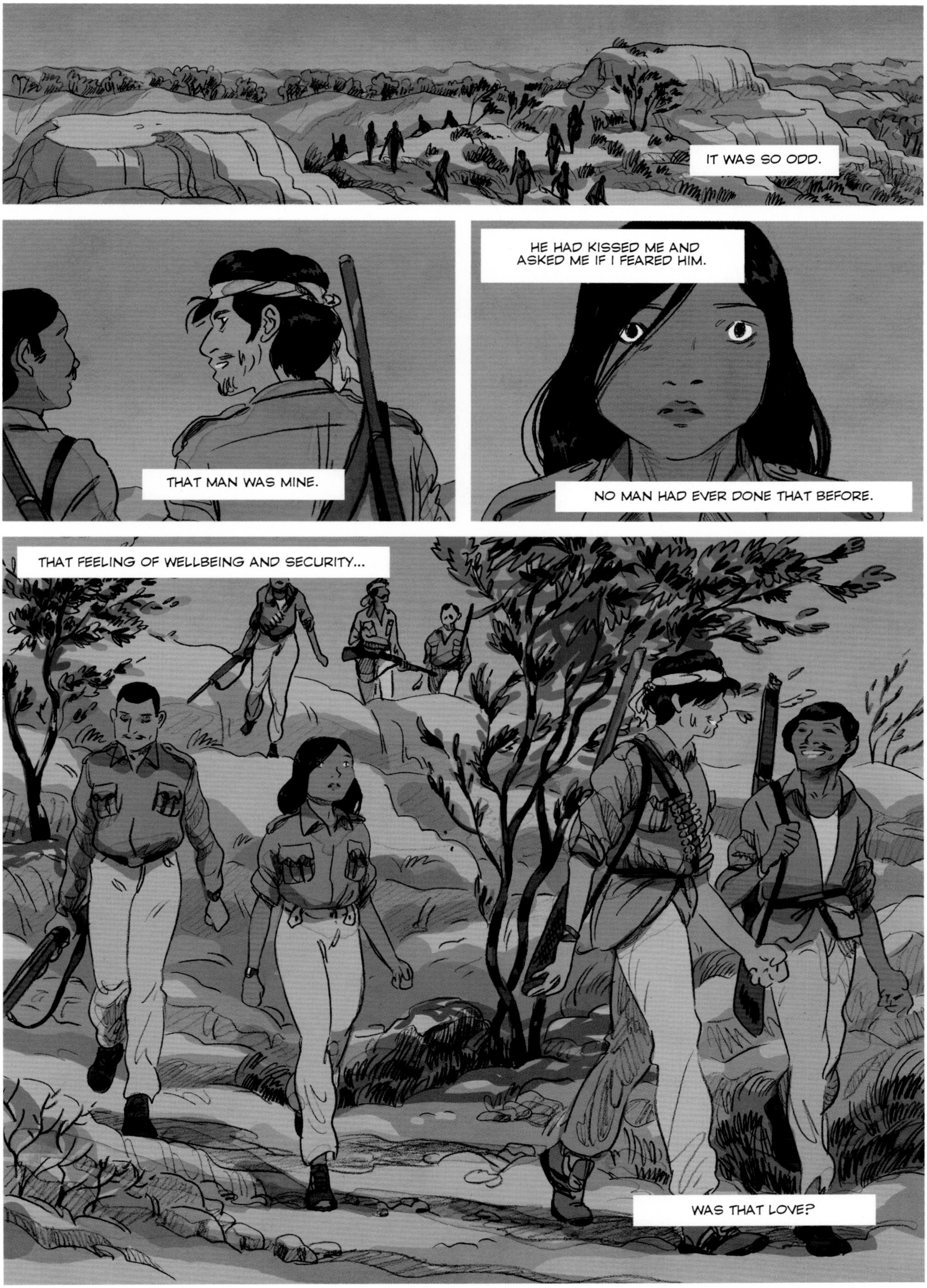
IT WAS SO ODD.
THAT MAN WAS MINE.
HE HAD KISSED ME AND ASKED ME IF I FEARED HIM.
NO MAN HAD EVER DONE THAT BEFORE.
THAT FEELING OF WELLBEING AND SECURITY...
WAS THAT LOVE?

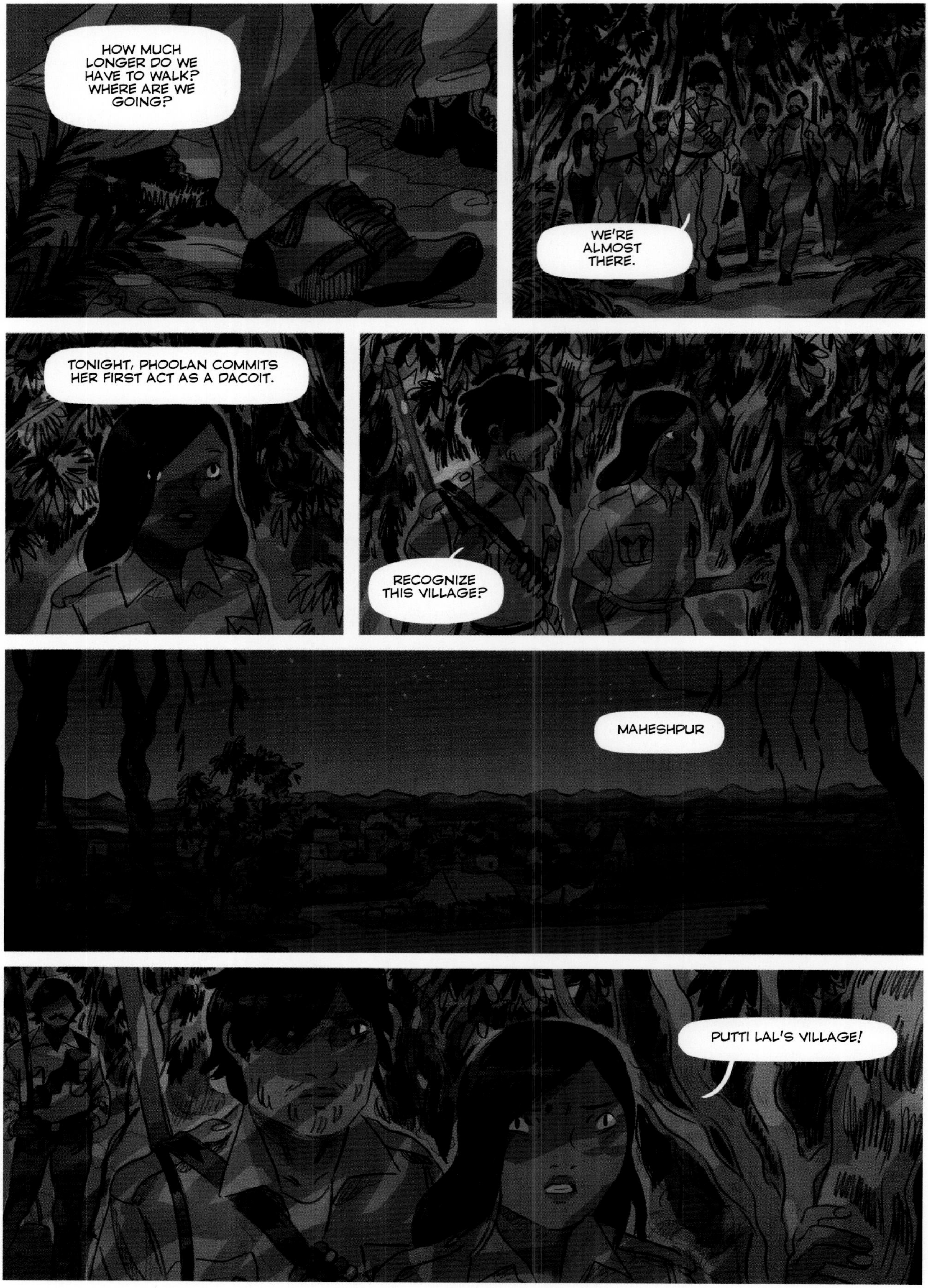
HOW MUCH LONGER DO WE HAVE TO WALK? WHERE ARE WE GOING?
WE'RE ALMOST THERE.
TONIGHT, PHOOLAN COMMITS HER FIRST ACT AS A DACOIT.
RECOGNIZE THIS VILLAGE?
MAHESHPUR
PUTTI LAL'S VILLAGE!

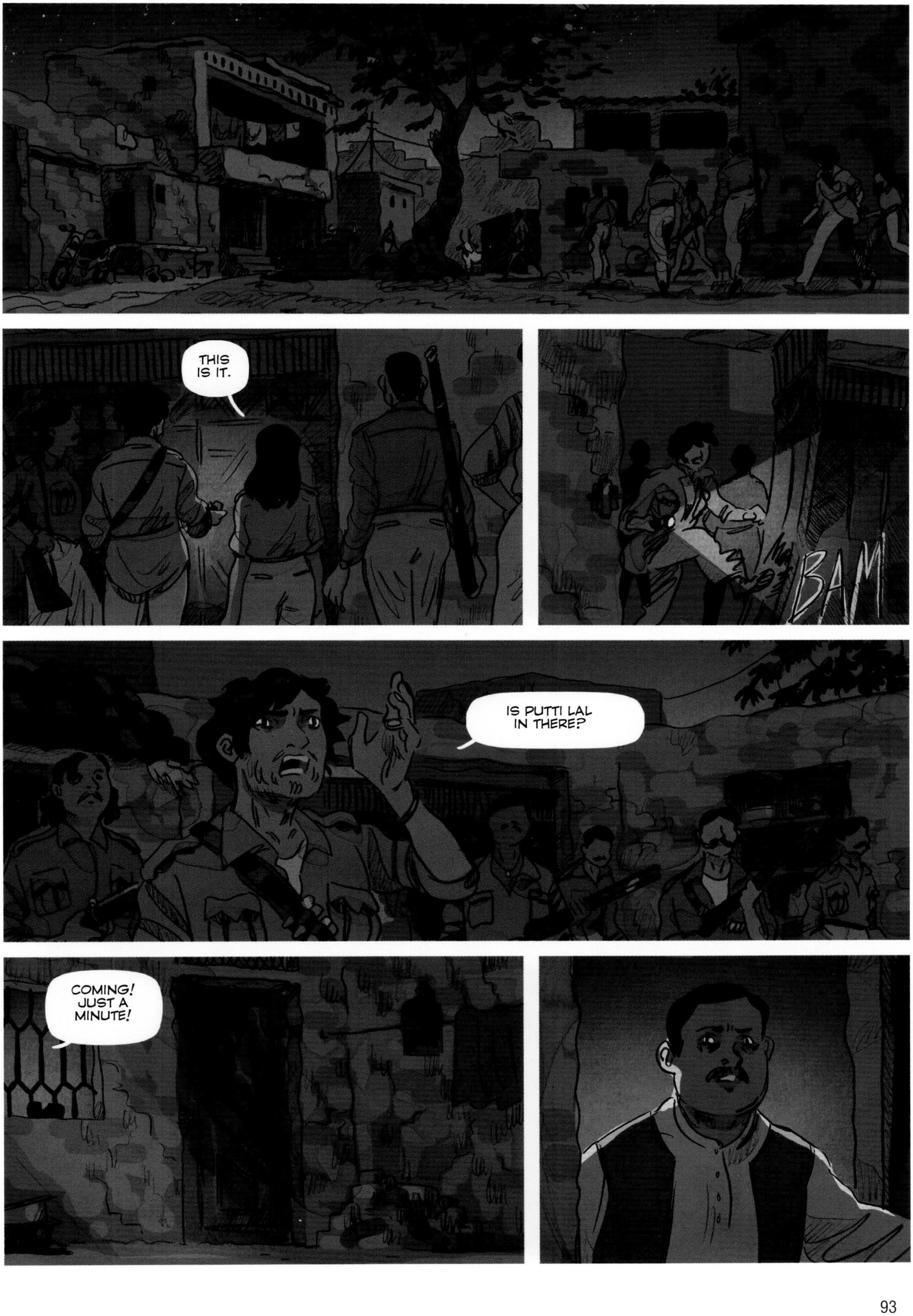
THIS IS IT.
BAM
IS PUTTI LAL IN THERE?
COMING! JUST A MINUTE!

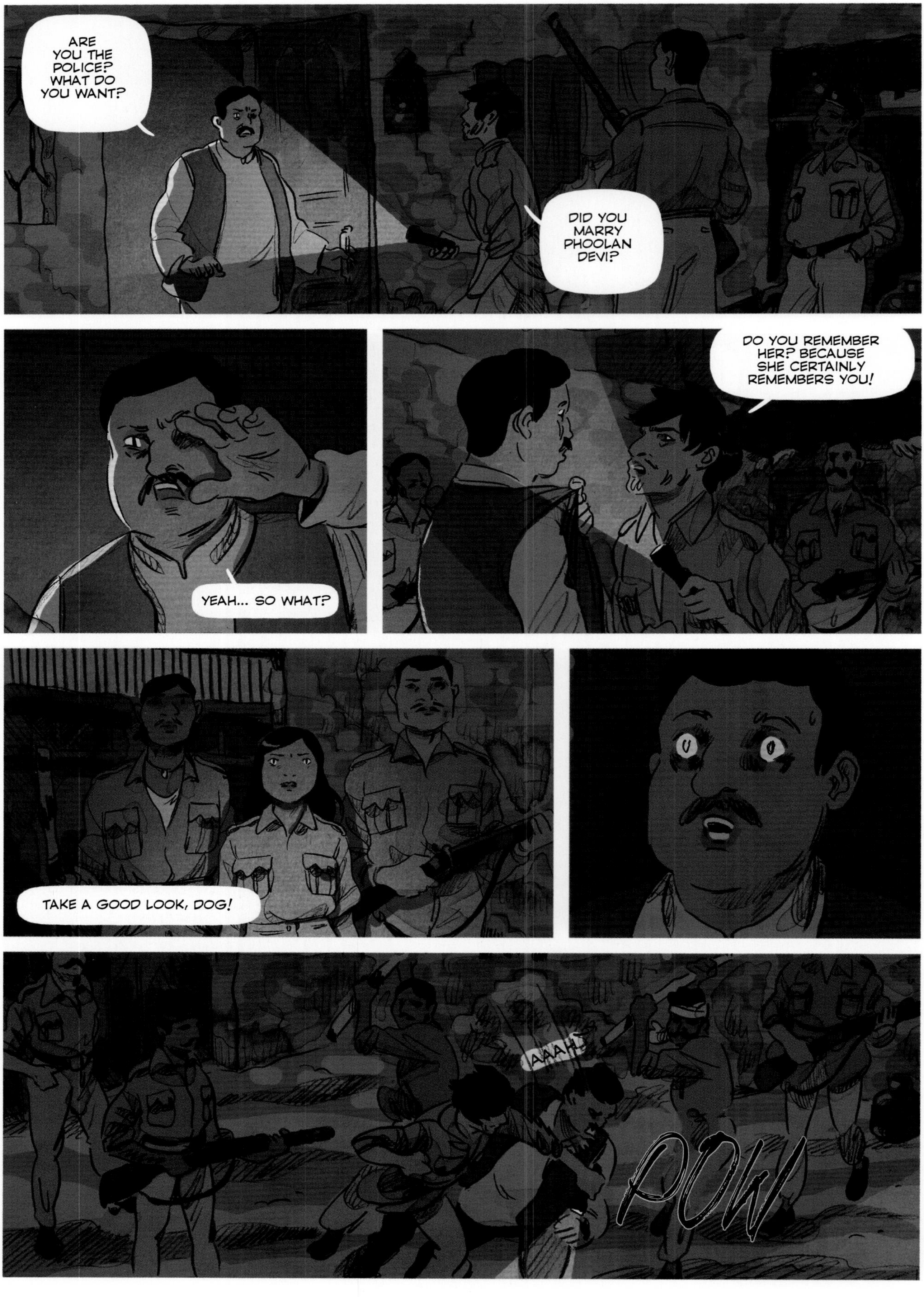
ARE YOU THE POLICE? WHAT DO YOU WANT?
DID YOU MARRY PHOOLAN DEVI?
YEAH... SO WHAT?
DO YOU REMEMBER HER? BECAUSE SHE CERTAINLY REMEMBERS YOU!
TAKE A GOOD LOOK, DOG!
AAAH!
POW

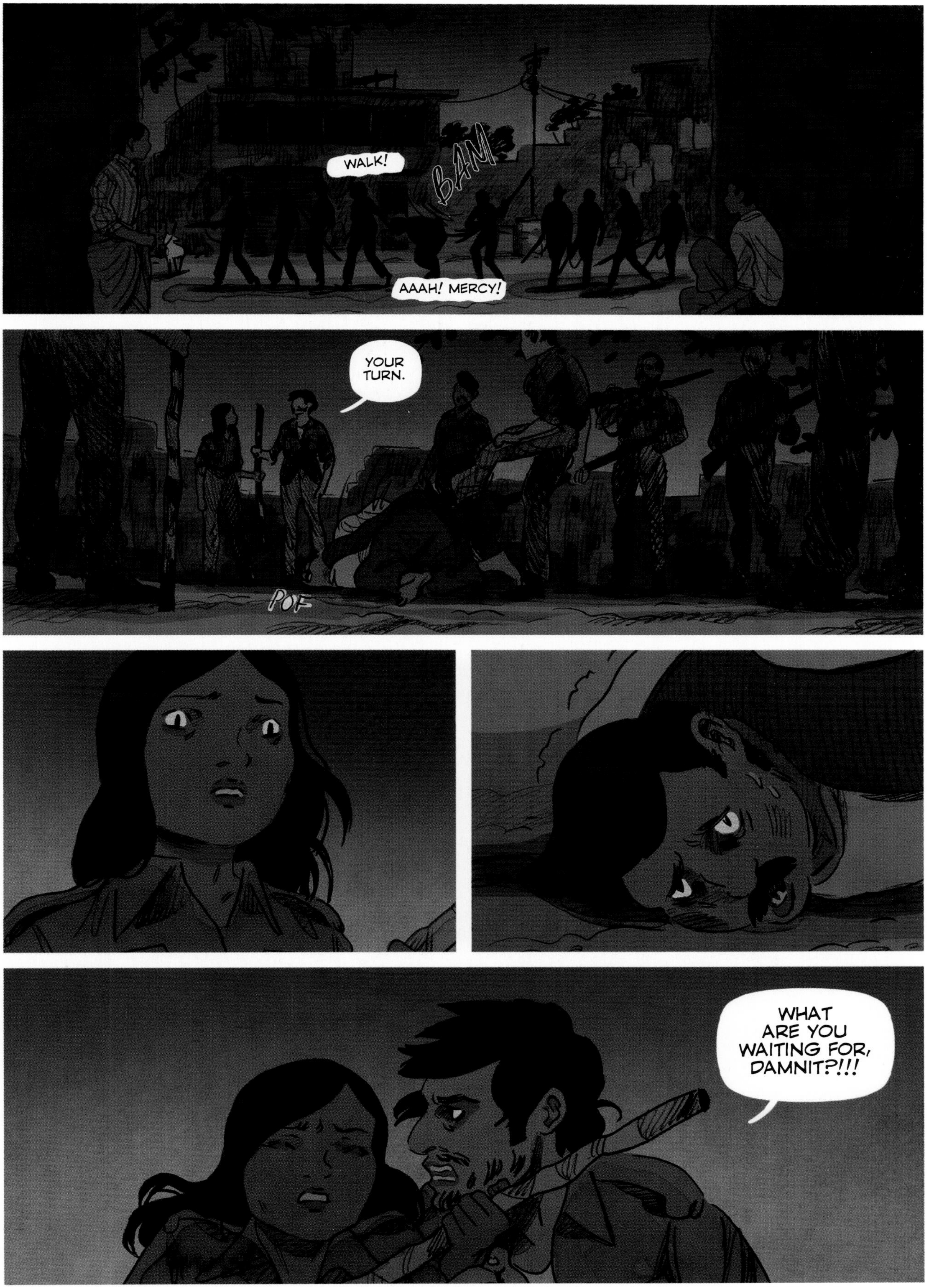
WALK!
BAM
AAAH! MERCY!
YOUR TURN.
POF
WHAT ARE YOU WAITING FOR, DAMNIT?!!!

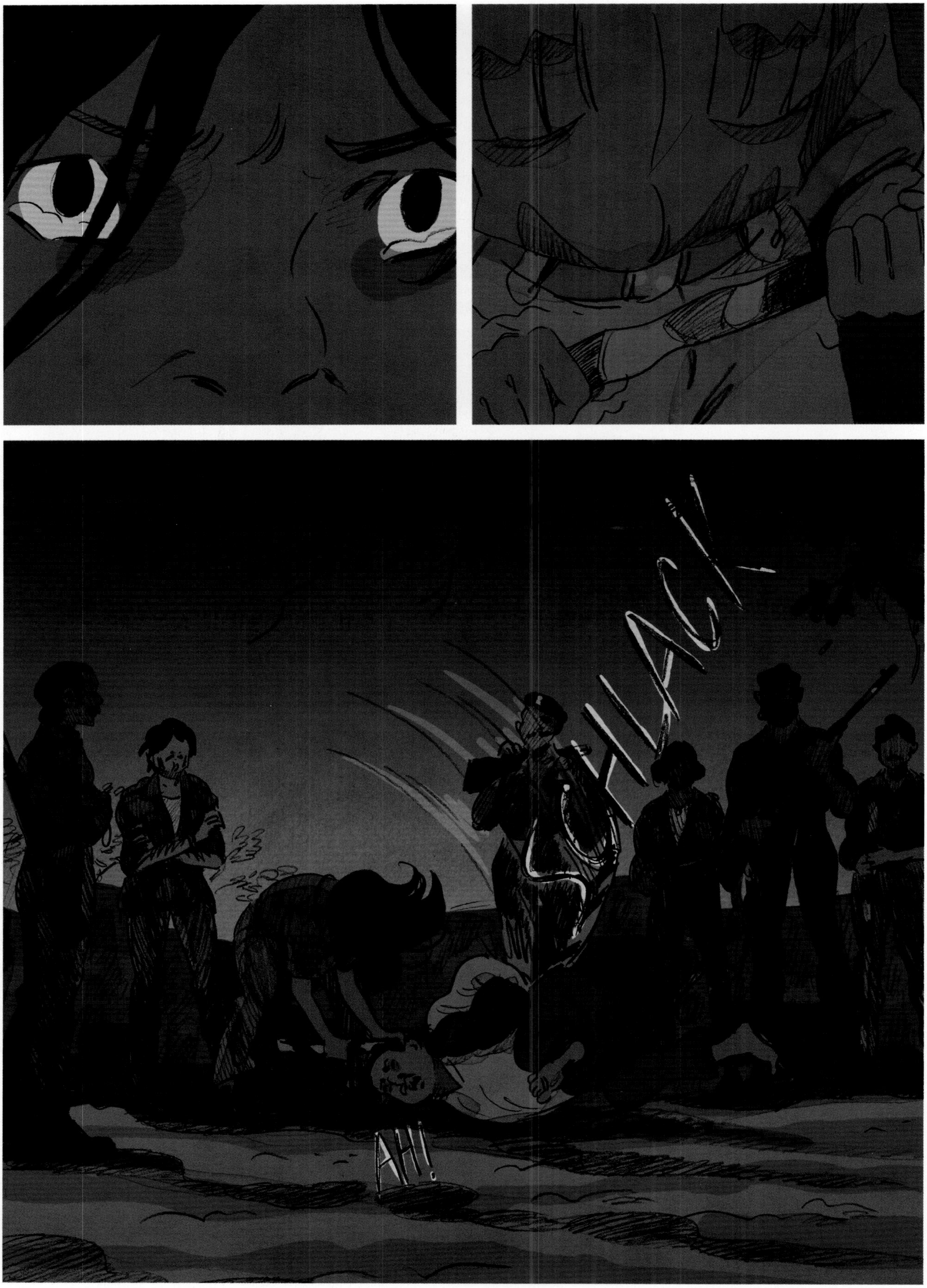
WHACK!
AH!

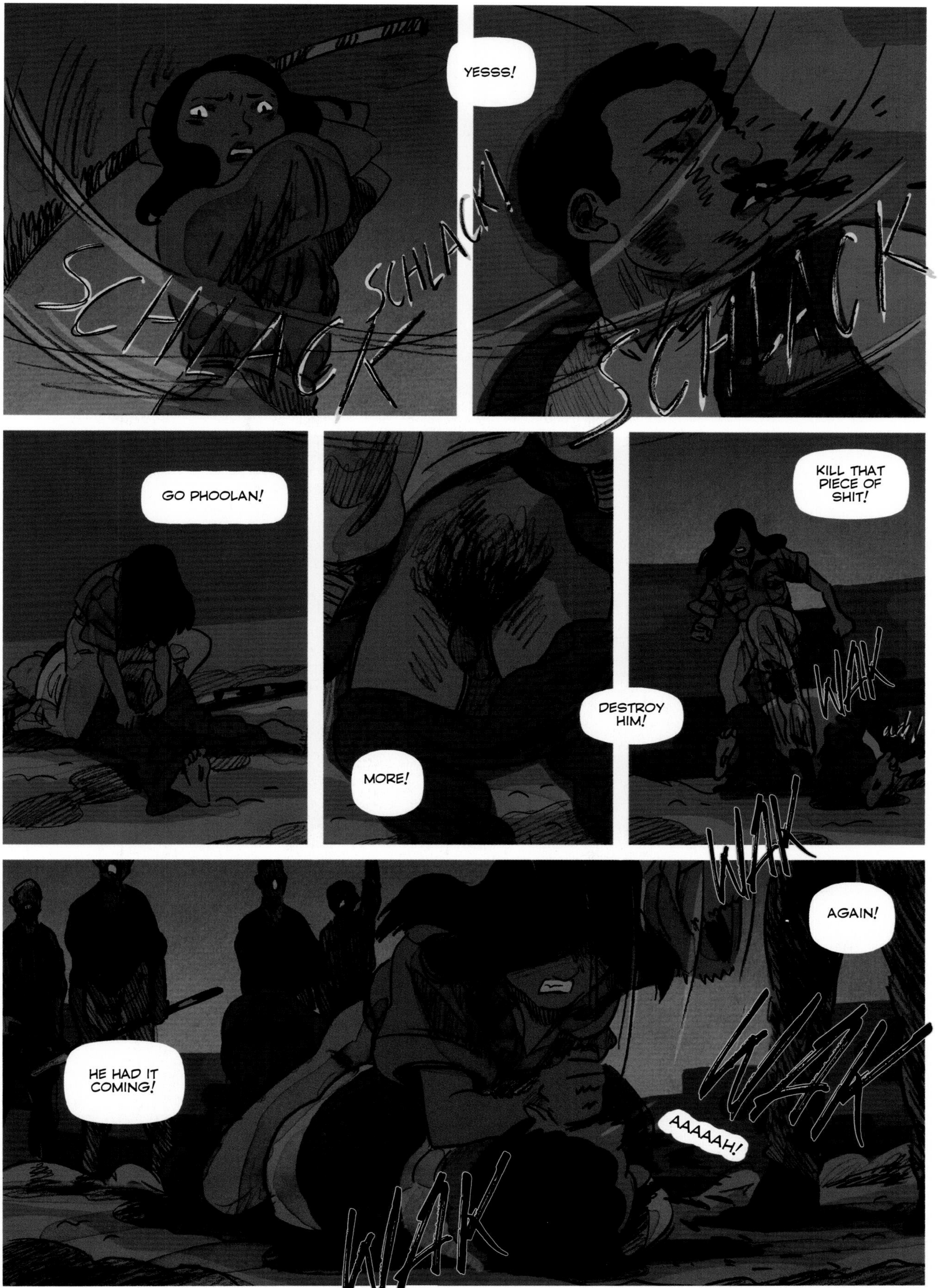
SCHLACK
SCHLACK!
YESSS!
SCHLACK
GO PHOOLAN!
DESTROY HIM!
MORE!
KILL THAT PIECE OF SHIT!
WAK
WAK
WAK
AGAIN!
HE HAD IT COMING!
WAK
AAAAAH!
WAK

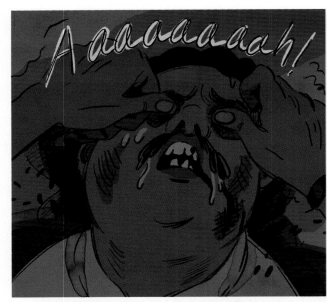

Aaaaaaaah!

PHOOLAN!

THAT'S ENOUGH!

IF YOU WANT TO KEEP GOING, I'LL GET YOU A RIFLE.

DO YOU WANT TO KILL HIM?

NO.

HE DOESN'T DESERVE TO DIE!

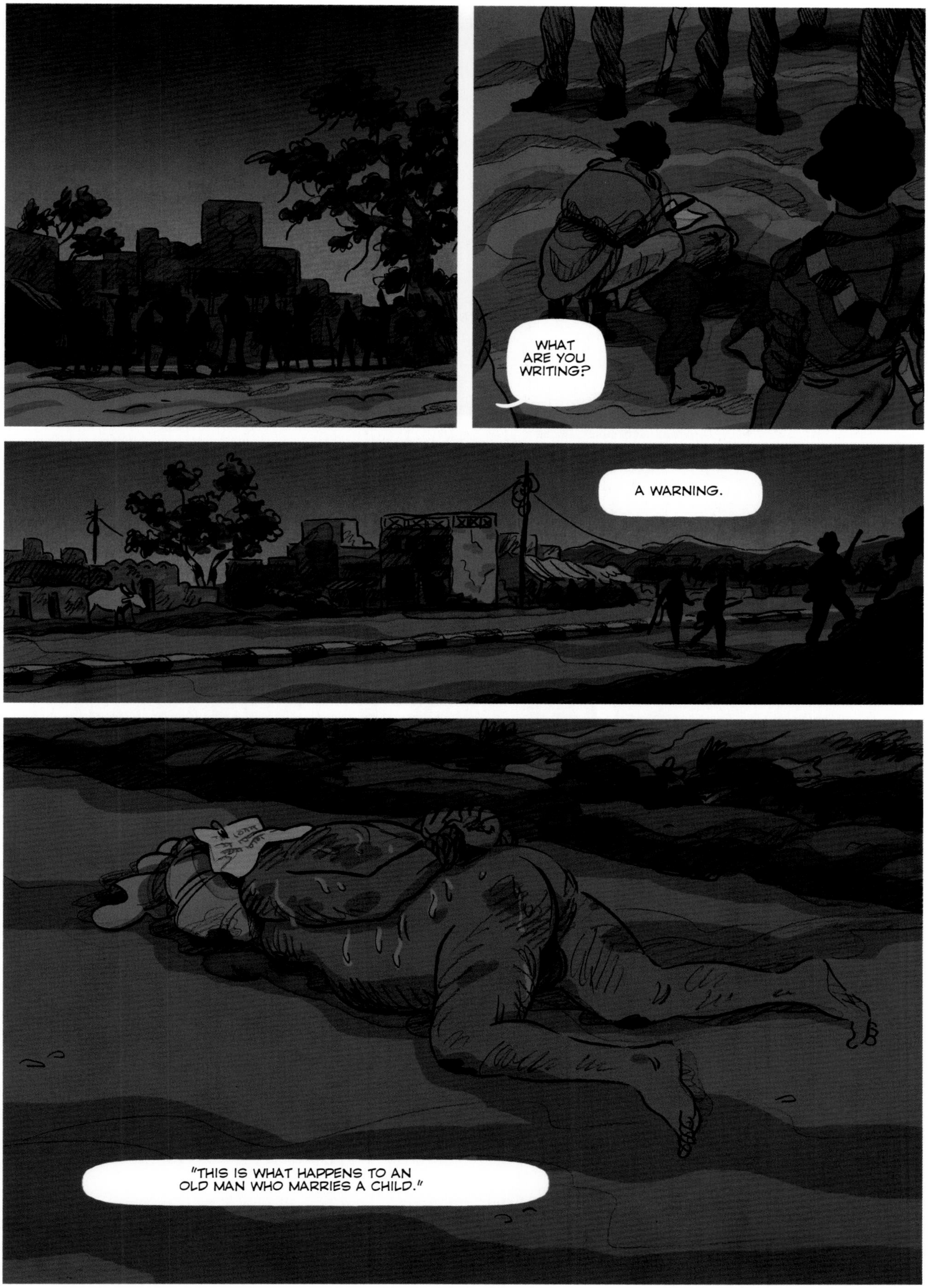
WHAT ARE YOU WRITING?
A WARNING.
"THIS IS WHAT HAPPENS TO AN OLD MAN WHO MARRIES A CHILD."

DID I STILL WANT TO GO HOME? NO.

DID I BELIEVE IN A NEW GOD? YES.

KEEP YOUR EYES ON THE TARGET.

DID I HAVE HOPE FOR MY LIFE AGAIN? YES.

MAKE SURE YOUR LEGS ARE STEADY. THE RECOIL WILL HIT YOUR SHOULDER.

GO AHEAD, FIRE!

ah!

BAM

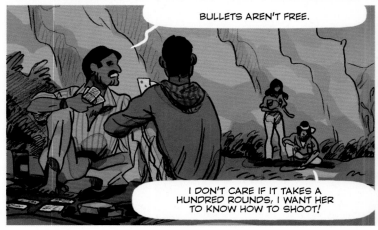

BULLETS AREN'T FREE.

I DON'T CARE IF IT TAKES A HUNDRED ROUNDS, I WANT HER TO KNOW HOW TO SHOOT!

AGAIN.

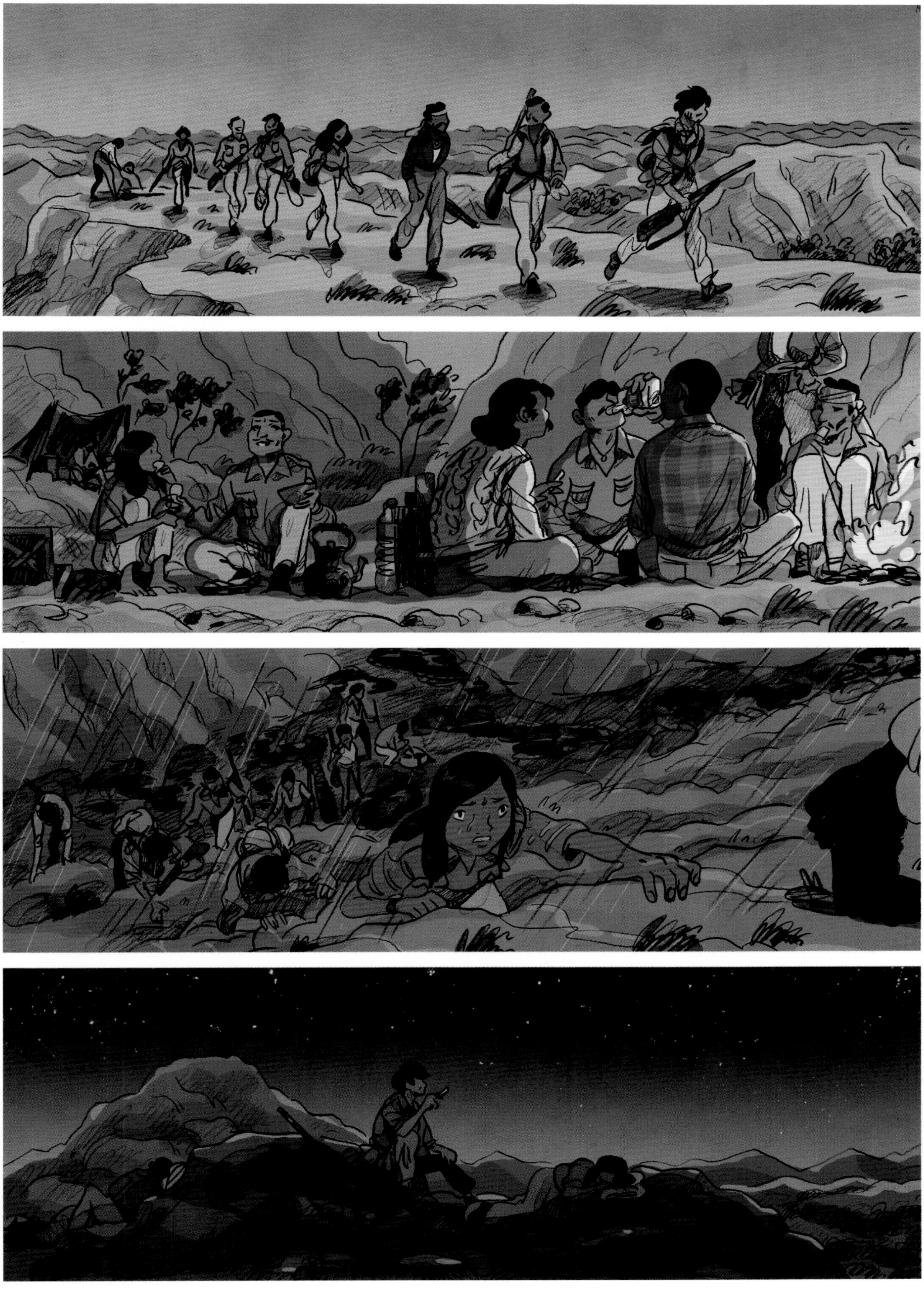

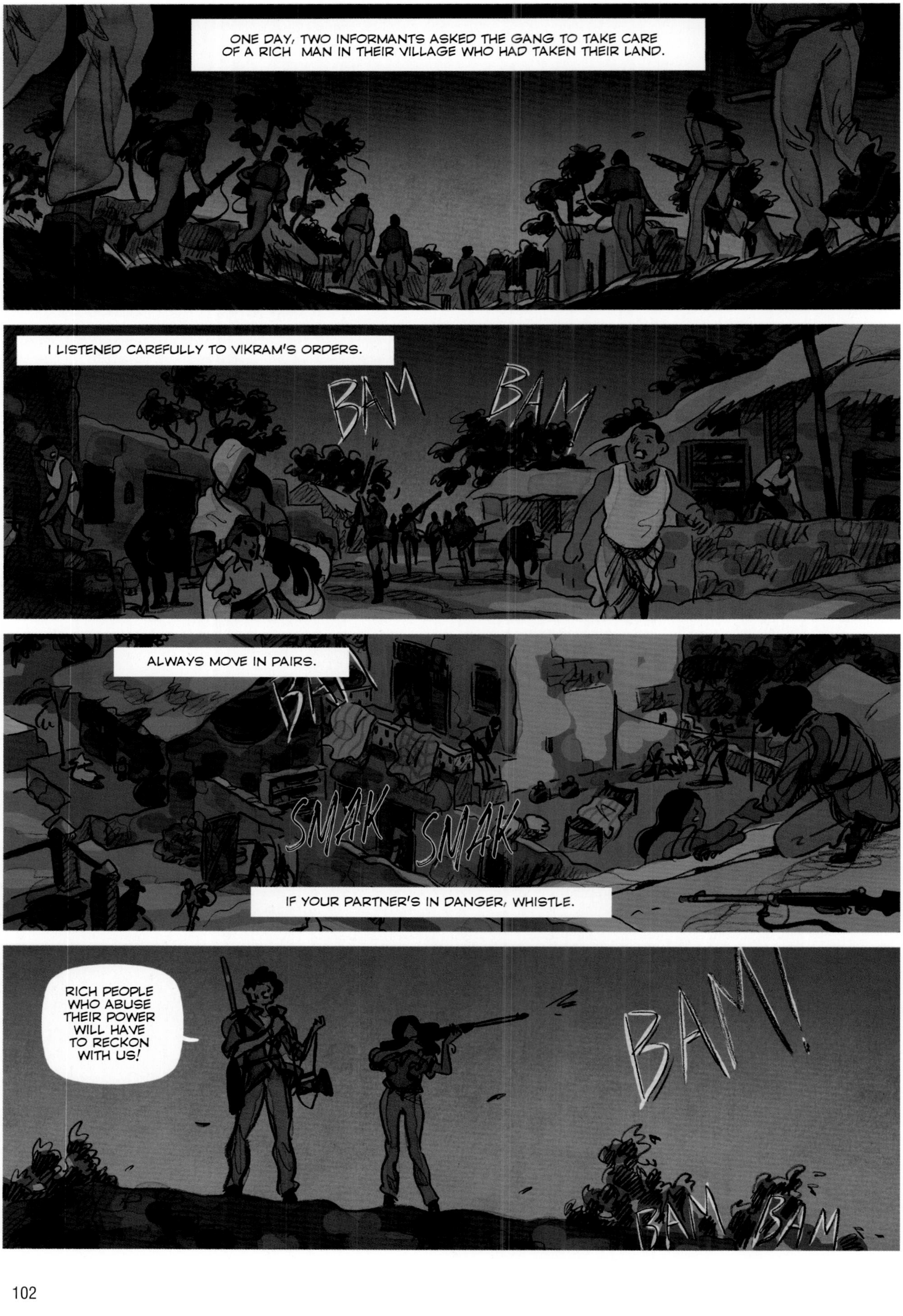

ONE DAY, TWO INFORMANTS ASKED THE GANG TO TAKE CARE OF A RICH MAN IN THEIR VILLAGE WHO HAD TAKEN THEIR LAND.
I LISTENED CAREFULLY TO VIKRAM'S ORDERS.
BAM
BAM
ALWAYS MOVE IN PAIRS.
SMAK
SMAK
IF YOUR PARTNER'S IN DANGER, WHISTLE.
RICH PEOPLE WHO ABUSE THEIR POWER WILL HAVE TO RECKON WITH US!
BAM!
BAM
BAM

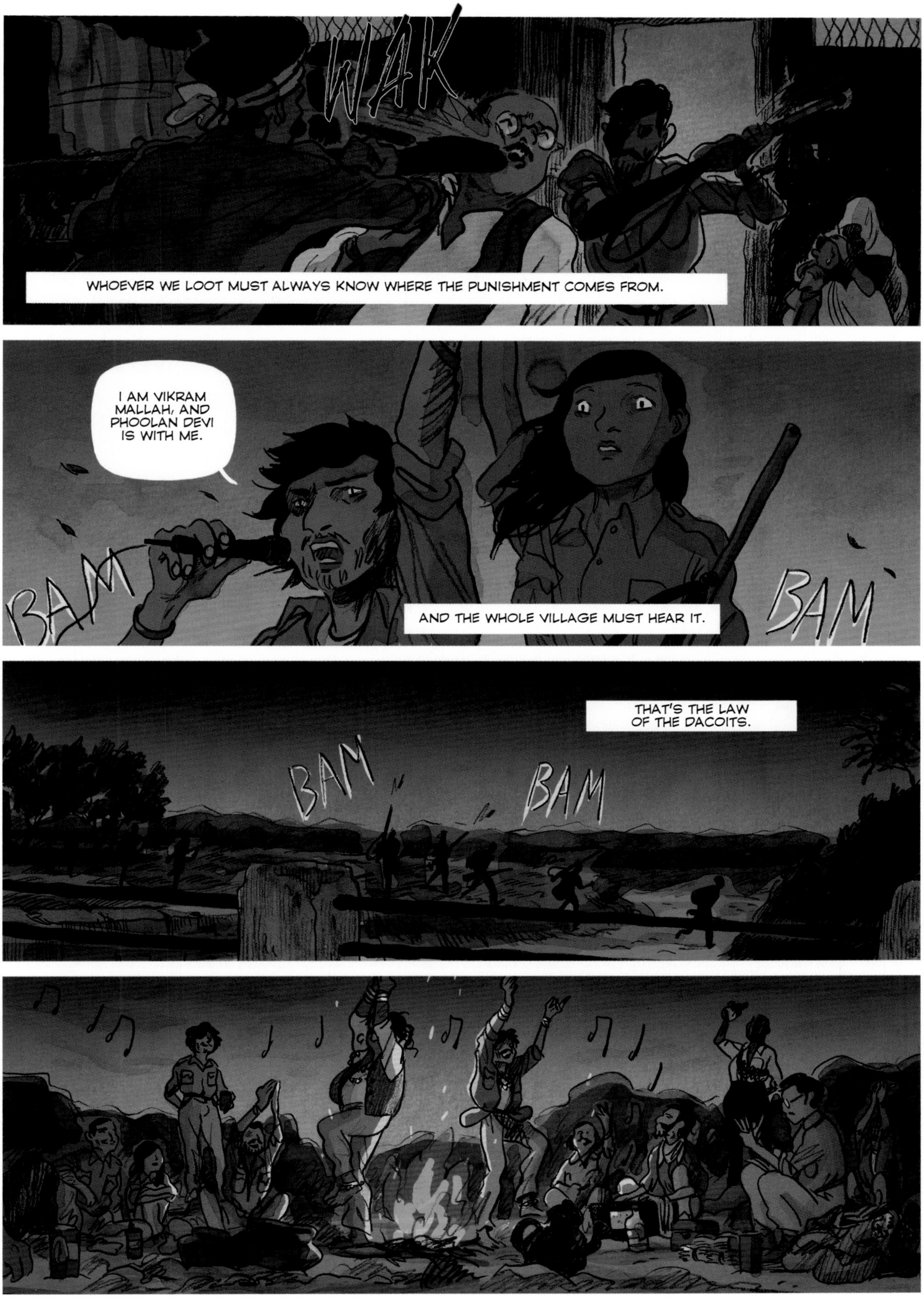
WAK
WHOEVER WE LOOT MUST ALWAYS KNOW WHERE THE PUNISHMENT COMES FROM.
I AM VIKRAM MALLAH, AND PHOOLAN DEVI IS WITH ME.
BAM
AND THE WHOLE VILLAGE MUST HEAR IT.
BAM
THAT'S THE LAW OF THE DACOITS.
BAM
BAM

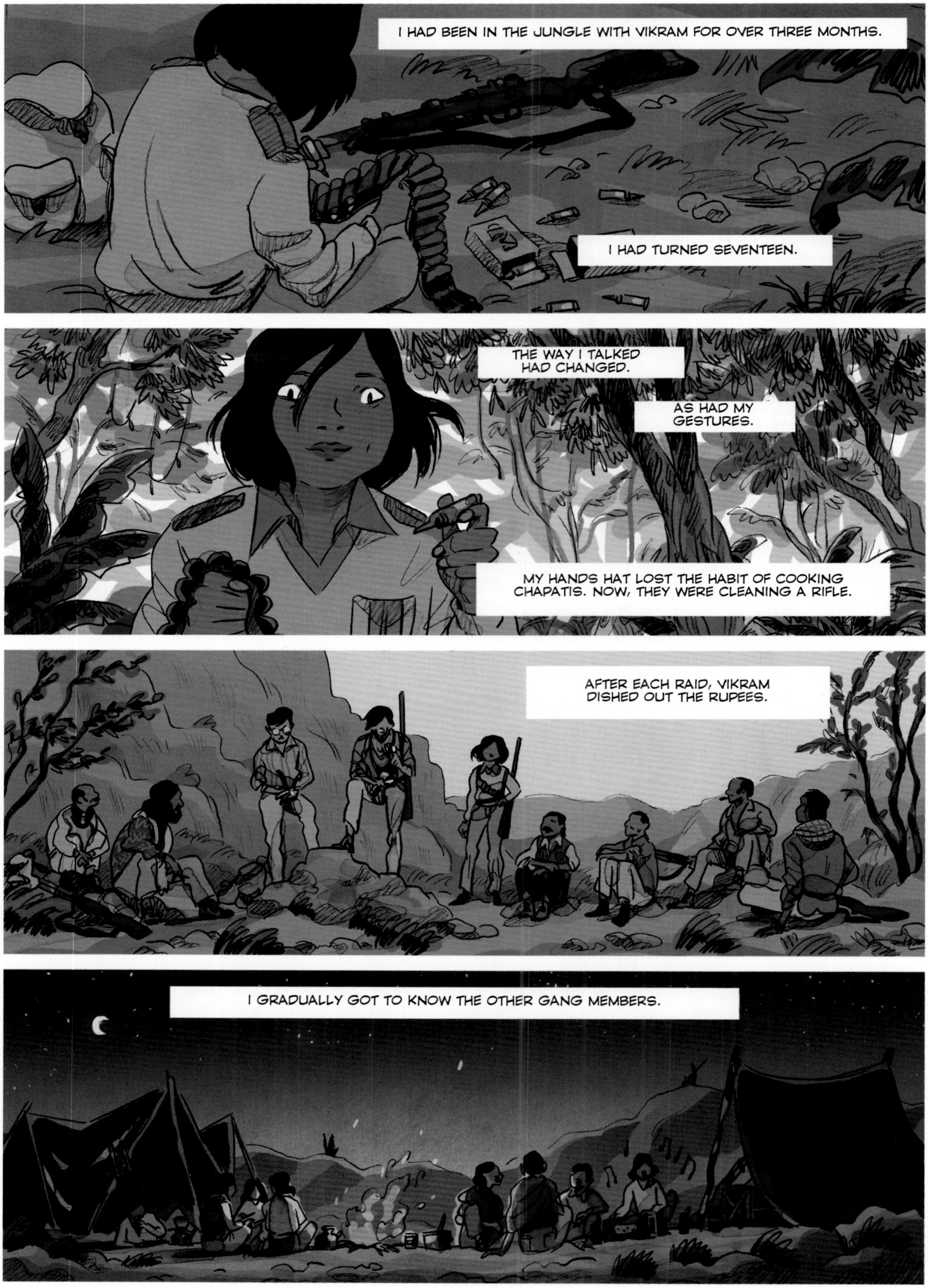
I HAD BEEN IN THE JUNGLE WITH VIKRAM FOR OVER THREE MONTHS.
I HAD TURNED SEVENTEEN.
THE WAY I TALKED HAD CHANGED.
AS HAD MY GESTURES.
MY HANDS HAT LOST THE HABIT OF COOKING CHAPATIS. NOW, THEY WERE CLEANING A RIFLE.
AFTER EACH RAID, VIKRAM DISHED OUT THE RUPEES.
I GRADUALLY GOT TO KNOW THE OTHER GANG MEMBERS.

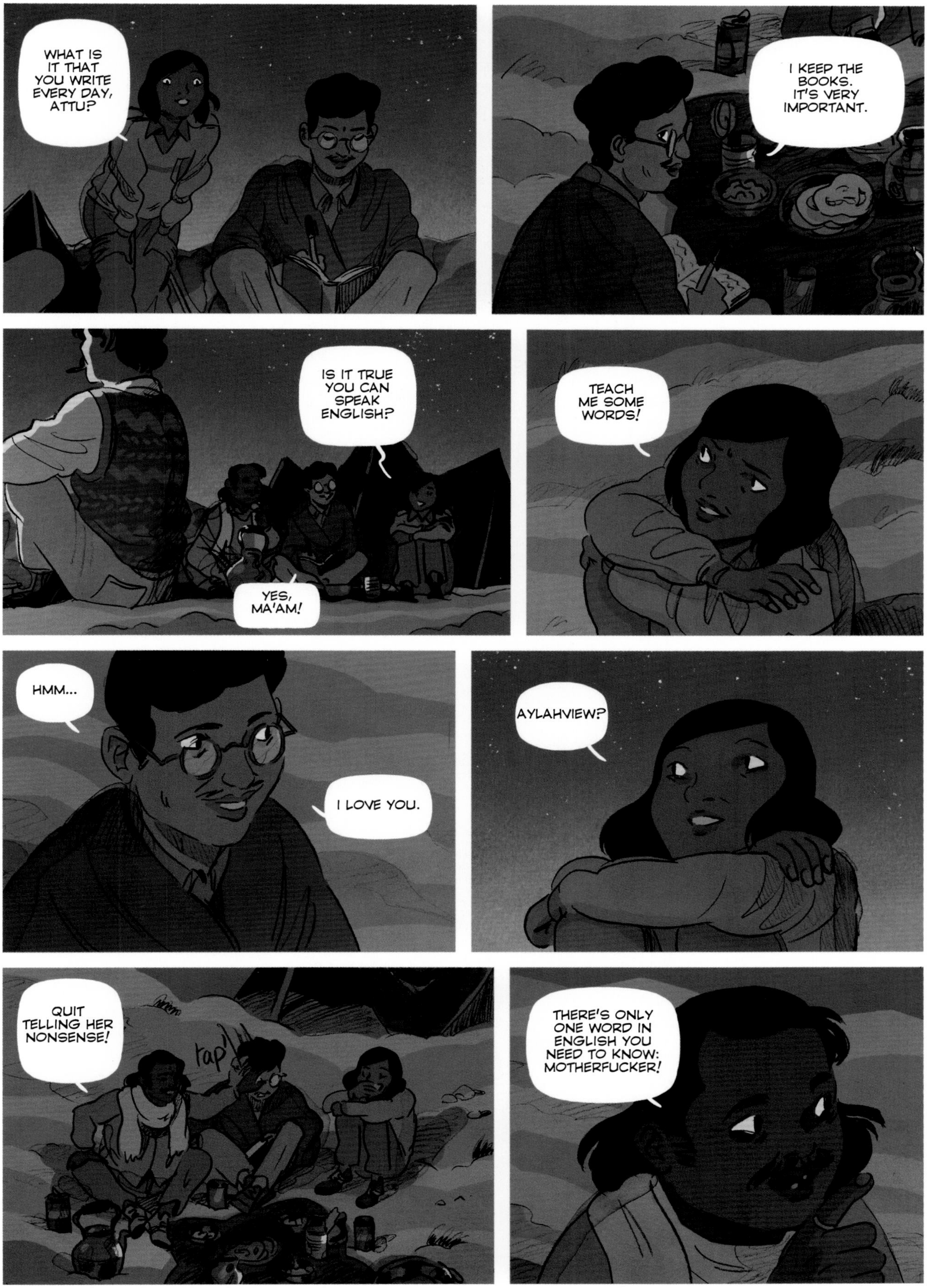
WHAT IS IT THAT YOU WRITE EVERY DAY, ATTU?
I KEEP THE BOOKS. IT'S VERY IMPORTANT.
IS IT TRUE YOU CAN SPEAK ENGLISH?
YES, MA'AM!
TEACH ME SOME WORDS!
HMM...
I LOVE YOU.
AYLAHVIEW?
QUIT TELLING HER NONSENSE!
rap!
THERE'S ONLY ONE WORD IN ENGLISH YOU NEED TO KNOW: MOTHERFUCKER!

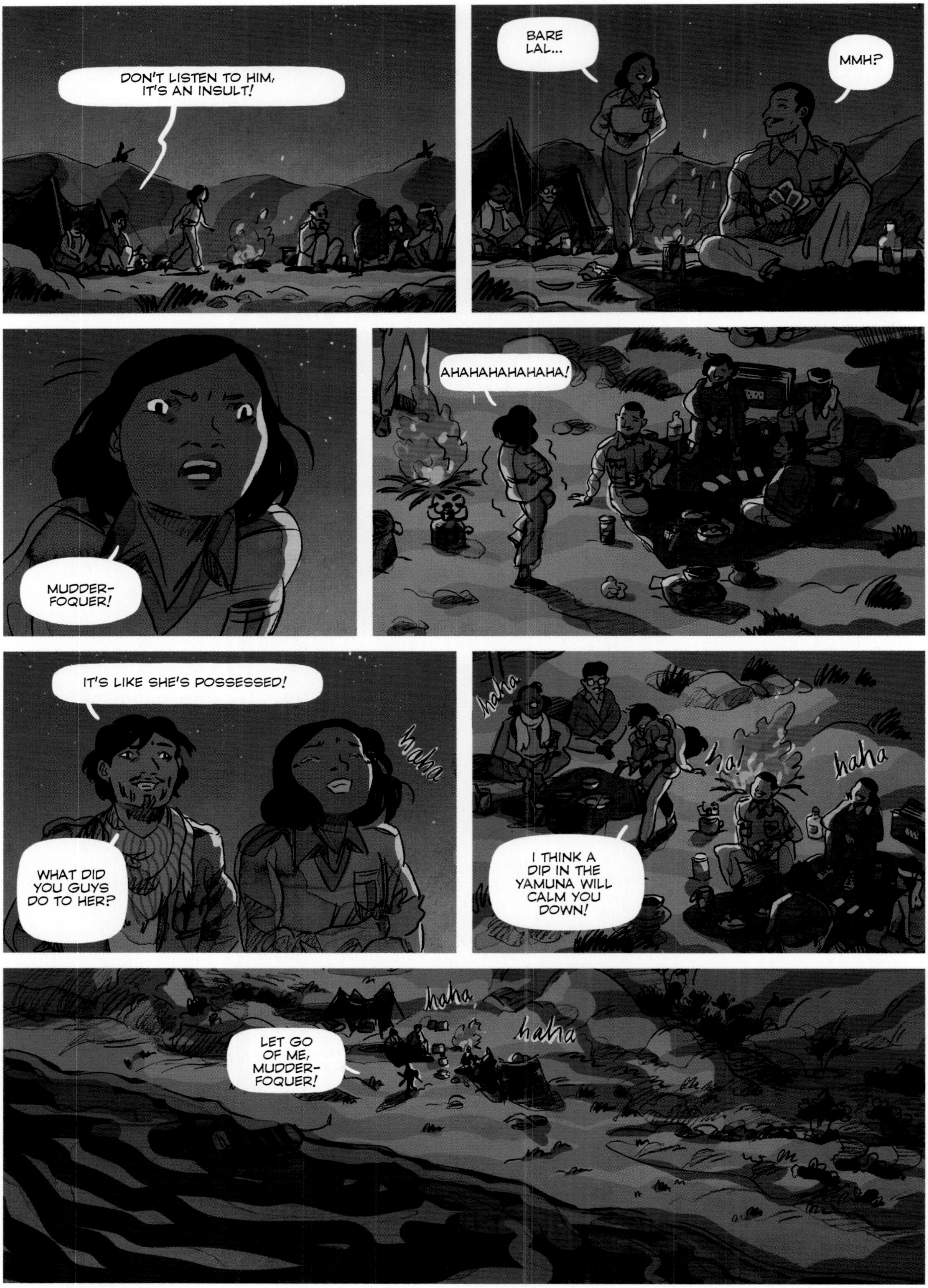
DON'T LISTEN TO HIM, IT'S AN INSULT!
BARE LAL...
MMH?
MUDDER-FOQUER!
AHAHAHAHAHAHA!
IT'S LIKE SHE'S POSSESSED!
WHAT DID YOU GUYS DO TO HER?
haha
haha
ha!
haha
I THINK A DIP IN THE YAMUNA WILL CALM YOU DOWN!
haha
haha
LET GO OF ME, MUDDER-FOQUER!

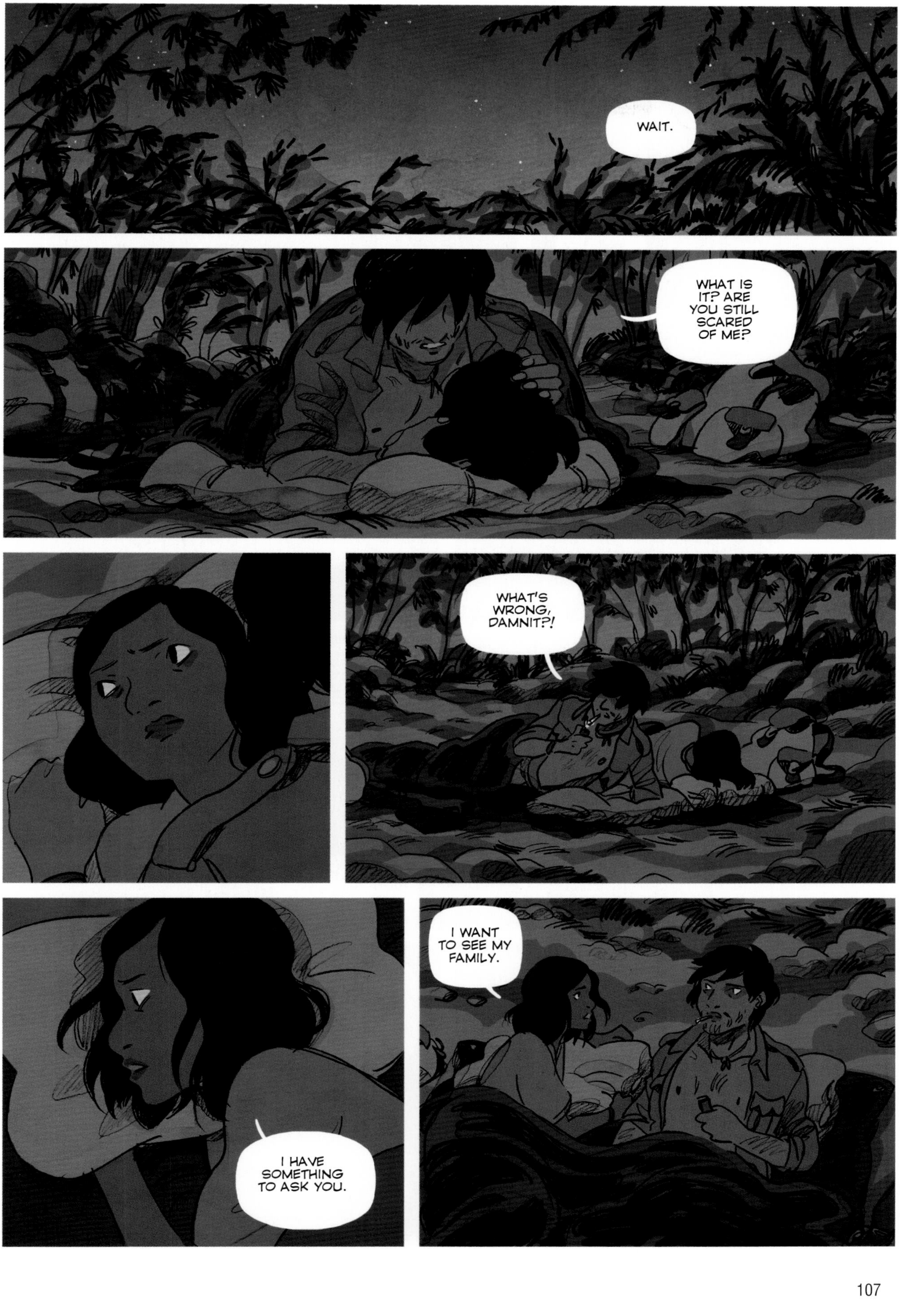
WAIT.
WHAT IS IT? ARE YOU STILL SCARED OF ME?
WHAT'S WRONG, DAMNIT?!
I HAVE SOMETHING TO ASK YOU.
I WANT TO SEE MY FAMILY.

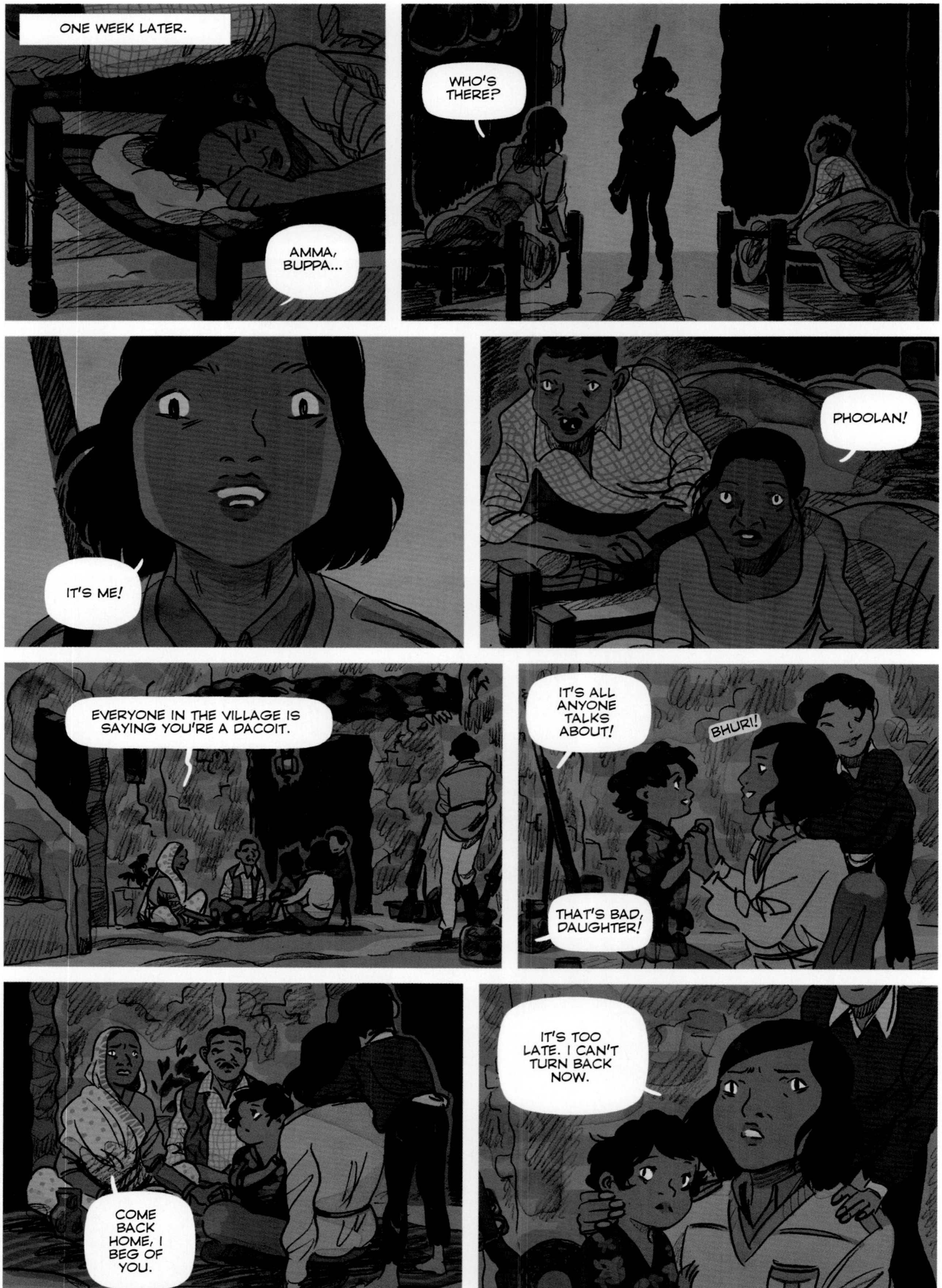
ONE WEEK LATER.
AMMA, BUPPA...
WHO'S THERE?
IT'S ME!
PHOOLAN!
EVERYONE IN THE VILLAGE IS SAYING YOU'RE A DACOIT.
IT'S ALL ANYONE TALKS ABOUT!
BHURI!
THAT'S BAD, DAUGHTER!
COME BACK HOME, I BEG OF YOU.
IT'S TOO LATE. I CAN'T TURN BACK NOW.

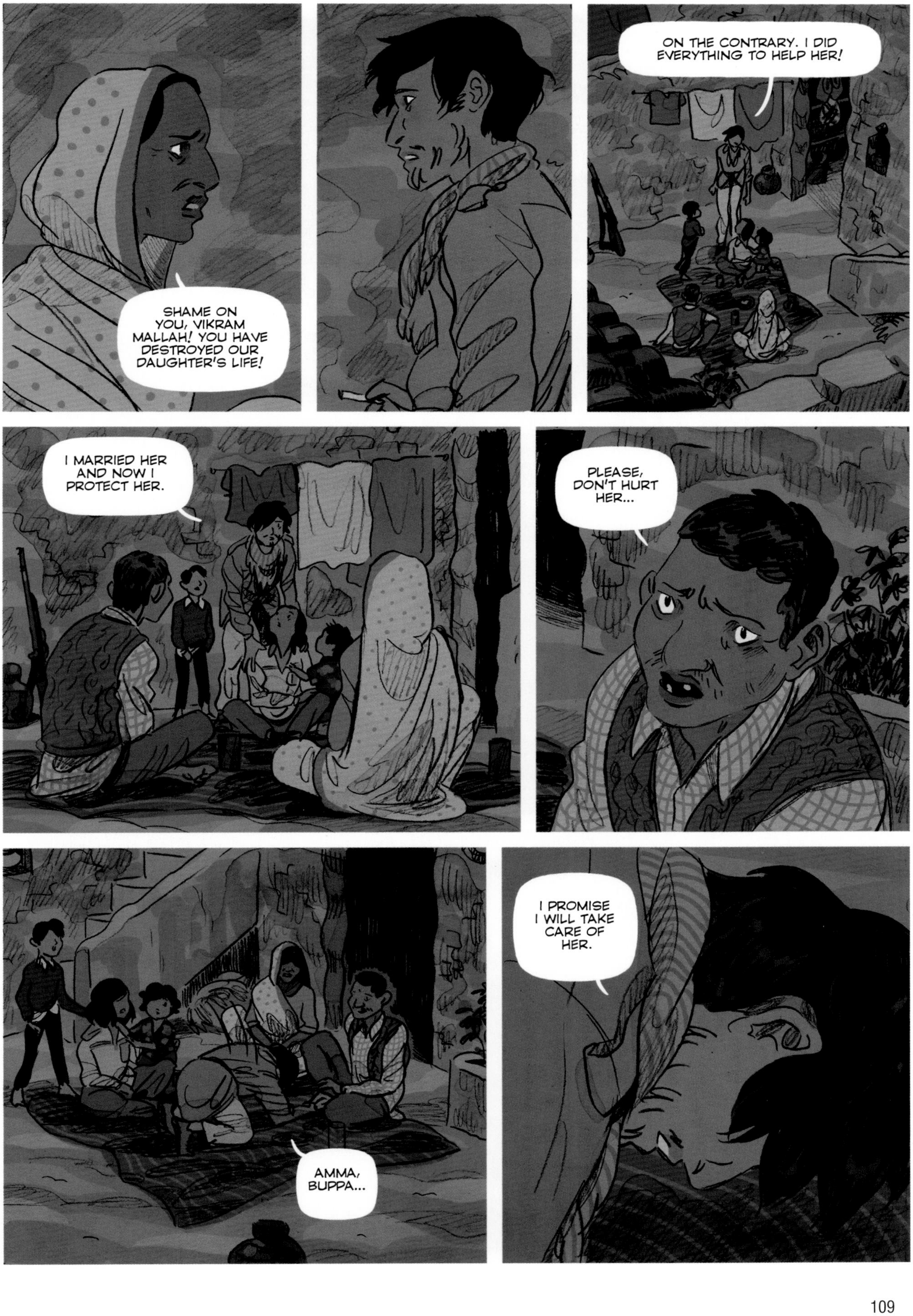
SHAME ON YOU, VIKRAM MALLAH! YOU HAVE DESTROYED OUR DAUGHTER'S LIFE!
ON THE CONTRARY. I DID EVERYTHING TO HELP HER!
I MARRIED HER AND NOW I PROTECT HER.
PLEASE, DON'T HURT HER...
AMMA, BUPPA...
I PROMISE I WILL TAKE CARE OF HER.

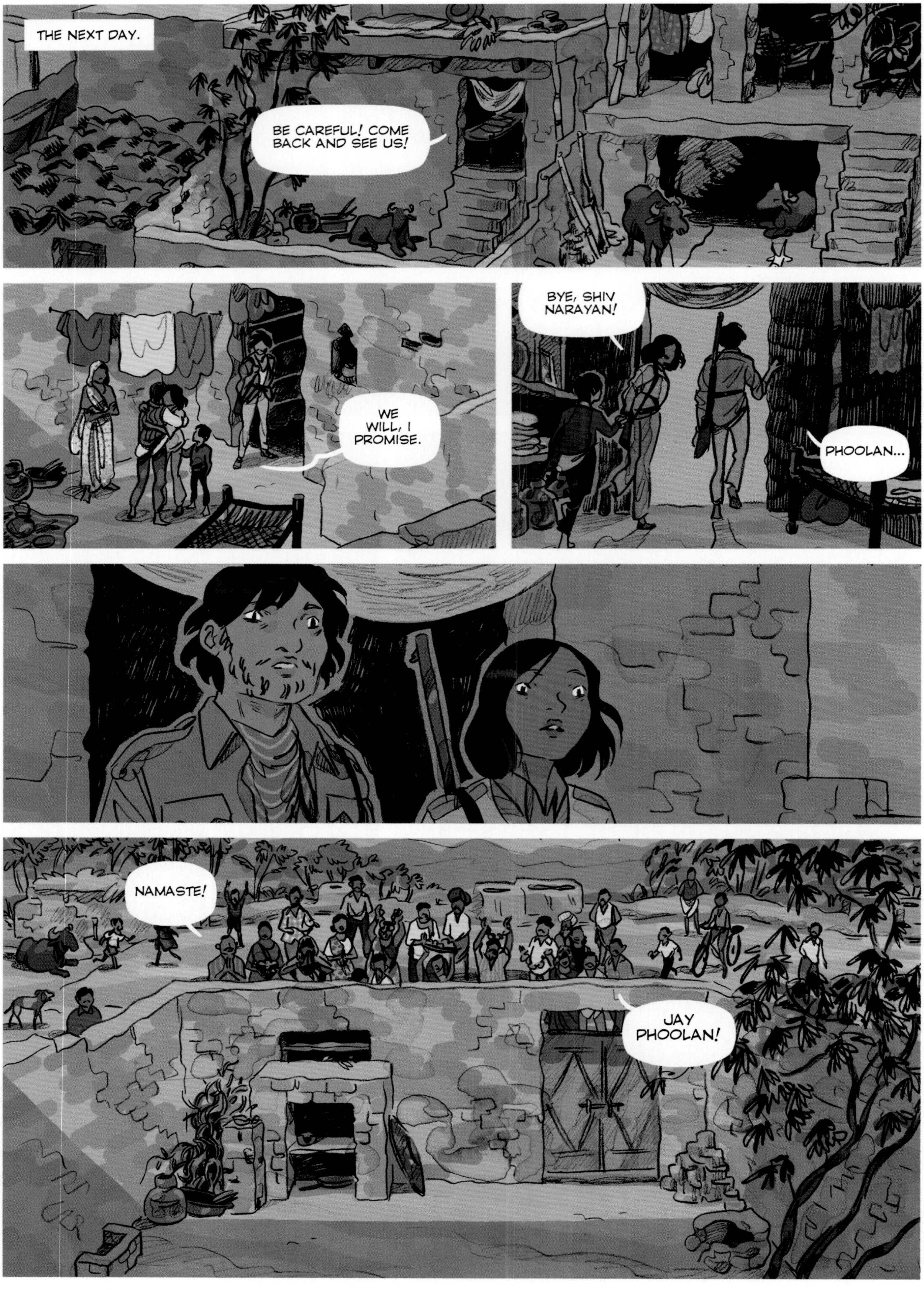
THE NEXT DAY.
BE CAREFUL! COME BACK AND SEE US!
WE WILL, I PROMISE.
BYE, SHIV NARAYAN!
PHOOLAN...
NAMASTE!
JAY PHOOLAN!

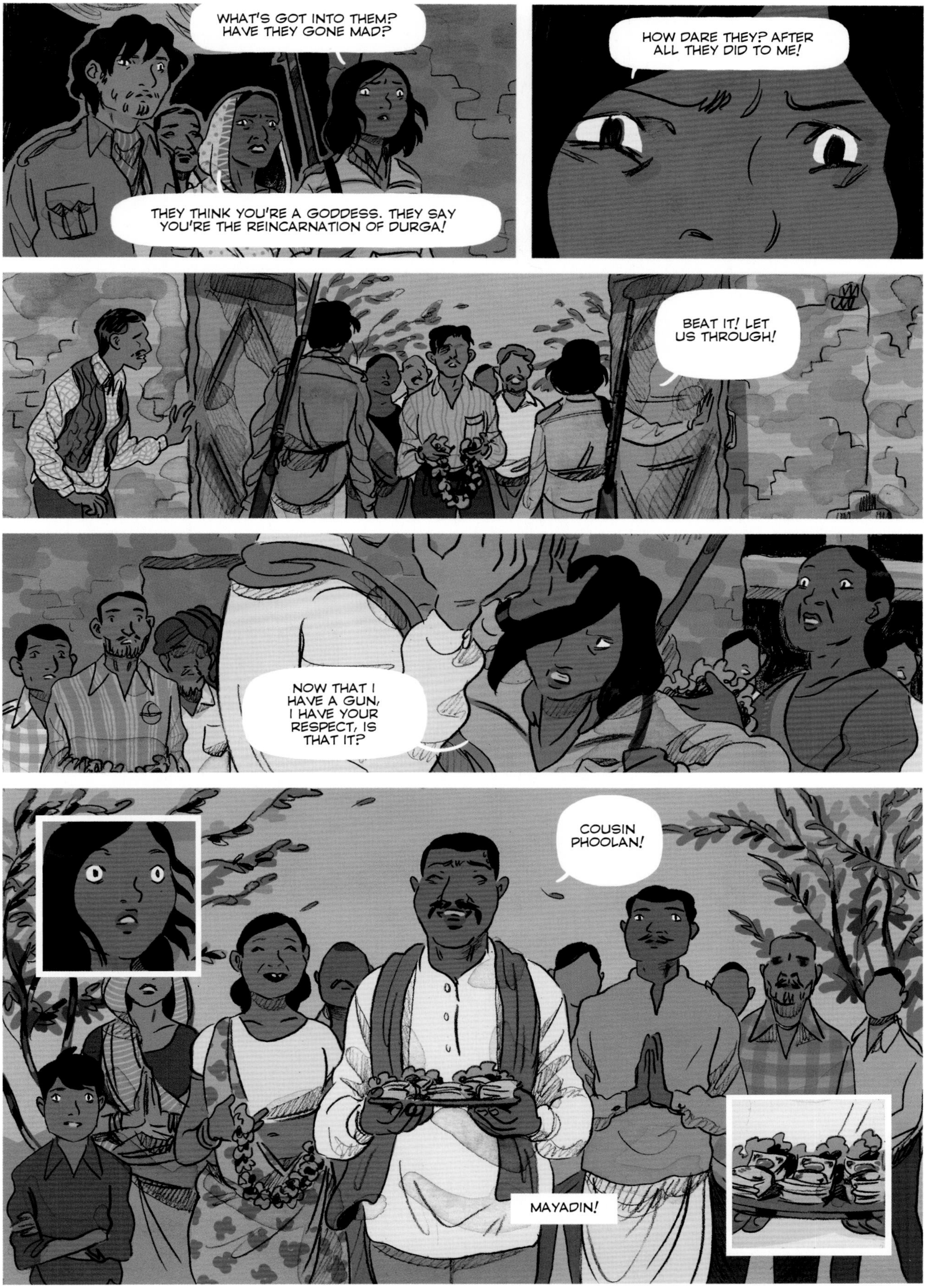
WHAT'S GOT INTO THEM? HAVE THEY GONE MAD?
THEY THINK YOU'RE A GODDESS. THEY SAY YOU'RE THE REINCARNATION OF DURGA!
HOW DARE THEY? AFTER ALL THEY DID TO ME!
BEAT IT! LET US THROUGH!
NOW THAT I HAVE A GUN, I HAVE YOUR RESPECT, IS THAT IT?
COUSIN PHOOLAN!
MAYADIN!

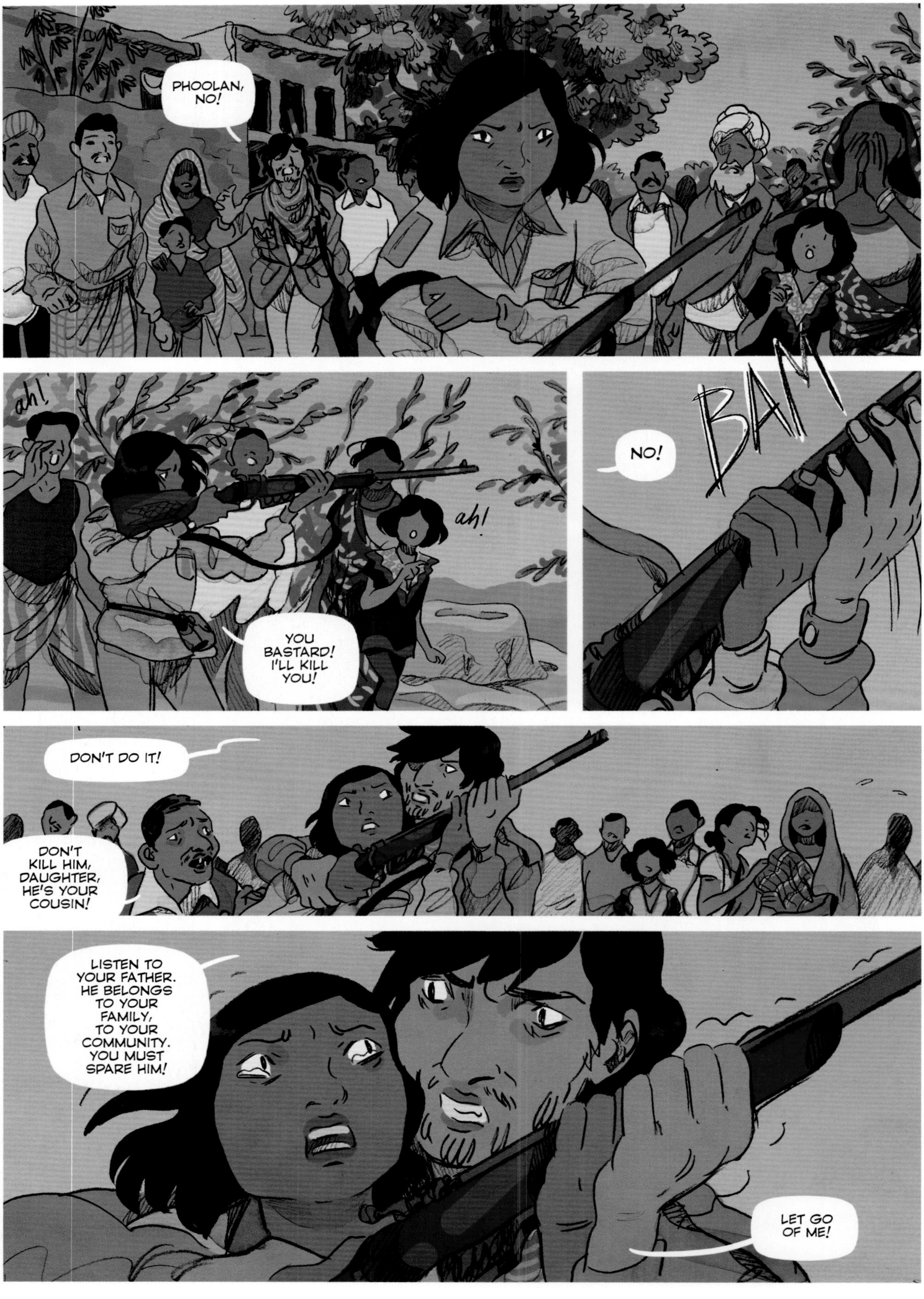
PHOOLAN, NO!
ah!
ah!
YOU BASTARD! I'LL KILL YOU!
NO!
BAM
DON'T DO IT!
DON'T KILL HIM, DAUGHTER, HE'S YOUR COUSIN!
LISTEN TO YOUR FATHER. HE BELONGS TO YOUR FAMILY, TO YOUR COMMUNITY. YOU MUST SPARE HIM!
LET GO OF ME!

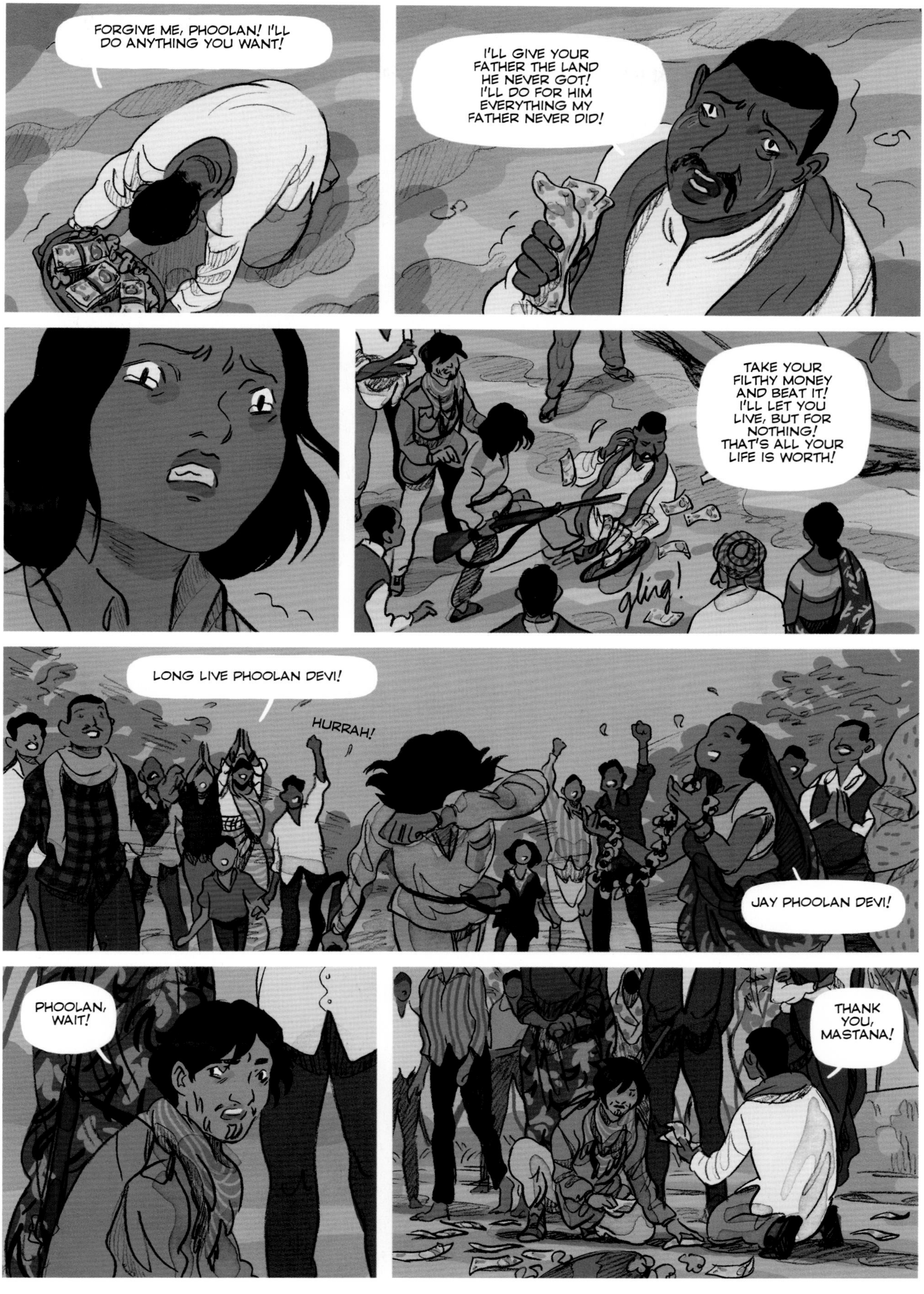
FORGIVE ME, PHOOLAN! I'LL DO ANYTHING YOU WANT!
I'LL GIVE YOUR FATHER THE LAND HE NEVER GOT! I'LL DO FOR HIM EVERYTHING MY FATHER NEVER DID!
TAKE YOUR FILTHY MONEY AND BEAT IT! I'LL LET YOU LIVE, BUT FOR NOTHING! THAT'S ALL YOUR LIFE IS WORTH!
gling!
LONG LIVE PHOOLAN DEVI!
HURRAH!
JAY PHOOLAN DEVI!
PHOOLAN, WAIT!
THANK YOU, MASTANA!

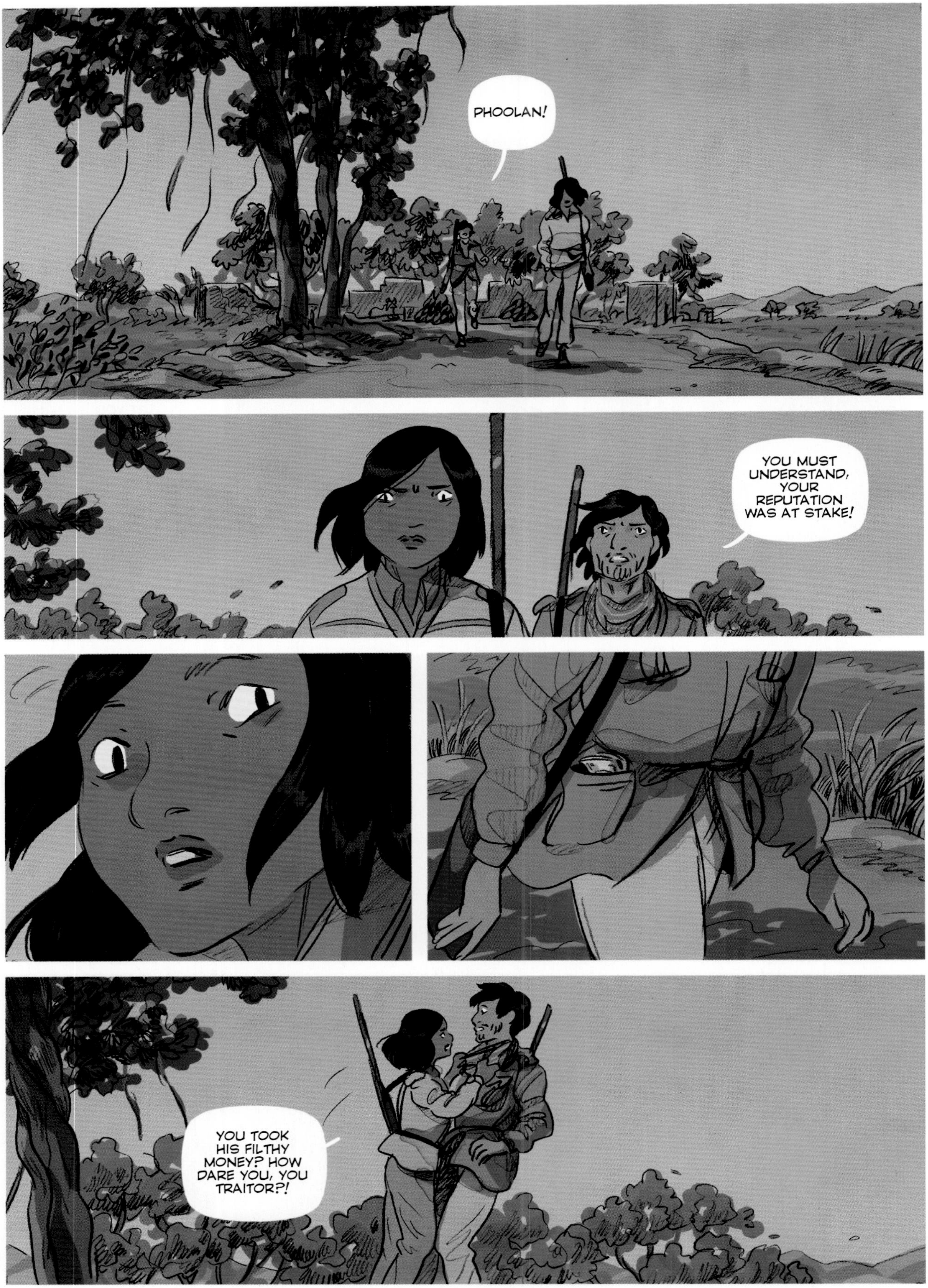
PHOOLAN!
YOU MUST UNDERSTAND, YOUR REPUTATION WAS AT STAKE!
YOU TOOK HIS FILTHY MONEY? HOW DARE YOU, YOU TRAITOR?!

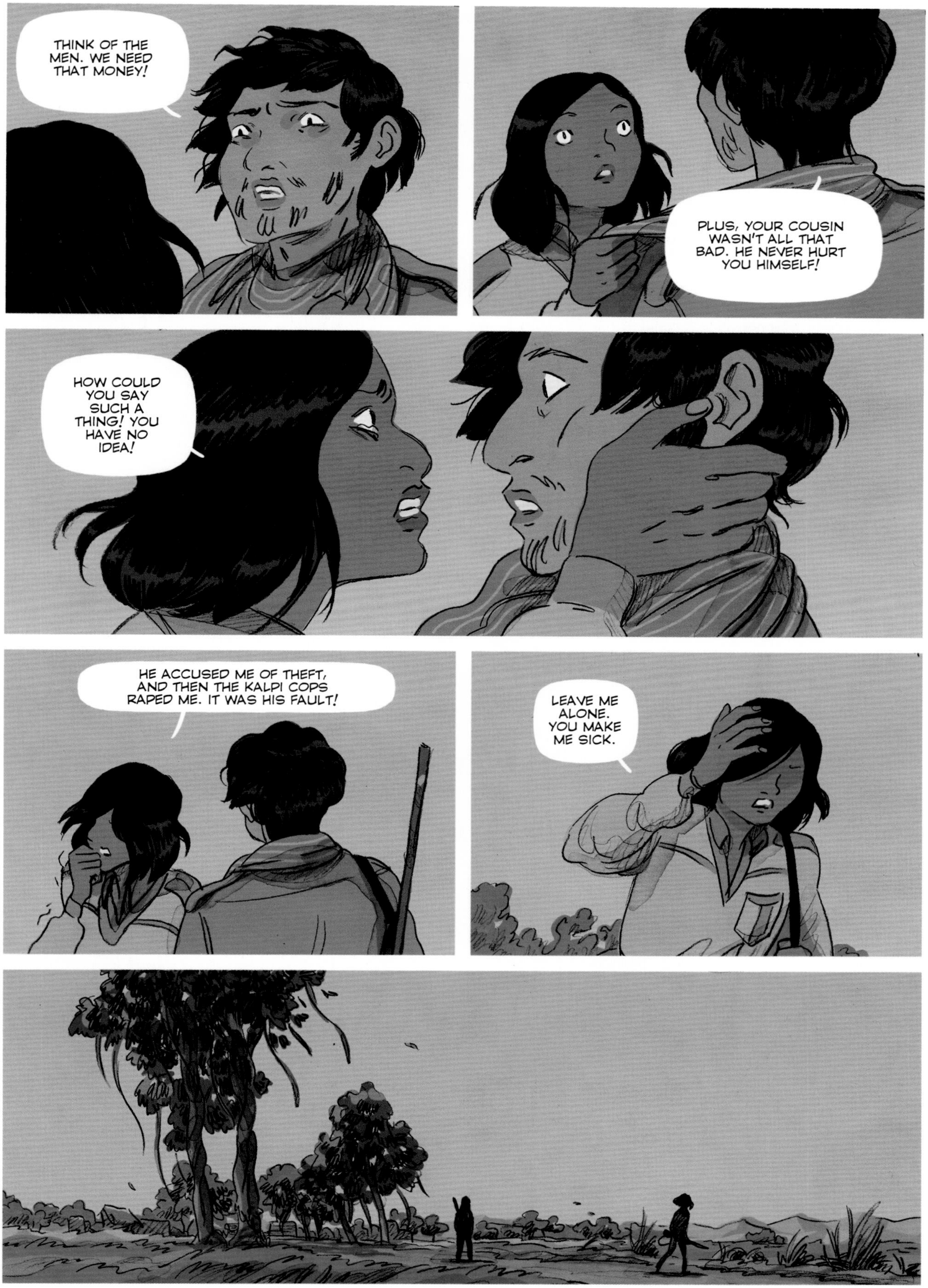
THINK OF THE MEN. WE NEED THAT MONEY!
PLUS, YOUR COUSIN WASN'T ALL THAT BAD. HE NEVER HURT YOU HIMSELF!
HOW COULD YOU SAY SUCH A THING! YOU HAVE NO IDEA!
HE ACCUSED ME OF THEFT, AND THEN THE KALPI COPS RAPED ME. IT WAS HIS FAULT!
LEAVE ME ALONE. YOU MAKE ME SICK.

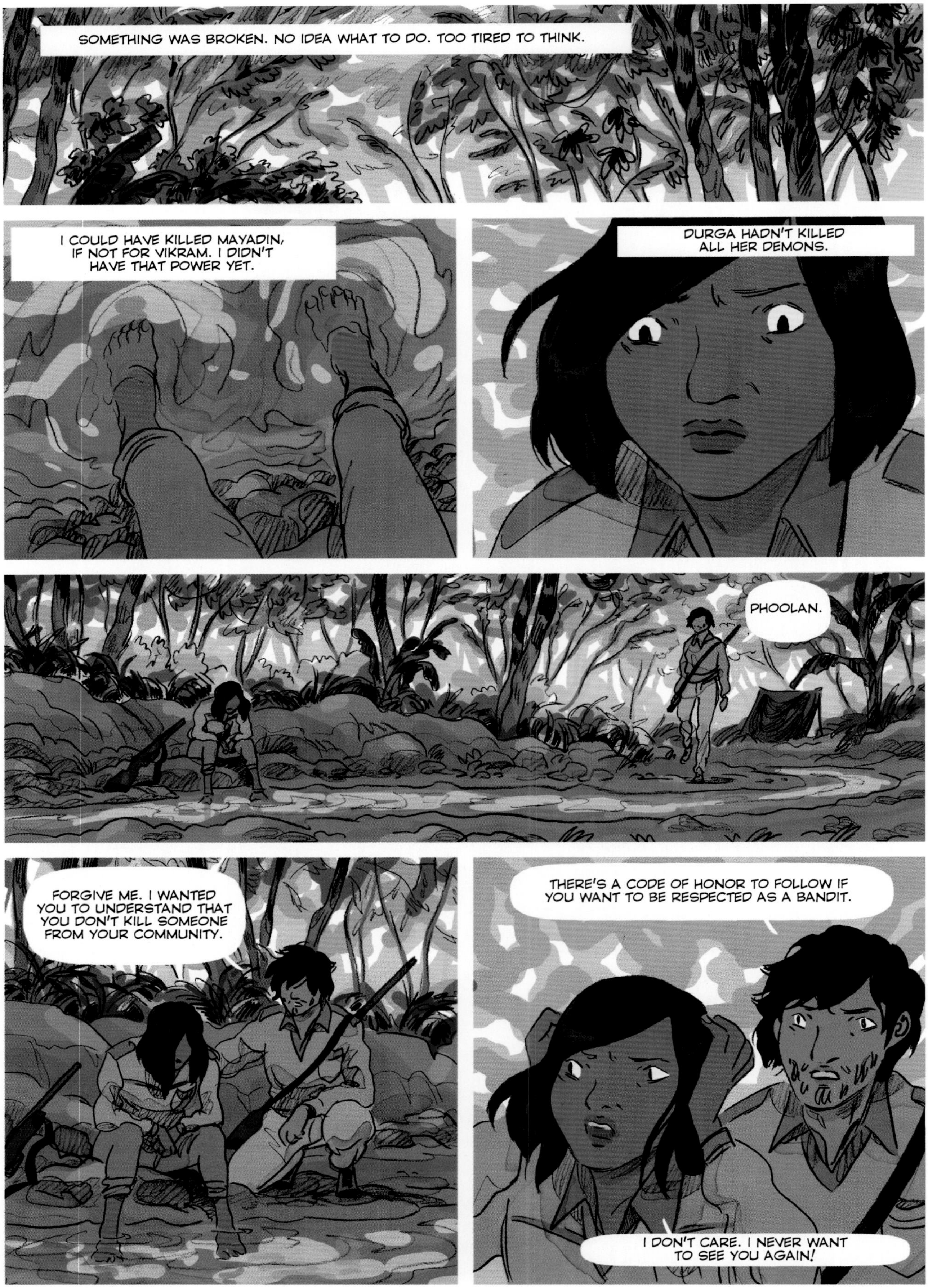
SOMETHING WAS BROKEN. NO IDEA WHAT TO DO. TOO TIRED TO THINK.
I COULD HAVE KILLED MAYADIN, IF NOT FOR VIKRAM. I DIDN'T HAVE THAT POWER YET.
DURGA HADN'T KILLED ALL HER DEMONS.
PHOOLAN.
FORGIVE ME. I WANTED YOU TO UNDERSTAND THAT YOU DON'T KILL SOMEONE FROM YOUR COMMUNITY.
THERE'S A CODE OF HONOR TO FOLLOW IF YOU WANT TO BE RESPECTED AS A BANDIT.
I DON'T CARE. I NEVER WANT TO SEE YOU AGAIN!

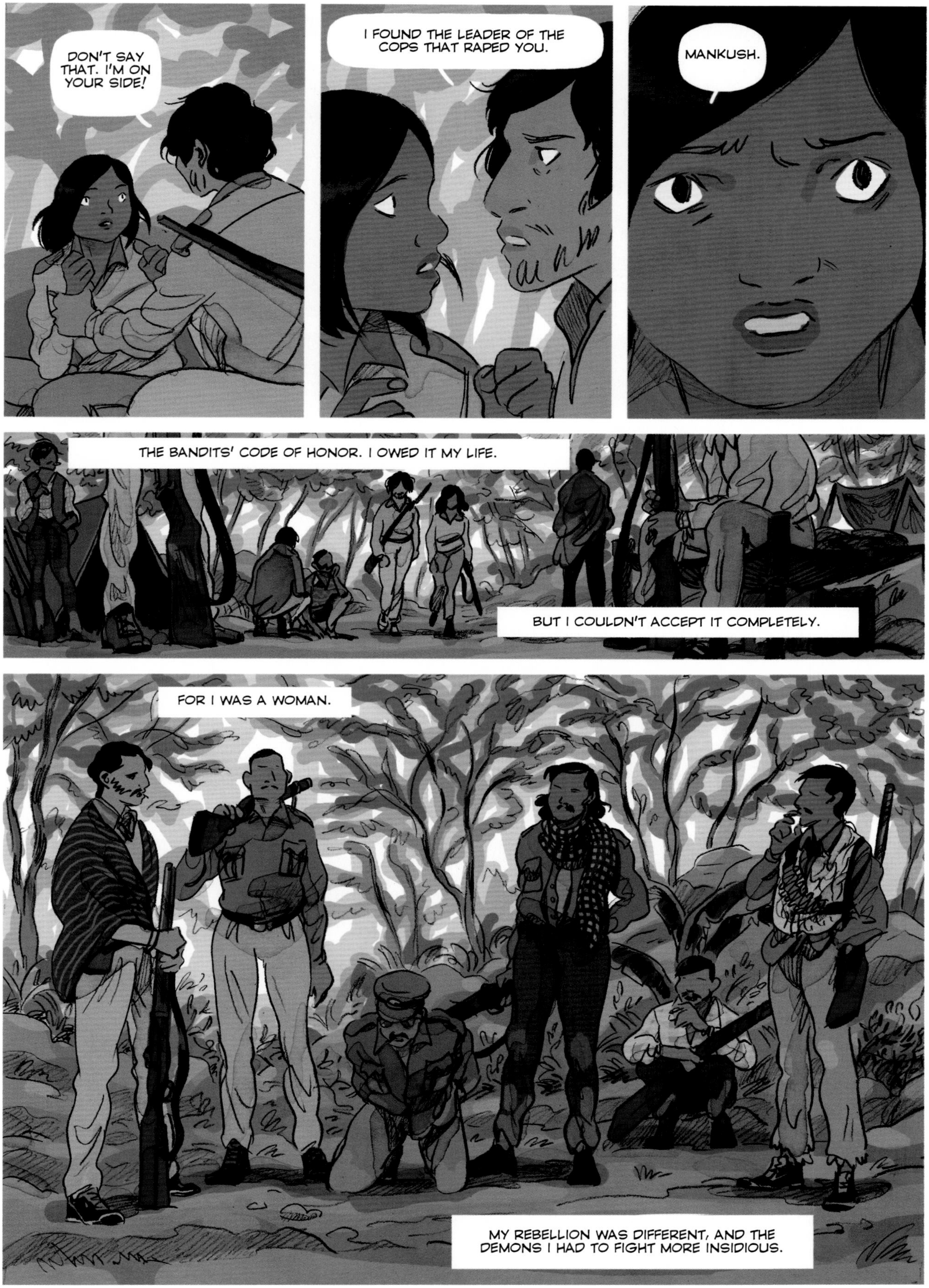
DON'T SAY THAT. I'M ON YOUR SIDE!
I FOUND THE LEADER OF THE COPS THAT RAPED YOU.
MANKUSH.
THE BANDITS' CODE OF HONOR. I OWED IT MY LIFE.
BUT I COULDN'T ACCEPT IT COMPLETELY.
FOR I WAS A WOMAN.
MY REBELLION WAS DIFFERENT, AND THE DEMONS I HAD TO FIGHT MORE INSIDIOUS.

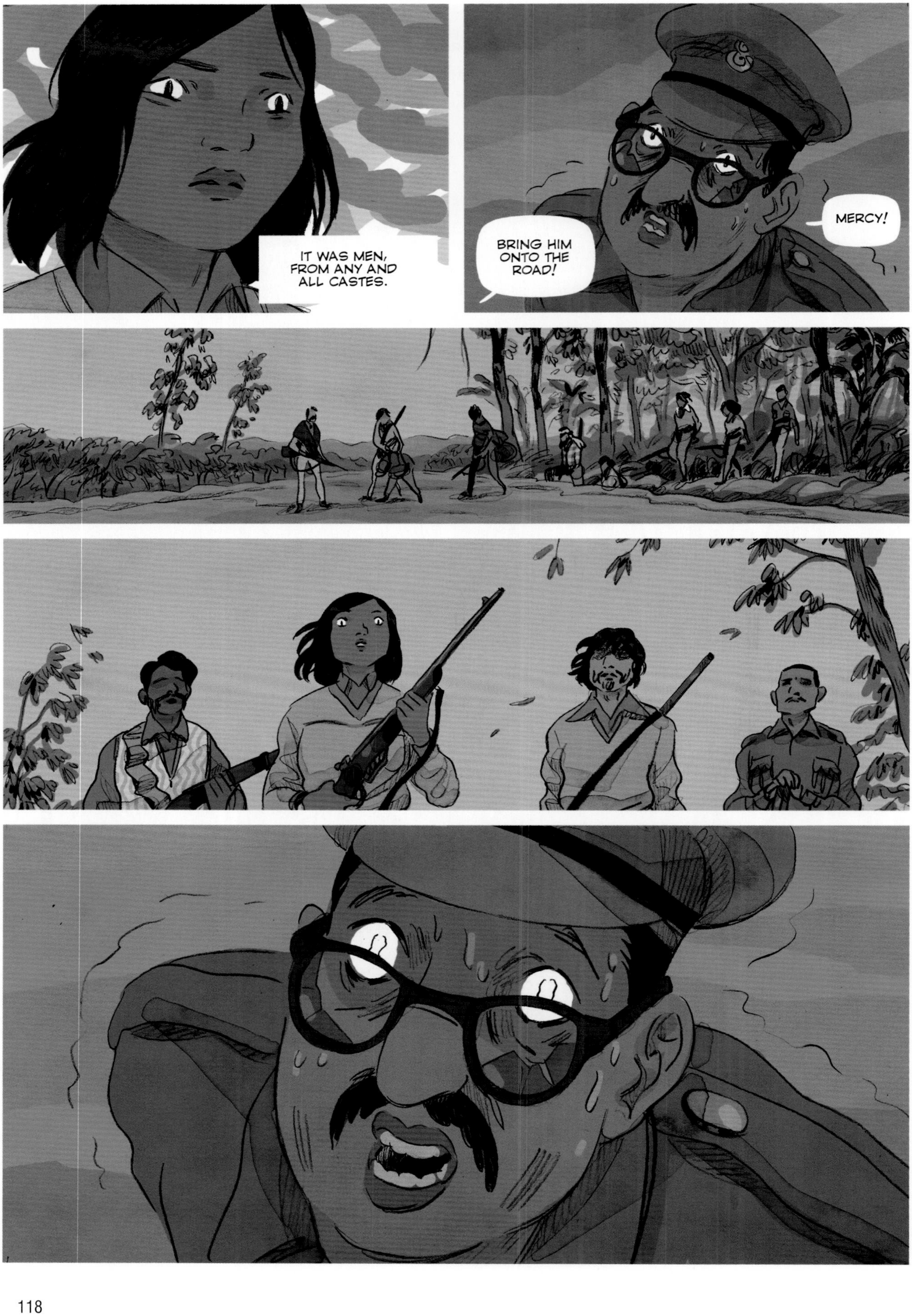
IT WAS MEN, FROM ANY AND ALL CASTES.
BRING HIM ONTO THE ROAD!
MERCY!

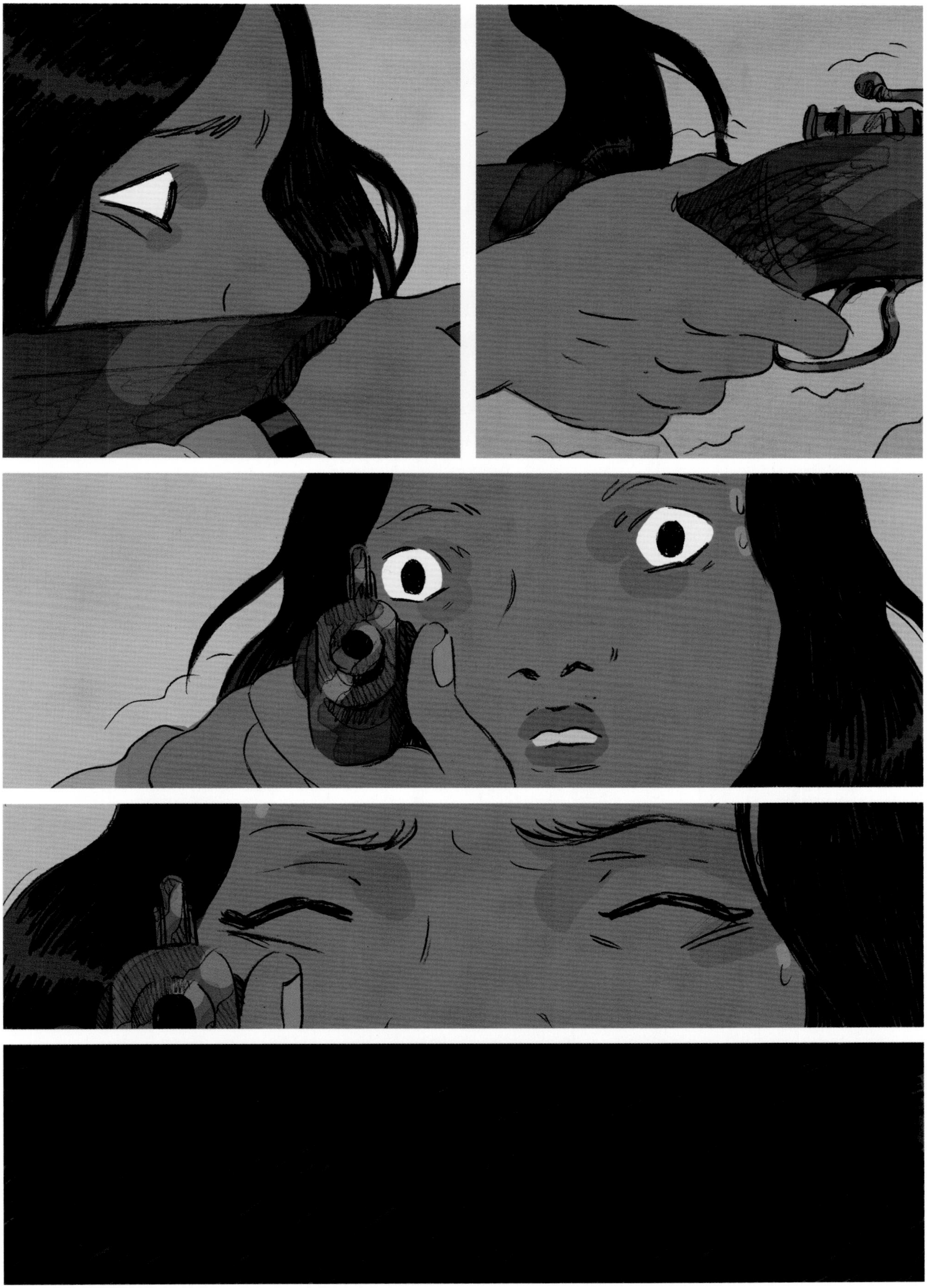

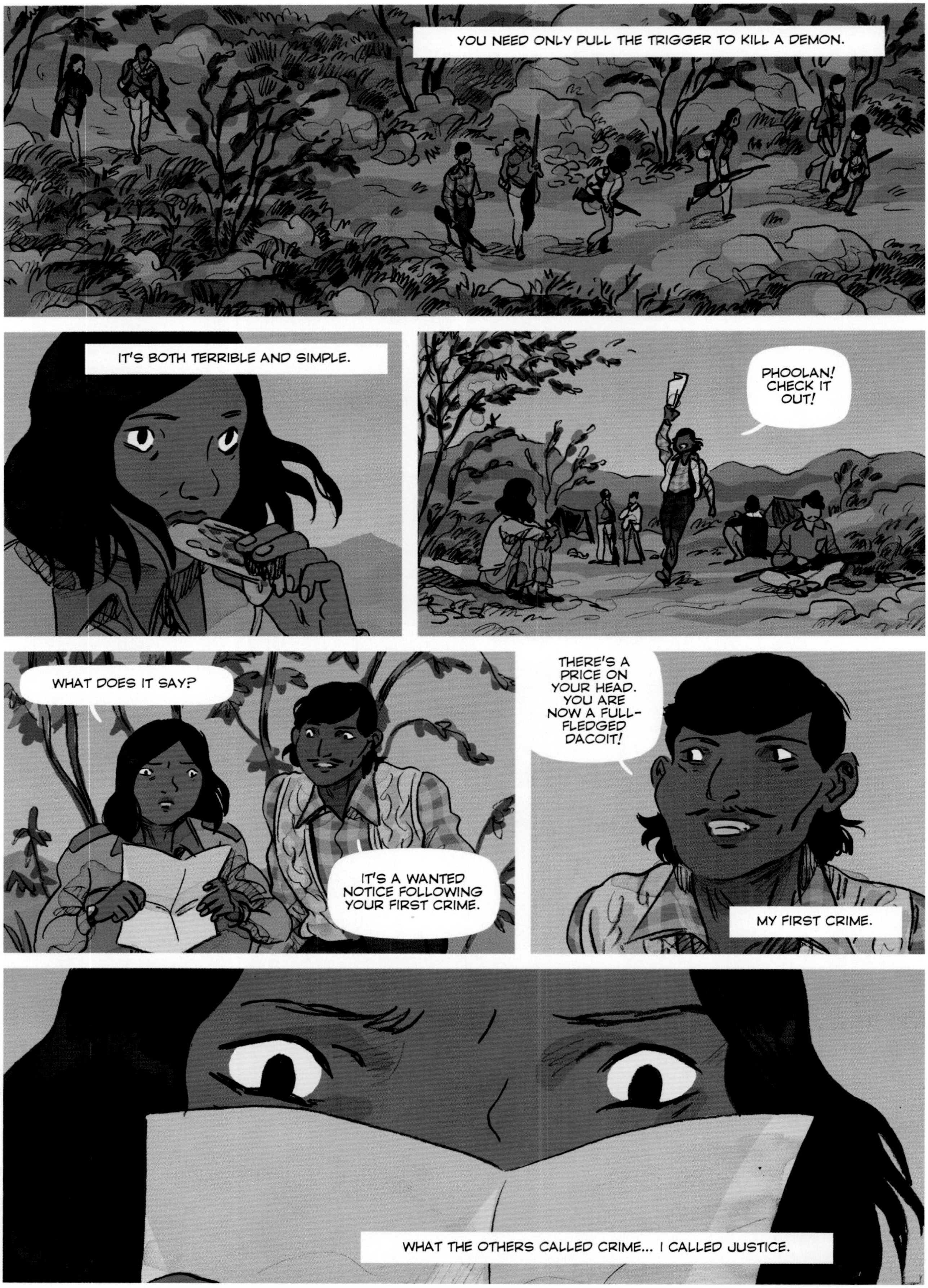
YOU NEED ONLY PULL THE TRIGGER TO KILL A DEMON.
IT'S BOTH TERRIBLE AND SIMPLE.
PHOOLAN! CHECK IT OUT!
WHAT DOES IT SAY?
IT'S A WANTED NOTICE FOLLOWING YOUR FIRST CRIME.
THERE'S A PRICE ON YOUR HEAD. YOU ARE NOW A FULL-FLEDGED DACOIT!
MY FIRST CRIME.
WHAT THE OTHERS CALLED CRIME... I CALLED JUSTICE.

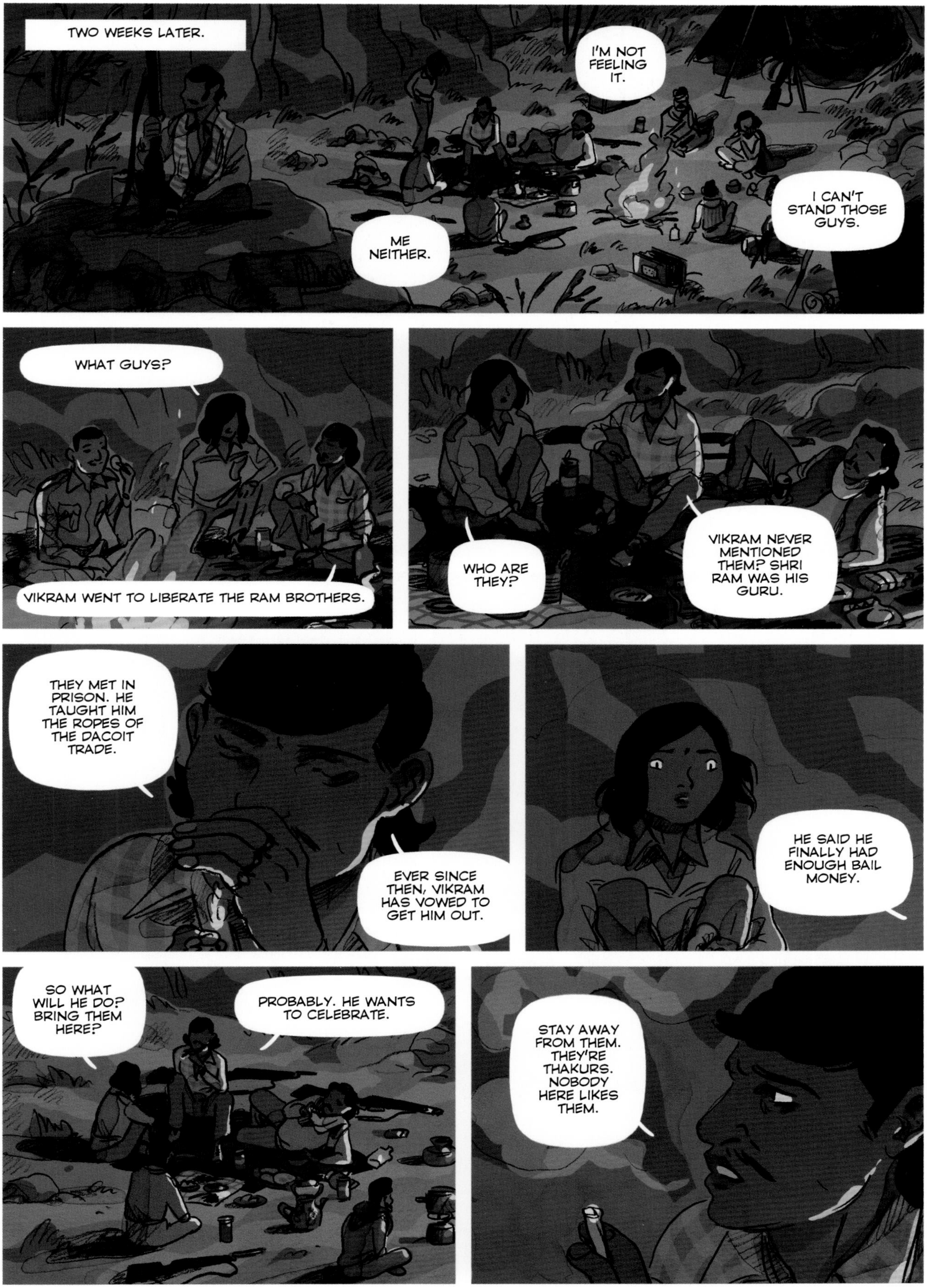
TWO WEEKS LATER.
I'M NOT FEELING IT.
I CAN'T STAND THOSE GUYS.
ME NEITHER.
WHAT GUYS?
VIKRAM WENT TO LIBERATE THE RAM BROTHERS.
WHO ARE THEY?
VIKRAM NEVER MENTIONED THEM? SHRI RAM WAS HIS GURU.
THEY MET IN PRISON. HE TAUGHT HIM THE ROPES OF THE DACOIT TRADE.
EVER SINCE THEN, VIKRAM HAS VOWED TO GET HIM OUT.
HE SAID HE FINALLY HAD ENOUGH BAIL MONEY.
SO WHAT WILL HE DO? BRING THEM HERE?
PROBABLY. HE WANTS TO CELEBRATE.
STAY AWAY FROM THEM. THEY'RE THAKURS. NOBODY HERE LIKES THEM.

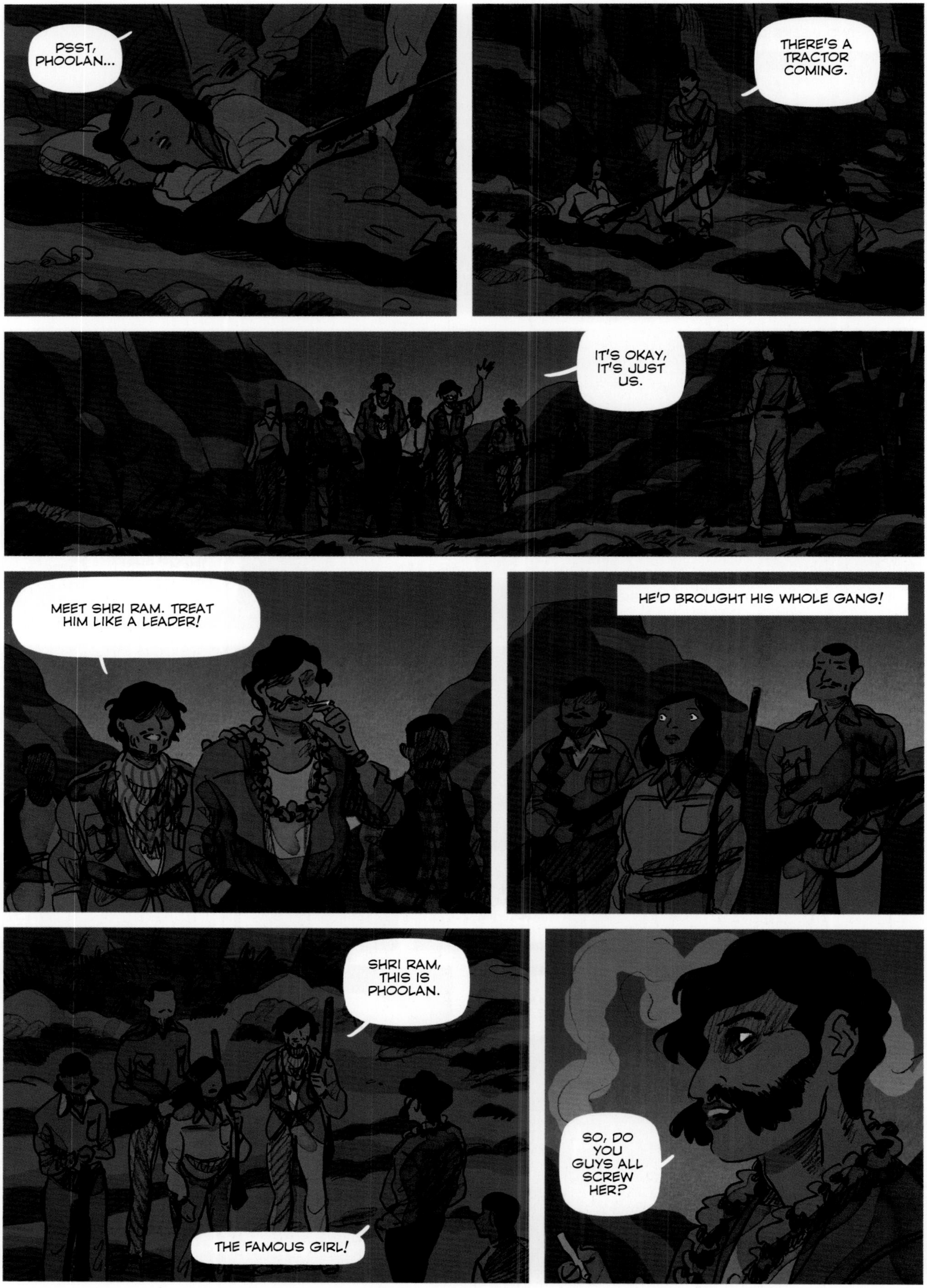
PSST, PHOOLAN...
THERE'S A TRACTOR COMING.
IT'S OKAY, IT'S JUST US.
MEET SHRI RAM. TREAT HIM LIKE A LEADER!
HE'D BROUGHT HIS WHOLE GANG!
SHRI RAM, THIS IS PHOOLAN.
THE FAMOUS GIRL!
SO, DO YOU GUYS ALL SCREW HER?

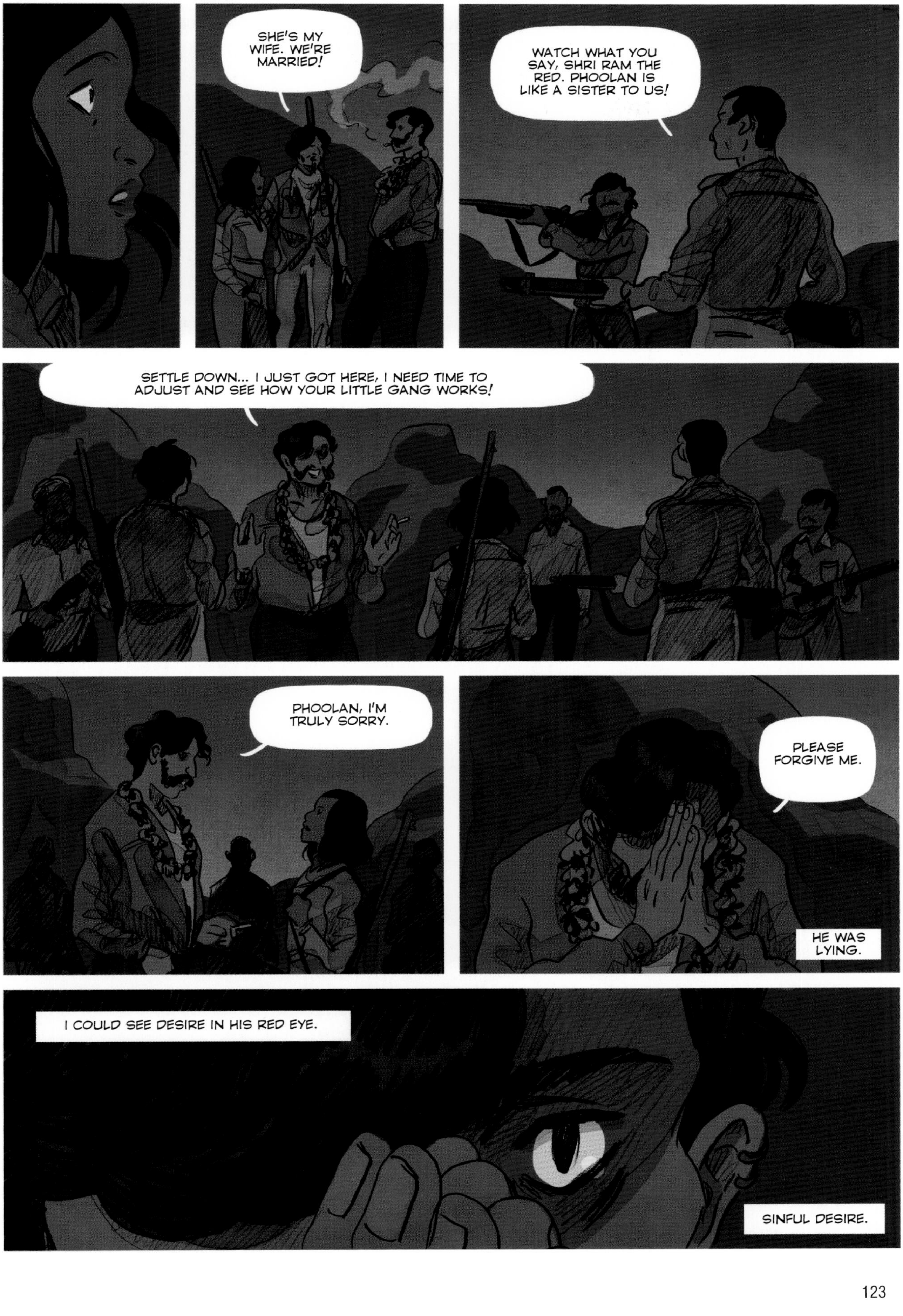
SHE'S MY WIFE. WE'RE MARRIED!
WATCH WHAT YOU SAY, SHRI RAM THE RED. PHOOLAN IS LIKE A SISTER TO US!
SETTLE DOWN... I JUST GOT HERE, I NEED TIME TO ADJUST AND SEE HOW YOUR LITTLE GANG WORKS!
PHOOLAN, I'M TRULY SORRY.
PLEASE FORGIVE ME.
HE WAS LYING.
I COULD SEE DESIRE IN HIS RED EYE.
SINFUL DESIRE.

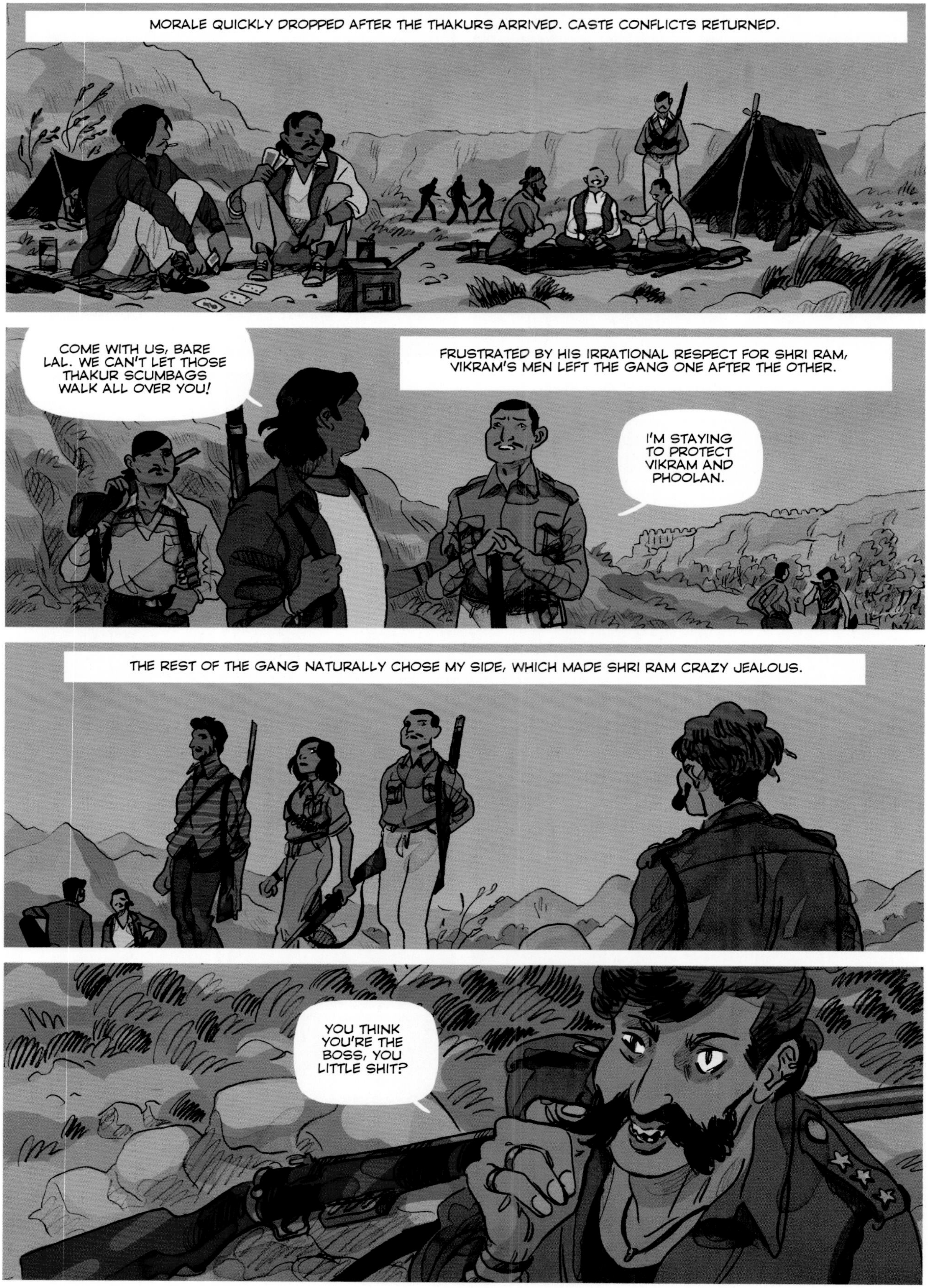
MORALE QUICKLY DROPPED AFTER THE THAKURS ARRIVED. CASTE CONFLICTS RETURNED.
COME WITH US, BARE LAL. WE CAN'T LET THOSE THAKUR SCUMBAGS WALK ALL OVER YOU!
FRUSTRATED BY HIS IRRATIONAL RESPECT FOR SHRI RAM, VIKRAM'S MEN LEFT THE GANG ONE AFTER THE OTHER.
I'M STAYING TO PROTECT VIKRAM AND PHOOLAN.
THE REST OF THE GANG NATURALLY CHOSE MY SIDE, WHICH MADE SHRI RAM CRAZY JEALOUS.
YOU THINK YOU'RE THE BOSS, YOU LITTLE SHIT?

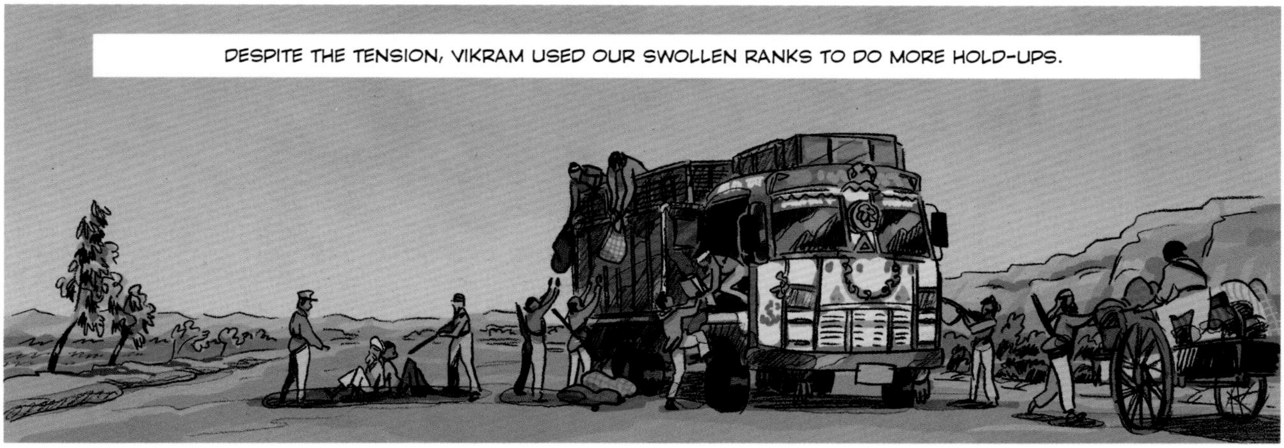
DESPITE THE TENSION, VIKRAM USED OUR SWOLLEN RANKS TO DO MORE HOLD-UPS.

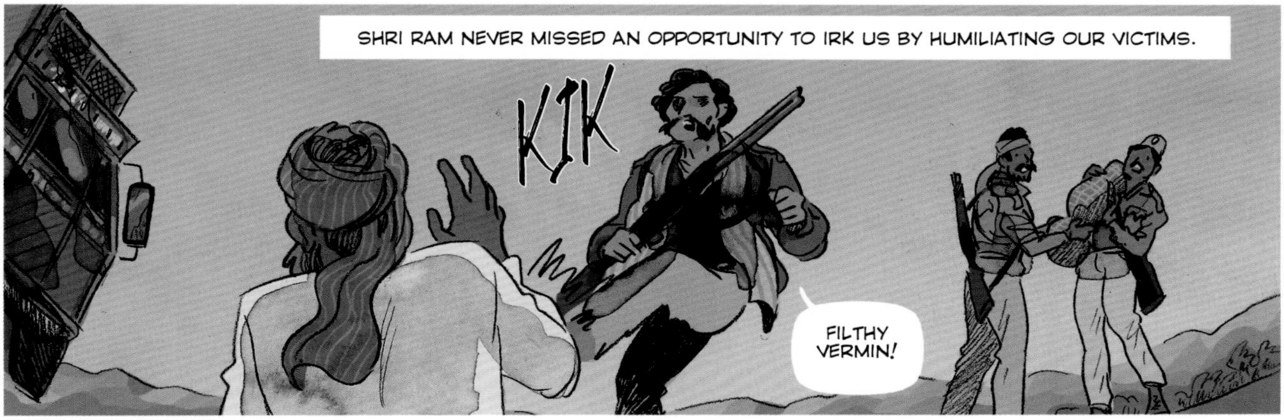
SHRI RAM NEVER MISSED AN OPPORTUNITY TO IRK US BY HUMILIATING OUR VICTIMS.
KIK
FILTHY VERMIN!

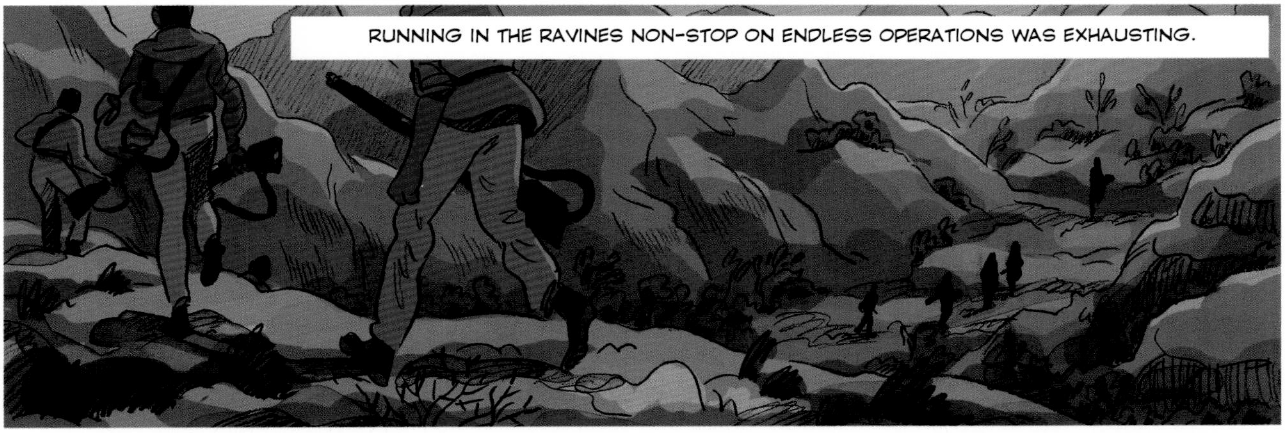
RUNNING IN THE RAVINES NON-STOP ON ENDLESS OPERATIONS WAS EXHAUSTING.

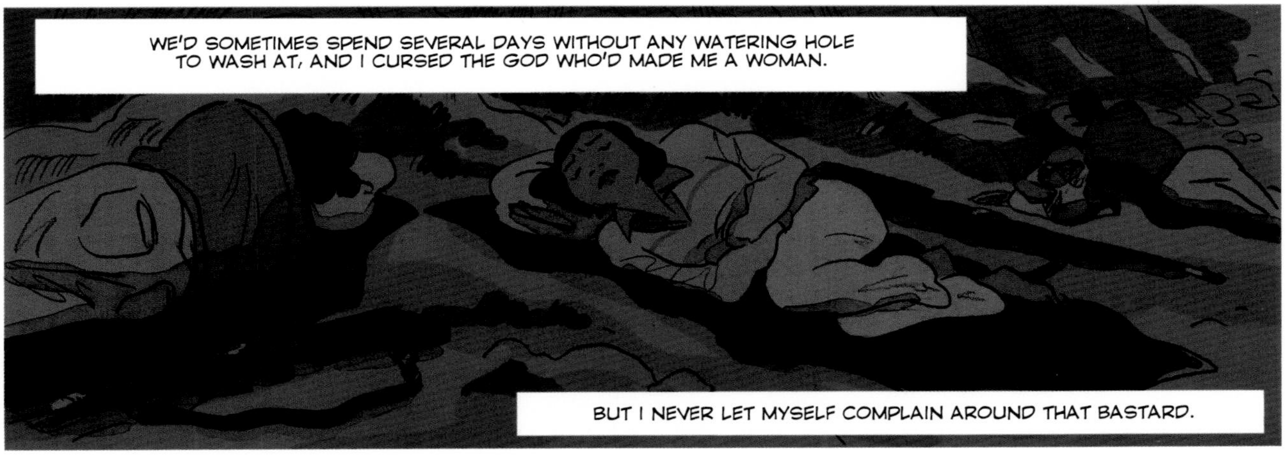
WE'D SOMETIMES SPEND SEVERAL DAYS WITHOUT ANY WATERING HOLE TO WASH AT, AND I CURSED THE GOD WHO'D MADE ME A WOMAN.
BUT I NEVER LET MYSELF COMPLAIN AROUND THAT BASTARD.

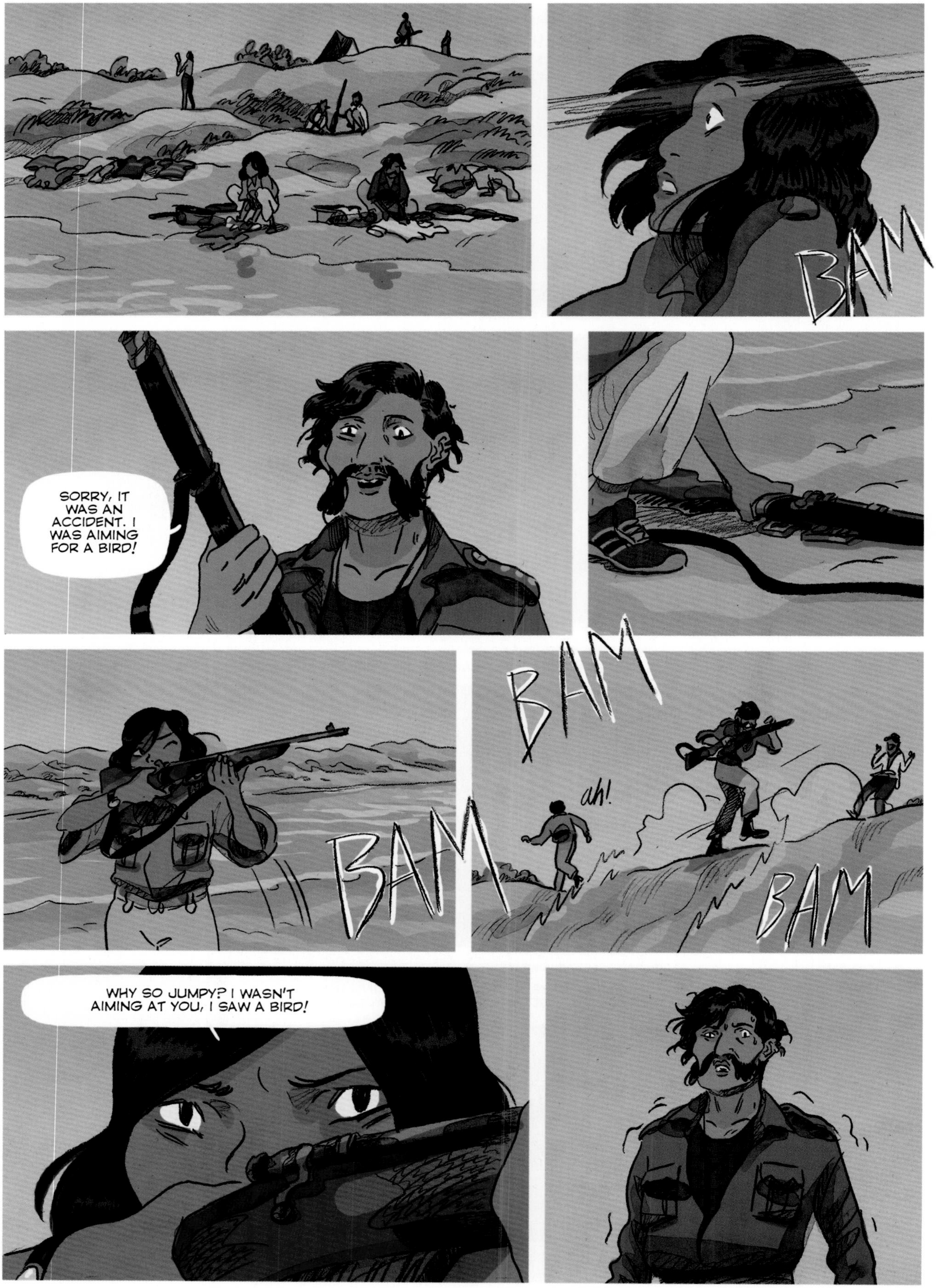
BAM
SORRY, IT WAS AN ACCIDENT. I WAS AIMING FOR A BIRD!
BAM
BAM
ah!
BAM
WHY SO JUMPY? I WASN'T AIMING AT YOU, I SAW A BIRD!

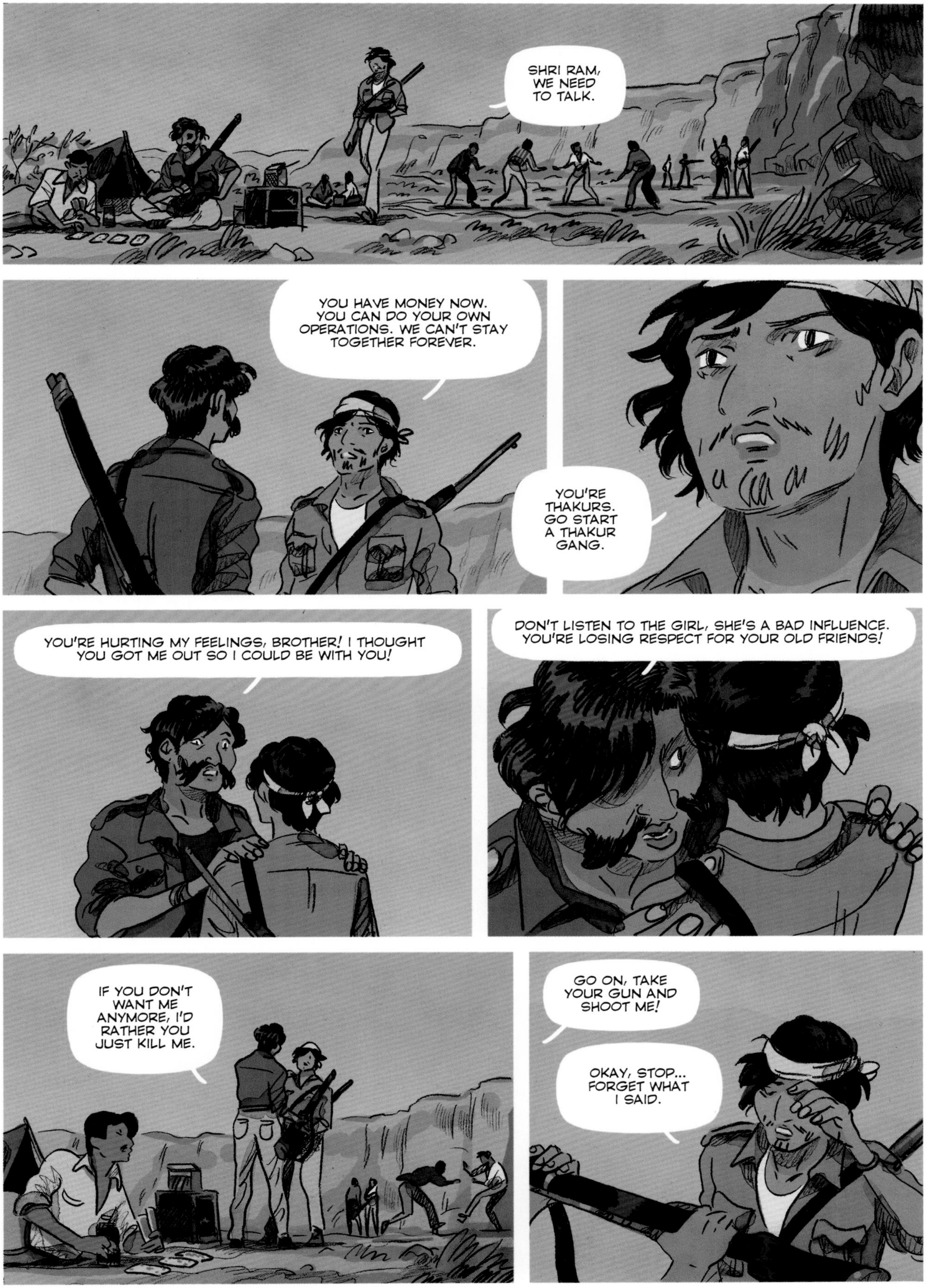
SHRI RAM, WE NEED TO TALK.
YOU HAVE MONEY NOW. YOU CAN DO YOUR OWN OPERATIONS. WE CAN'T STAY TOGETHER FOREVER.
YOU'RE THAKURS. GO START A THAKUR GANG.
YOU'RE HURTING MY FEELINGS, BROTHER! I THOUGHT YOU GOT ME OUT SO I COULD BE WITH YOU!
DON'T LISTEN TO THE GIRL, SHE'S A BAD INFLUENCE. YOU'RE LOSING RESPECT FOR YOUR OLD FRIENDS!
IF YOU DON'T WANT ME ANYMORE, I'D RATHER YOU JUST KILL ME.
GO ON, TAKE YOUR GUN AND SHOOT ME!
OKAY, STOP... FORGET WHAT I SAID.

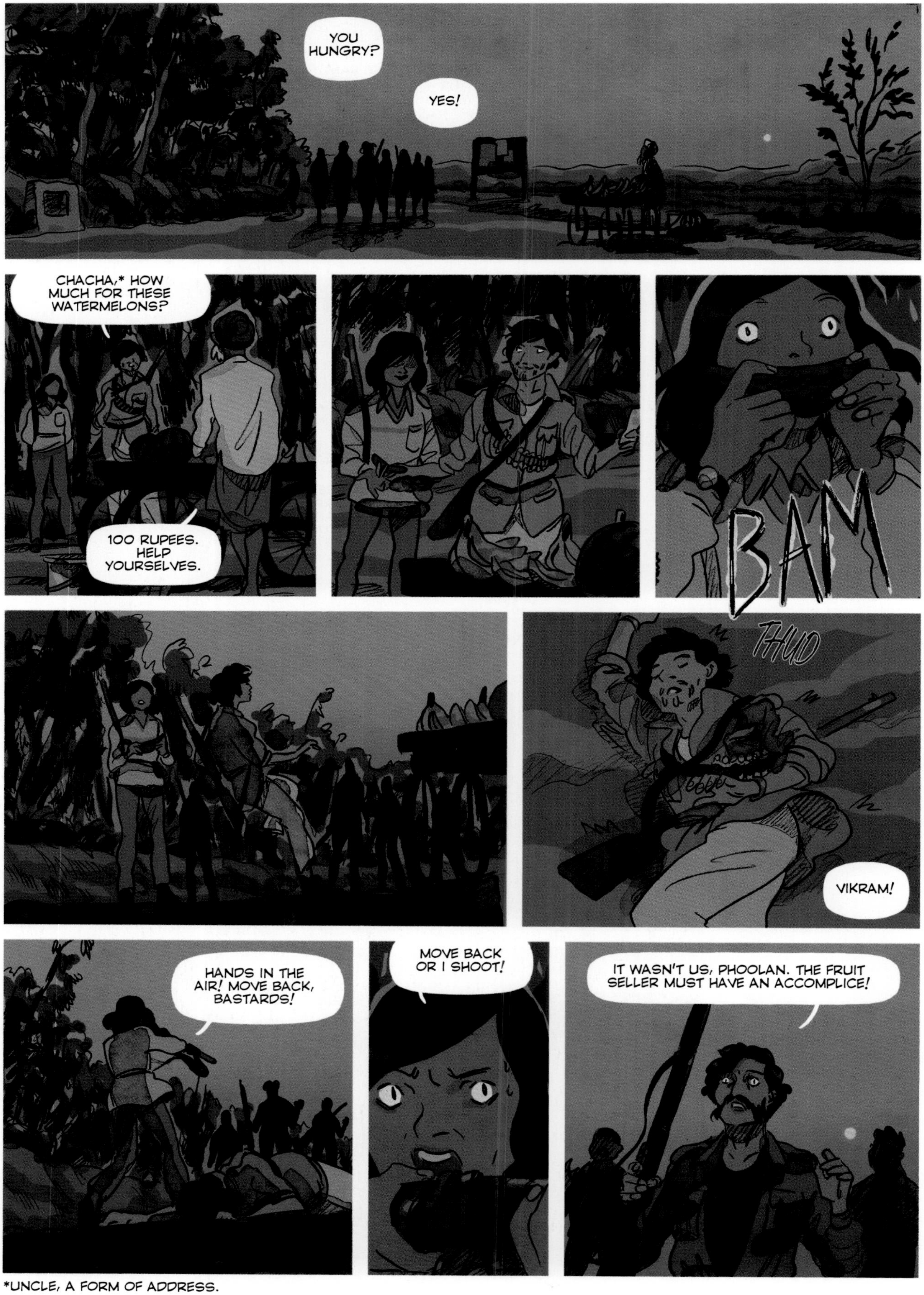
YOU HUNGRY?
YES!
CHACHA,* HOW MUCH FOR THESE WATERMELONS?
100 RUPEES. HELP YOURSELVES.
BAM
THUD
VIKRAM!
HANDS IN THE AIR! MOVE BACK, BASTARDS!
MOVE BACK OR I SHOOT!
IT WASN'T US, PHOOLAN. THE FRUIT SELLER MUST HAVE AN ACCOMPLICE!

*UNCLE, A FORM OF ADDRESS.

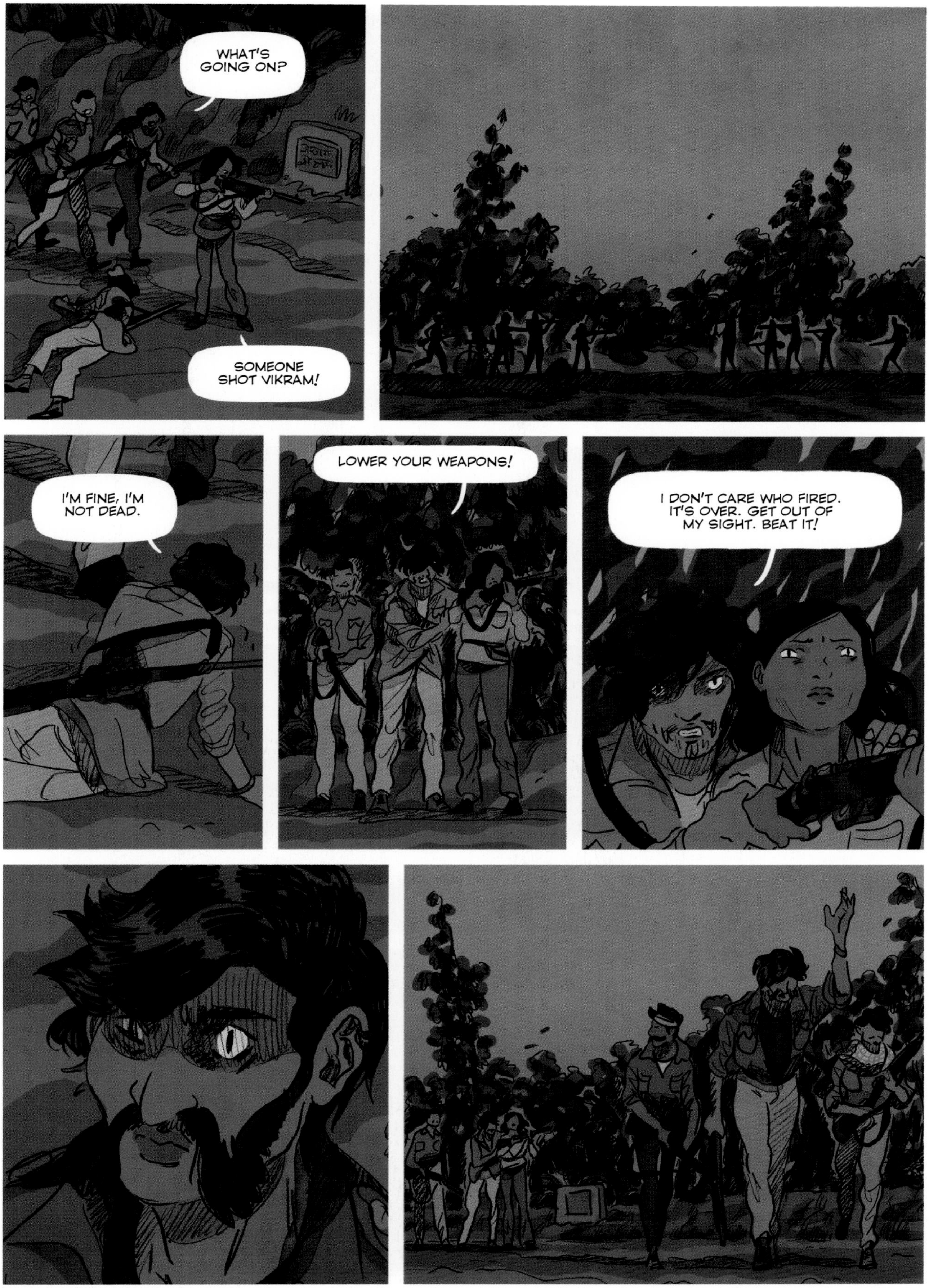
WHAT'S GOING ON?
SOMEONE SHOT VIKRAM!
I'M FINE, I'M NOT DEAD.
LOWER YOUR WEAPONS!
I DON'T CARE WHO FIRED. IT'S OVER. GET OUT OF MY SIGHT. BEAT IT!

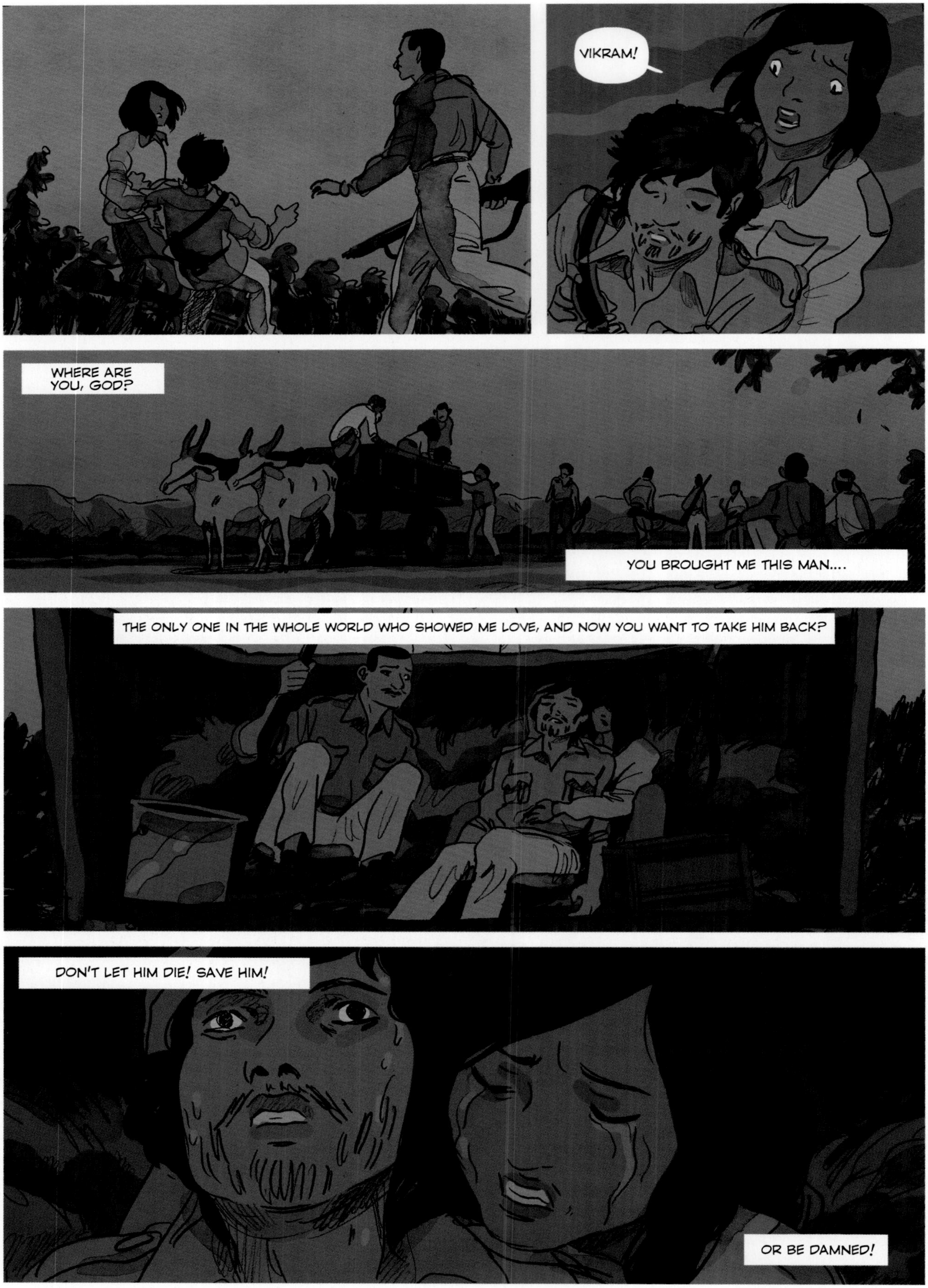
VIKRAM!
WHERE ARE YOU, GOD?
YOU BROUGHT ME THIS MAN....
THE ONLY ONE IN THE WHOLE WORLD WHO SHOWED ME LOVE, AND NOW YOU WANT TO TAKE HIM BACK?
DON'T LET HIM DIE! SAVE HIM!
OR BE DAMNED!

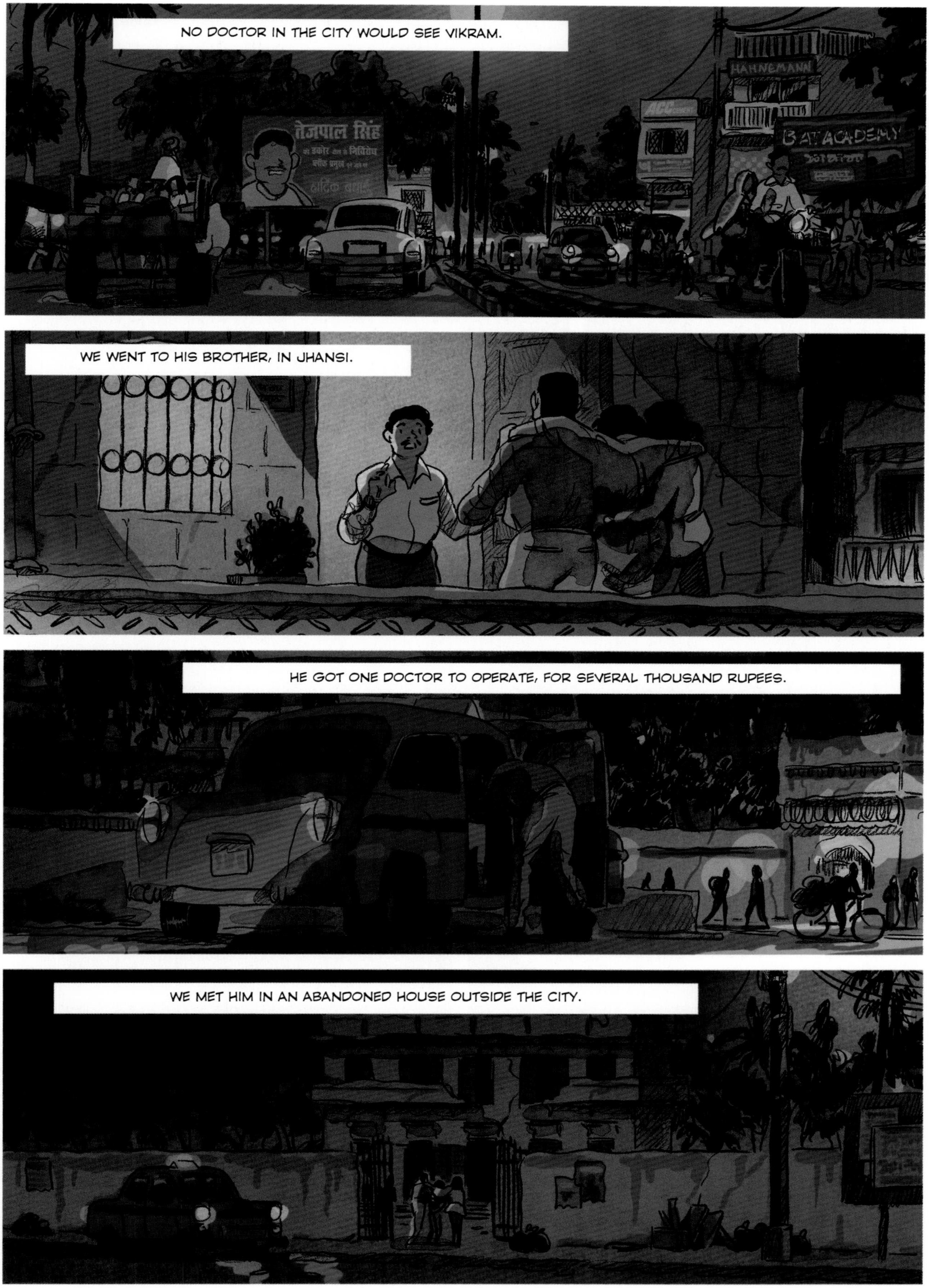
NO DOCTOR IN THE CITY WOULD SEE VIKRAM.
HAHNEMANN
BAT ACADEMY
WE WENT TO HIS BROTHER, IN JHANSI.
HE GOT ONE DOCTOR TO OPERATE, FOR SEVERAL THOUSAND RUPEES.
WE MET HIM IN AN ABANDONED HOUSE OUTSIDE THE CITY.

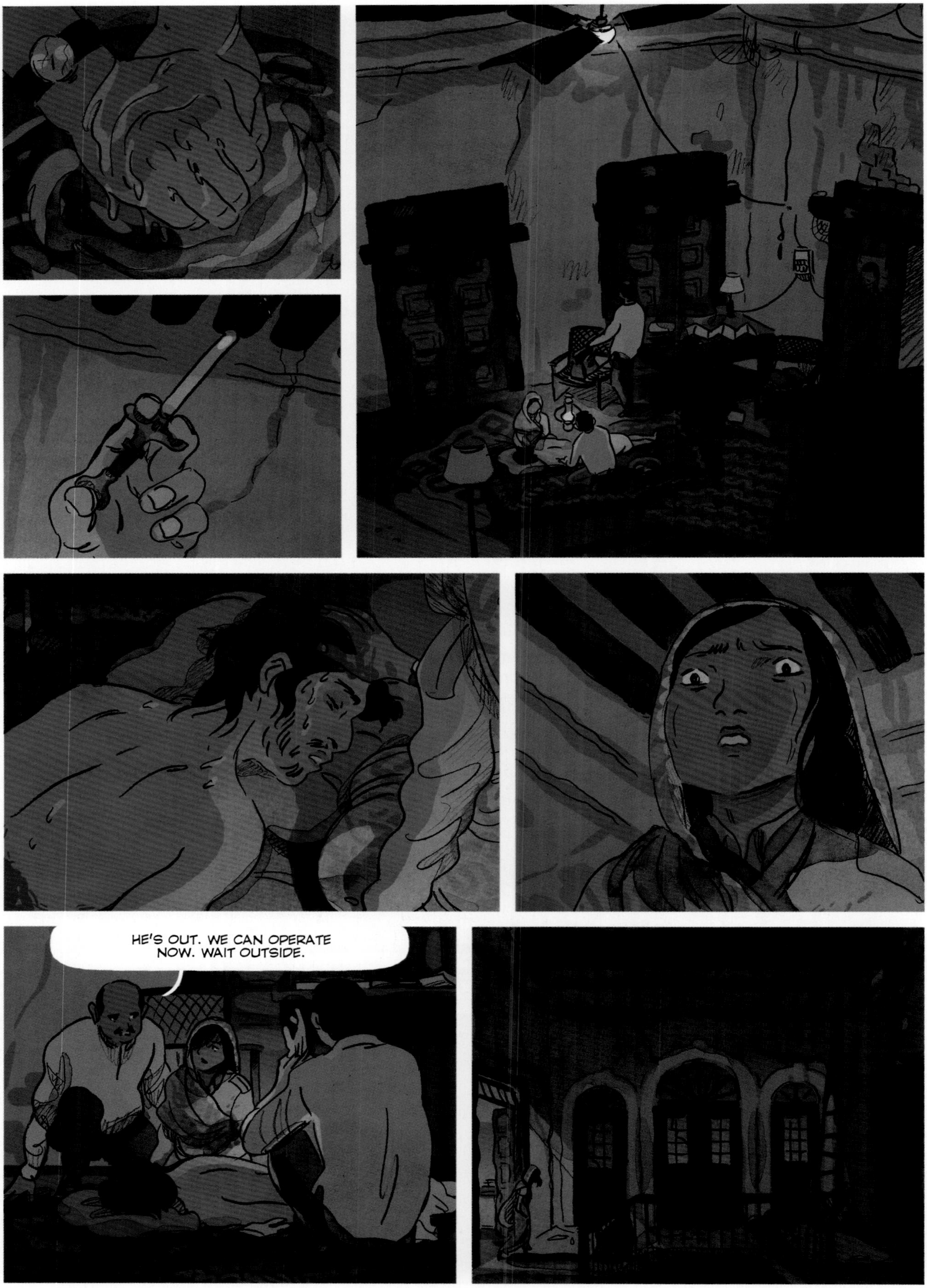
HE'S OUT. WE CAN OPERATE NOW. WAIT OUTSIDE.

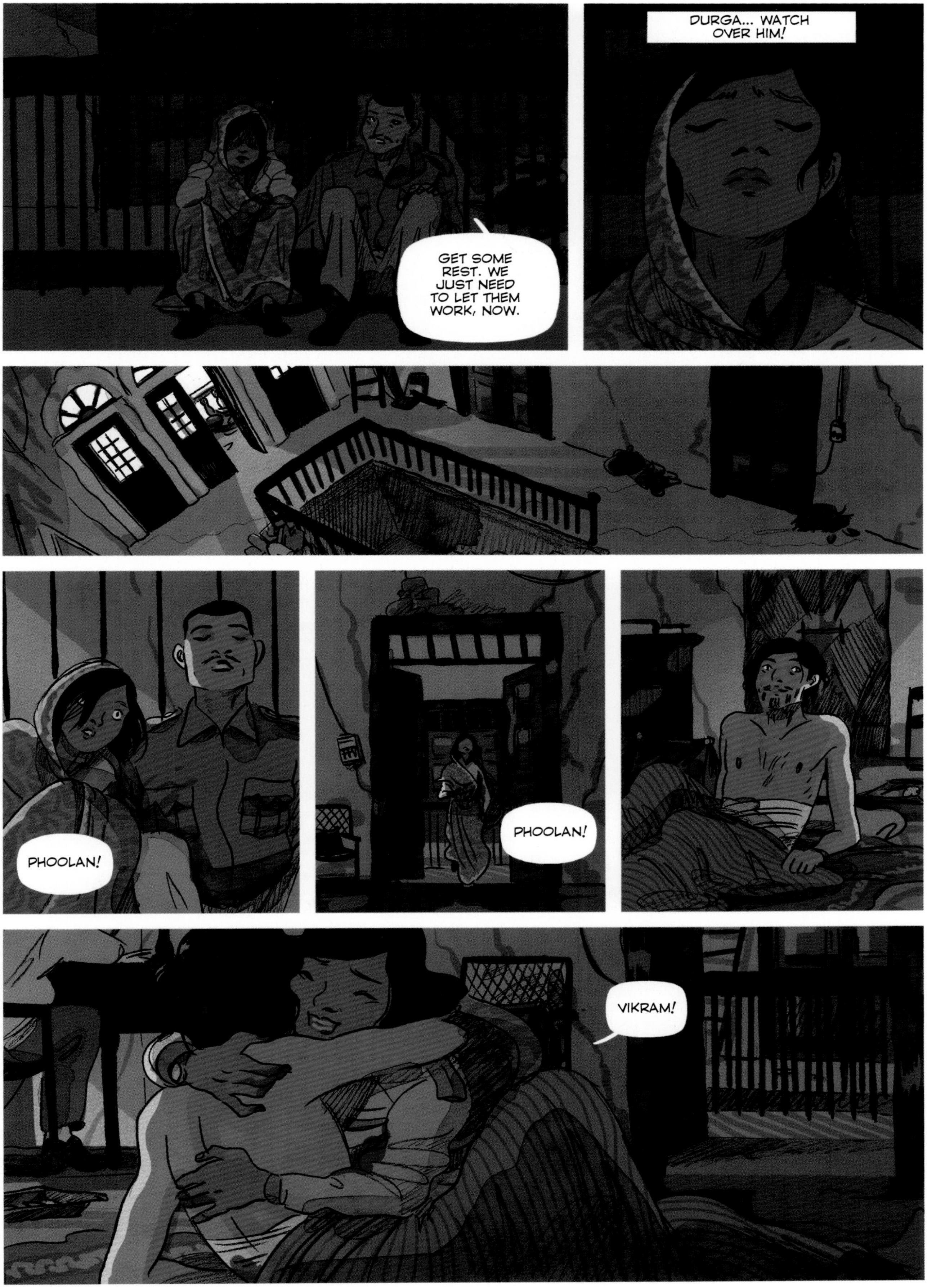
GET SOME REST. WE JUST NEED TO LET THEM WORK, NOW.
DURGA... WATCH OVER HIM!
PHOOLAN!
PHOOLAN!
VIKRAM!

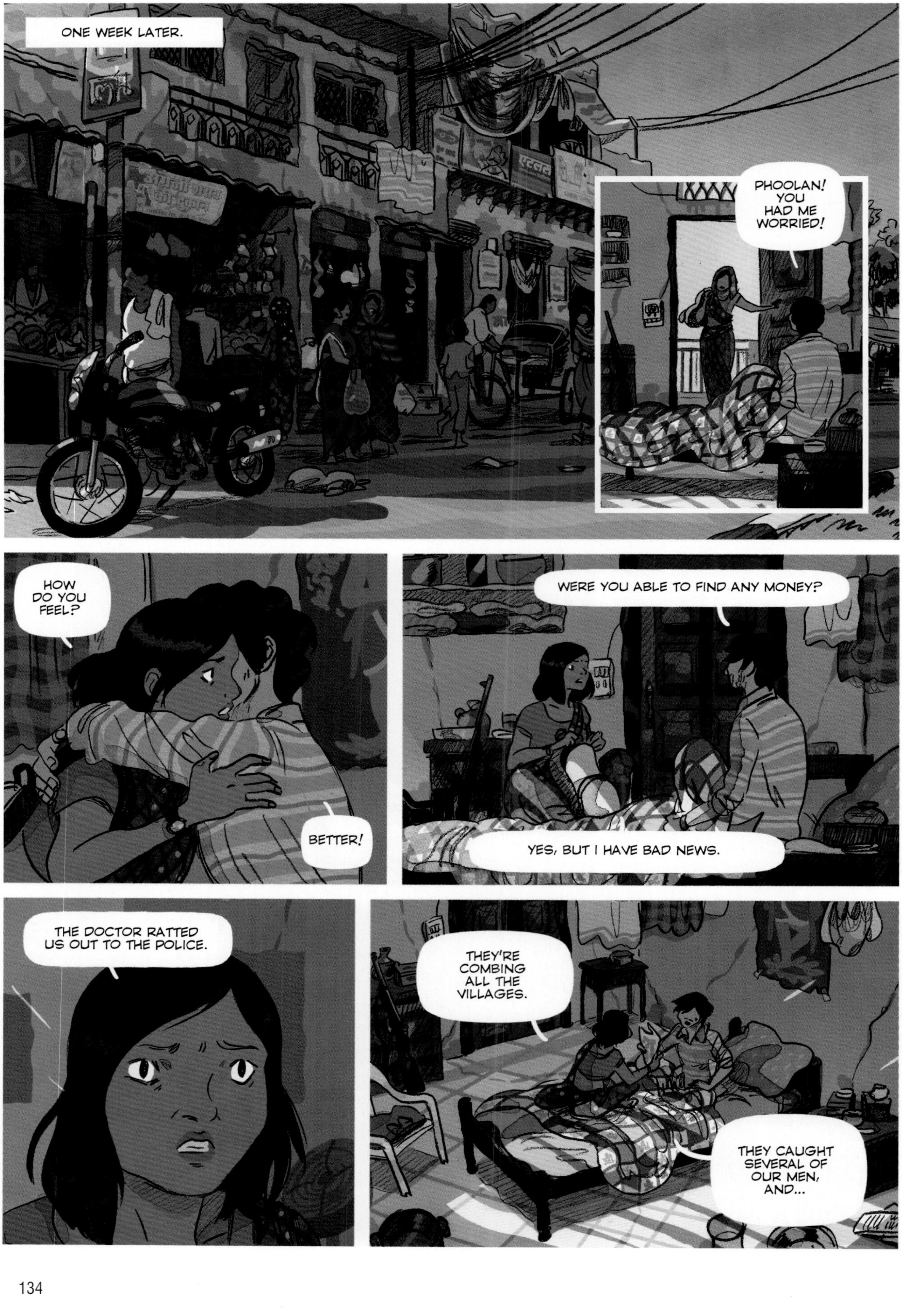

ONE WEEK LATER.
PHOOLAN! YOU HAD ME WORRIED!
HOW DO YOU FEEL?
BETTER!
WERE YOU ABLE TO FIND ANY MONEY?
YES, BUT I HAVE BAD NEWS.
THE DOCTOR RATTED US OUT TO THE POLICE.
THEY'RE COMBING ALL THE VILLAGES.
THEY CAUGHT SEVERAL OF OUR MEN, AND...

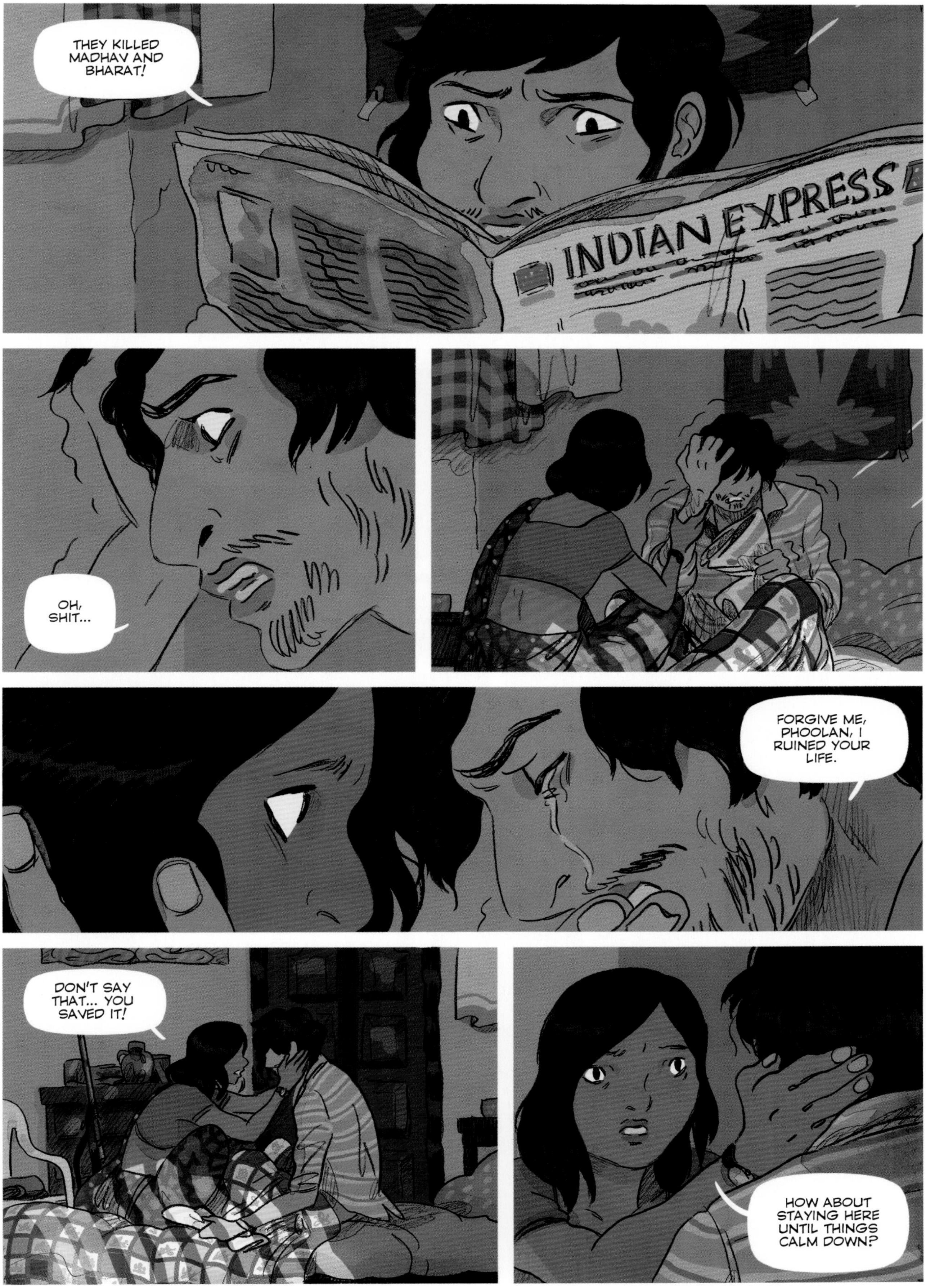
THEY KILLED MADHAV AND BHARAT!
INDIAN EXPRESS
OH, SHIT...
FORGIVE ME, PHOOLAN, I RUINED YOUR LIFE.
DON'T SAY THAT... YOU SAVED IT!
HOW ABOUT STAYING HERE UNTIL THINGS CALM DOWN?

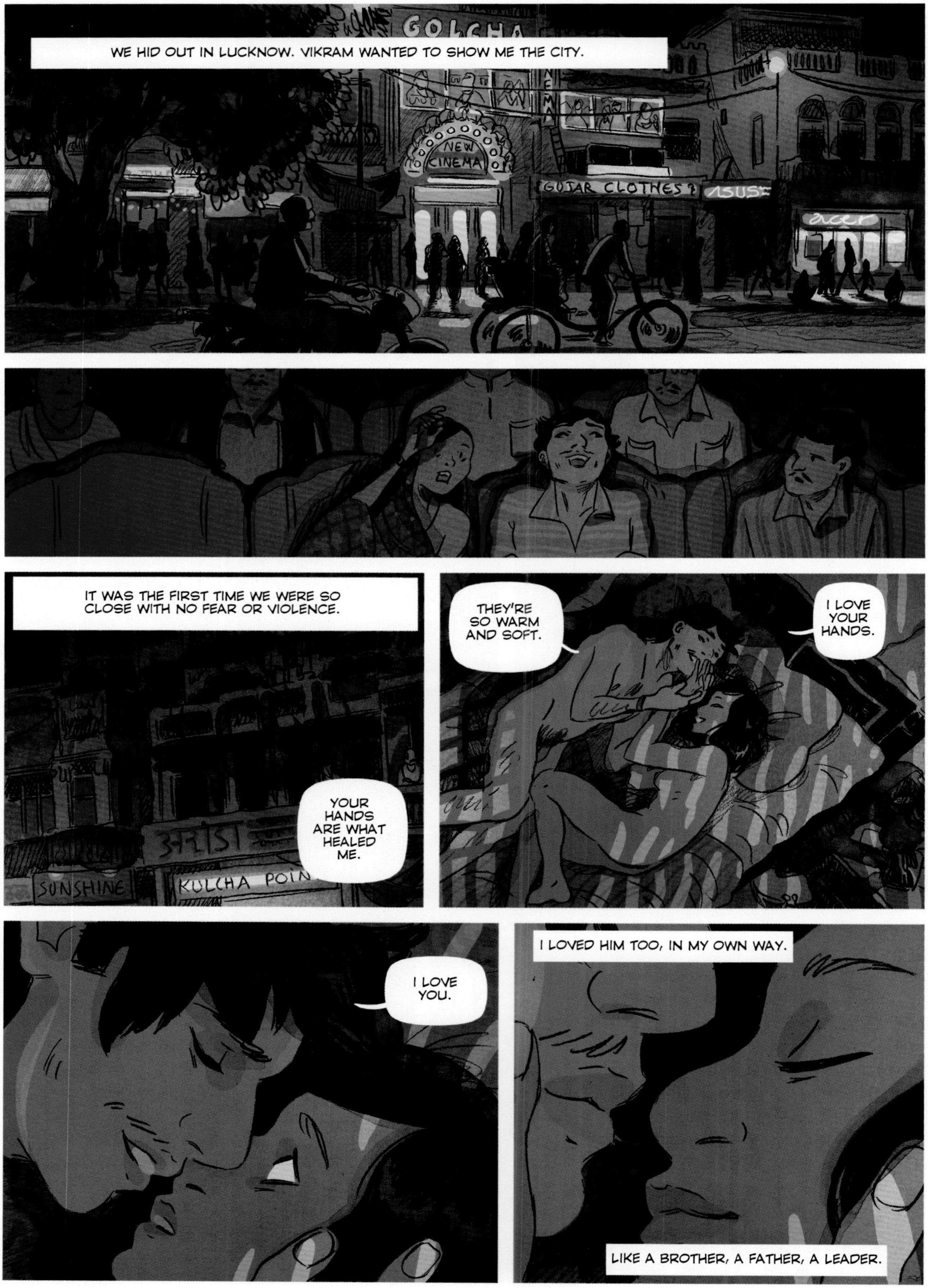

WE HID OUT IN LUCKNOW. VIKRAM WANTED TO SHOW ME THE CITY.
GOLCHA
NEW CINEMA
GUJAR CLOTHES
ASUS
acer
IT WAS THE FIRST TIME WE WERE SO CLOSE WITH NO FEAR OR VIOLENCE.
YOUR HANDS ARE WHAT HEALED ME.
SUNSHINE
KULCHA POIN
THEY'RE SO WARM AND SOFT.
I LOVE YOUR HANDS.
I LOVE YOU.
I LOVED HIM TOO, IN MY OWN WAY.
LIKE A BROTHER, A FATHER, A LEADER.

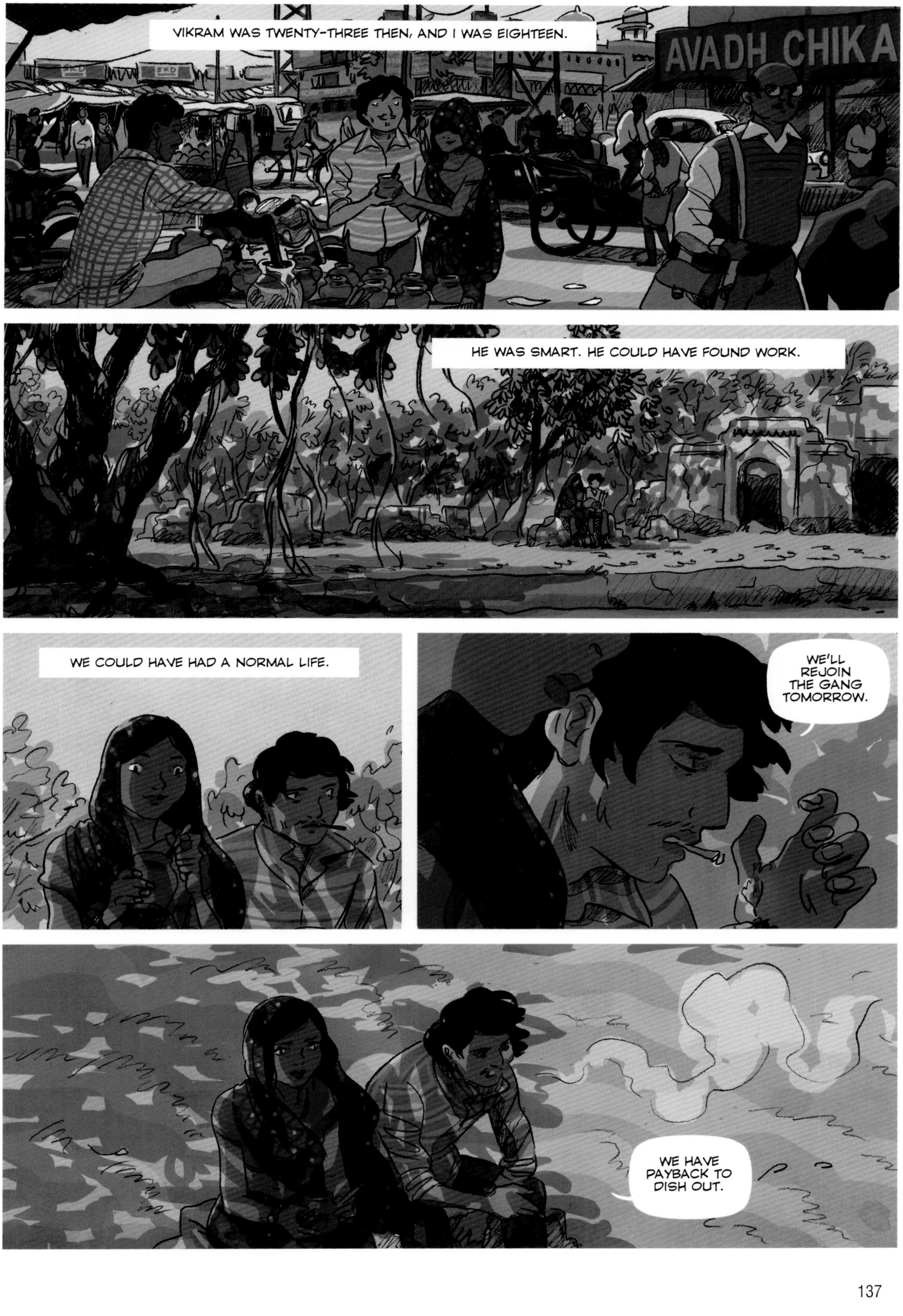
VIKRAM WAS TWENTY-THREE THEN, AND I WAS EIGHTEEN.
AVADH CHIKA
HE WAS SMART. HE COULD HAVE FOUND WORK.
WE COULD HAVE HAD A NORMAL LIFE.
WE'LL REJOIN THE GANG TOMORROW.
WE HAVE PAYBACK TO DISH OUT.

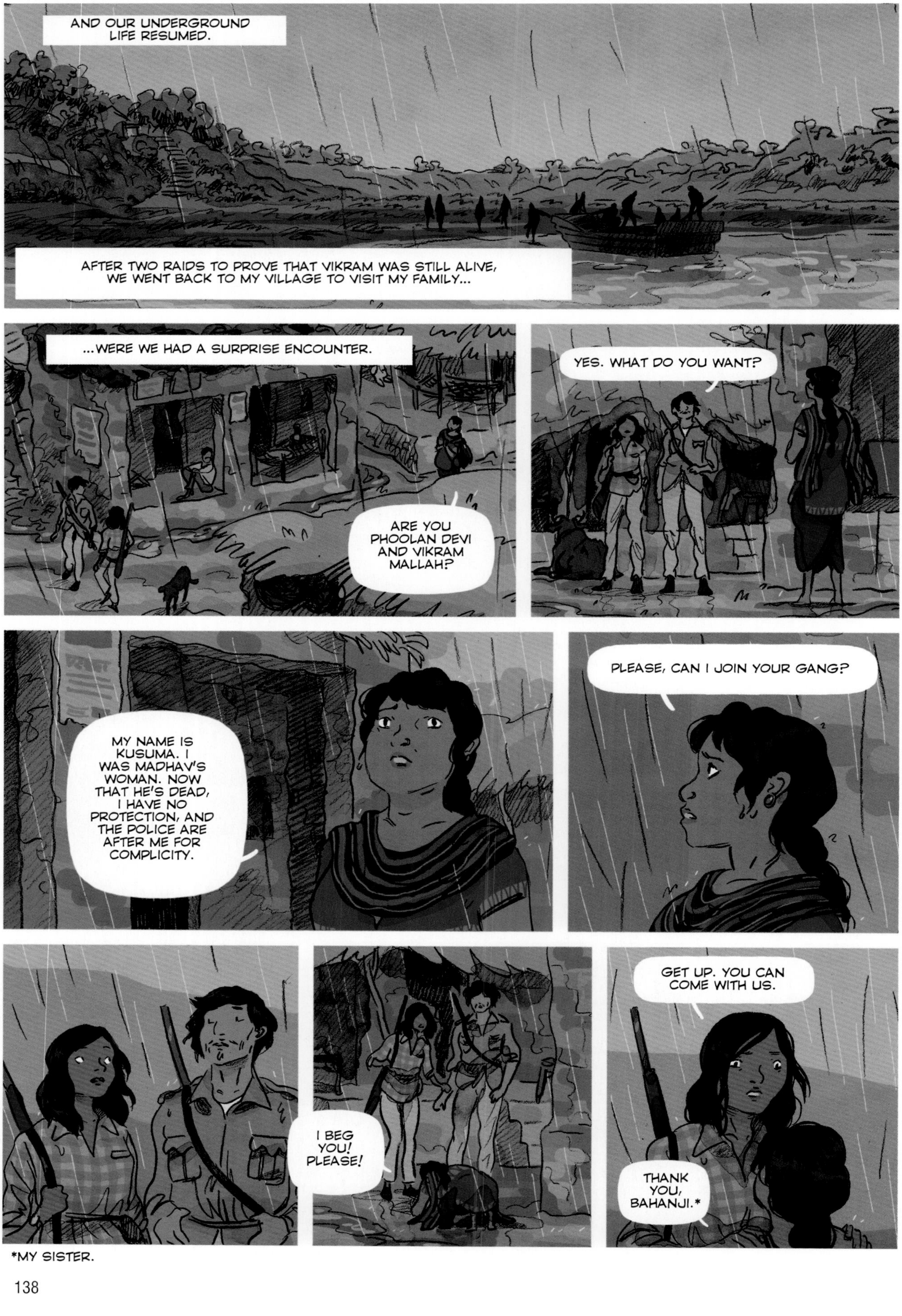
AND OUR UNDERGROUND LIFE RESUMED.
AFTER TWO RAIDS TO PROVE THAT VIKRAM WAS STILL ALIVE, WE WENT BACK TO MY VILLAGE TO VISIT MY FAMILY...
...WERE WE HAD A SURPRISE ENCOUNTER.
ARE YOU PHOOLAN DEVI AND VIKRAM MALLAH?
YES. WHAT DO YOU WANT?
MY NAME IS KUSUMA. I WAS MADHAV'S WOMAN. NOW THAT HE'S DEAD, I HAVE NO PROTECTION, AND THE POLICE ARE AFTER ME FOR COMPLICITY.
PLEASE, CAN I JOIN YOUR GANG?
I BEG YOU! PLEASE!
GET UP. YOU CAN COME WITH US.
THANK YOU, BAHANJI.*

*MY SISTER.

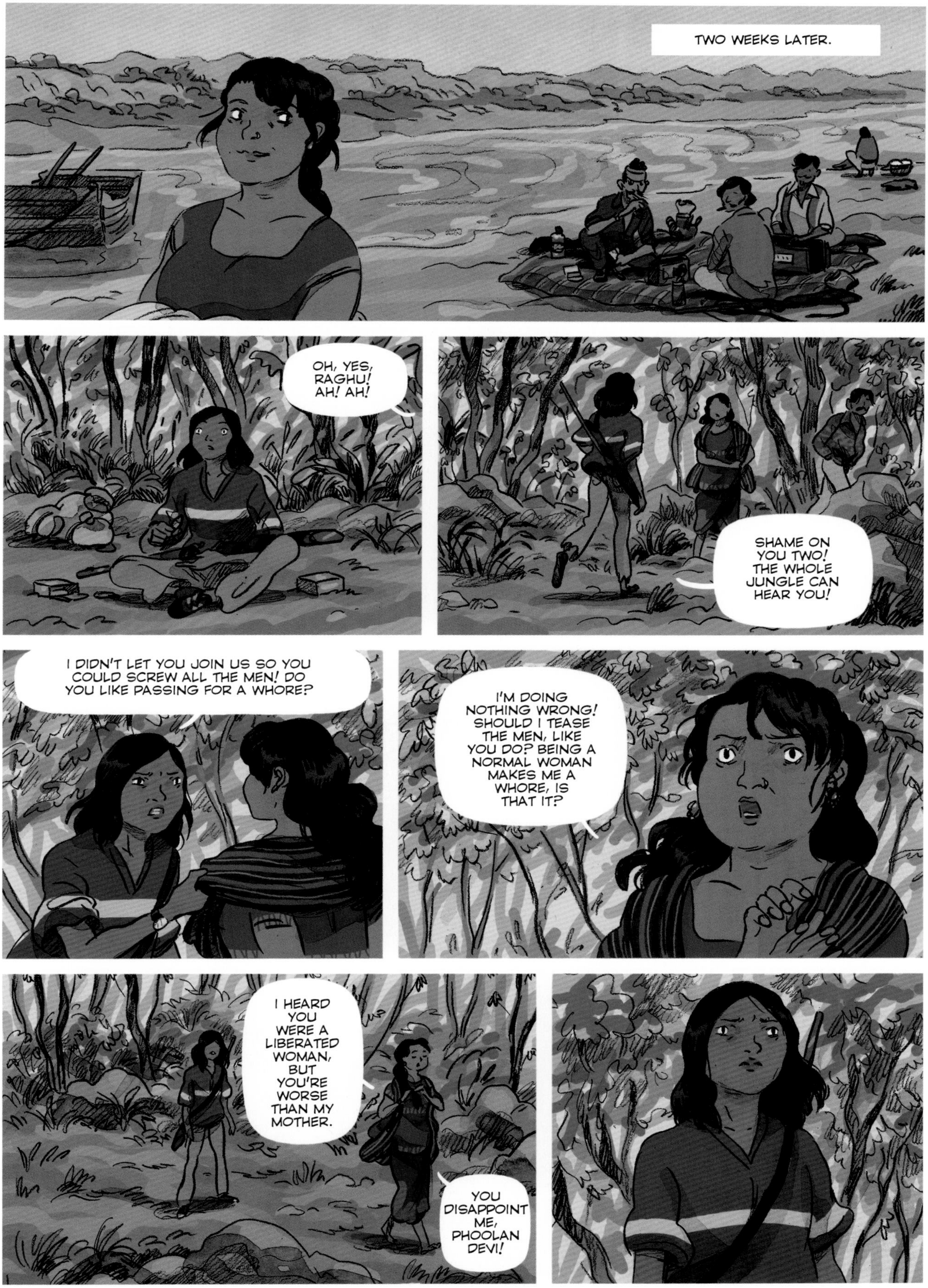
TWO WEEKS LATER.
OH, YES, RAGHU! AH! AH!
SHAME ON YOU TWO! THE WHOLE JUNGLE CAN HEAR YOU!
I DIDN'T LET YOU JOIN US SO YOU COULD SCREW ALL THE MEN! DO YOU LIKE PASSING FOR A WHORE?
I'M DOING NOTHING WRONG! SHOULD I TEASE THE MEN, LIKE YOU DO? BEING A NORMAL WOMAN MAKES ME A WHORE, IS THAT IT?
I HEARD YOU WERE A LIBERATED WOMAN, BUT YOU'RE WORSE THAN MY MOTHER.
YOU DISAPPOINT ME, PHOOLAN DEVI!

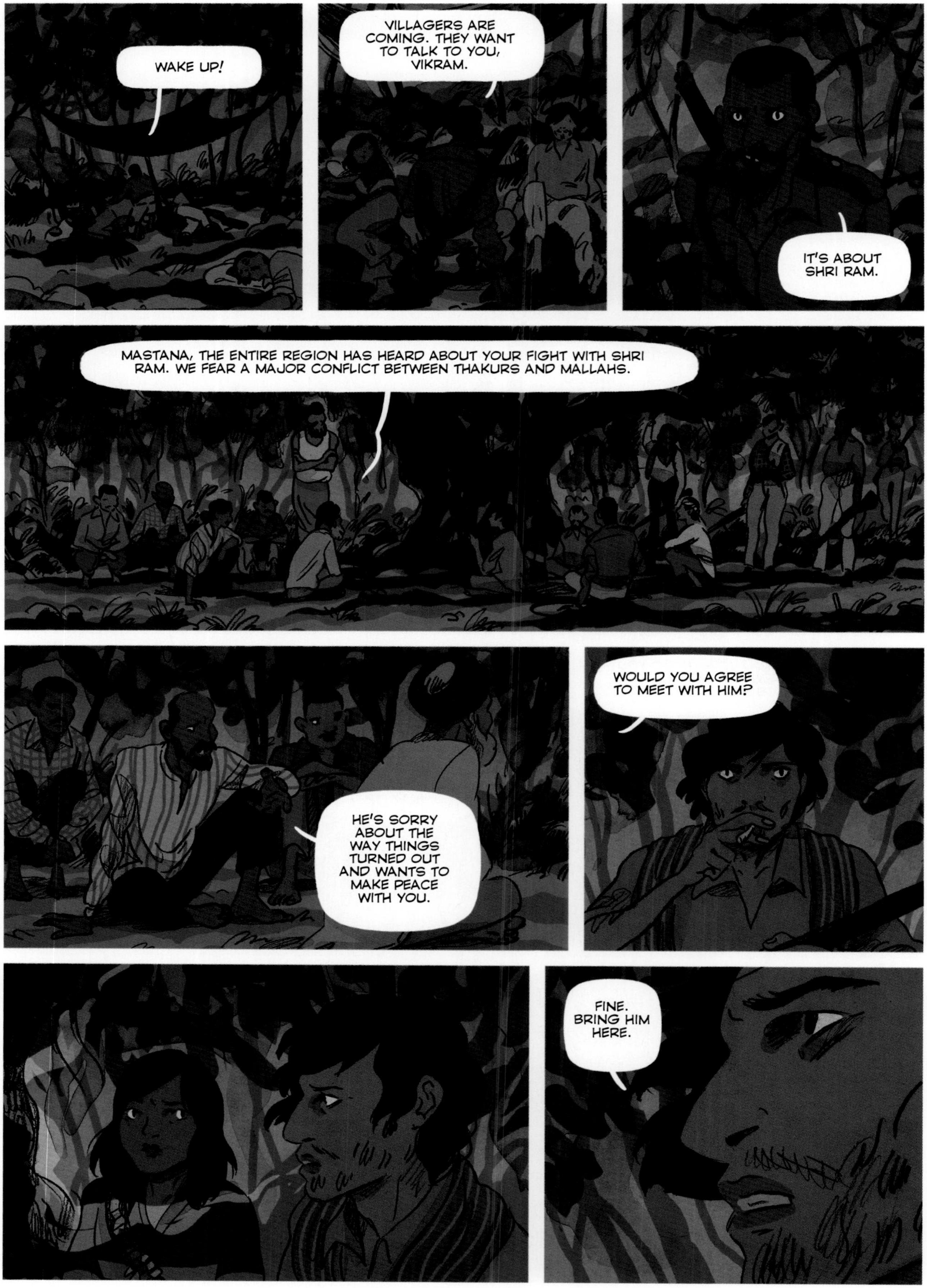
WAKE UP!
VILLAGERS ARE COMING. THEY WANT TO TALK TO YOU, VIKRAM.
IT'S ABOUT SHRI RAM.
MASTANA, THE ENTIRE REGION HAS HEARD ABOUT YOUR FIGHT WITH SHRI RAM. WE FEAR A MAJOR CONFLICT BETWEEN THAKURS AND MALLAHS.
HE'S SORRY ABOUT THE WAY THINGS TURNED OUT AND WANTS TO MAKE PEACE WITH YOU.
WOULD YOU AGREE TO MEET WITH HIM?
FINE. BRING HIM HERE.

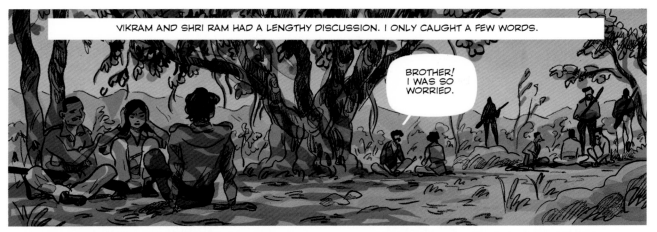

VIKRAM AND SHRI RAM HAD A LENGTHY DISCUSSION. I ONLY CAUGHT A FEW WORDS.

BROTHER! I WAS SO WORRIED.

ONE HOUR LATER.

WELL?

WE MADE A DEAL. HE WANTS TO PAY ME BACK THE BAIL MONEY SO WE'RE EVEN.

HE ASKED ME FOR TWO DAYS, TO GIVE HIM TIME TO FIND THE MONEY. THEN, WE WILL SEPARATE FOR GOOD, NO HARD FEELINGS.

CAN'T YOU SEE HE'S MOCKING YOU? WE WERE SUPPOSED TO KILL HIM!

THAT WAS A BAD IDEA. THE PEASANTS ARE RIGHT. WE MUST AVOID A BLOODBATH AT ALL COSTS!

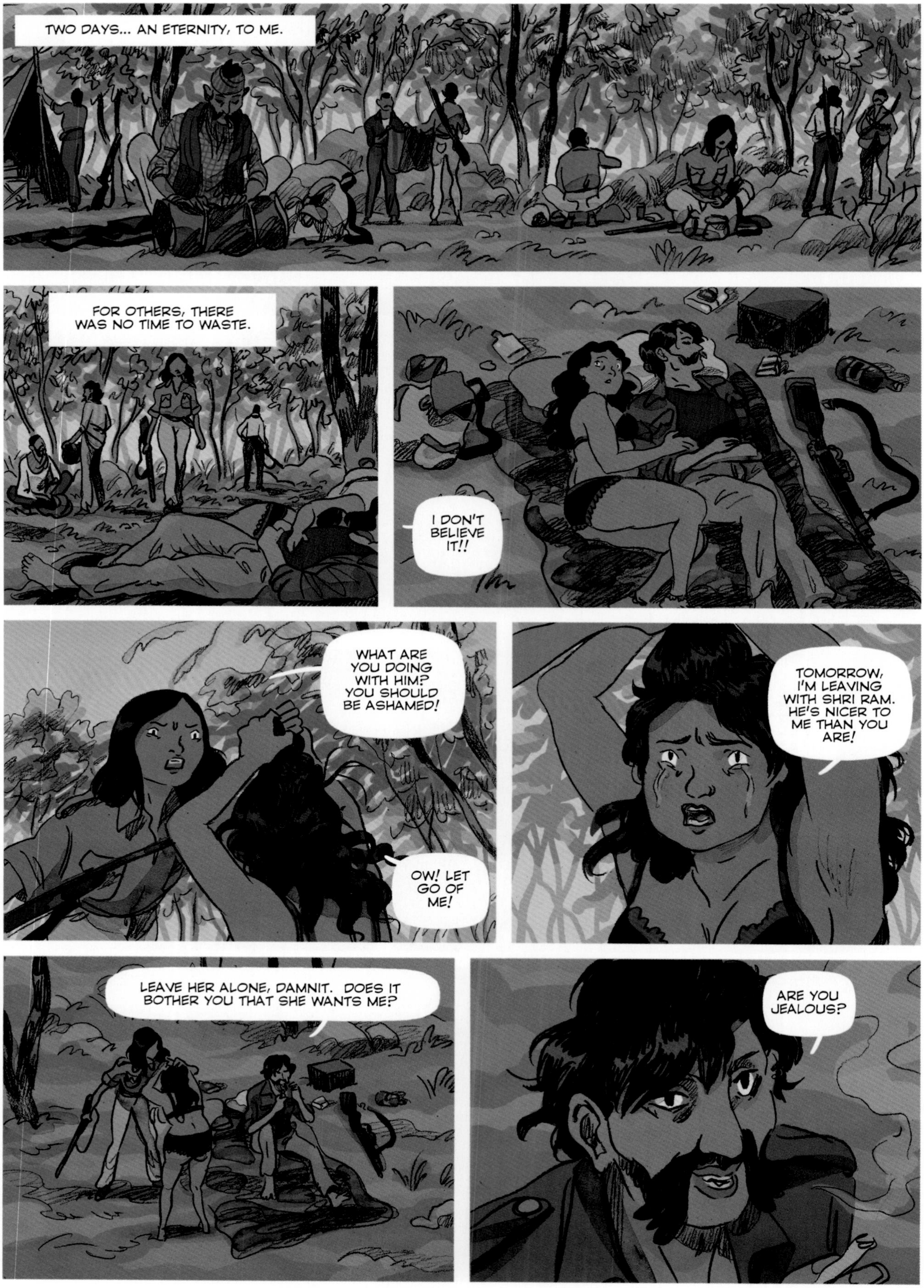
TWO DAYS... AN ETERNITY, TO ME.
FOR OTHERS, THERE WAS NO TIME TO WASTE.
I DON'T BELIEVE IT!!
WHAT ARE YOU DOING WITH HIM? YOU SHOULD BE ASHAMED!
OW! LET GO OF ME!
TOMORROW, I'M LEAVING WITH SHRI RAM. HE'S NICER TO ME THAN YOU ARE!
LEAVE HER ALONE, DAMNIT. DOES IT BOTHER YOU THAT SHE WANTS ME?
ARE YOU JEALOUS?

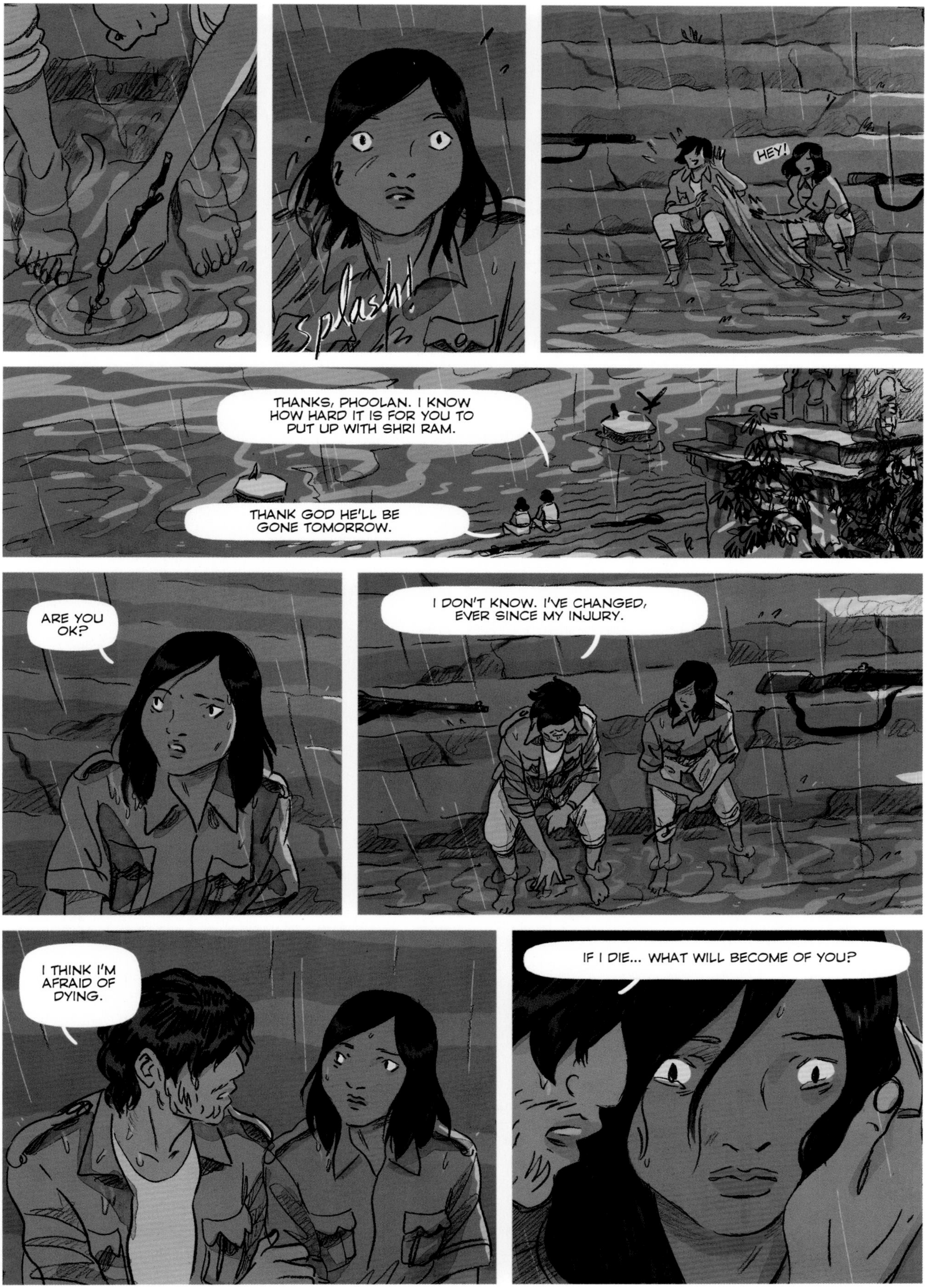
splash!
HEY!
THANKS, PHOOLAN. I KNOW HOW HARD IT IS FOR YOU TO PUT UP WITH SHRI RAM.
THANK GOD HE'LL BE GONE TOMORROW.
ARE YOU OK?
I DON'T KNOW. I'VE CHANGED, EVER SINCE MY INJURY.
I THINK I'M AFRAID OF DYING.
IF I DIE... WHAT WILL BECOME OF YOU?

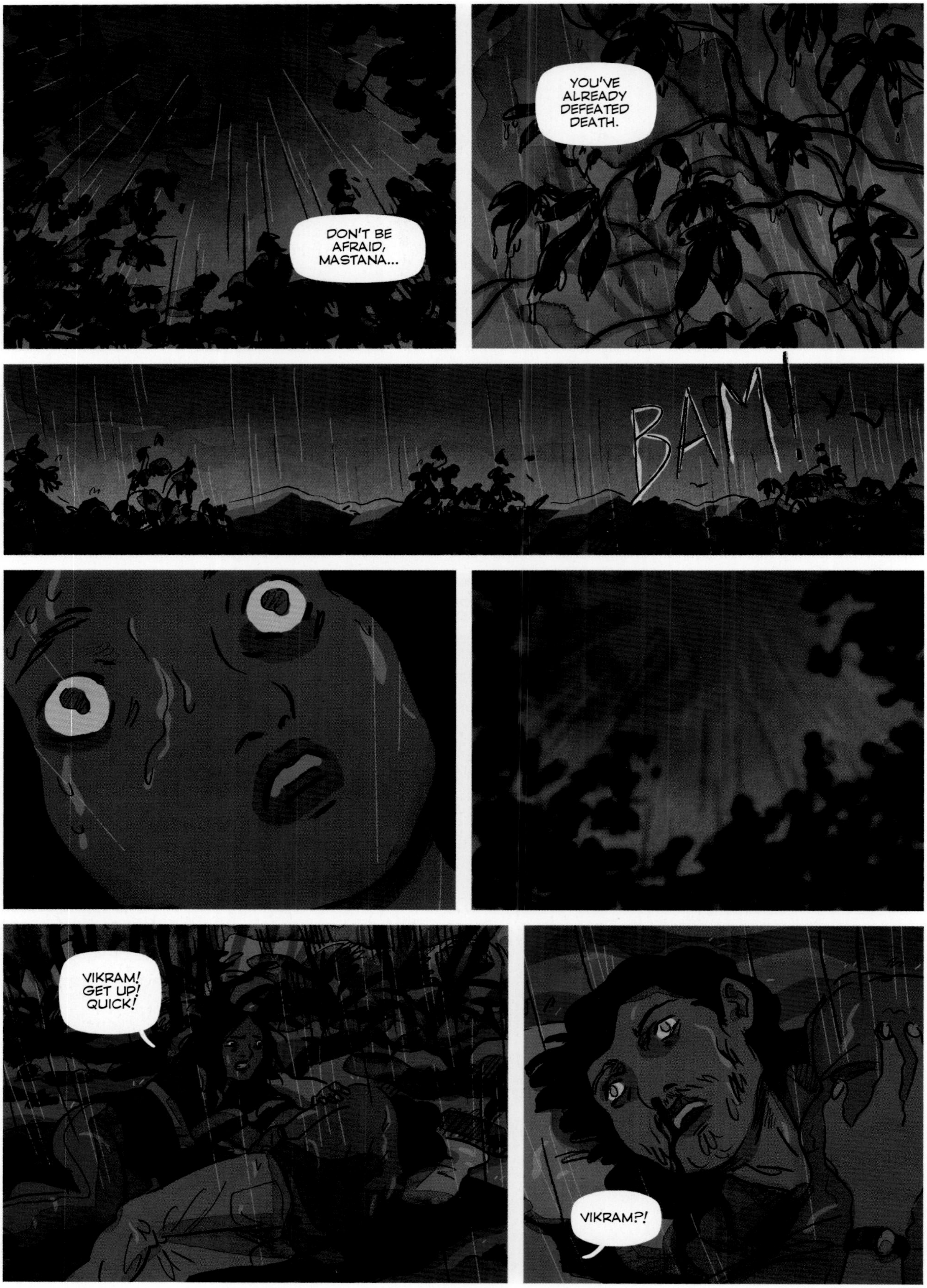
DON'T BE AFRAID, MASTANA...
YOU'VE ALREADY DEFEATED DEATH.
BAM!
VIKRAM! GET UP! QUICK!
VIKRAM?!

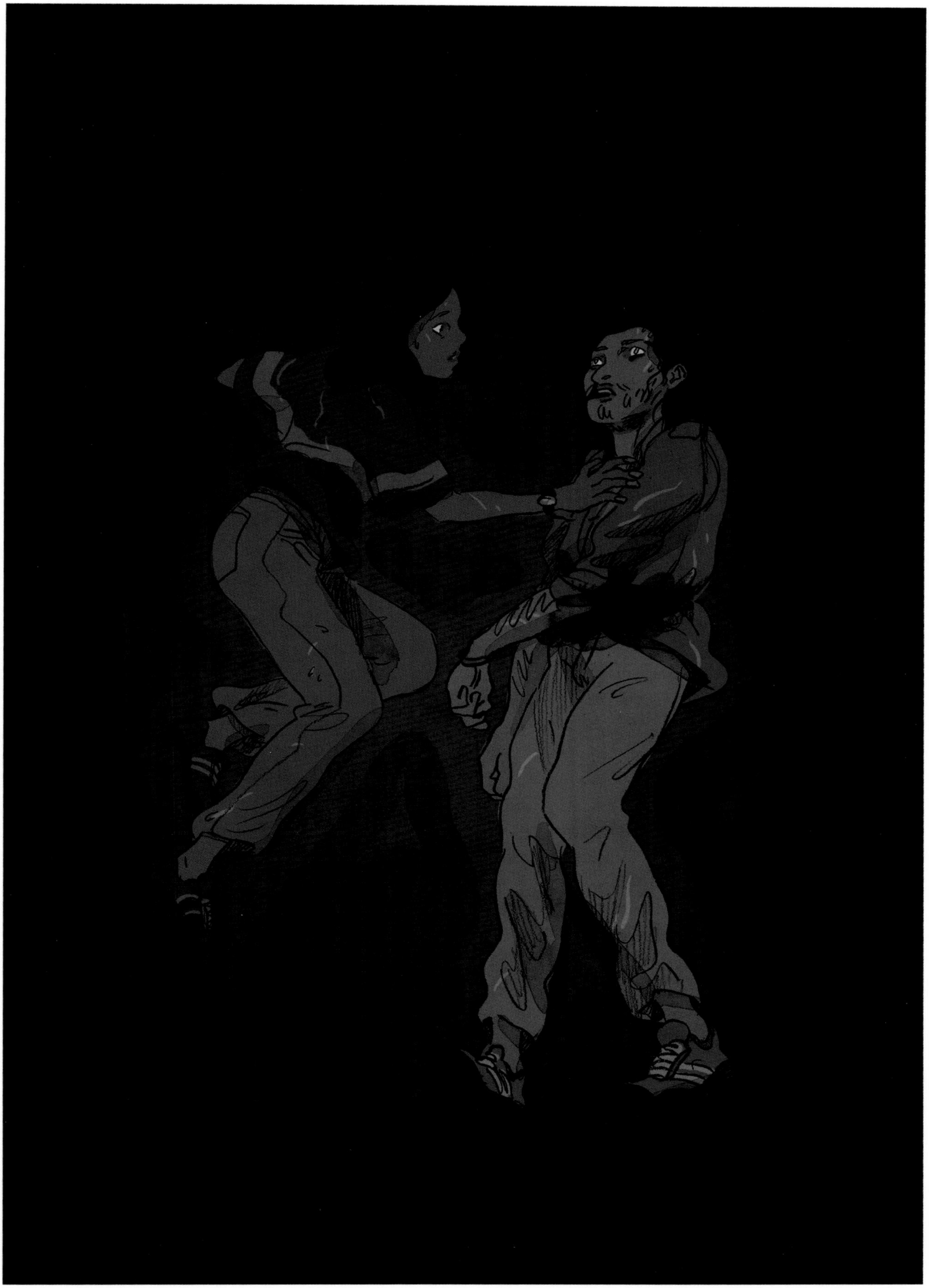

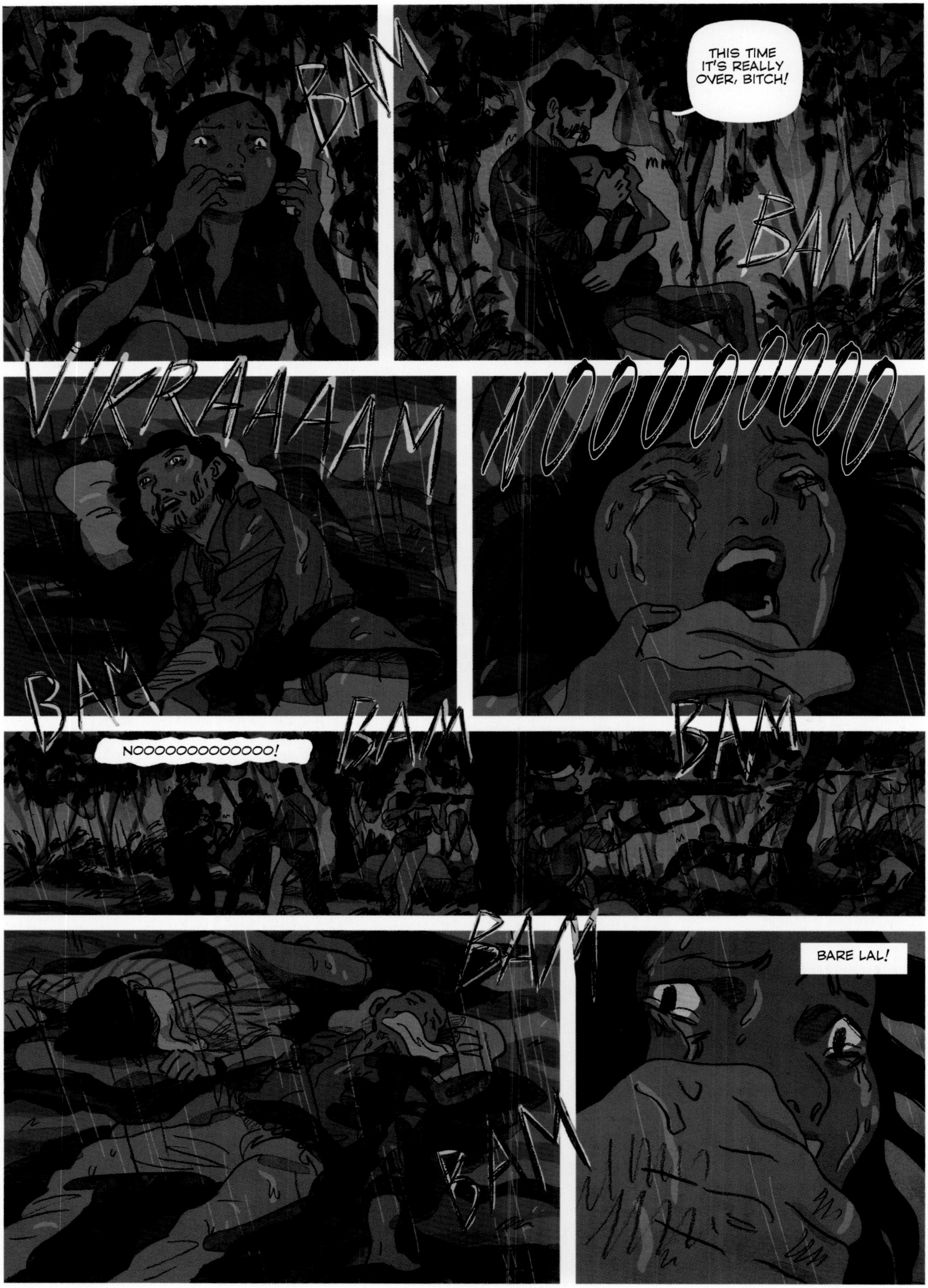
BAM
THIS TIME IT'S REALLY OVER, BITCH!
BAM
VIRRAAAAAM
NOOOOOOOOO
BAM
NOOOOOOOOOOOOOO!
BAM
BAM
BAM
BAM
BARE LAL!

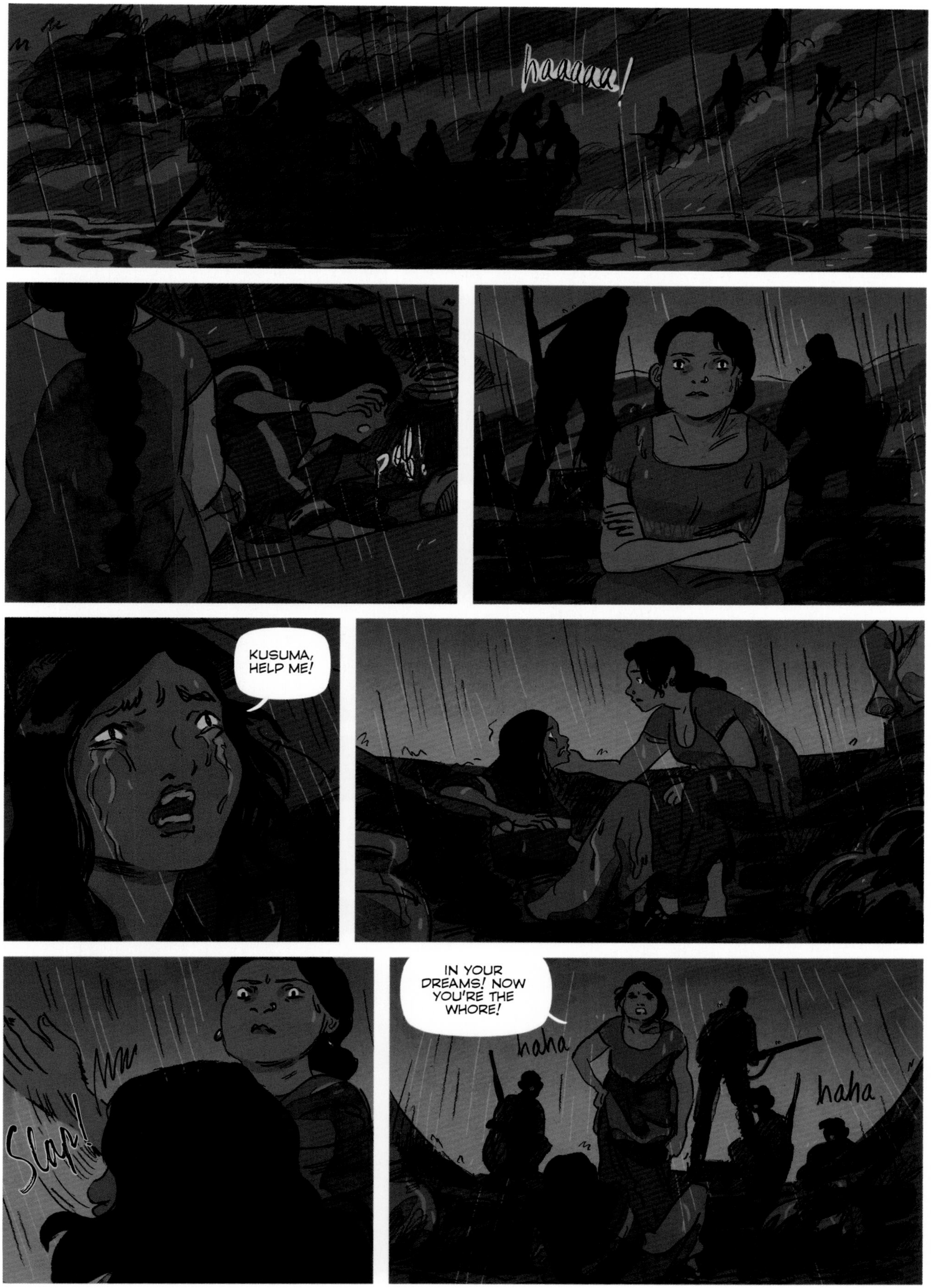
haaaaa!
Paf!
KUSUMA, HELP ME!
Slap!
IN YOUR DREAMS! NOW YOU'RE THE WHORE!
haha
haha

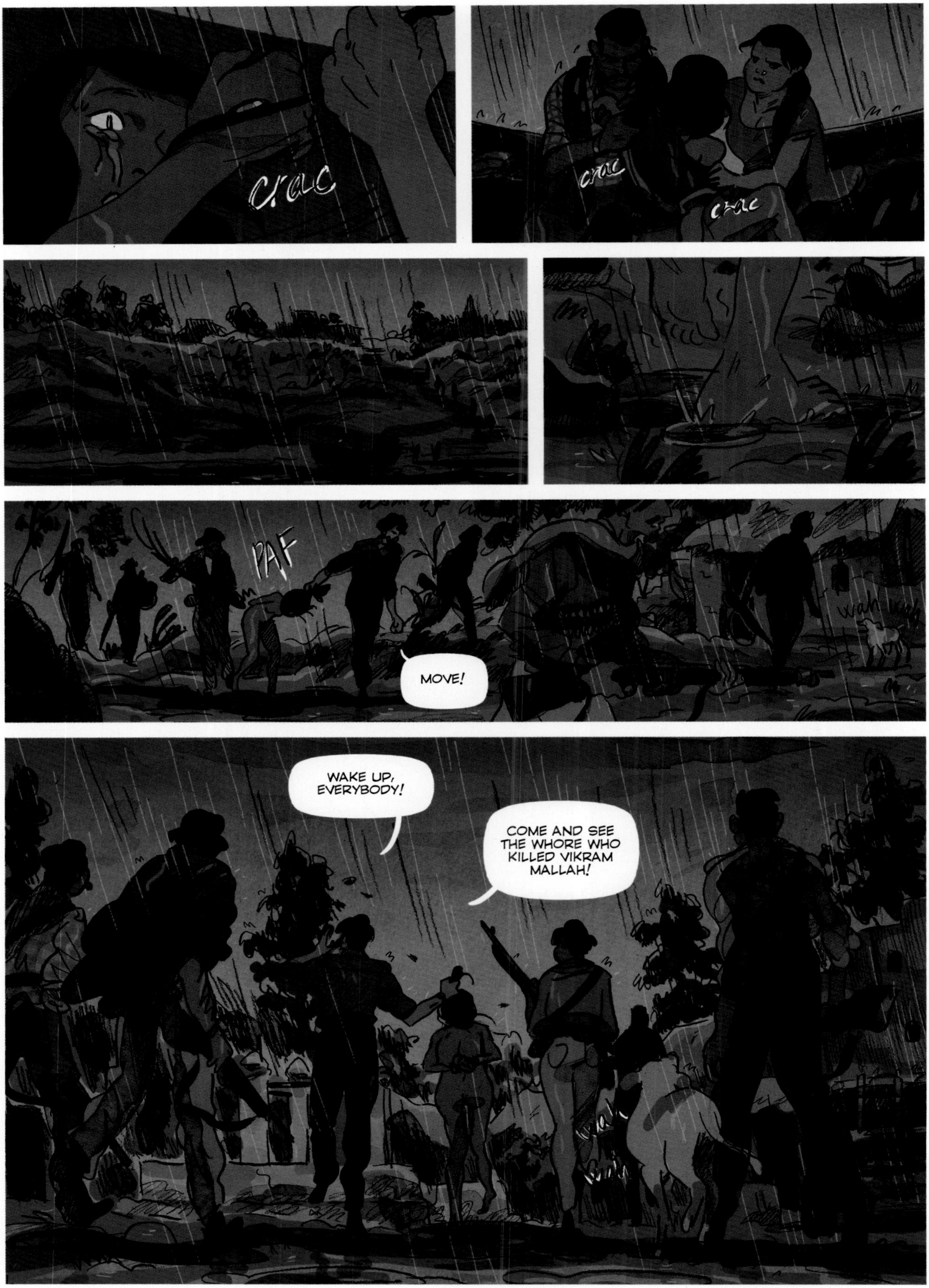
crac
crac
crac
PAF
MOVE!
wah
WAKE UP, EVERYBODY!
COME AND SEE THE WHORE WHO KILLED VIKRAM MALLAH!

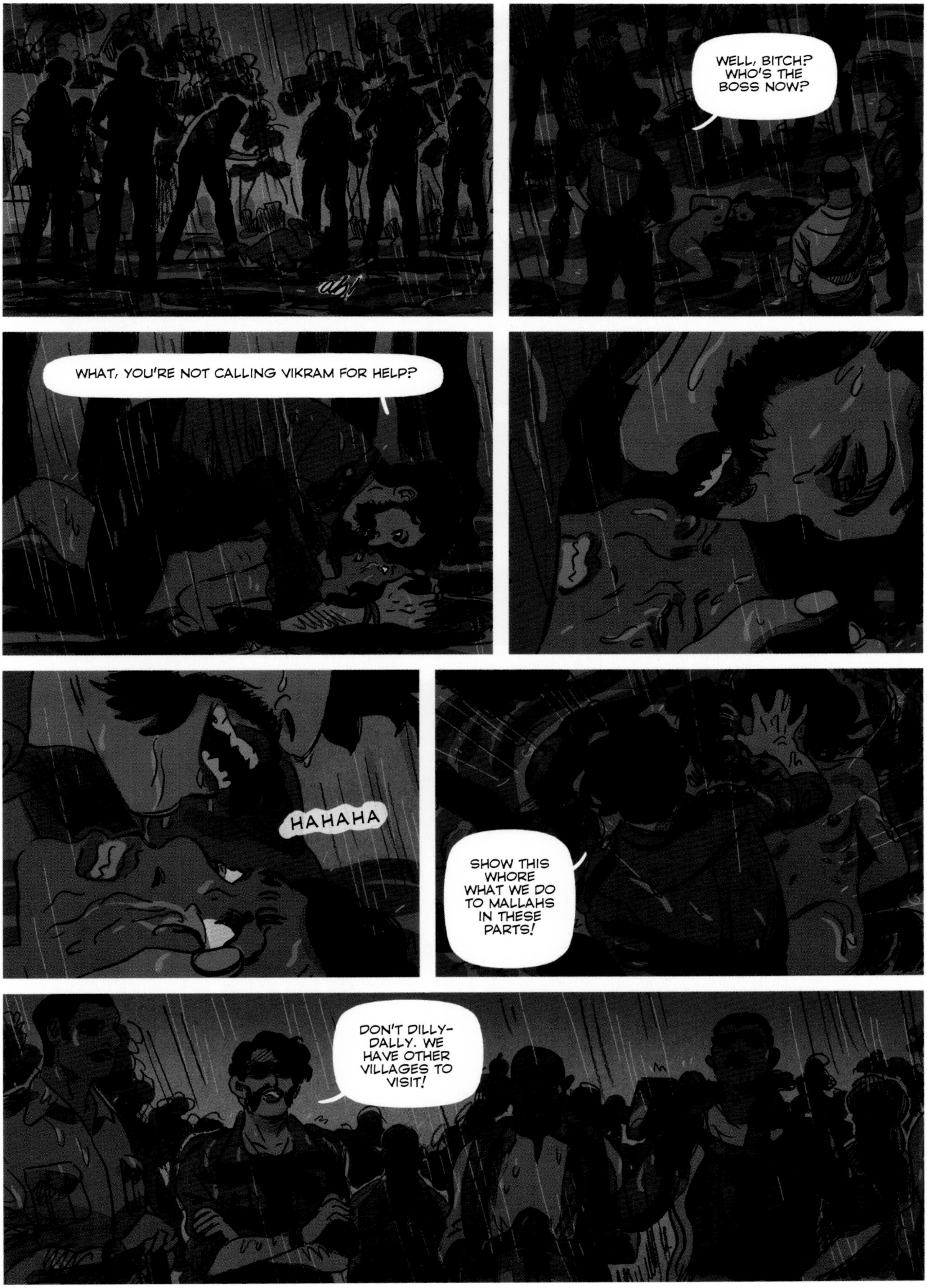
WELL, BITCH? WHO'S THE BOSS NOW?
WHAT, YOU'RE NOT CALLING VIKRAM FOR HELP?
HAHAHA
SHOW THIS WHORE WHAT WE DO TO MALLAHS IN THESE PARTS!
DON'T DILLY-DALLY. WE HAVE OTHER VILLAGES TO VISIT!

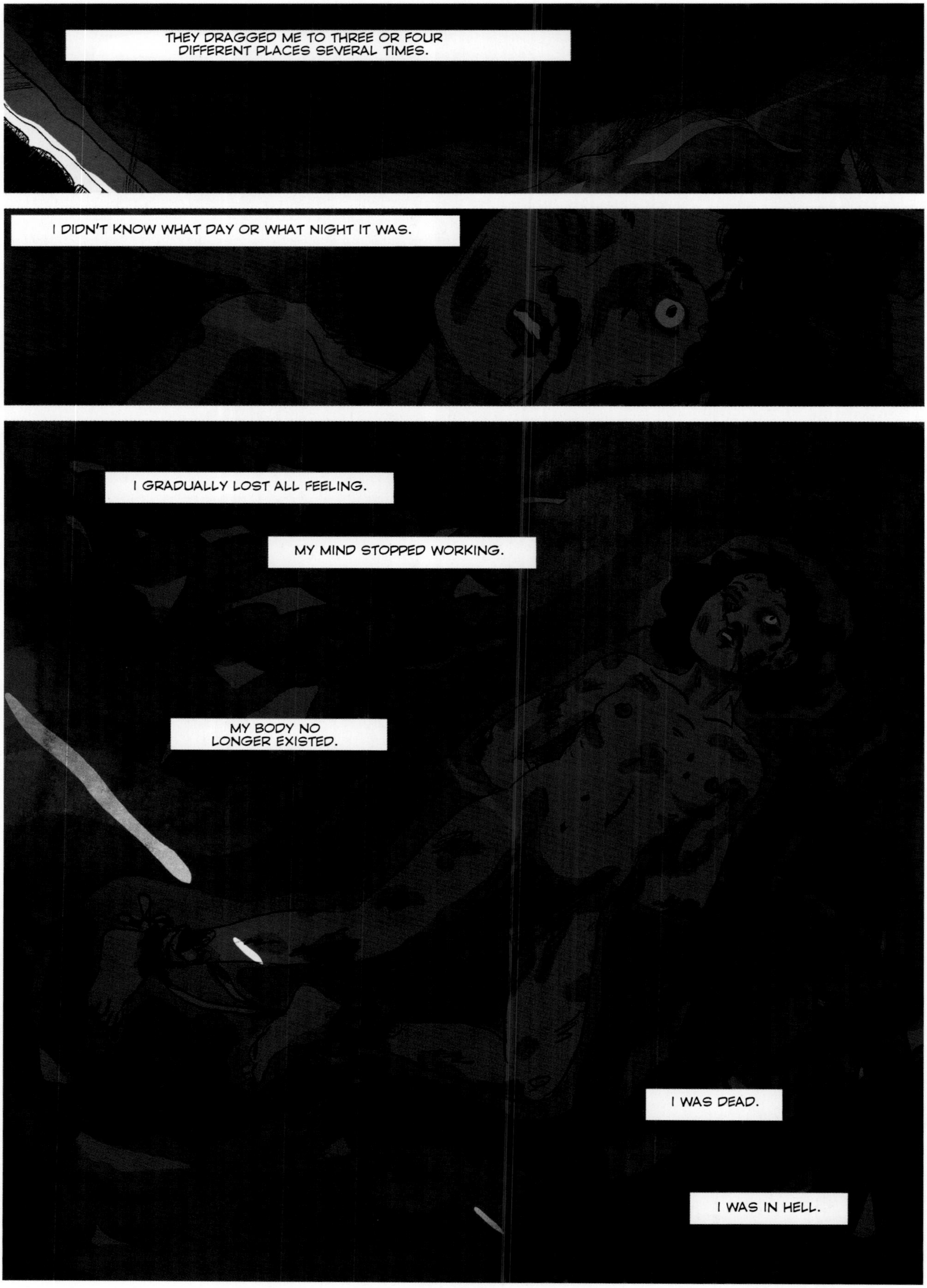
THEY DRAGGED ME TO THREE OR FOUR DIFFERENT PLACES SEVERAL TIMES.
I DIDN'T KNOW WHAT DAY OR WHAT NIGHT IT WAS.
I GRADUALLY LOST ALL FEELING.
MY MIND STOPPED WORKING.
MY BODY NO LONGER EXISTED.
I WAS DEAD.
I WAS IN HELL.

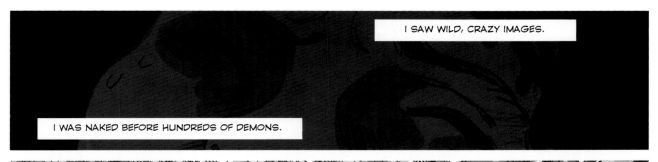

I SAW WILD, CRAZY IMAGES.

I WAS NAKED BEFORE HUNDREDS OF DEMONS.

I CALLED OUT TO THE GODS FOR HELP.

I SAW MYSELF RUNNING IN THE JUNGLE.

BUT THE DEMONS WERE ALWAYS THERE.

UGLY GHOSTS THAT REEKED OF DEATH.

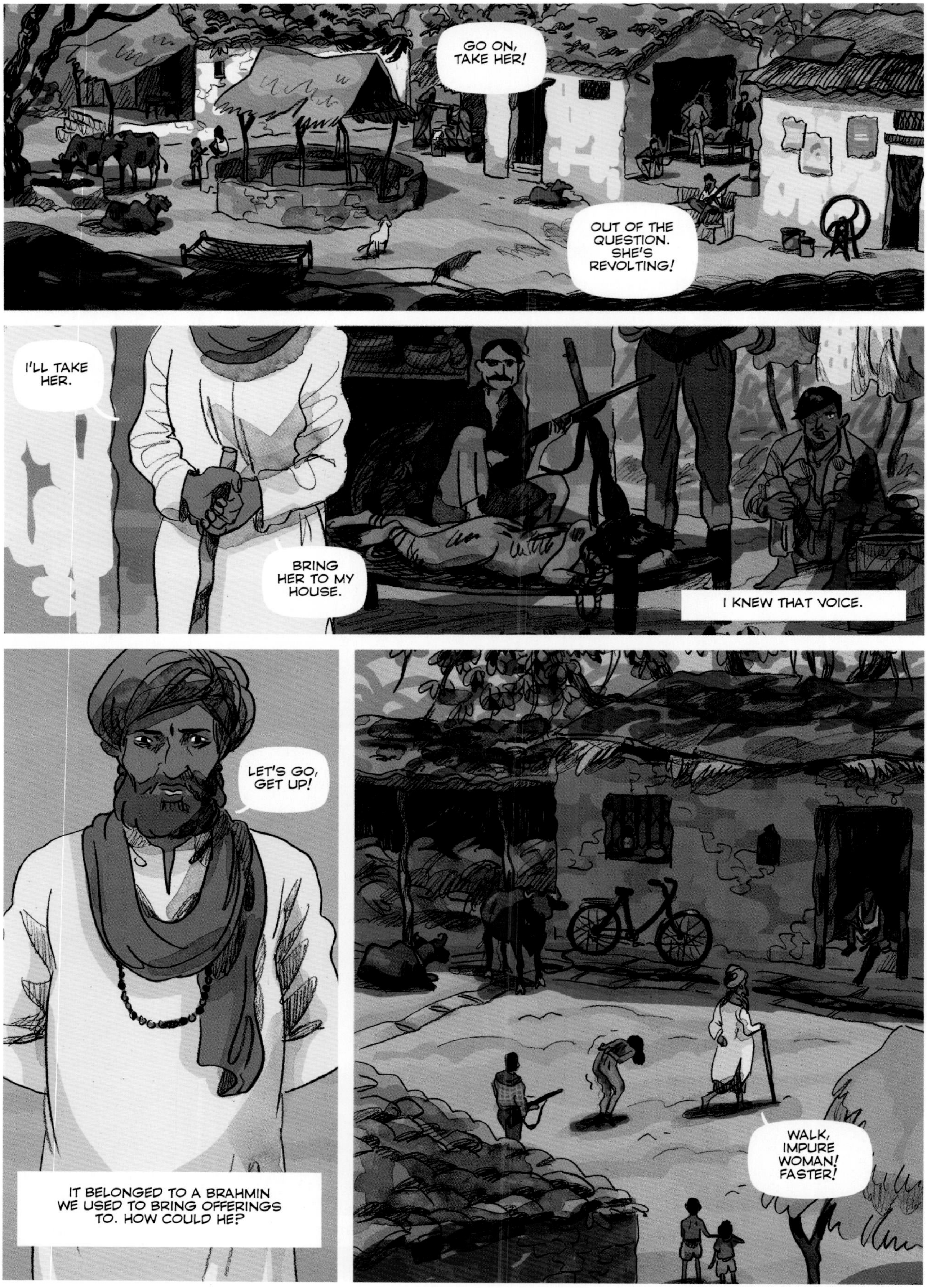
GO ON, TAKE HER!
OUT OF THE QUESTION. SHE'S REVOLTING!
I'LL TAKE HER.
BRING HER TO MY HOUSE.
I KNEW THAT VOICE.
LET'S GO, GET UP!
IT BELONGED TO A BRAHMIN WE USED TO BRING OFFERINGS TO. HOW COULD HE?
WALK, IMPURE WOMAN! FASTER!

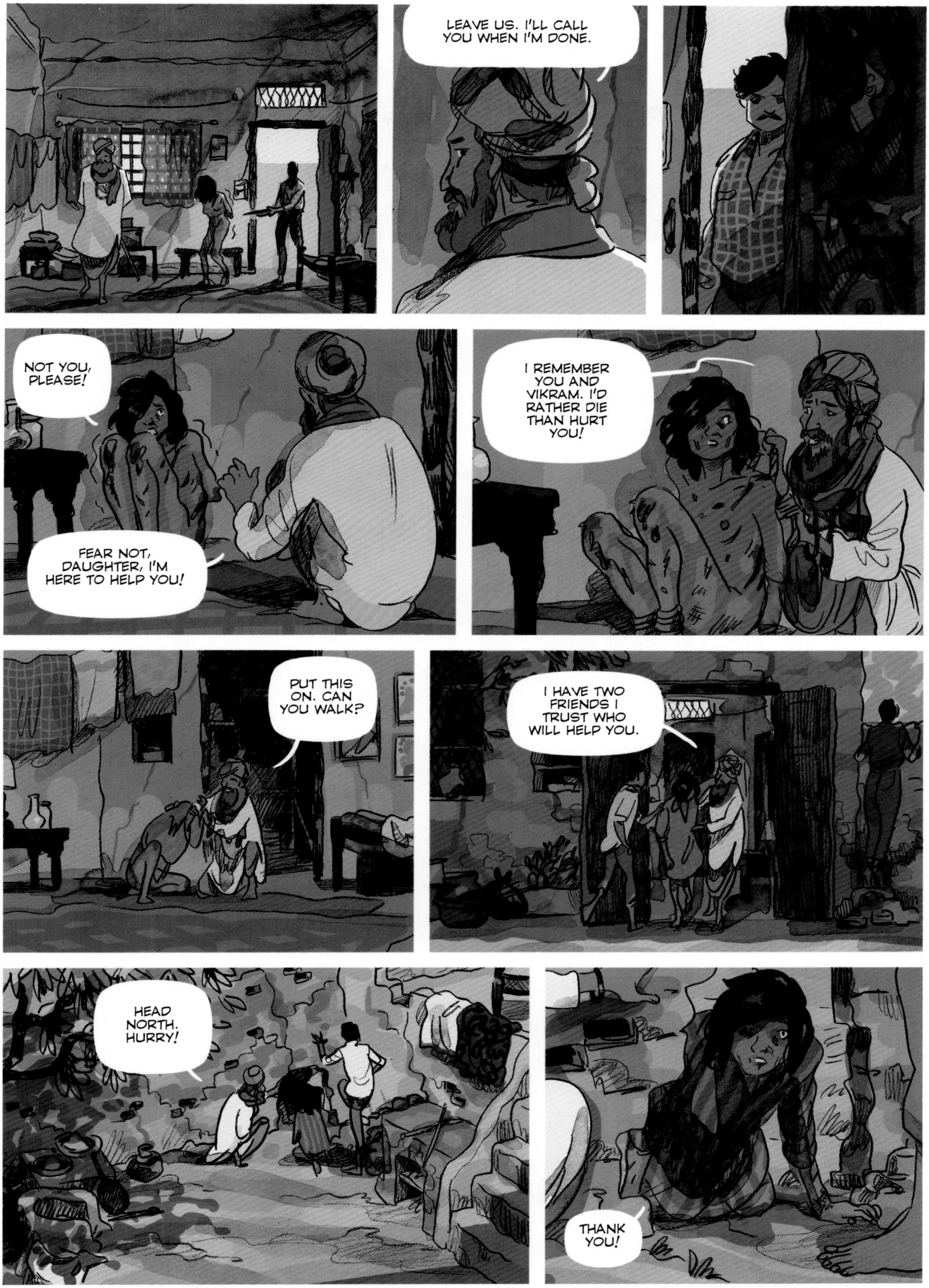
LEAVE US. I'LL CALL YOU WHEN I'M DONE.
NOT YOU, PLEASE!
FEAR NOT, DAUGHTER, I'M HERE TO HELP YOU!
I REMEMBER YOU AND VIKRAM. I'D RATHER DIE THAN HURT YOU!
PUT THIS ON. CAN YOU WALK?
I HAVE TWO FRIENDS I TRUST WHO WILL HELP YOU.
HEAD NORTH. HURRY!
THANK YOU!

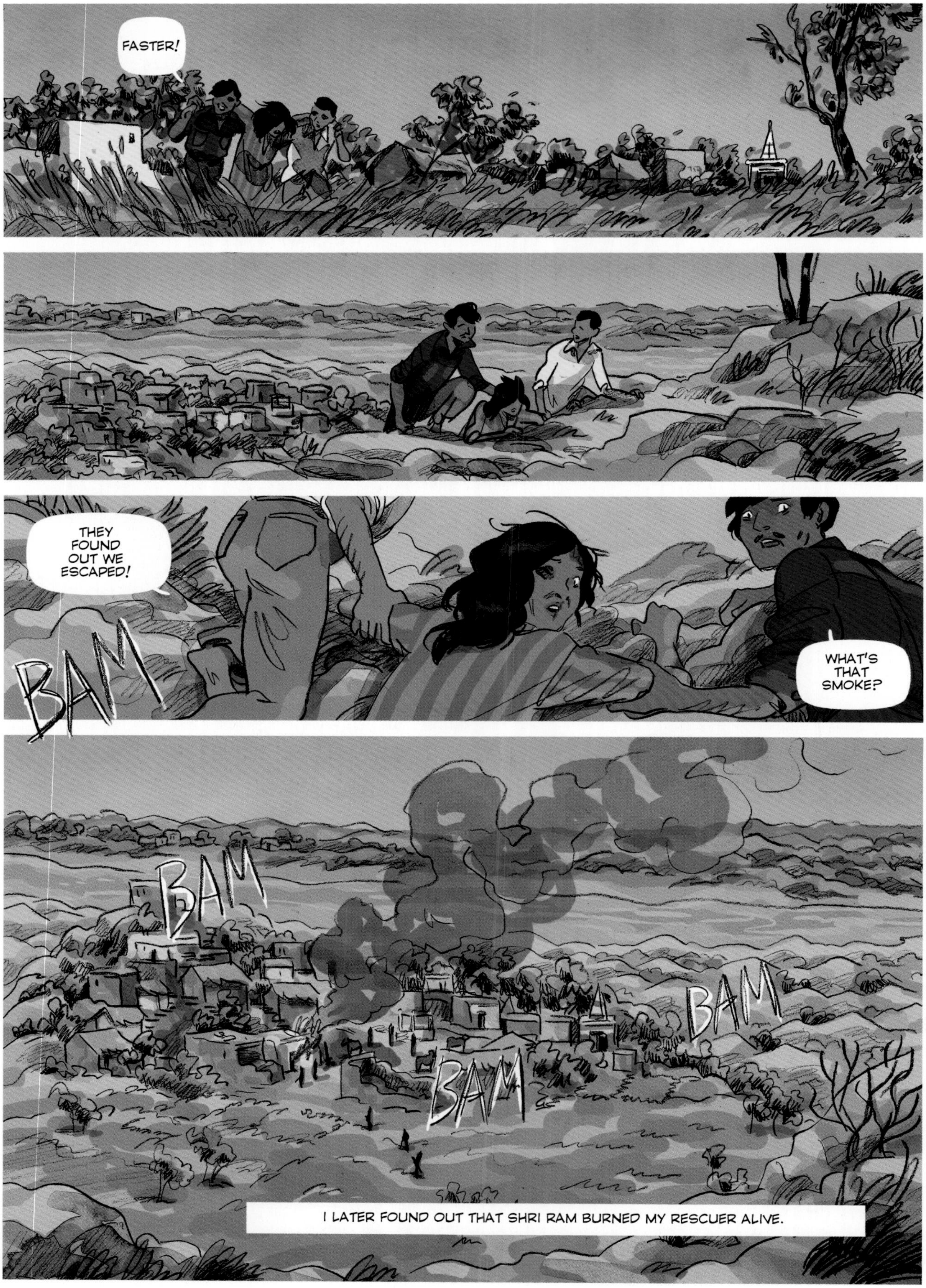
FASTER!
THEY FOUND OUT WE ESCAPED!
BAM
WHAT'S THAT SMOKE?
BAM
BAM
BAM
I LATER FOUND OUT THAT SHRI RAM BURNED MY RESCUER ALIVE.

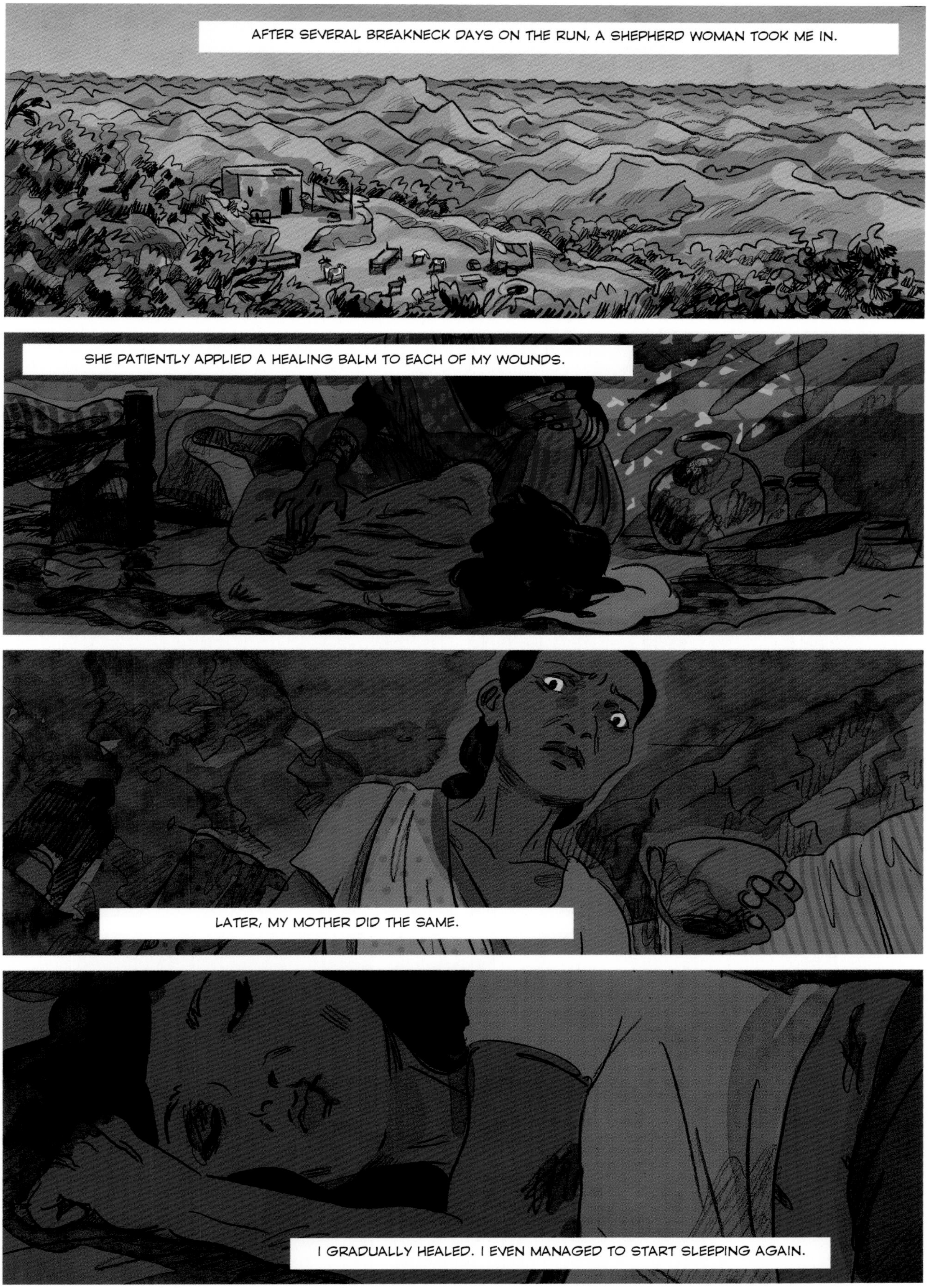
AFTER SEVERAL BREAKNECK DAYS ON THE RUN, A SHEPHERD WOMAN TOOK ME IN.
SHE PATIENTLY APPLIED A HEALING BALM TO EACH OF MY WOUNDS.
LATER, MY MOTHER DID THE SAME.
I GRADUALLY HEALED. I EVEN MANAGED TO START SLEEPING AGAIN.

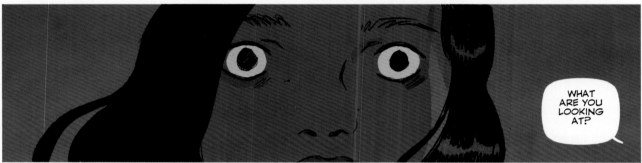

WHAT ARE YOU LOOKING AT?

THE SUN. I WONDER WHERE IT HIDES EVERY NIGHT...

IT'S NOT HIDING! WE CAN'T SEE IT ANYMORE BECAUSE THE EARTH ROTATES.

WAY OVER THERE IS THE BORDER OF OUR COUNTRY.

WHAT'S A COUNTRY?

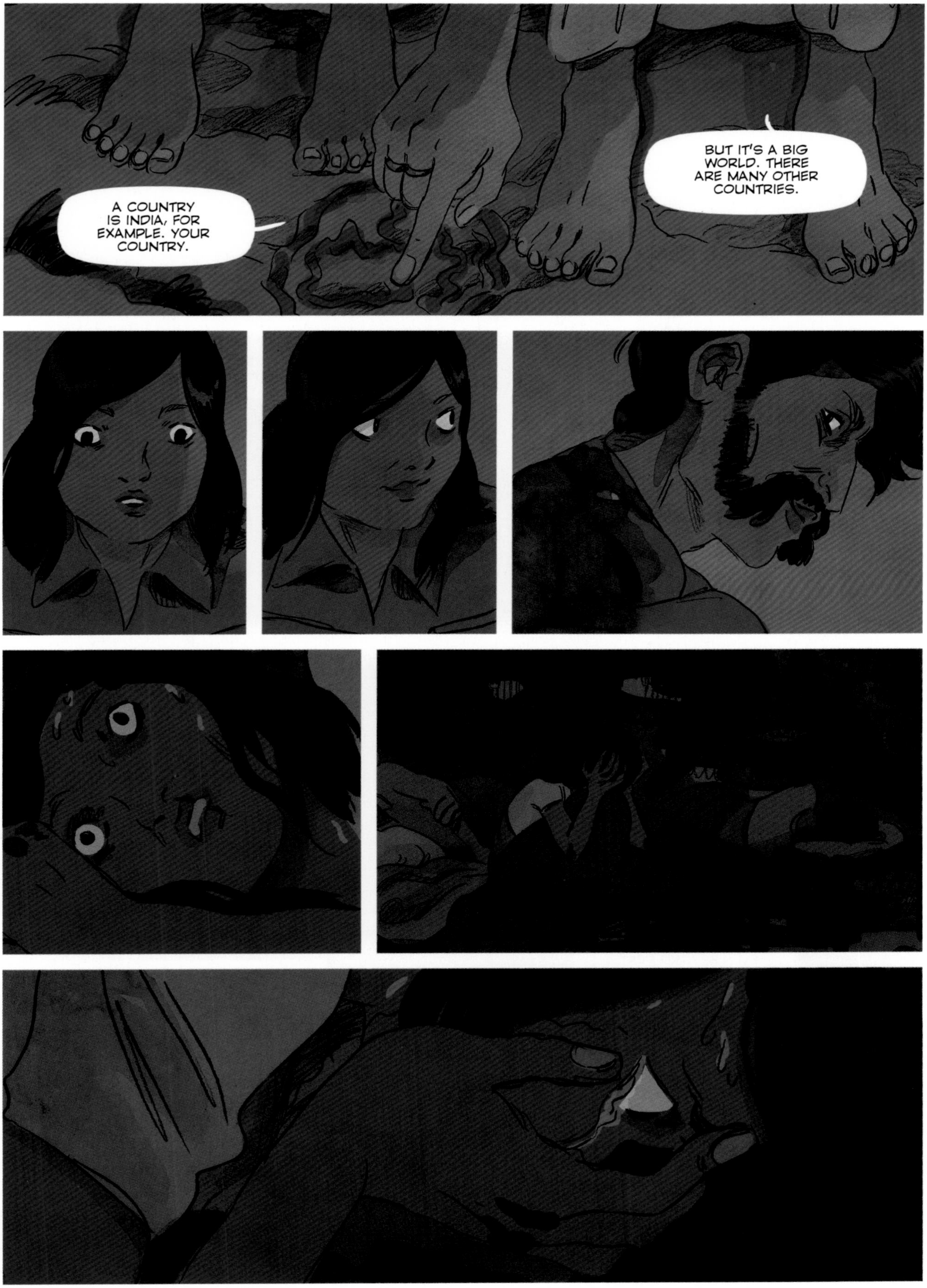
A COUNTRY IS INDIA, FOR EXAMPLE. YOUR COUNTRY.
BUT IT'S A BIG WORLD. THERE ARE MANY OTHER COUNTRIES.

CUT HIM INTO PIECES.

LET HIM LOSE HIS BODY PIECE BY PIECE WHILE ALIVE.

LET HIM SEE ME THROW THEM TO THE DOGS, DAY AFTER DAY.

LET THE DOGS EAT HIM, FIGHT OVER HIS FLESH AND GNAW ON HIS BONES.

SHRI RAM.

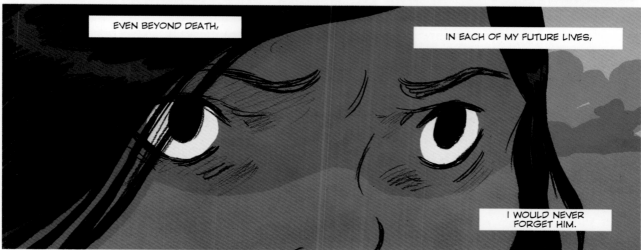

EVEN BEYOND DEATH,

IN EACH OF MY FUTURE LIVES,

I WOULD NEVER FORGET HIM.

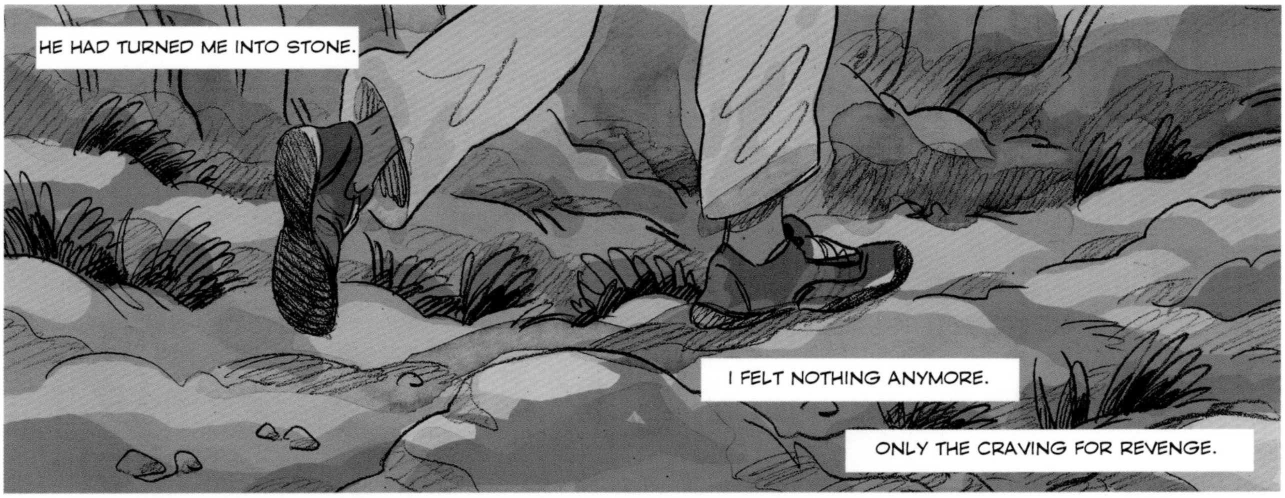
HE HAD TURNED ME INTO STONE.
I FELT NOTHING ANYMORE.
ONLY THE CRAVING FOR REVENGE.

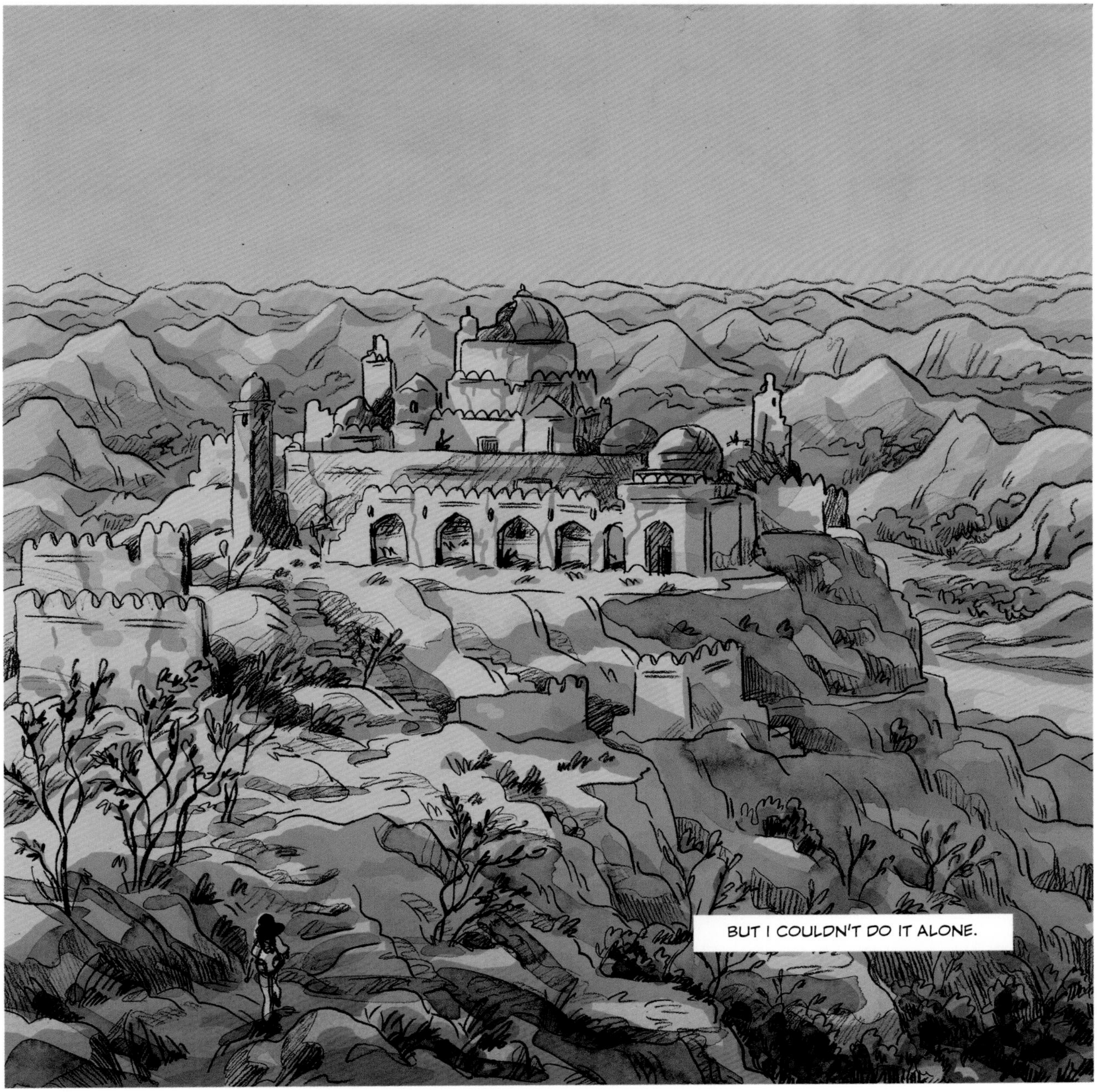
BUT I COULDN'T DO IT ALONE.

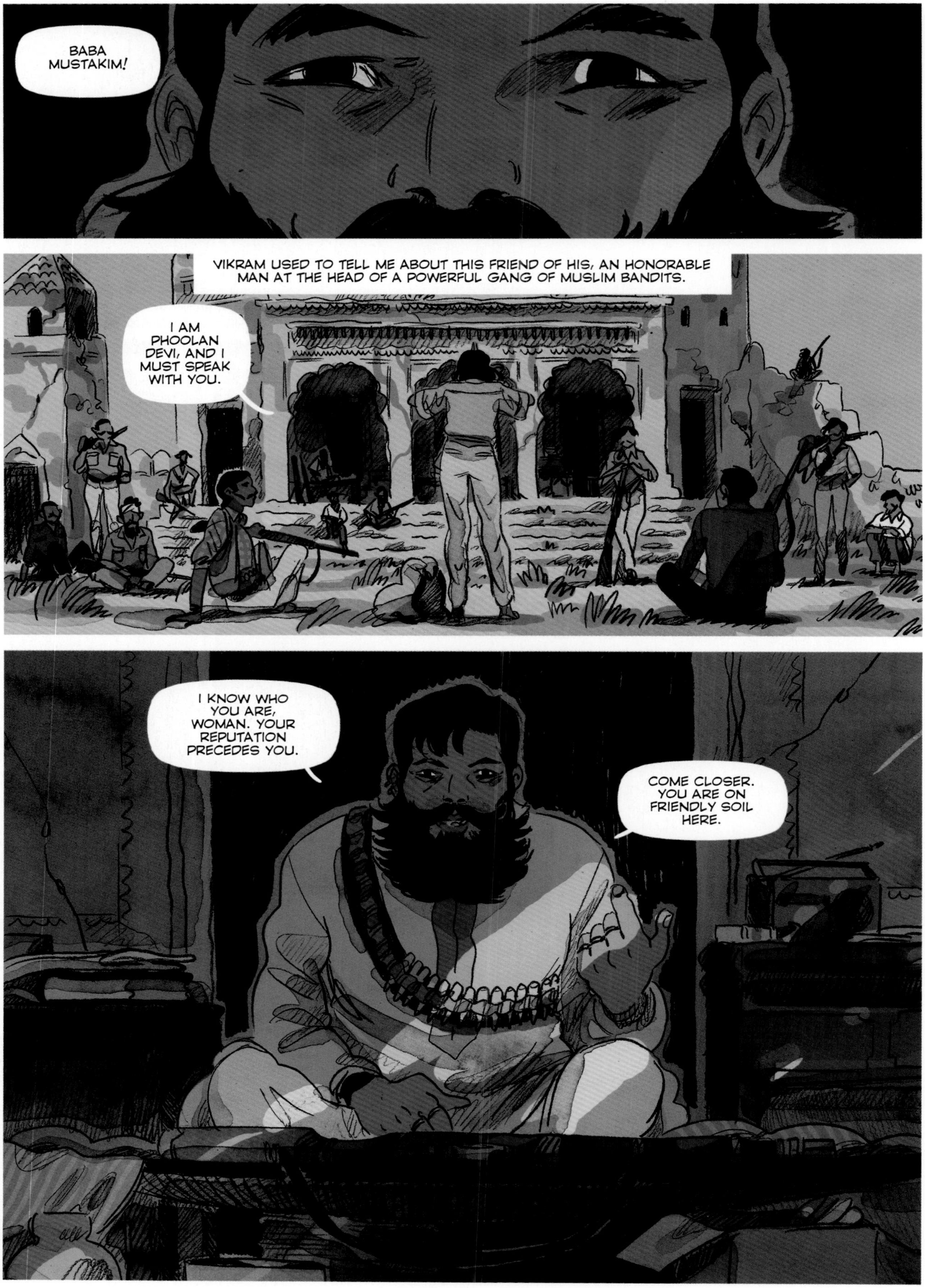
BABA MUSTAKIM!
VIKRAM USED TO TELL ME ABOUT THIS FRIEND OF HIS, AN HONORABLE MAN AT THE HEAD OF A POWERFUL GANG OF MUSLIM BANDITS.
I AM PHOOLAN DEVI, AND I MUST SPEAK WITH YOU.
I KNOW WHO YOU ARE, WOMAN. YOUR REPUTATION PRECEDES YOU.
COME CLOSER. YOU ARE ON FRIENDLY SOIL HERE.

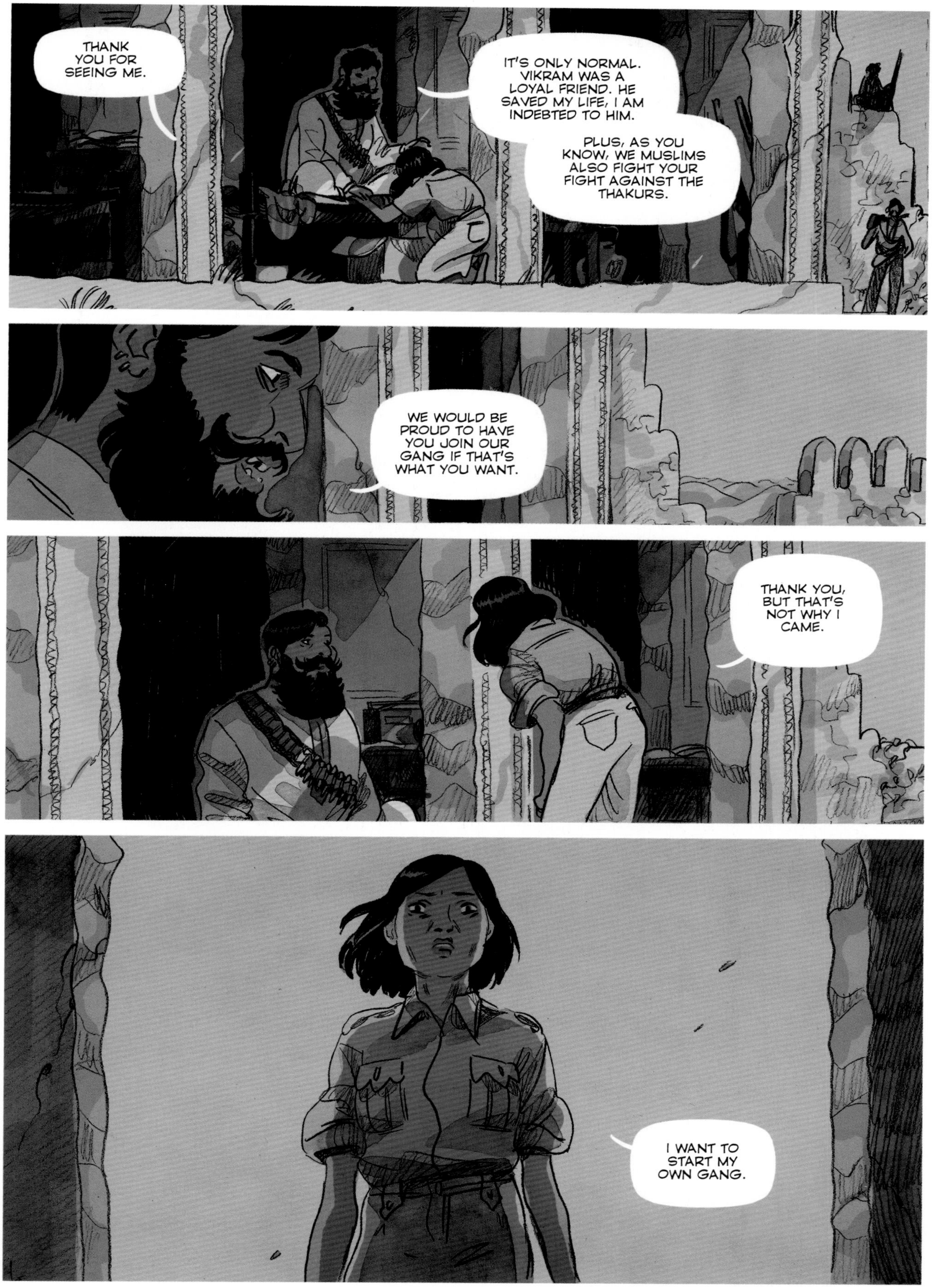
THANK YOU FOR SEEING ME.
IT'S ONLY NORMAL. VIKRAM WAS A LOYAL FRIEND. HE SAVED MY LIFE, I AM INDEBTED TO HIM.
PLUS, AS YOU KNOW, WE MUSLIMS ALSO FIGHT YOUR FIGHT AGAINST THE THAKURS.
WE WOULD BE PROUD TO HAVE YOU JOIN OUR GANG IF THAT'S WHAT YOU WANT.
THANK YOU, BUT THAT'S NOT WHY I CAME.
I WANT TO START MY OWN GANG.

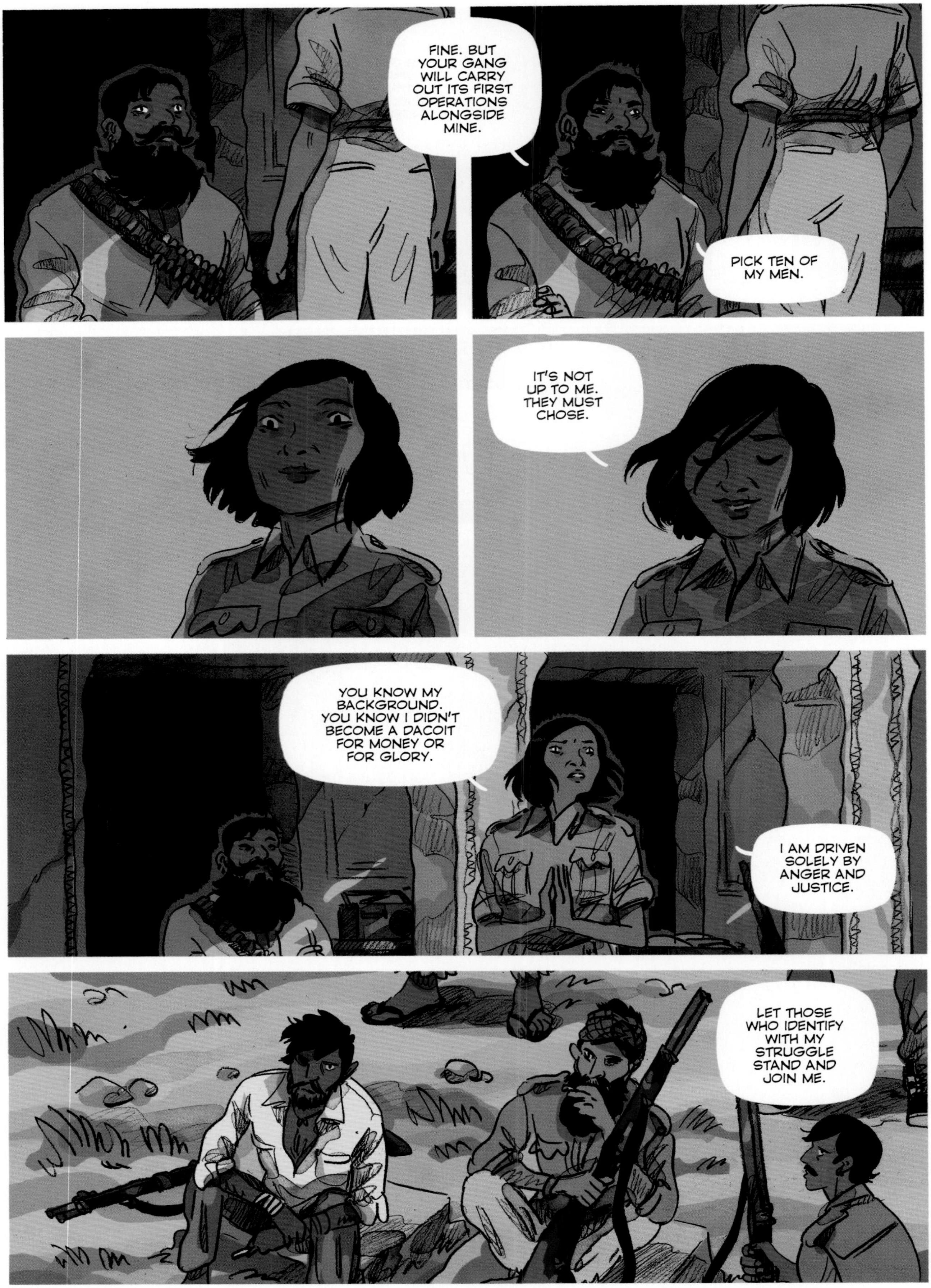
FINE. BUT YOUR GANG WILL CARRY OUT ITS FIRST OPERATIONS ALONGSIDE MINE.
PICK TEN OF MY MEN.
IT'S NOT UP TO ME. THEY MUST CHOSE.
YOU KNOW MY BACKGROUND. YOU KNOW I DIDN'T BECOME A DACOIT FOR MONEY OR FOR GLORY.
I AM DRIVEN SOLELY BY ANGER AND JUSTICE.
LET THOSE WHO IDENTIFY WITH MY STRUGGLE STAND AND JOIN ME.

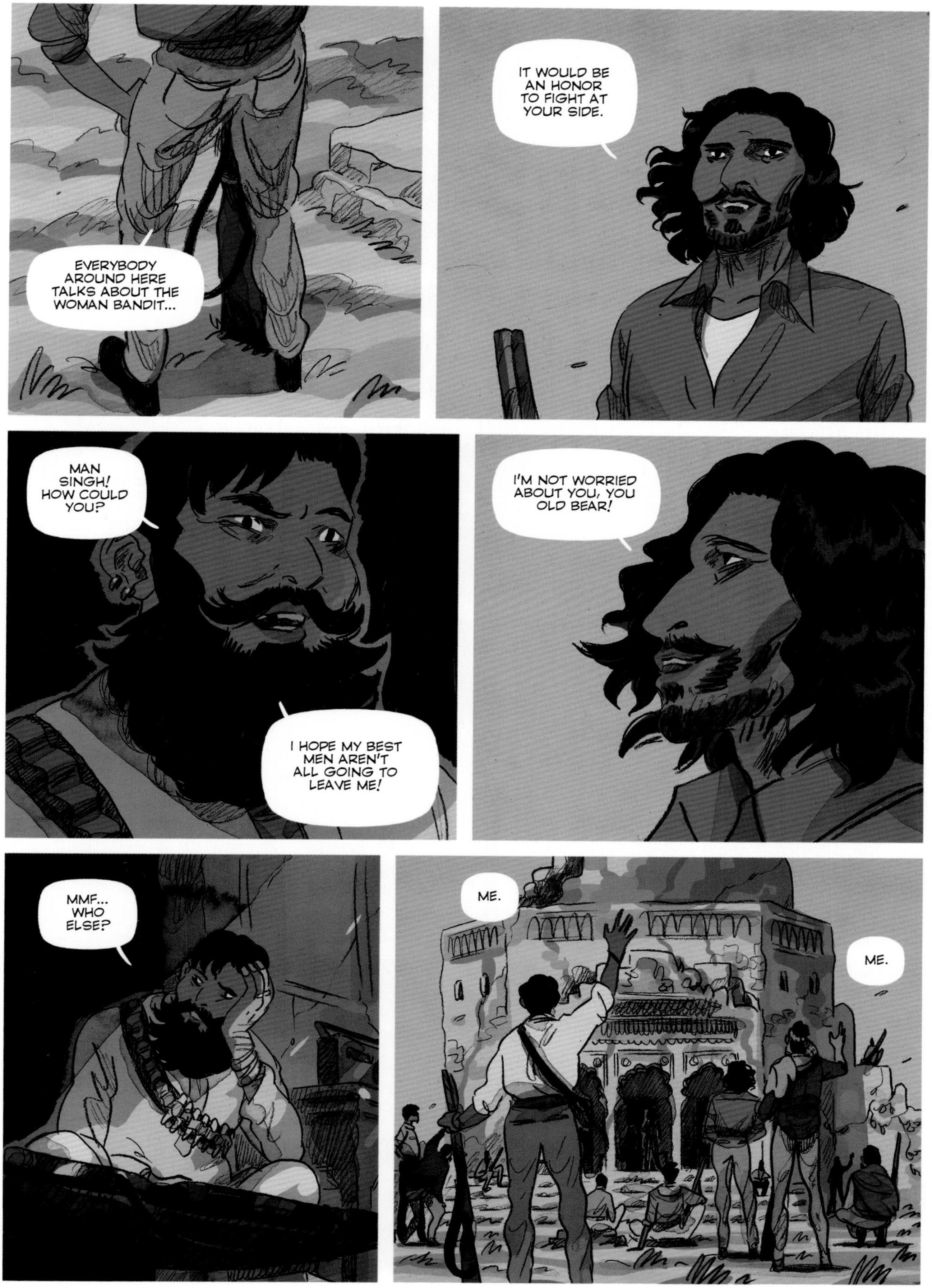
EVERYBODY AROUND HERE TALKS ABOUT THE WOMAN BANDIT...
IT WOULD BE AN HONOR TO FIGHT AT YOUR SIDE.
MAN SINGH! HOW COULD YOU?
I HOPE MY BEST MEN AREN'T ALL GOING TO LEAVE ME!
I'M NOT WORRIED ABOUT YOU, YOU OLD BEAR!
MMF... WHO ELSE?
ME.
ME.

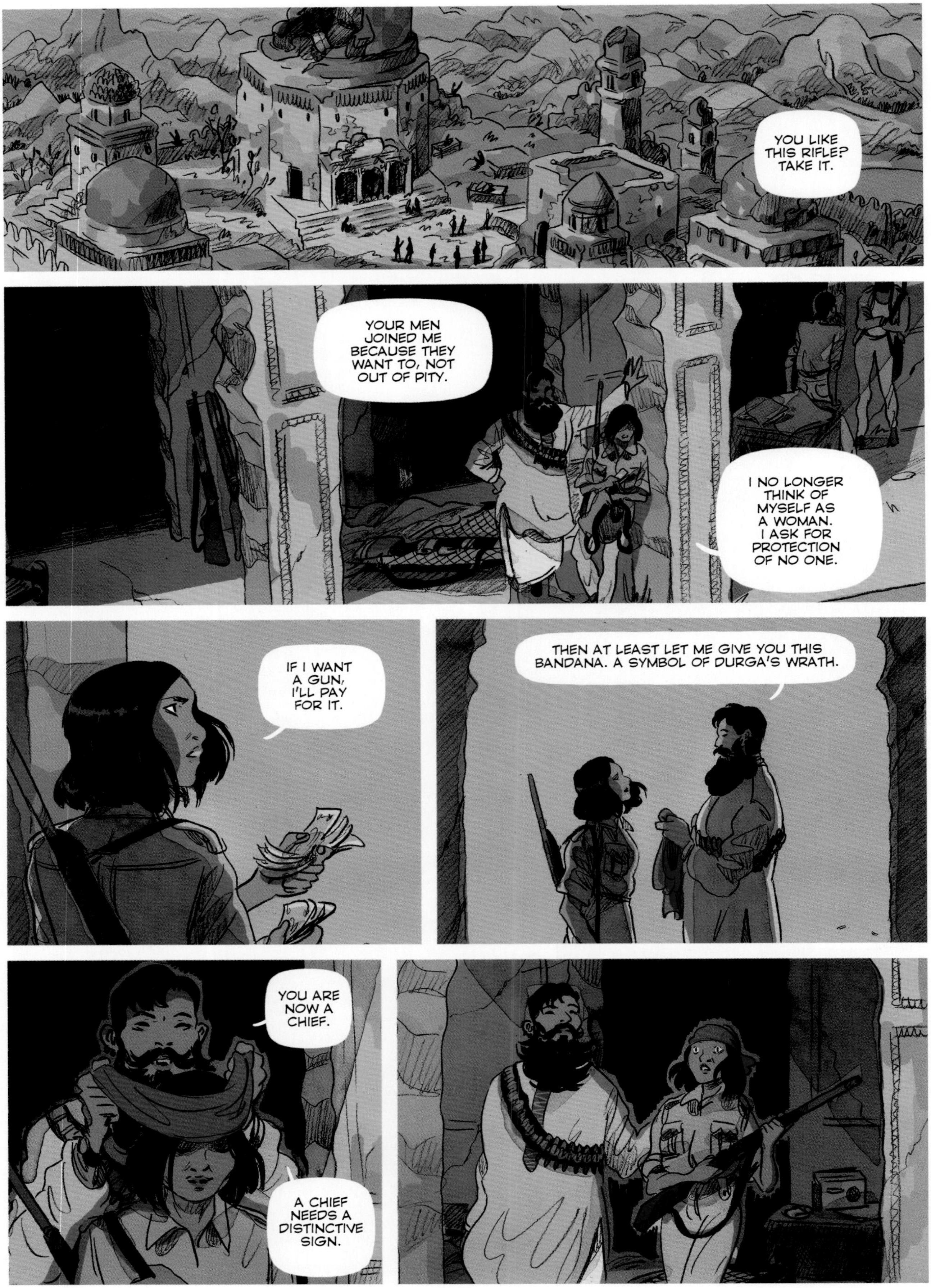
YOU LIKE THIS RIFLE? TAKE IT.
YOUR MEN JOINED ME BECAUSE THEY WANT TO, NOT OUT OF PITY.
I NO LONGER THINK OF MYSELF AS A WOMAN. I ASK FOR PROTECTION OF NO ONE.
IF I WANT A GUN, I'LL PAY FOR IT.
THEN AT LEAST LET ME GIVE YOU THIS BANDANA. A SYMBOL OF DURGA'S WRATH.
YOU ARE NOW A CHIEF.
A CHIEF NEEDS A DISTINCTIVE SIGN.

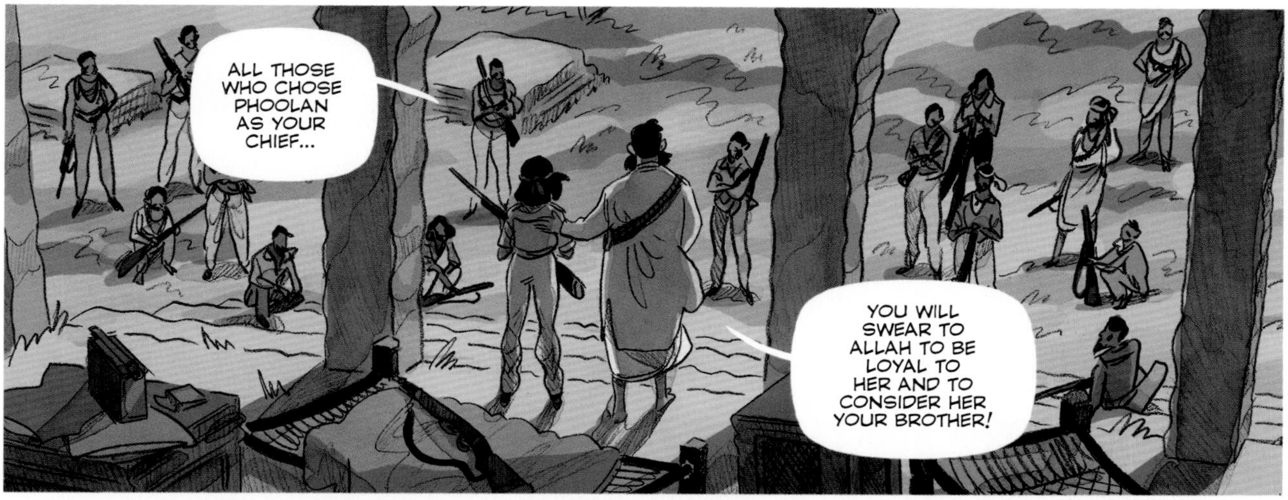
ALL THOSE WHO CHOSE PHOOLAN AS YOUR CHIEF...
YOU WILL SWEAR TO ALLAH TO BE LOYAL TO HER AND TO CONSIDER HER YOUR BROTHER!

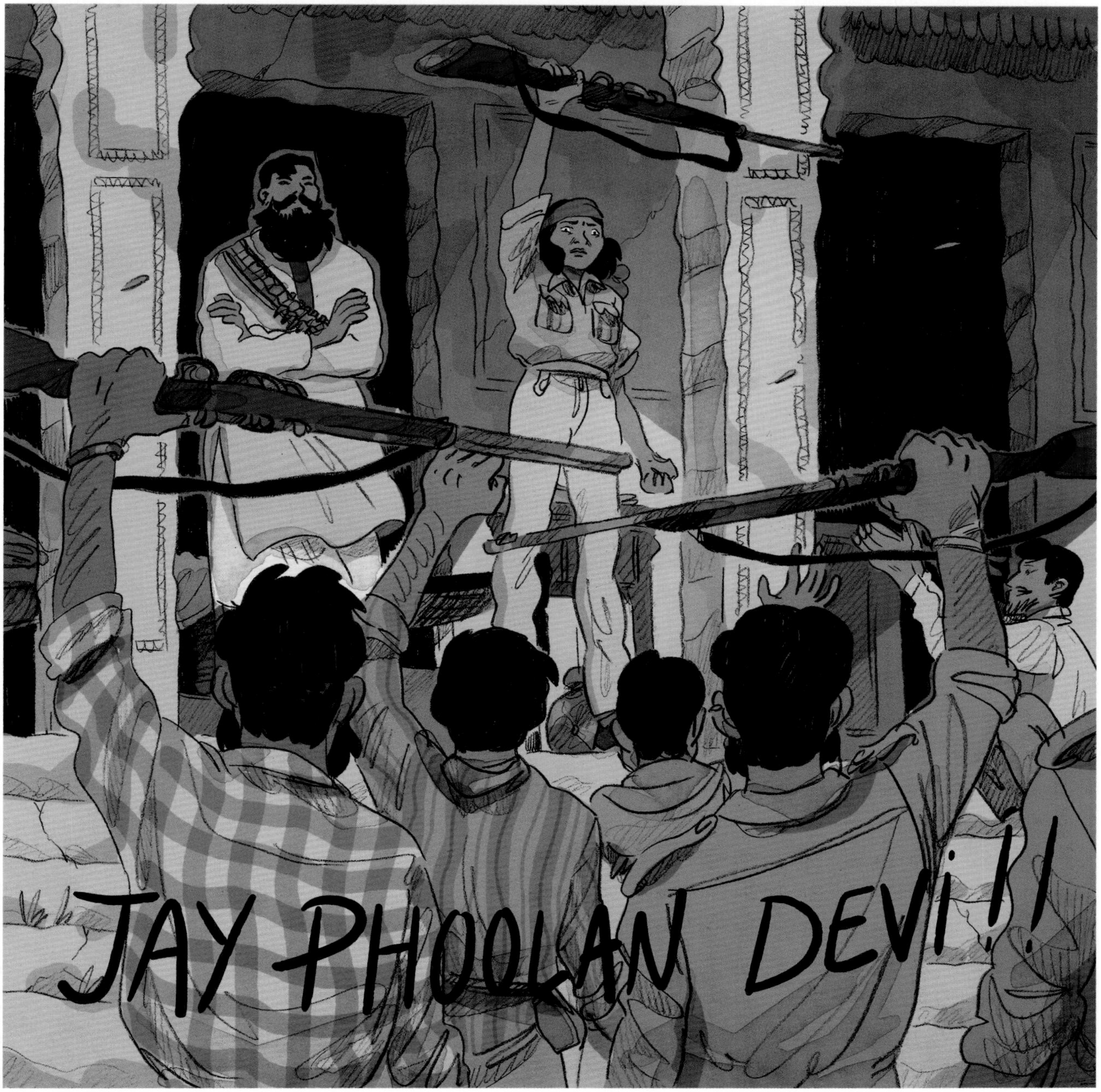
JAY PHOOLAN DEVI!!

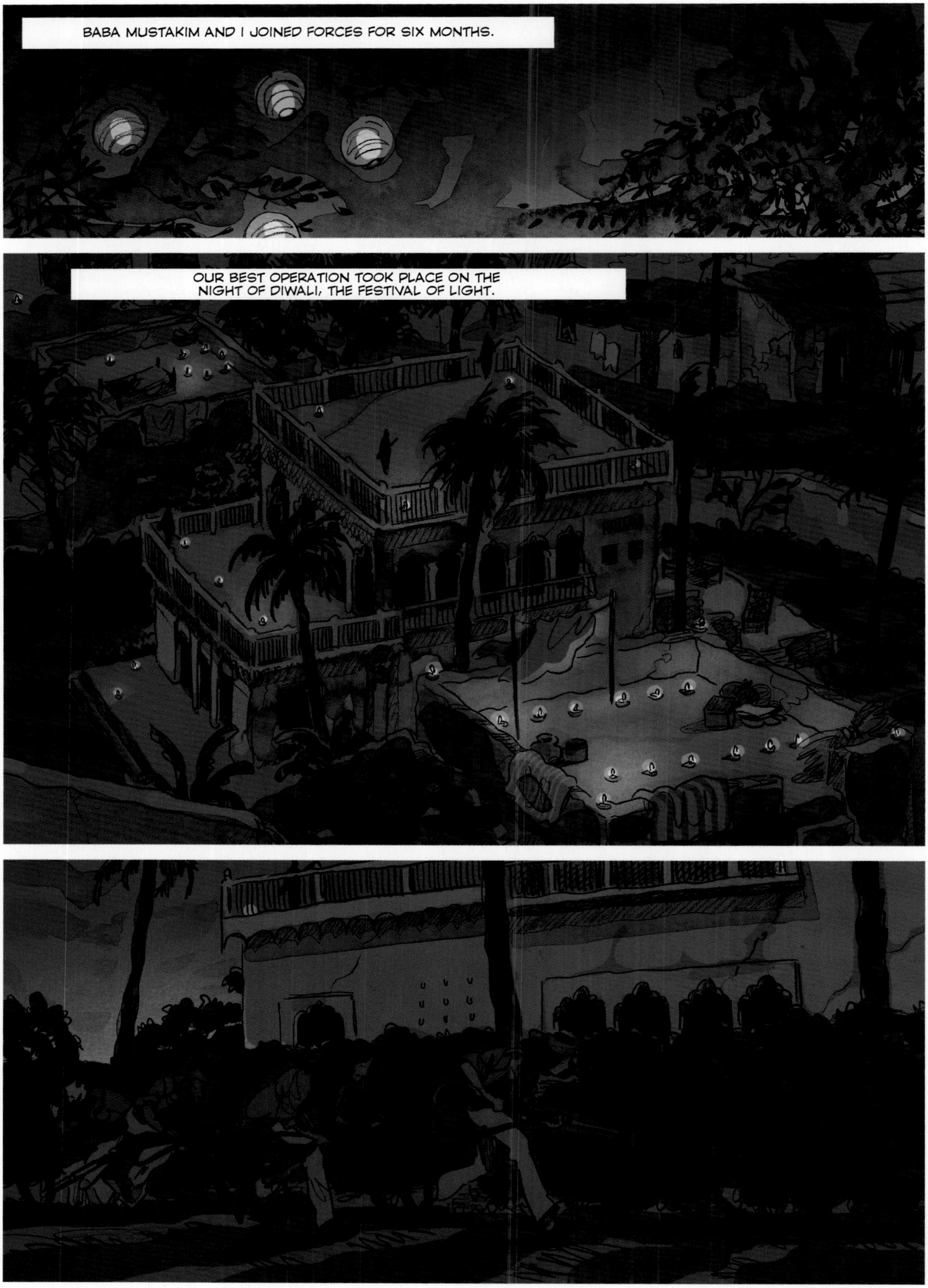
BABA MUSTAKIM AND I JOINED FORCES FOR SIX MONTHS.
OUR BEST OPERATION TOOK PLACE ON THE NIGHT OF DIWALI, THE FESTIVAL OF LIGHT.

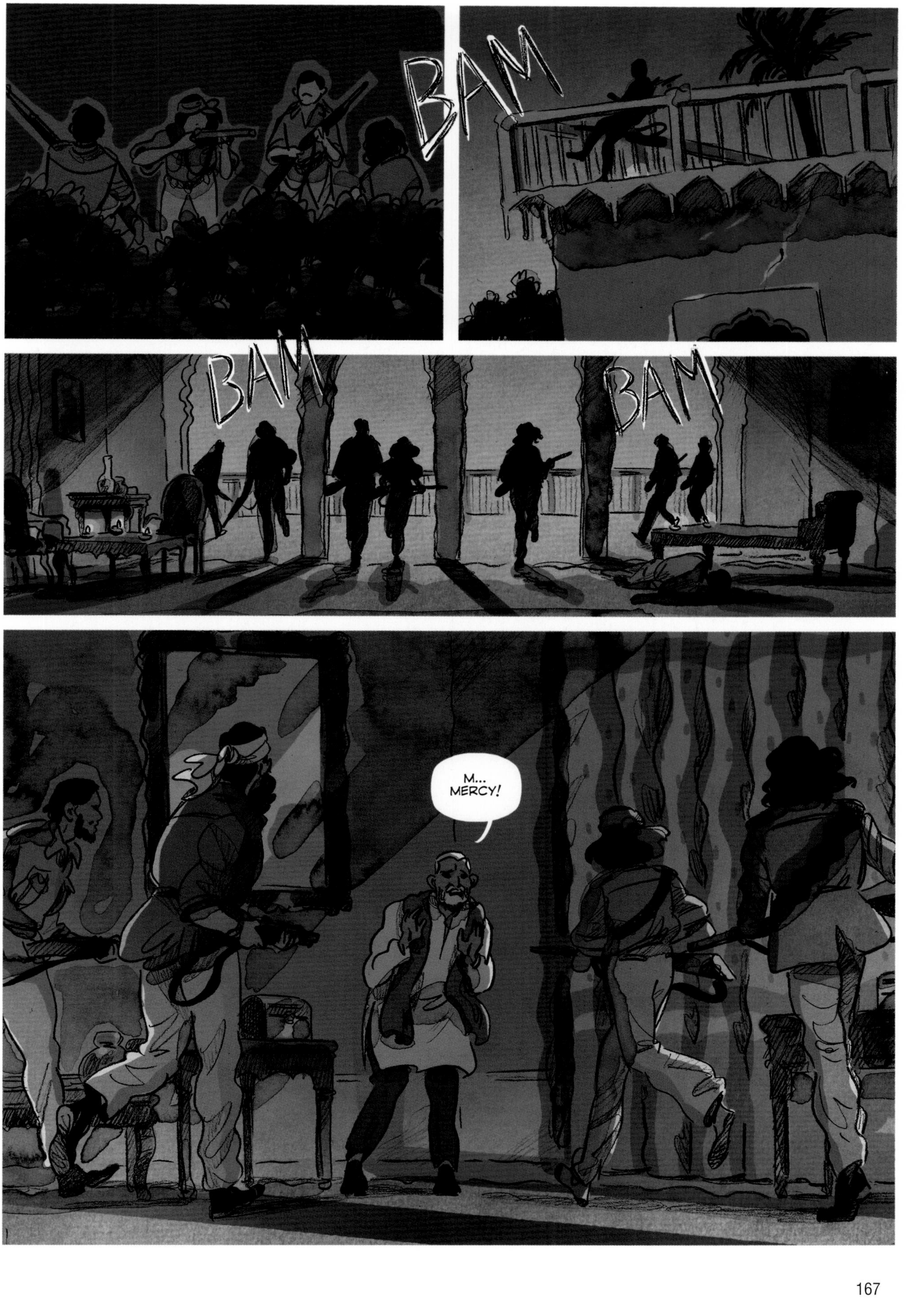
BAM
BAM
BAM
M... MERCY!

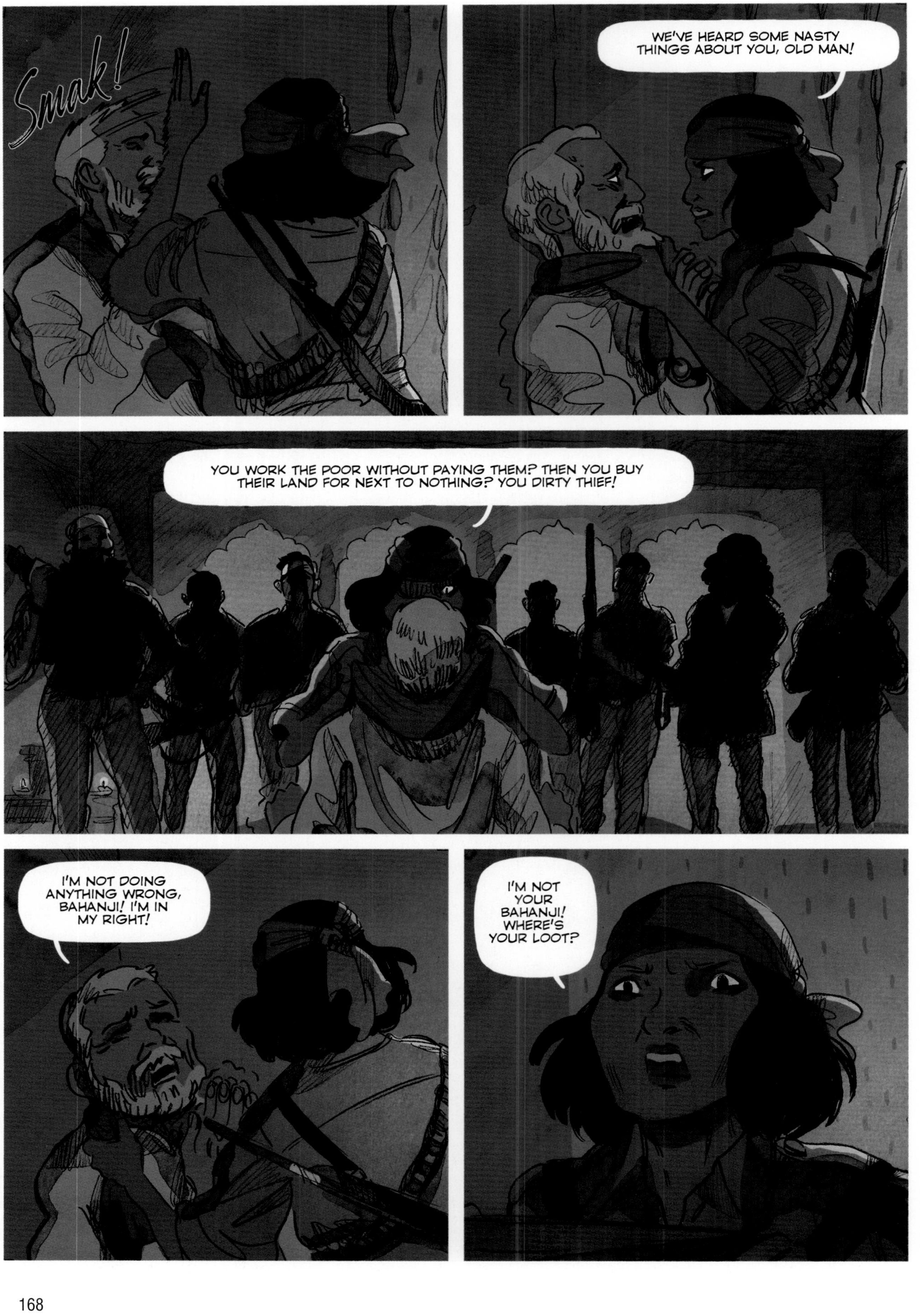
Smak!
WE'VE HEARD SOME NASTY THINGS ABOUT YOU, OLD MAN!
YOU WORK THE POOR WITHOUT PAYING THEM? THEN YOU BUY THEIR LAND FOR NEXT TO NOTHING? YOU DIRTY THIEF!
I'M NOT DOING ANYTHING WRONG, BAHANJI! I'M IN MY RIGHT!
I'M NOT YOUR BAHANJI! WHERE'S YOUR LOOT?

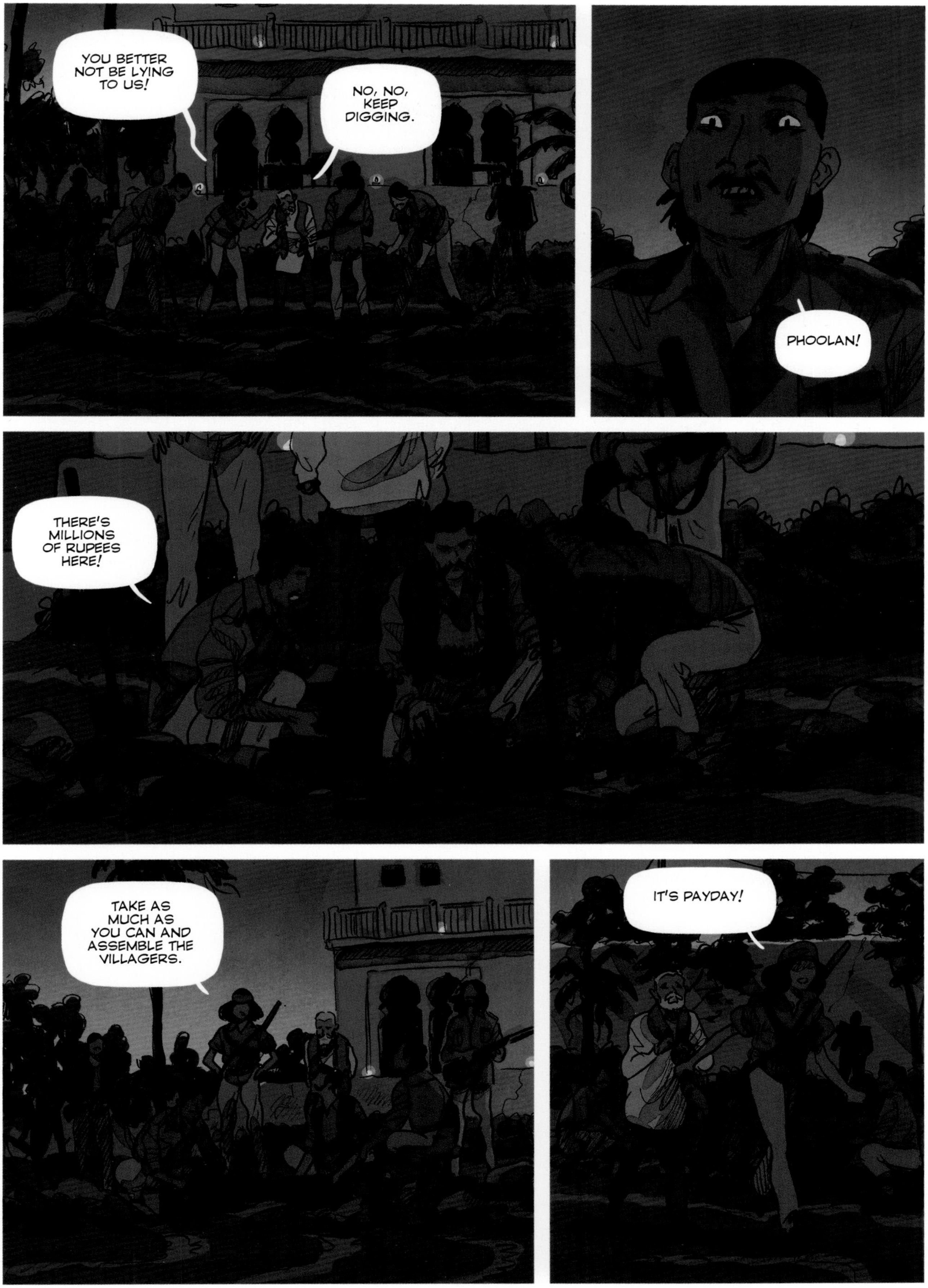

YOU BETTER NOT BE LYING TO US!
NO, NO, KEEP DIGGING.
PHOOLAN!
THERE'S MILLIONS OF RUPEES HERE!
TAKE AS MUCH AS YOU CAN AND ASSEMBLE THE VILLAGERS.
IT'S PAYDAY!

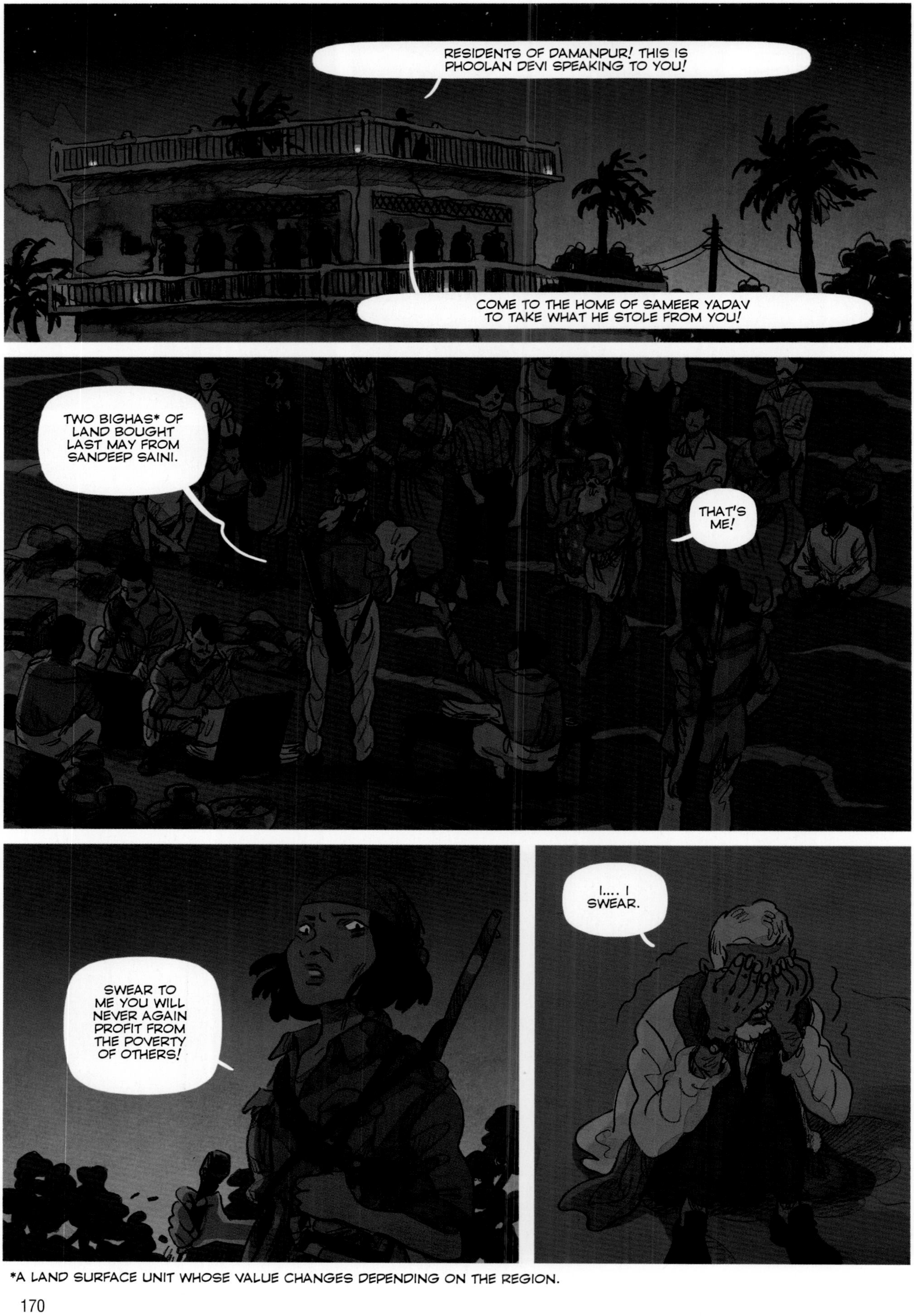
RESIDENTS OF DAMANPUR! THIS IS PHOOLAN DEVI SPEAKING TO YOU!
COME TO THE HOME OF SAMEER YADAV TO TAKE WHAT HE STOLE FROM YOU!
TWO BIGHAS* OF LAND BOUGHT LAST MAY FROM SANDEEP SAINI.
THAT'S ME!
SWEAR TO ME YOU WILL NEVER AGAIN PROFIT FROM THE POVERTY OF OTHERS!
I.... I SWEAR.

*A LAND SURFACE UNIT WHOSE VALUE CHANGES DEPENDING ON THE REGION.

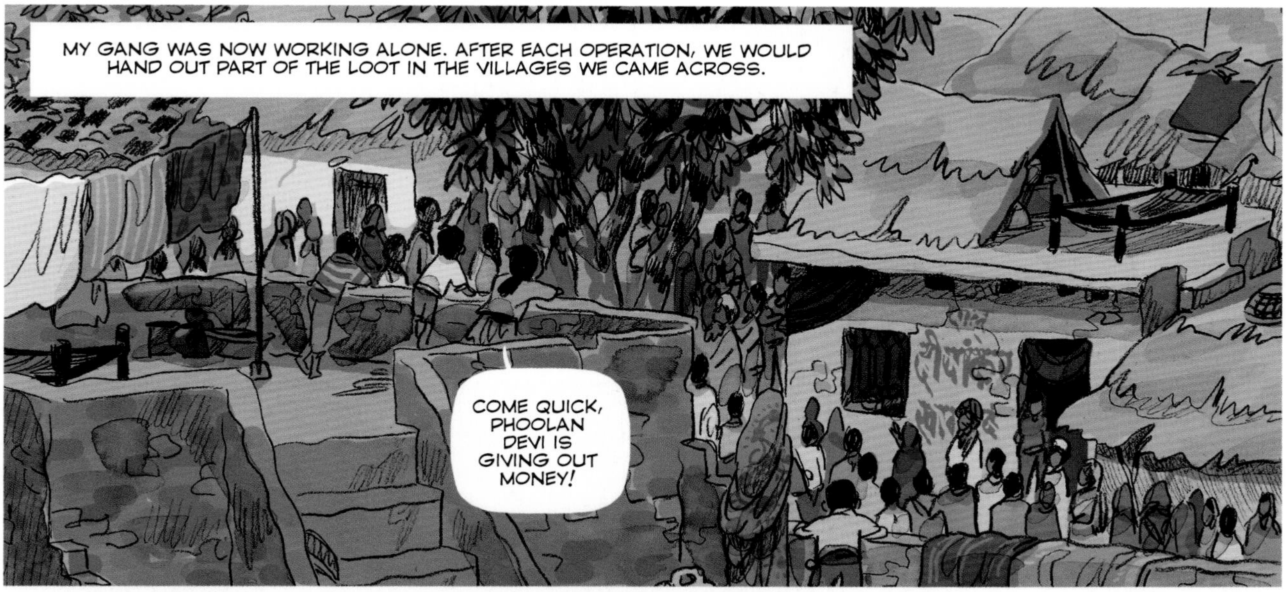
MY GANG WAS NOW WORKING ALONE. AFTER EACH OPERATION, WE WOULD HAND OUT PART OF THE LOOT IN THE VILLAGES WE CAME ACROSS.
COME QUICK, PHOOLAN DEVI IS GIVING OUT MONEY!

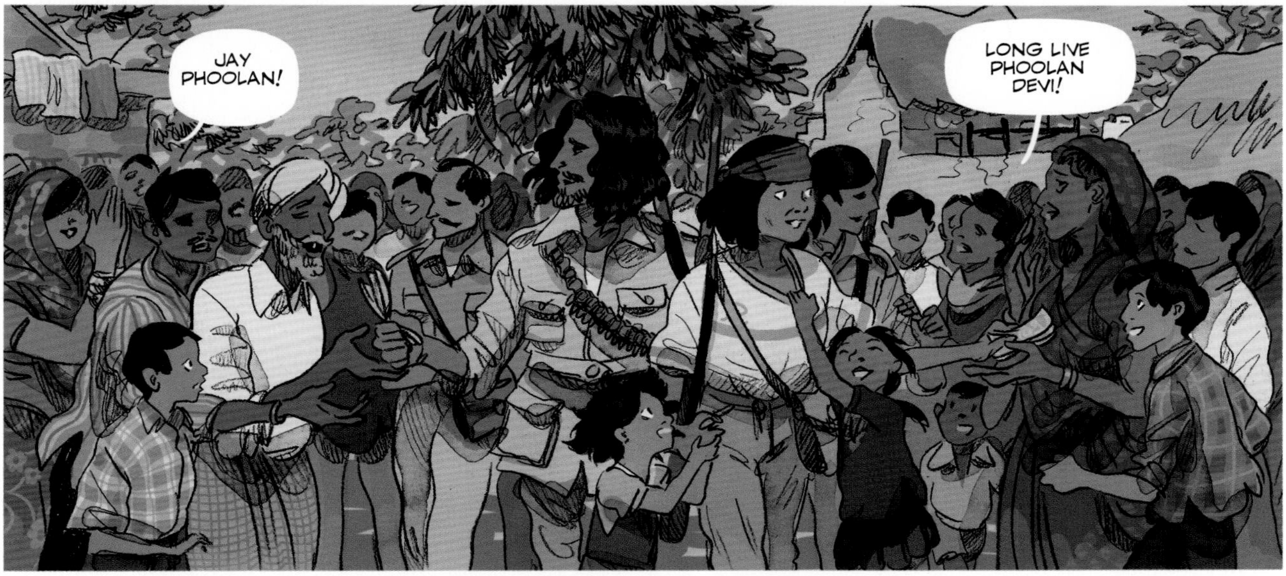
JAY PHOOLAN!
LONG LIVE PHOOLAN DEVI!

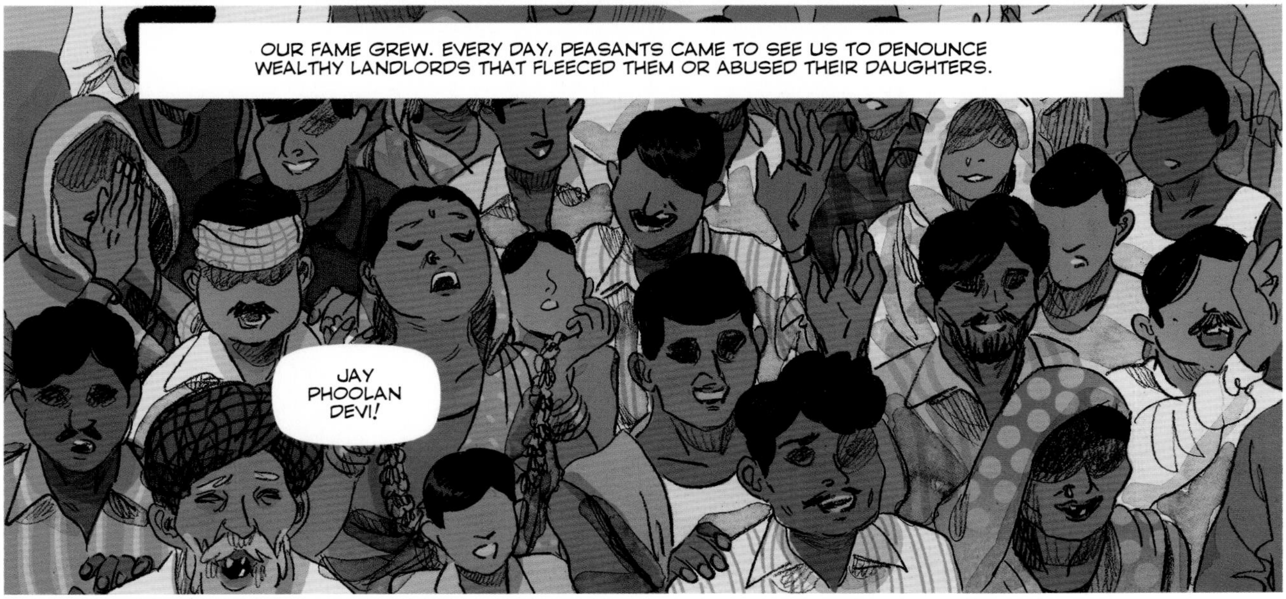
OUR FAME GREW. EVERY DAY, PEASANTS CAME TO SEE US TO DENOUNCE WEALTHY LANDLORDS THAT FLEECED THEM OR ABUSED THEIR DAUGHTERS.
JAY PHOOLAN DEVI!

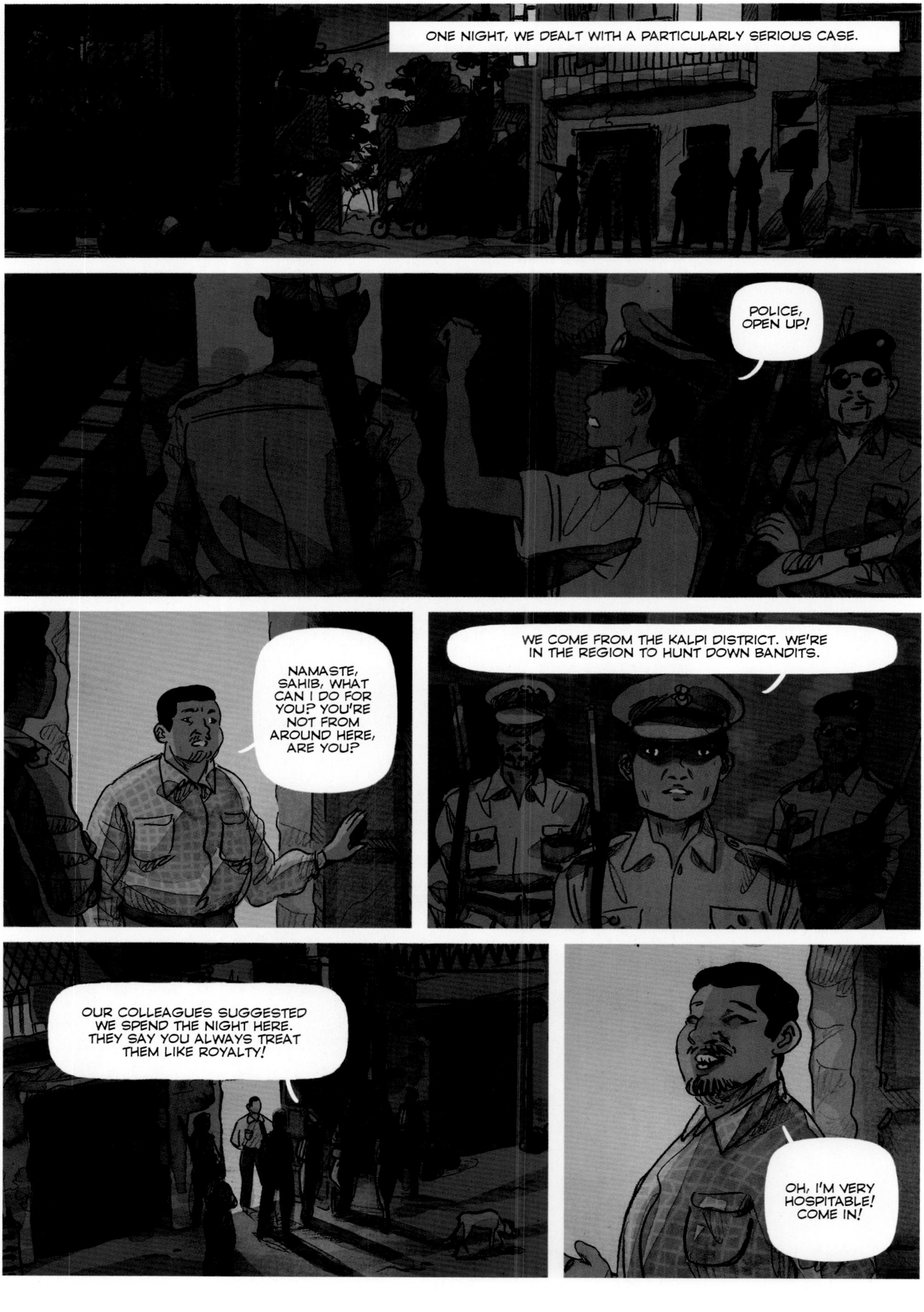
ONE NIGHT, WE DEALT WITH A PARTICULARLY SERIOUS CASE.
POLICE, OPEN UP!
NAMASTE, SAHIB, WHAT CAN I DO FOR YOU? YOU'RE NOT FROM AROUND HERE, ARE YOU?
WE COME FROM THE KALPI DISTRICT. WE'RE IN THE REGION TO HUNT DOWN BANDITS.
OUR COLLEAGUES SUGGESTED WE SPEND THE NIGHT HERE. THEY SAY YOU ALWAYS TREAT THEM LIKE ROYALTY!
OH, I'M VERY HOSPITABLE! COME IN!

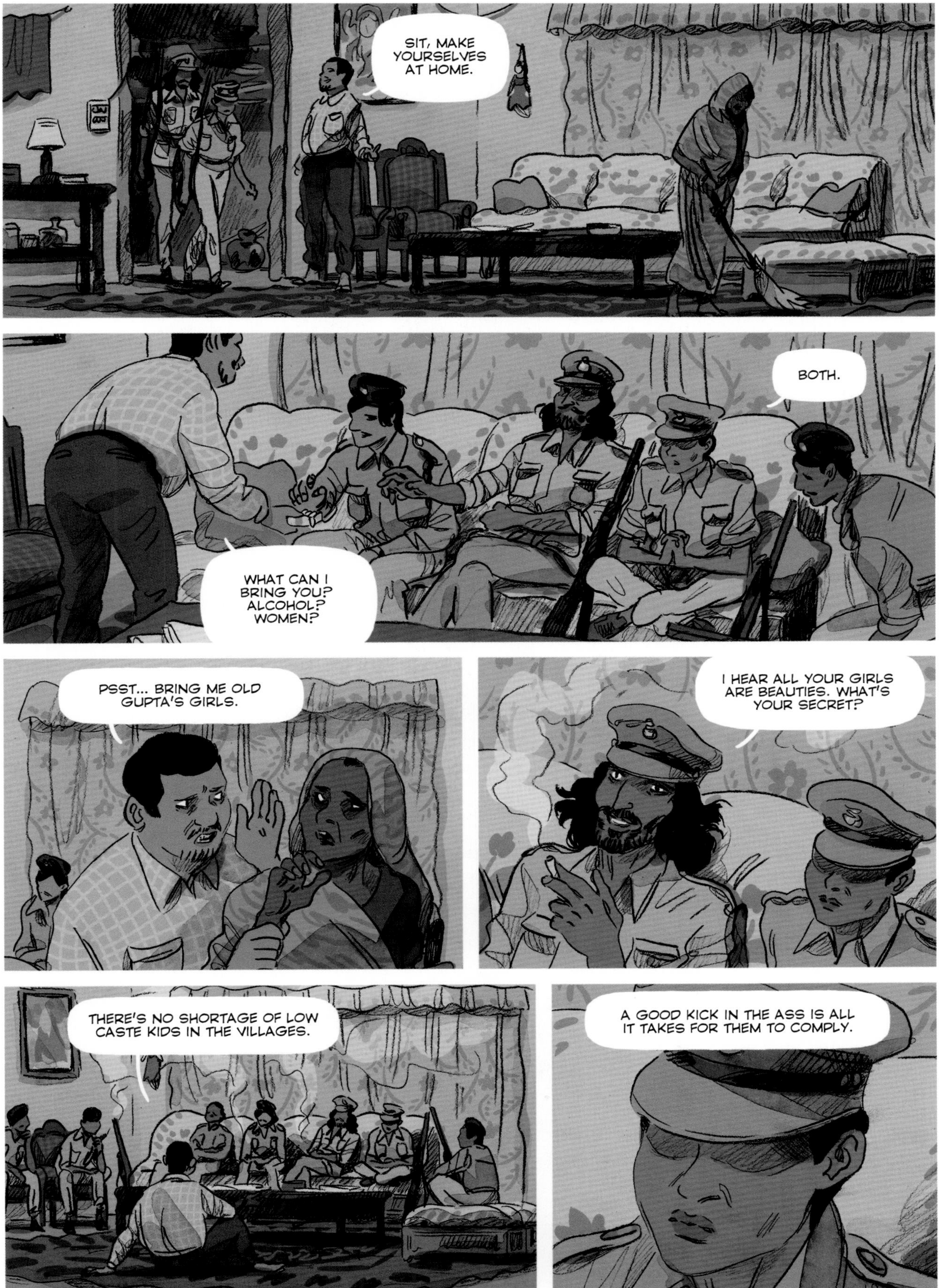
SIT, MAKE YOURSELVES AT HOME.
WHAT CAN I BRING YOU? ALCOHOL? WOMEN?
BOTH.
PSST... BRING ME OLD GUPTA'S GIRLS.
I HEAR ALL YOUR GIRLS ARE BEAUTIES. WHAT'S YOUR SECRET?
THERE'S NO SHORTAGE OF LOW CASTE KIDS IN THE VILLAGES.
A GOOD KICK IN THE ASS IS ALL IT TAKES FOR THEM TO COMPLY.

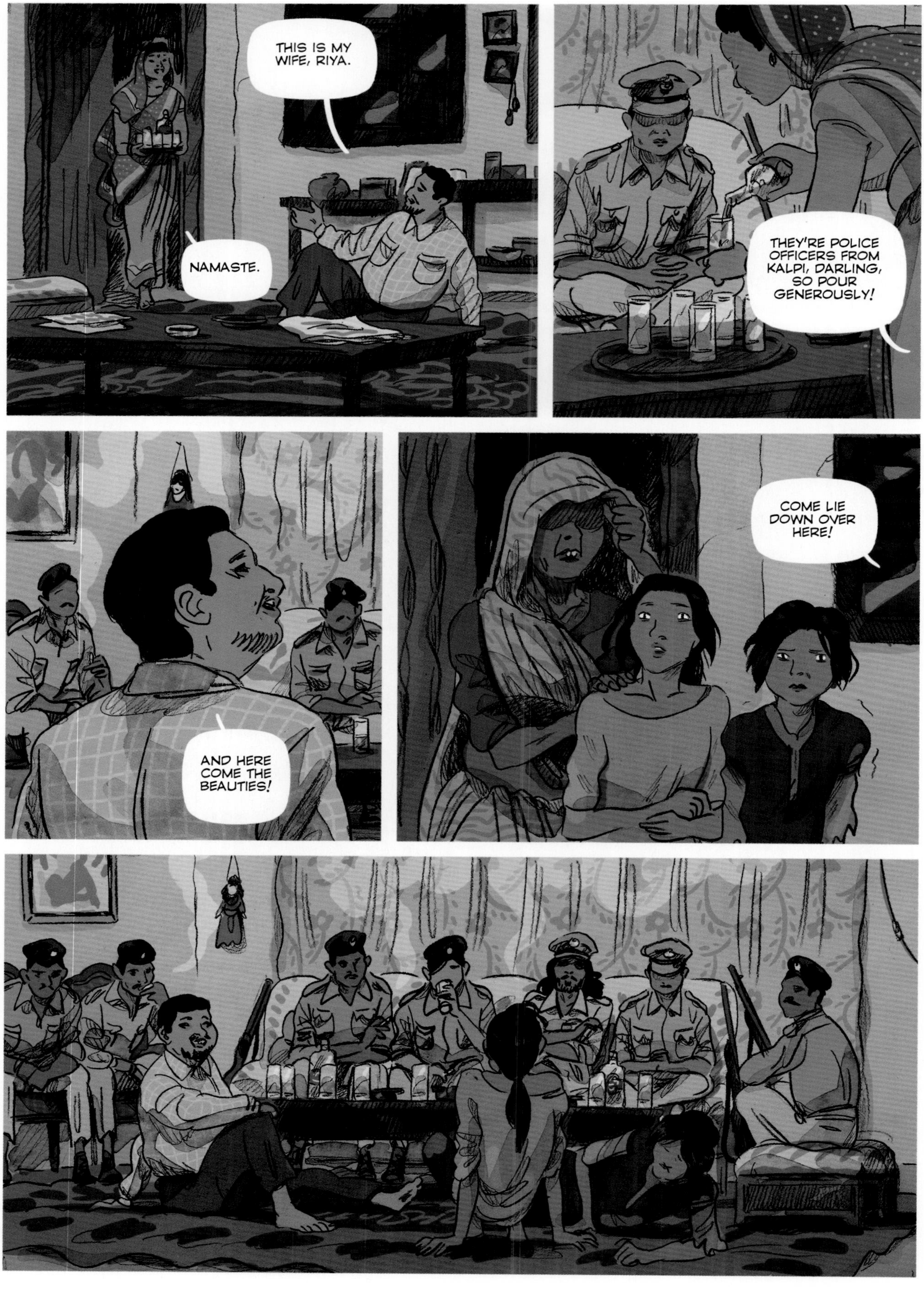
THIS IS MY WIFE, RIYA.
NAMASTE.
THEY'RE POLICE OFFICERS FROM KALPI, DARLING, SO POUR GENEROUSLY!
AND HERE COME THE BEAUTIES!
COME LIE DOWN OVER HERE!

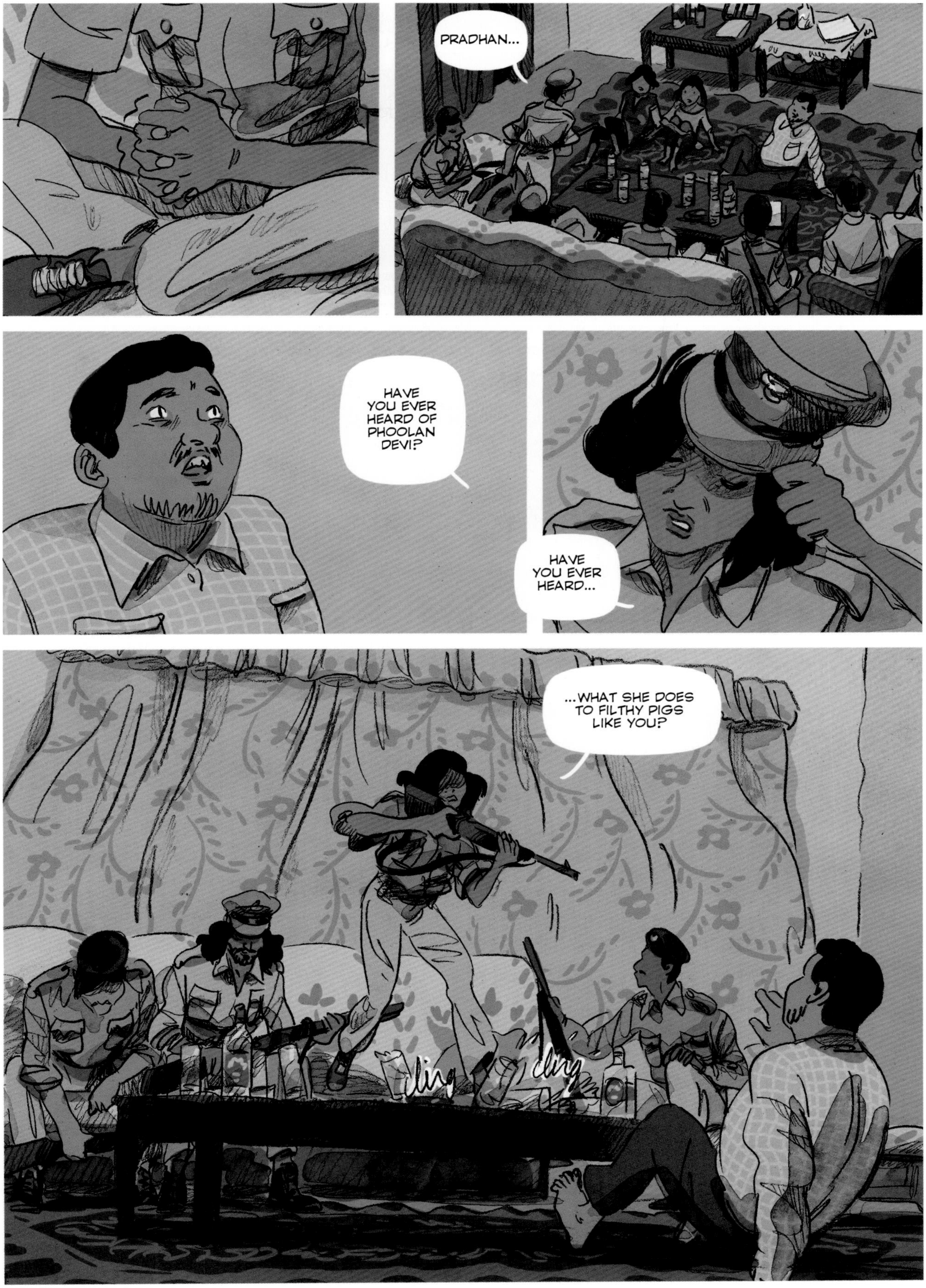
PRADHAN...
HAVE YOU EVER HEARD OF PHOOLAN DEVI?
HAVE YOU EVER HEARD...
...WHAT SHE DOES TO FILTHY PIGS LIKE YOU?
ding
ding

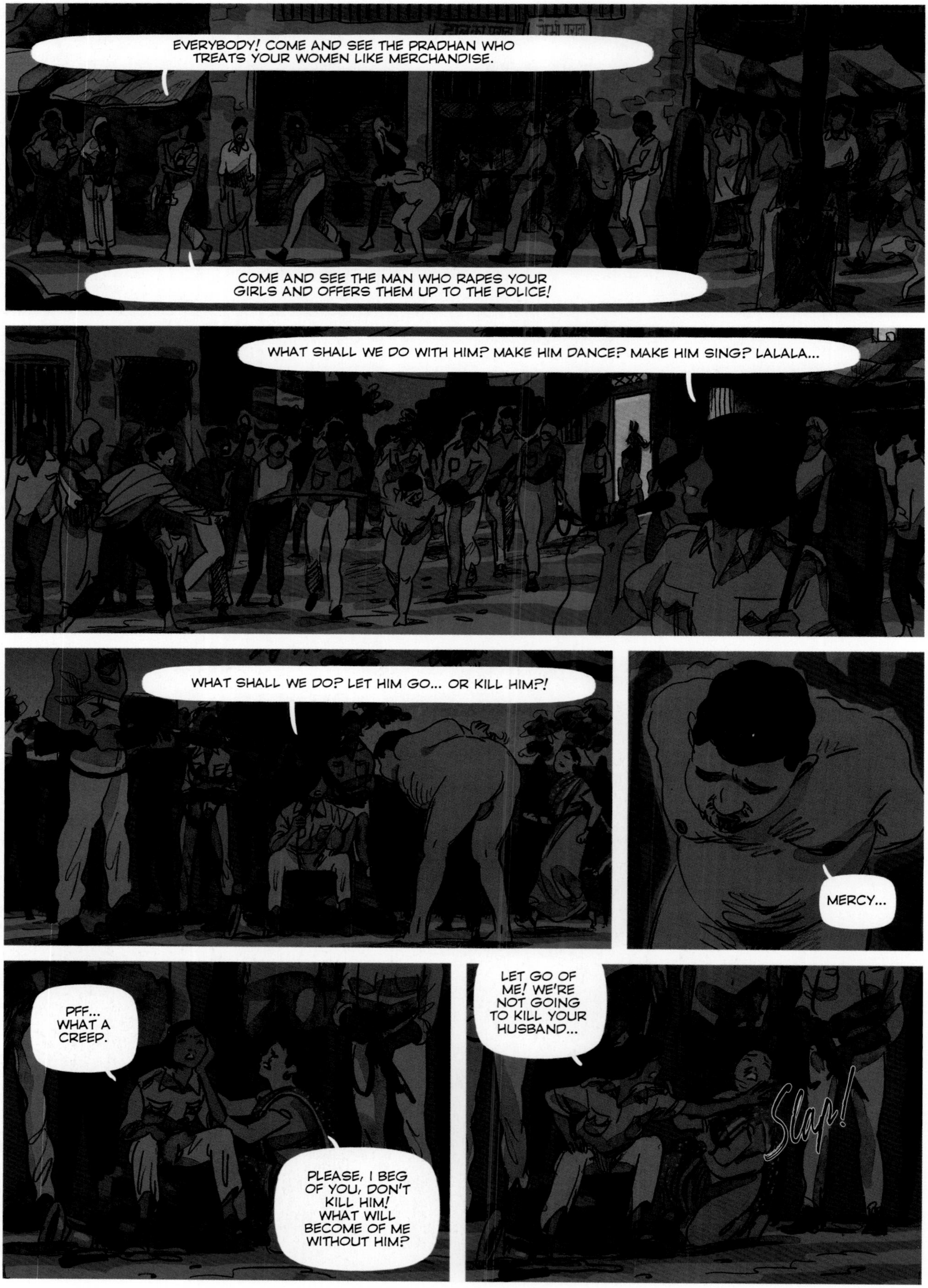
EVERYBODY! COME AND SEE THE PRADHAN WHO TREATS YOUR WOMEN LIKE MERCHANDISE.
COME AND SEE THE MAN WHO RAPES YOUR GIRLS AND OFFERS THEM UP TO THE POLICE!
WHAT SHALL WE DO WITH HIM? MAKE HIM DANCE? MAKE HIM SING? LALALA...
WHAT SHALL WE DO? LET HIM GO... OR KILL HIM?!
MERCY...
PFF... WHAT A CREEP.
PLEASE, I BEG OF YOU, DON'T KILL HIM! WHAT WILL BECOME OF ME WITHOUT HIM?
LET GO OF ME! WE'RE NOT GOING TO KILL YOUR HUSBAND...
Slap!

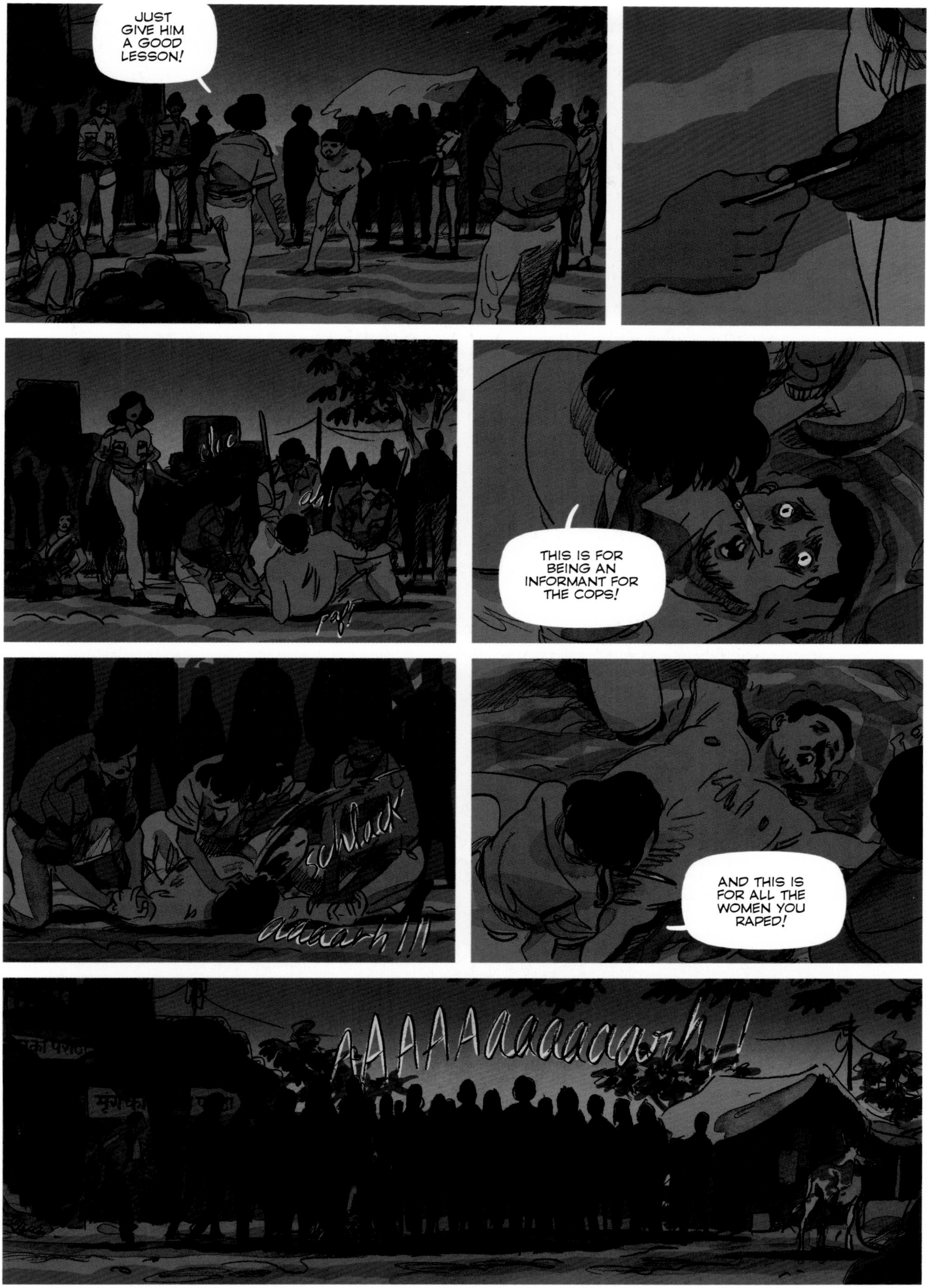
JUST GIVE HIM A GOOD LESSON!
THIS IS FOR BEING AN INFORMANT FOR THE COPS!
AND THIS IS FOR ALL THE WOMEN YOU RAPED!

BECAUSE EVERY DAY, LITTLE GIRLS HAVE ABORTIONS TO AVOID SHAME.

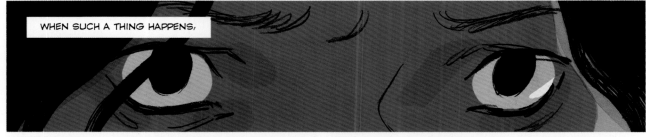

BECAUSE SOME OF THEM SET THEMSELVES ON FIRE OR THROW THEMSELVES INTO RIVERS OR WELLS.

WHEN SUCH A THING HAPPENS,

I WANT THE RAPIST TO KNOW:

PHOOLAN DEVI WILL PUNISH YOU.

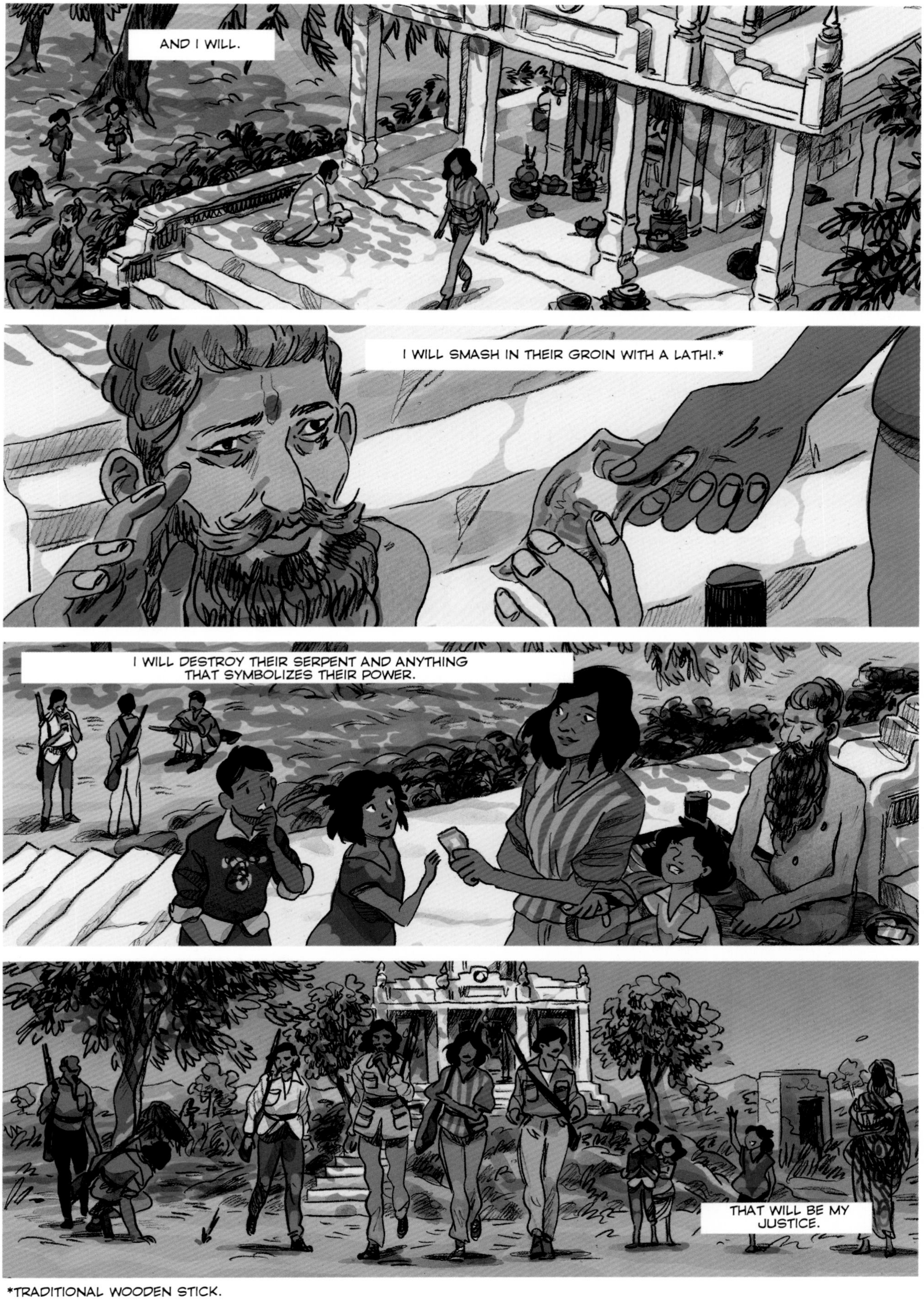
AND I WILL.
I WILL SMASH IN THEIR GROIN WITH A LATHI.*
I WILL DESTROY THEIR SERPENT AND ANYTHING THAT SYMBOLIZES THEIR POWER.
THAT WILL BE MY JUSTICE.

*TRADITIONAL WOODEN STICK.

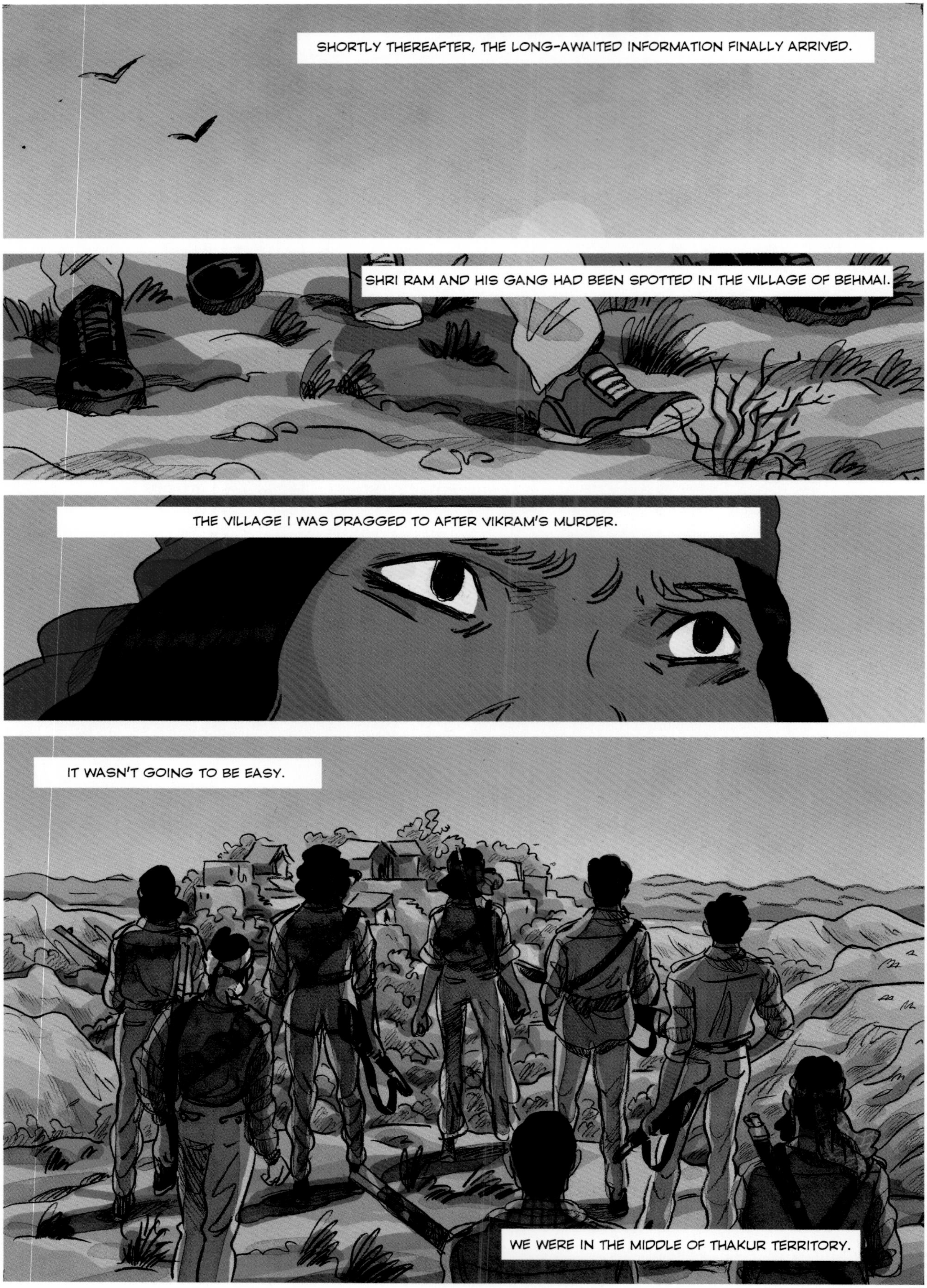
SHORTLY THEREAFTER, THE LONG-AWAITED INFORMATION FINALLY ARRIVED.
SHRI RAM AND HIS GANG HAD BEEN SPOTTED IN THE VILLAGE OF BEHMAI.
THE VILLAGE I WAS DRAGGED TO AFTER VIKRAM'S MURDER.
IT WASN'T GOING TO BE EASY.
WE WERE IN THE MIDDLE OF THAKUR TERRITORY.

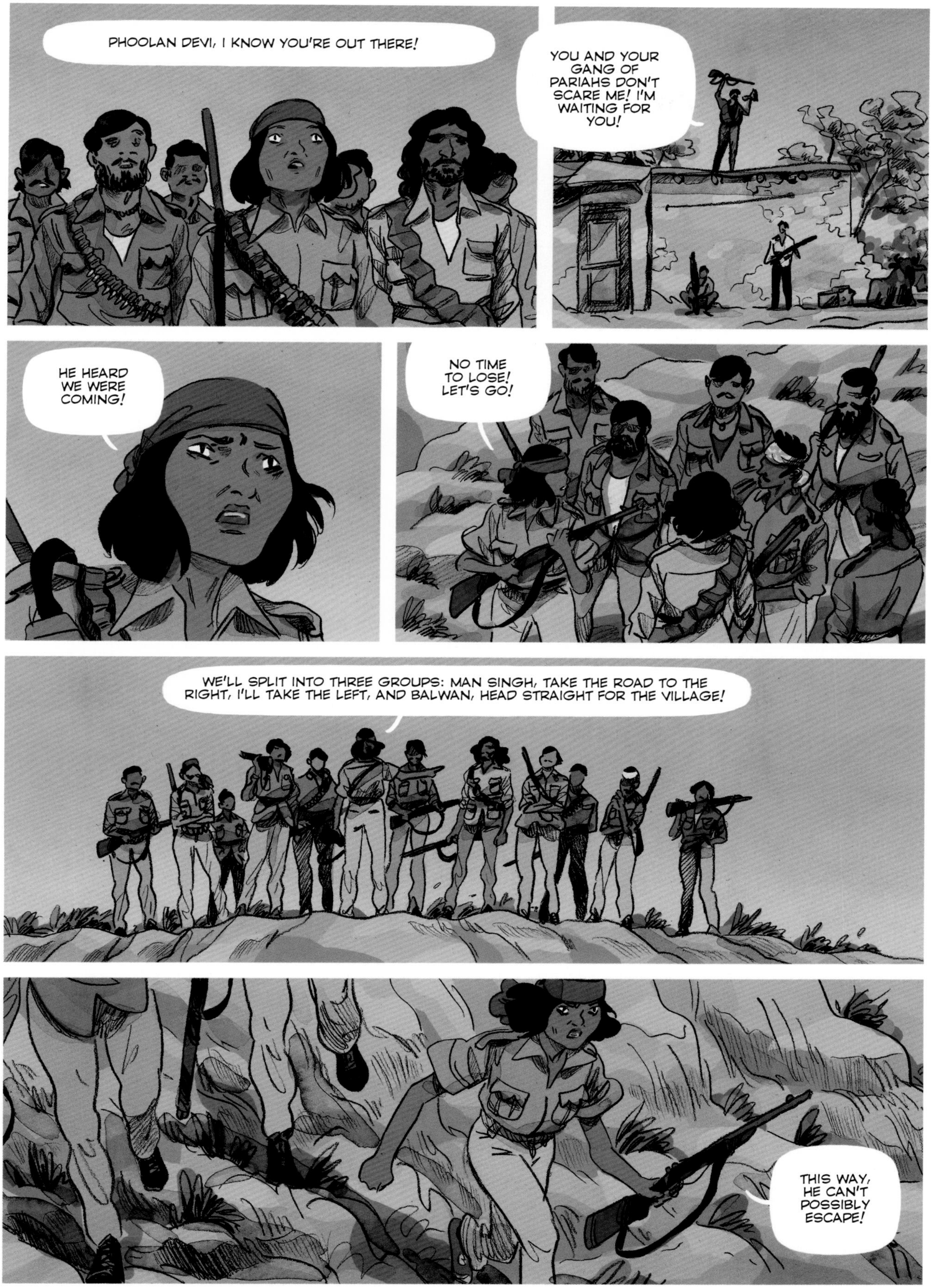
PHOOLAN DEVI, I KNOW YOU'RE OUT THERE!
YOU AND YOUR GANG OF PARIAHS DON'T SCARE ME! I'M WAITING FOR YOU!
HE HEARD WE WERE COMING!
NO TIME TO LOSE! LET'S GO!
WE'LL SPLIT INTO THREE GROUPS: MAN SINGH, TAKE THE ROAD TO THE RIGHT, I'LL TAKE THE LEFT, AND BALWAN, HEAD STRAIGHT FOR THE VILLAGE!
THIS WAY, HE CAN'T POSSIBLY ESCAPE!

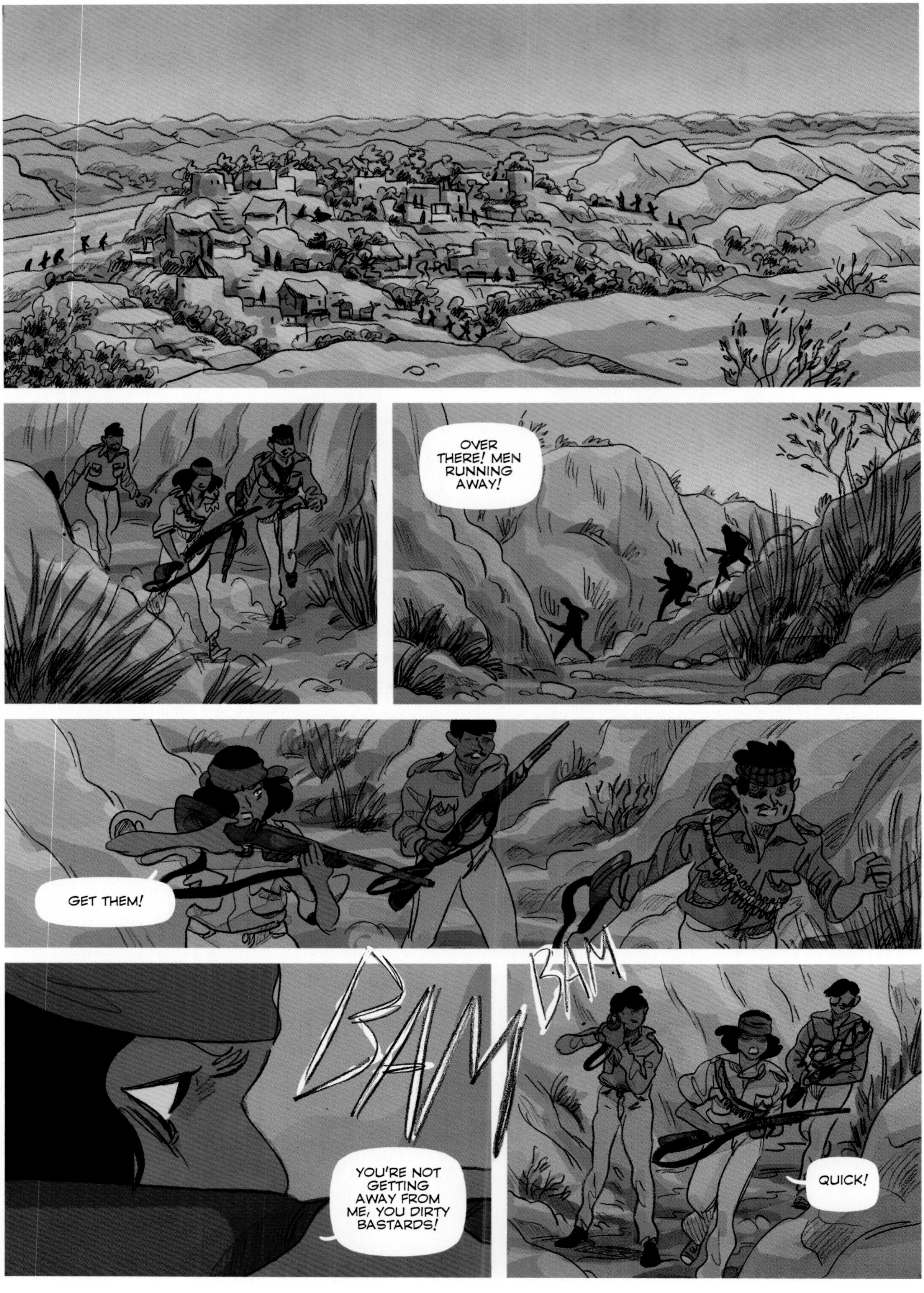
OVER THERE! MEN RUNNING AWAY!
GET THEM!
BAM
BAM
YOU'RE NOT GETTING AWAY FROM ME, YOU DIRTY BASTARDS!
QUICK!

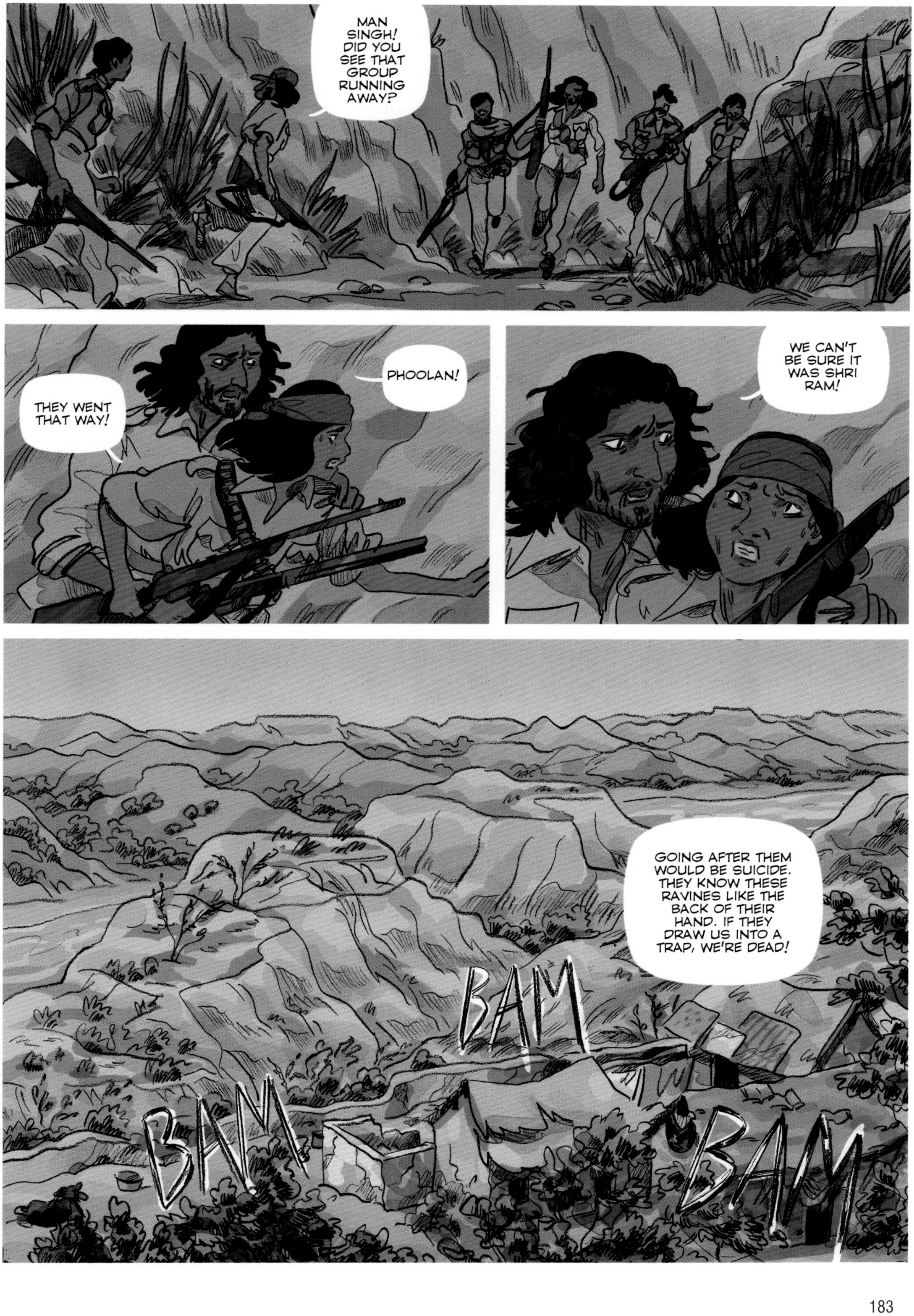
MAN SINGH! DID YOU SEE THAT GROUP RUNNING AWAY?
PHOOLAN!
THEY WENT THAT WAY!
WE CAN'T BE SURE IT WAS SHRI RAM!
GOING AFTER THEM WOULD BE SUICIDE. THEY KNOW THESE RAVINES LIKE THE BACK OF THEIR HAND. IF THEY DRAW US INTO A TRAP, WE'RE DEAD!
BAM
BAM
BAM

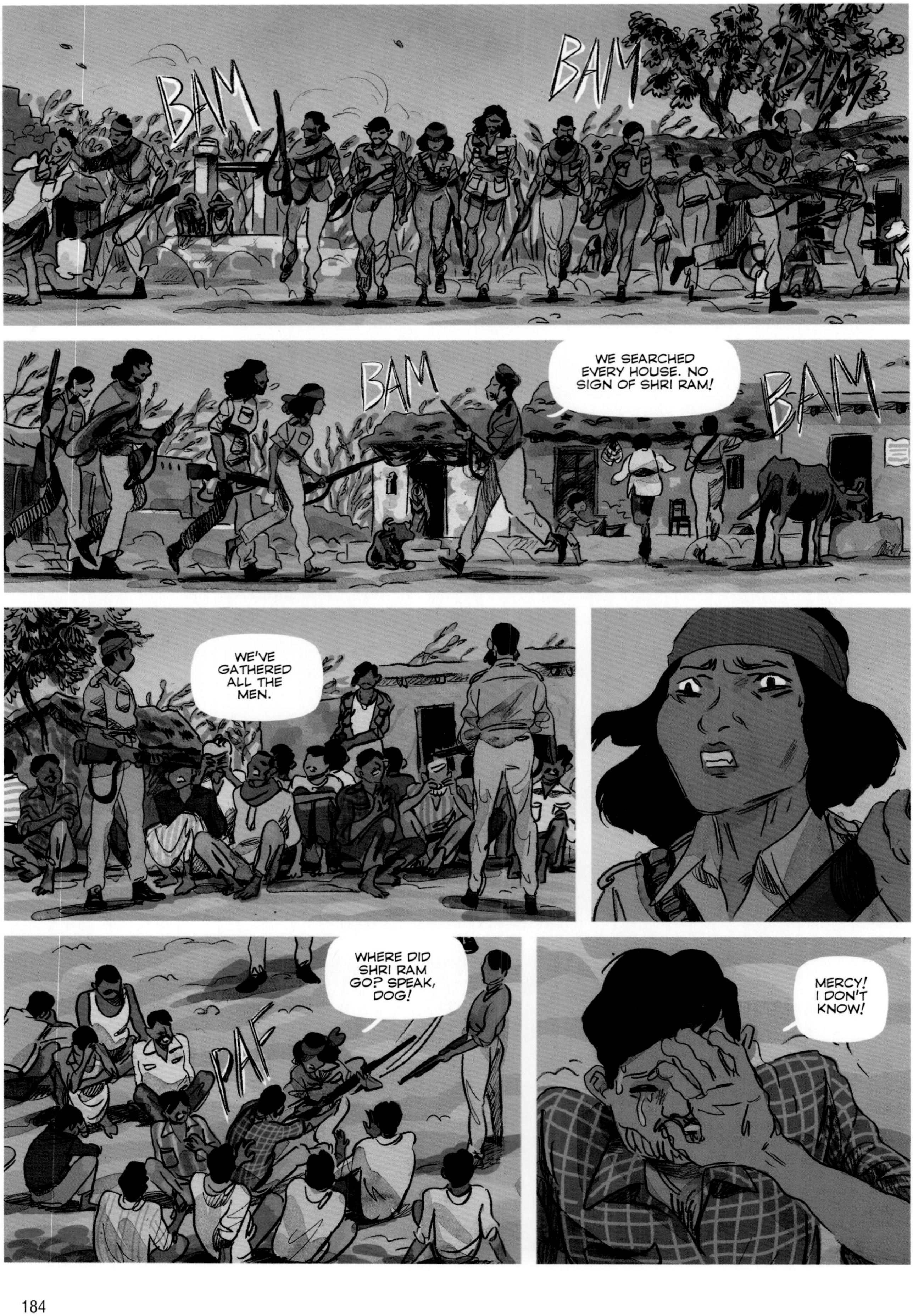
BAM
BAM
BAM
WE SEARCHED EVERY HOUSE. NO SIGN OF SHRI RAM!
BAM
BAM
WE'VE GATHERED ALL THE MEN.
WHERE DID SHRI RAM GO? SPEAK, DOG!
PAF
MERCY! I DON'T KNOW!

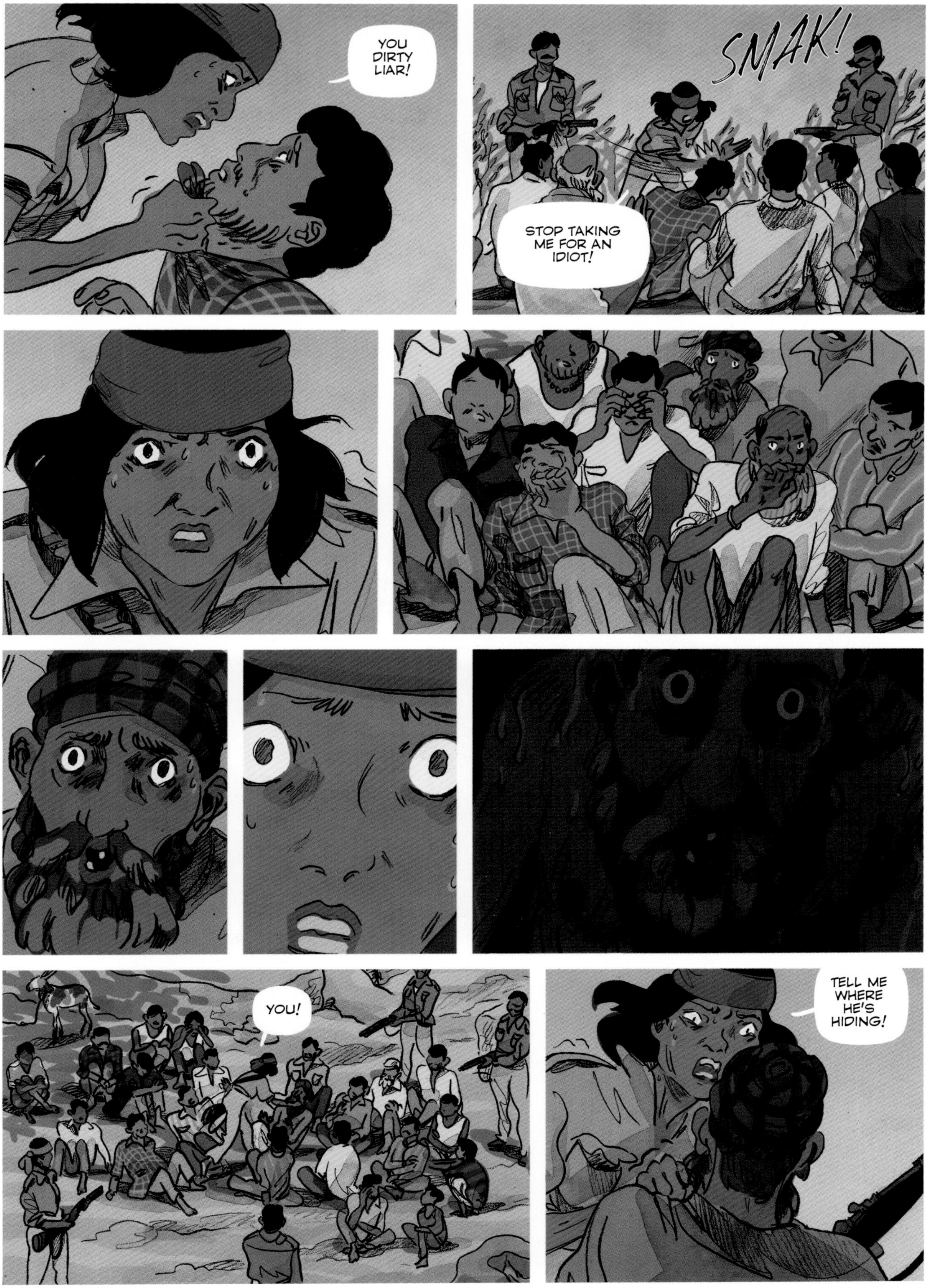
YOU DIRTY LIAR!
SMAK!
STOP TAKING ME FOR AN IDIOT!
YOU!
TELL ME WHERE HE'S HIDING!

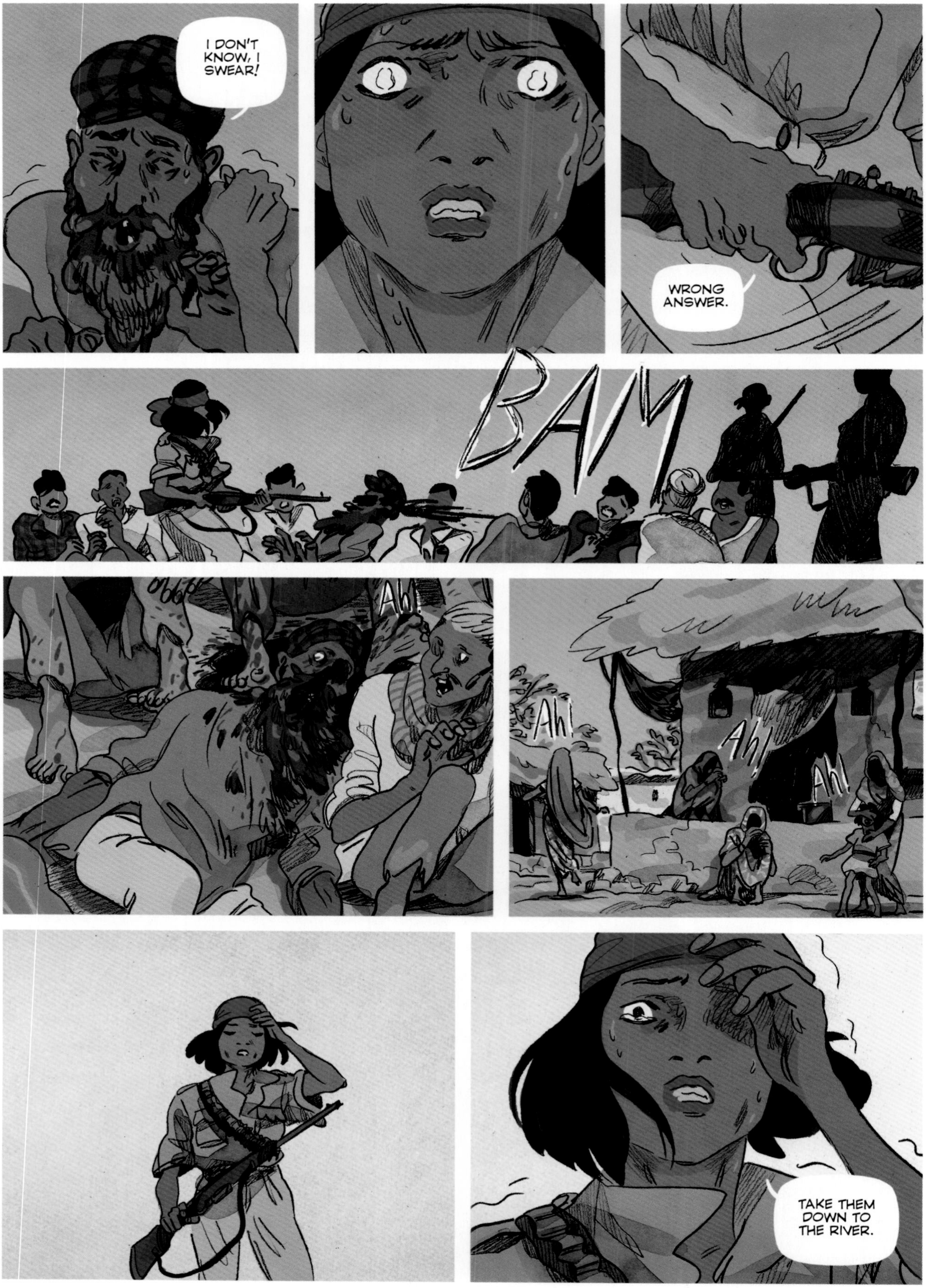
I DON'T KNOW, I SWEAR!
WRONG ANSWER.
BAM
Ah!
Ah!
Ah!
Ah!
TAKE THEM DOWN TO THE RIVER.

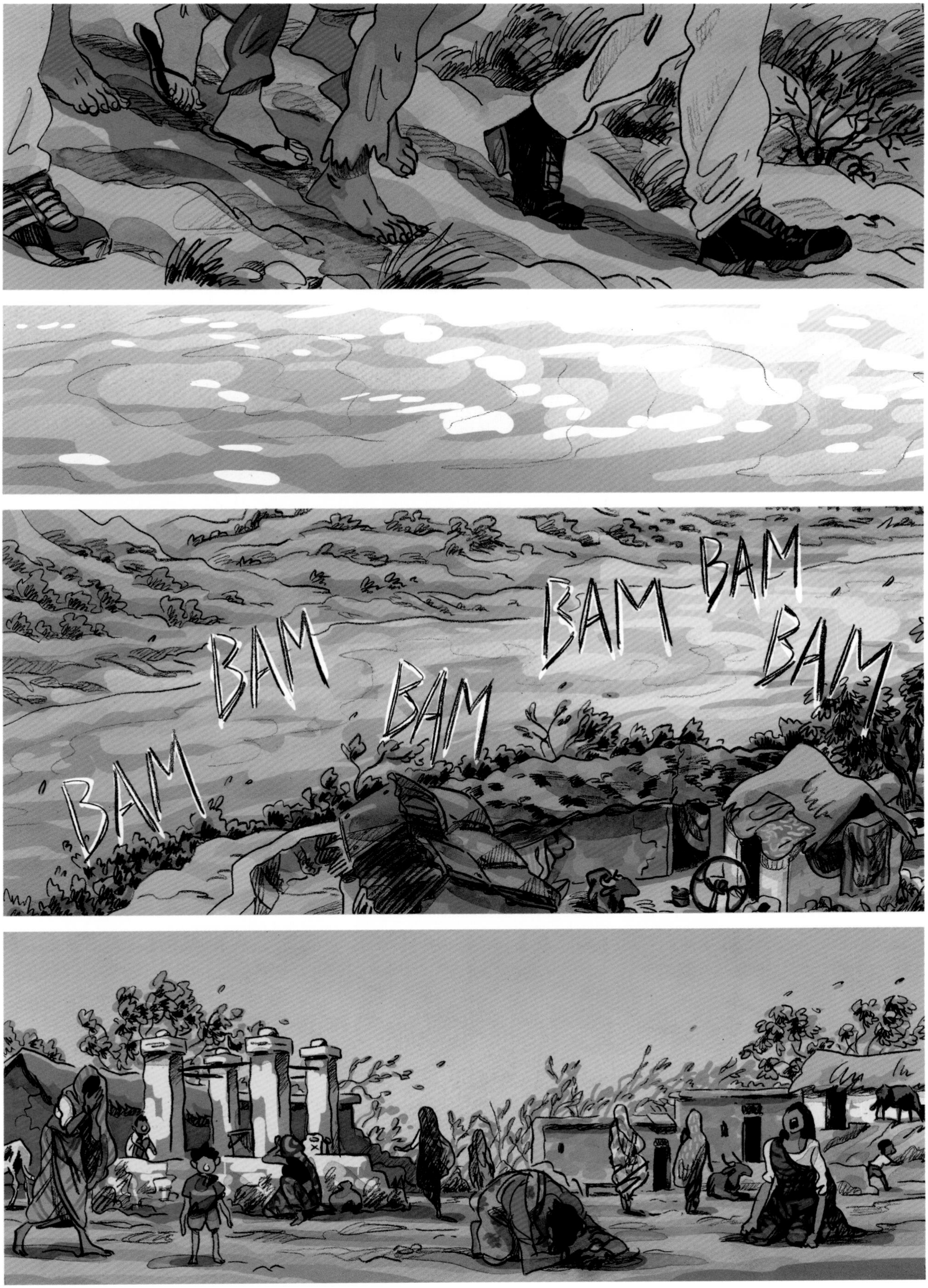
BAM
BAM
BAM
BAM
BAM
BAM

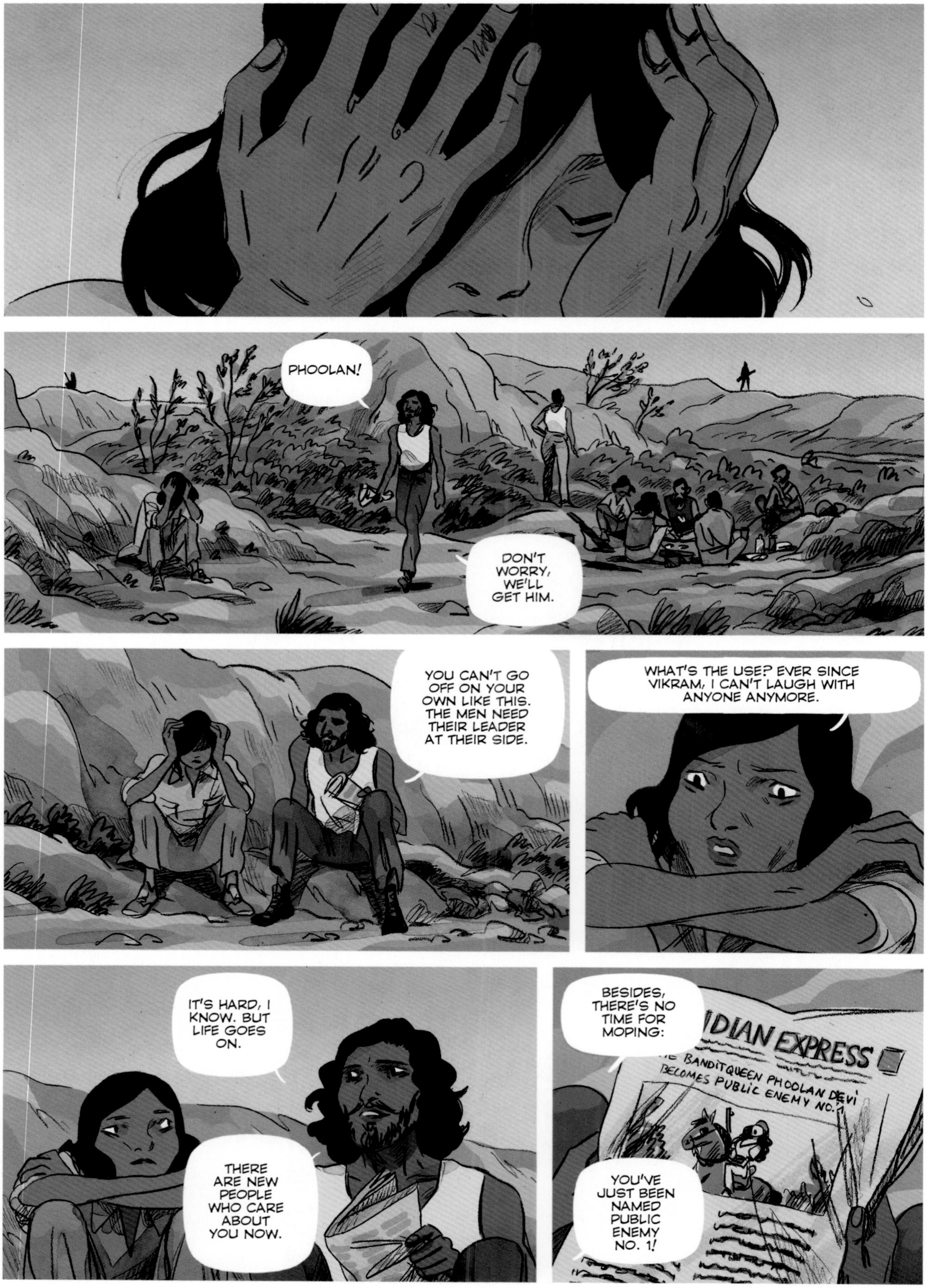
PHOOLAN!
DON'T WORRY, WE'LL GET HIM.
YOU CAN'T GO OFF ON YOUR OWN LIKE THIS. THE MEN NEED THEIR LEADER AT THEIR SIDE.
WHAT'S THE USE? EVER SINCE VIKRAM, I CAN'T LAUGH WITH ANYONE ANYMORE.
IT'S HARD, I KNOW. BUT LIFE GOES ON.
THERE ARE NEW PEOPLE WHO CARE ABOUT YOU NOW.
BESIDES, THERE'S NO TIME FOR MOPING:
NDIAN EXPRESS
THE BANDITQUEEN PHOOLAN DEVI BECOMES PUBLIC ENEMY NO. 1
YOU'VE JUST BEEN NAMED PUBLIC ENEMY NO. 1!

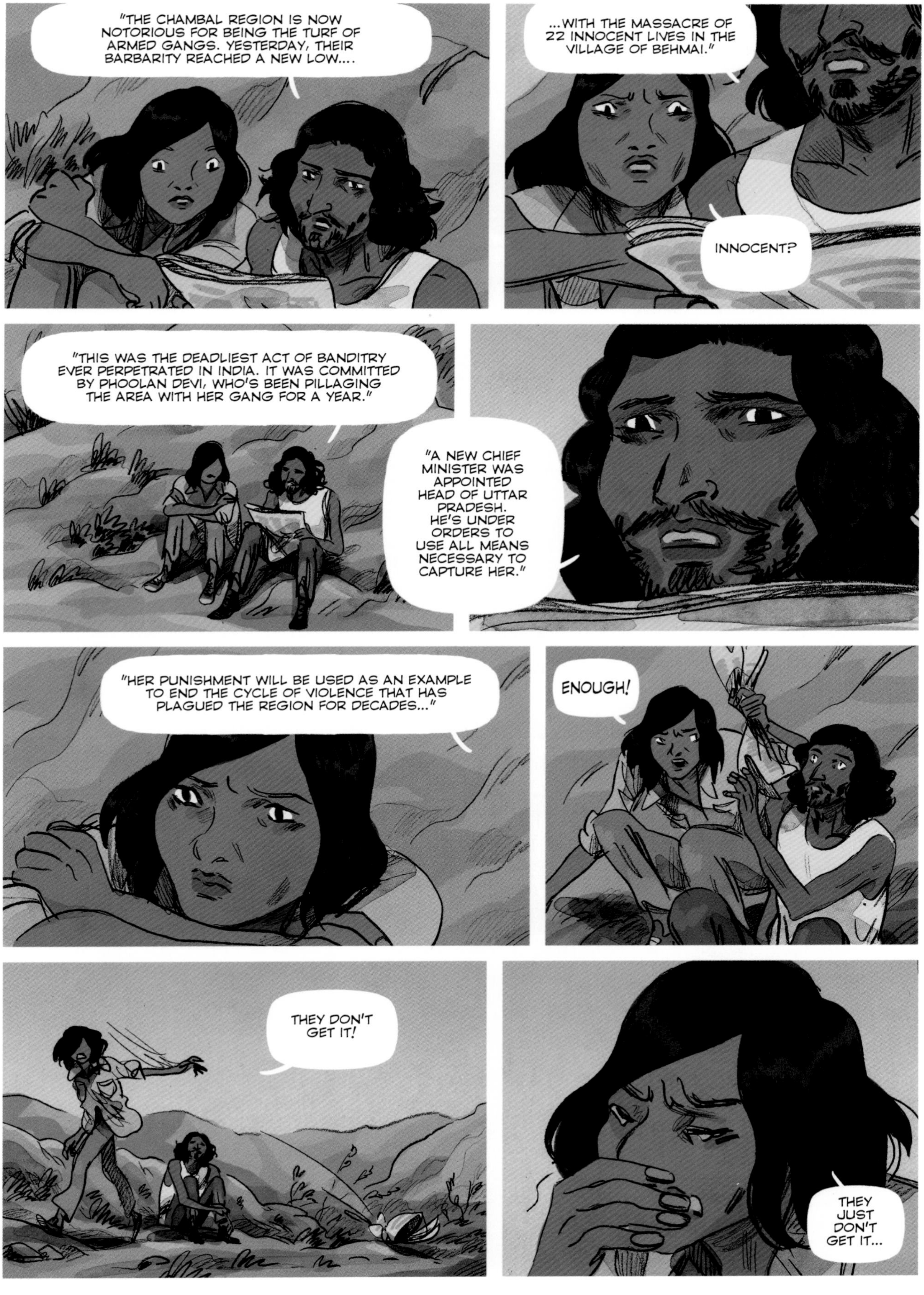
"THE CHAMBAL REGION IS NOW NOTORIOUS FOR BEING THE TURF OF ARMED GANGS. YESTERDAY, THEIR BARBARITY REACHED A NEW LOW....
...WITH THE MASSACRE OF 22 INNOCENT LIVES IN THE VILLAGE OF BEHMAI."
INNOCENT?
"THIS WAS THE DEADLIEST ACT OF BANDITRY EVER PERPETRATED IN INDIA. IT WAS COMMITTED BY PHOOLAN DEVI, WHO'S BEEN PILLAGING THE AREA WITH HER GANG FOR A YEAR."
"A NEW CHIEF MINISTER WAS APPOINTED HEAD OF UTTAR PRADESH. HE'S UNDER ORDERS TO USE ALL MEANS NECESSARY TO CAPTURE HER."
"HER PUNISHMENT WILL BE USED AS AN EXAMPLE TO END THE CYCLE OF VIOLENCE THAT HAS PLAGUED THE REGION FOR DECADES..."
ENOUGH!
THEY DON'T GET IT!
THEY JUST DON'T GET IT...

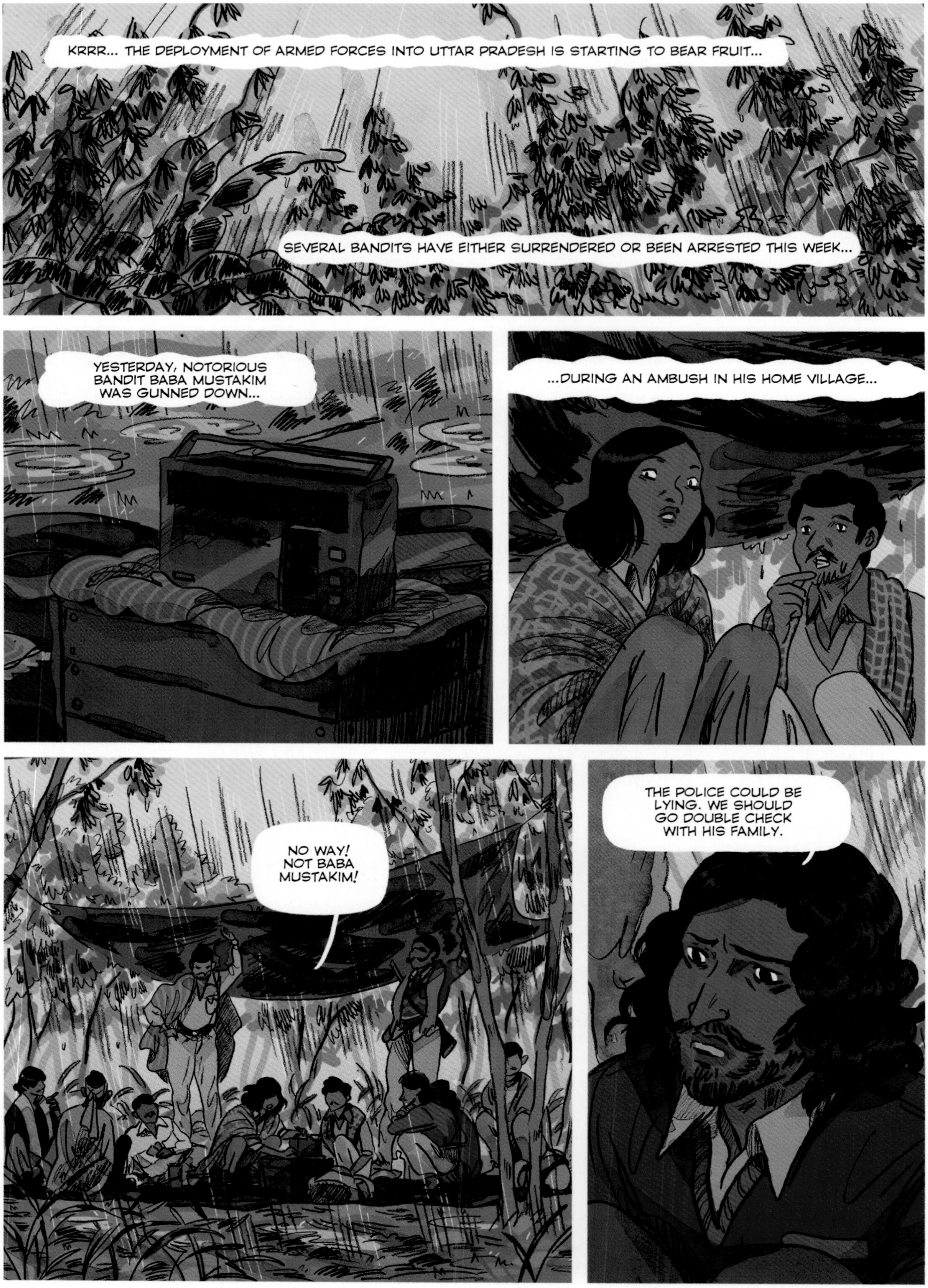
KRRR... THE DEPLOYMENT OF ARMED FORCES INTO UTTAR PRADESH IS STARTING TO BEAR FRUIT...
SEVERAL BANDITS HAVE EITHER SURRENDERED OR BEEN ARRESTED THIS WEEK...
YESTERDAY, NOTORIOUS BANDIT BABA MUSTAKIM WAS GUNNED DOWN...
...DURING AN AMBUSH IN HIS HOME VILLAGE...
NO WAY! NOT BABA MUSTAKIM!
THE POLICE COULD BE LYING. WE SHOULD GO DOUBLE CHECK WITH HIS FAMILY.

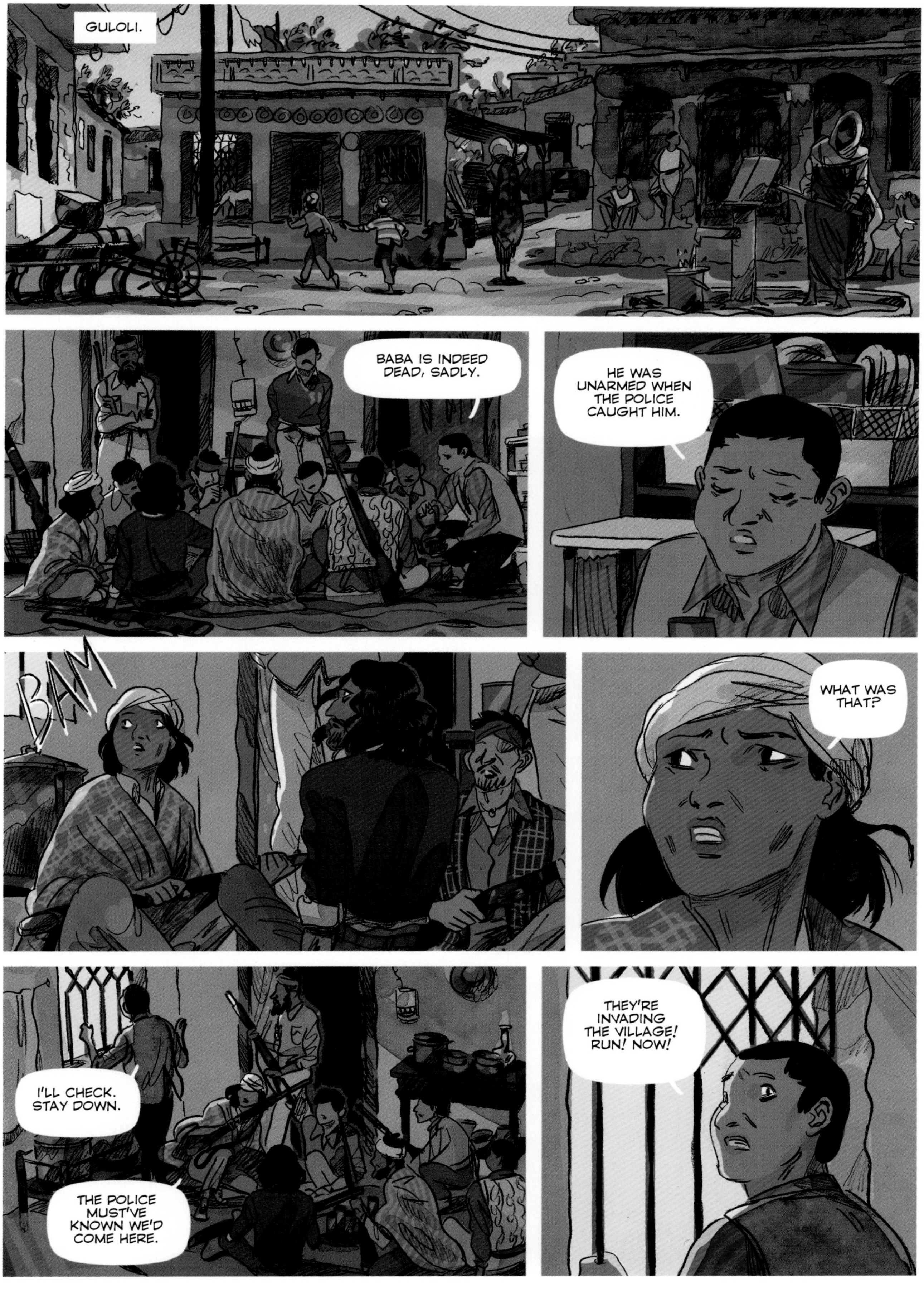
GULOLI.
BABA IS INDEED DEAD, SADLY.
HE WAS UNARMED WHEN THE POLICE CAUGHT HIM.
BAM
WHAT WAS THAT?
I'LL CHECK. STAY DOWN.
THE POLICE MUST'VE KNOWN WE'D COME HERE.
THEY'RE INVADING THE VILLAGE! RUN! NOW!

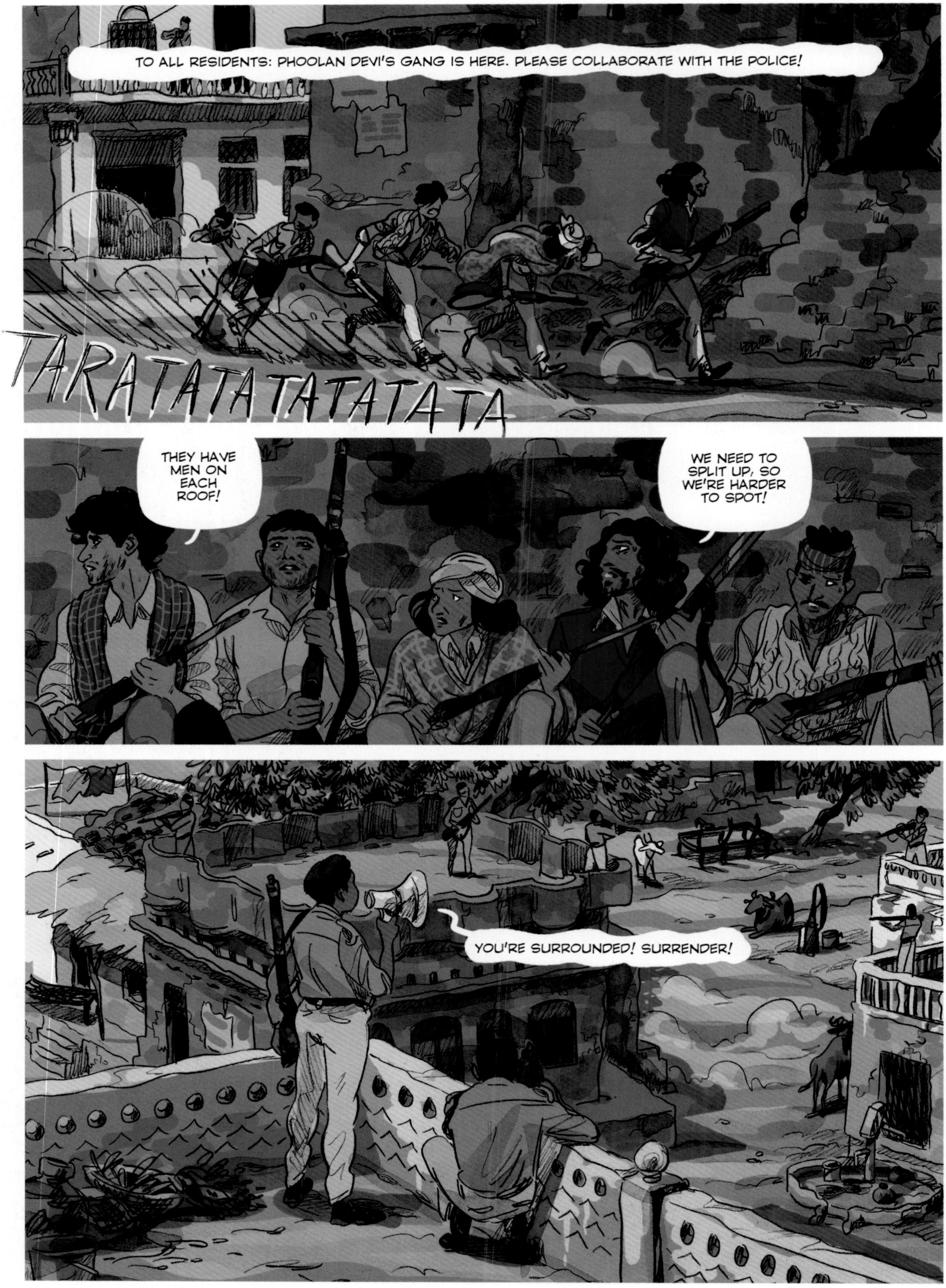
TO ALL RESIDENTS: PHOOLAN DEVI'S GANG IS HERE. PLEASE COLLABORATE WITH THE POLICE!
TARATATATATATATA
THEY HAVE MEN ON EACH ROOF!
WE NEED TO SPLIT UP, SO WE'RE HARDER TO SPOT!
YOU'RE SURROUNDED! SURRENDER!

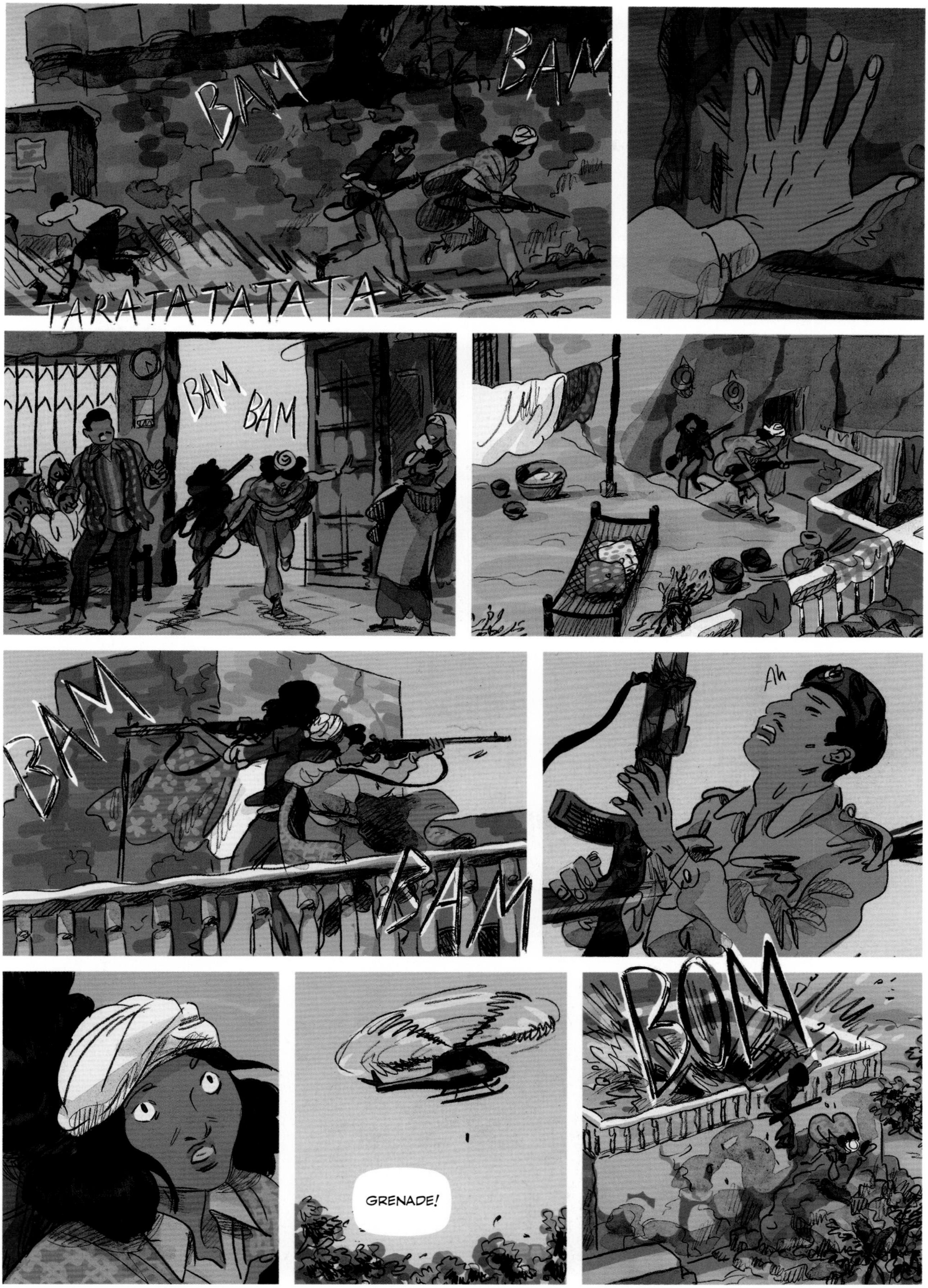
BAM
BAM
TARATATATATA
BAM
BAM
BAM
BAM
Ah
GRENADE!
BOM

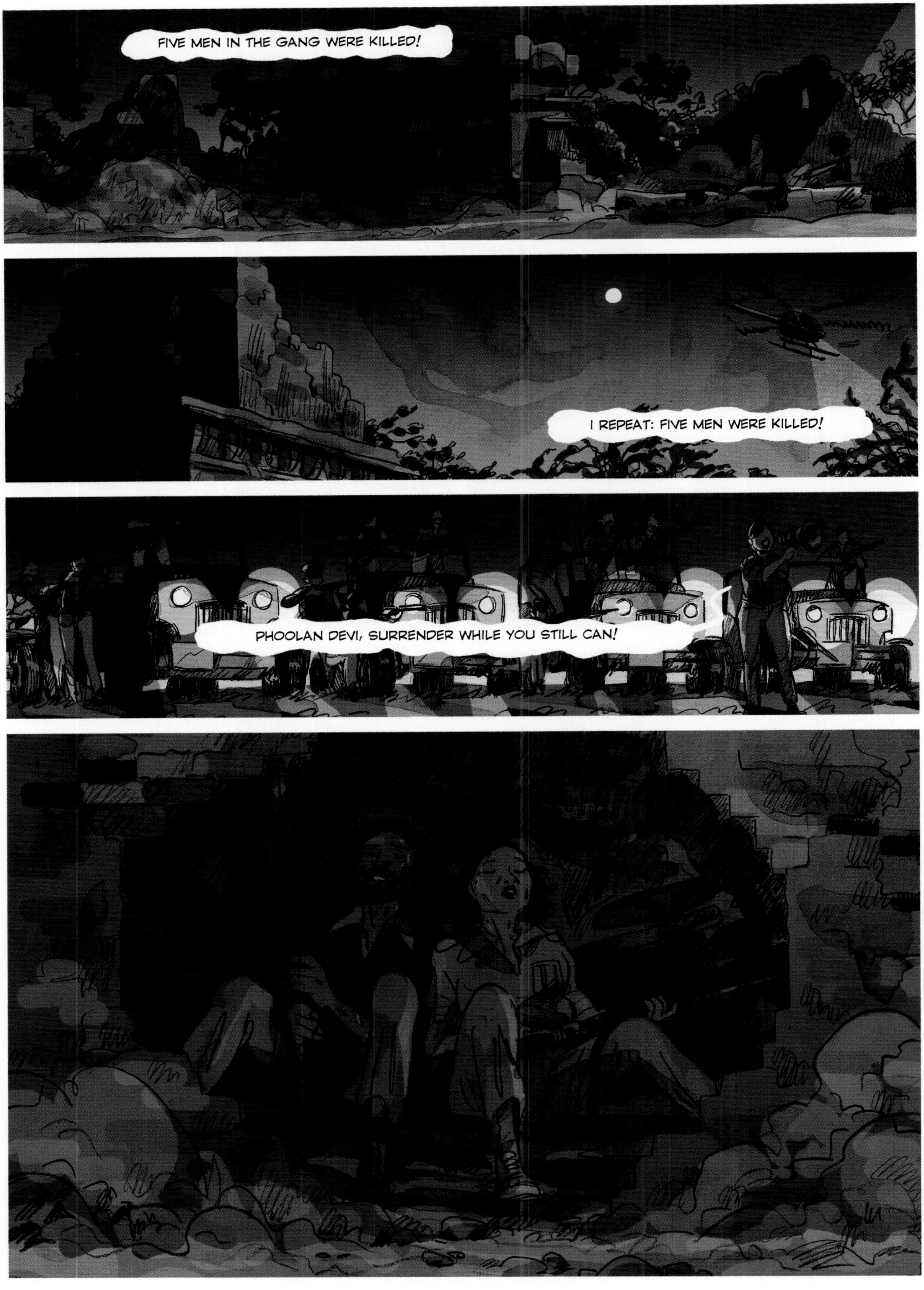
FIVE MEN IN THE GANG WERE KILLED!
I REPEAT: FIVE MEN WERE KILLED!
PHOOLAN DEVI, SURRENDER WHILE YOU STILL CAN!

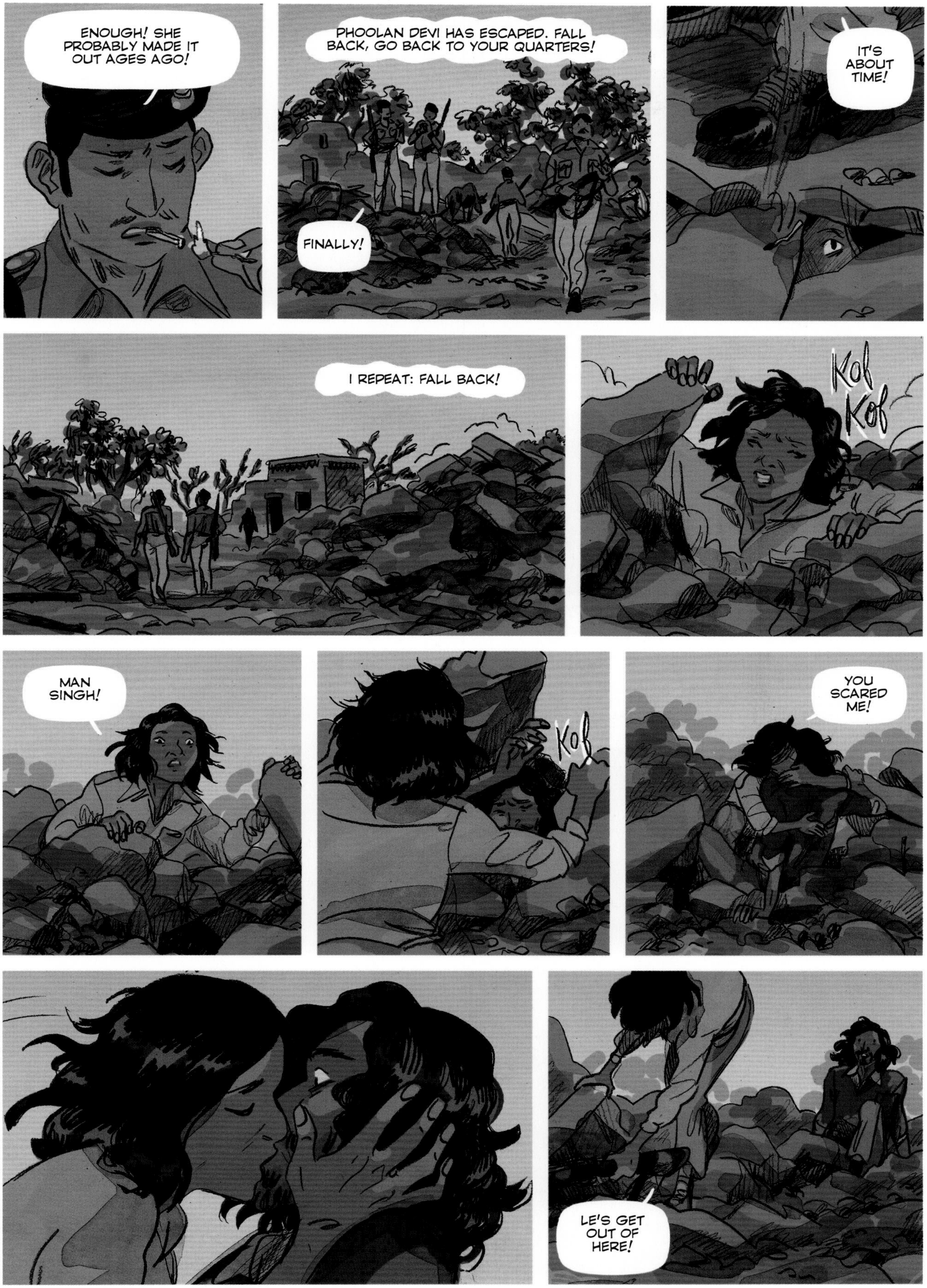
ENOUGH! SHE PROBABLY MADE IT OUT AGES AGO!
PHOOLAN DEVI HAS ESCAPED. FALL BACK, GO BACK TO YOUR QUARTERS!
FINALLY!
IT'S ABOUT TIME!
I REPEAT: FALL BACK!
KOF KOF
MAN SINGH!
KOF
YOU SCARED ME!
LE'S GET OUT OF HERE!

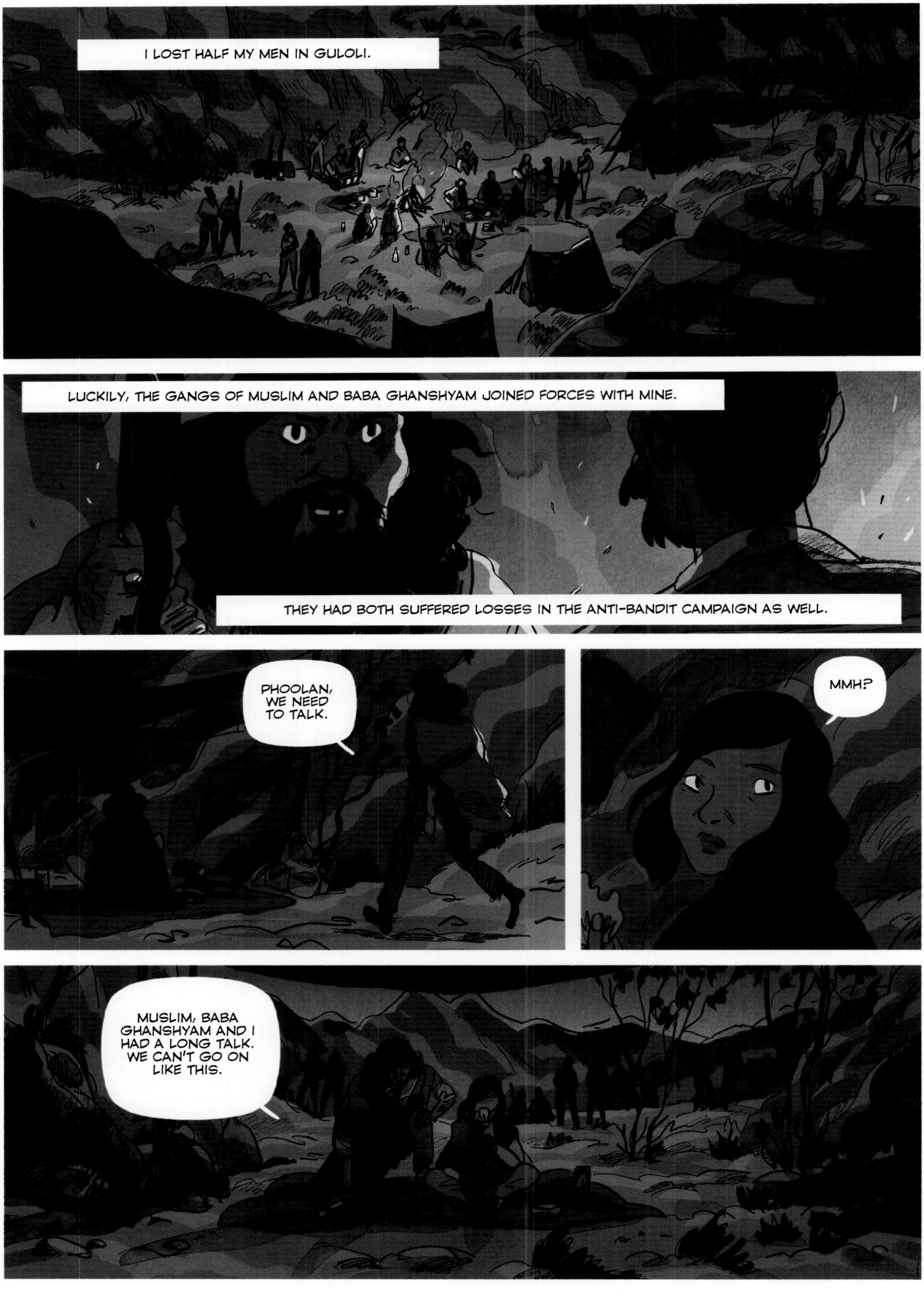
I LOST HALF MY MEN IN GULOLI.
LUCKILY, THE GANGS OF MUSLIM AND BABA GHANSHYAM JOINED FORCES WITH MINE.
THEY HAD BOTH SUFFERED LOSSES IN THE ANTI-BANDIT CAMPAIGN AS WELL.
PHOOLAN, WE NEED TO TALK.
MMH?
MUSLIM, BABA GHANSHYAM AND I HAD A LONG TALK. WE CAN'T GO ON LIKE THIS.

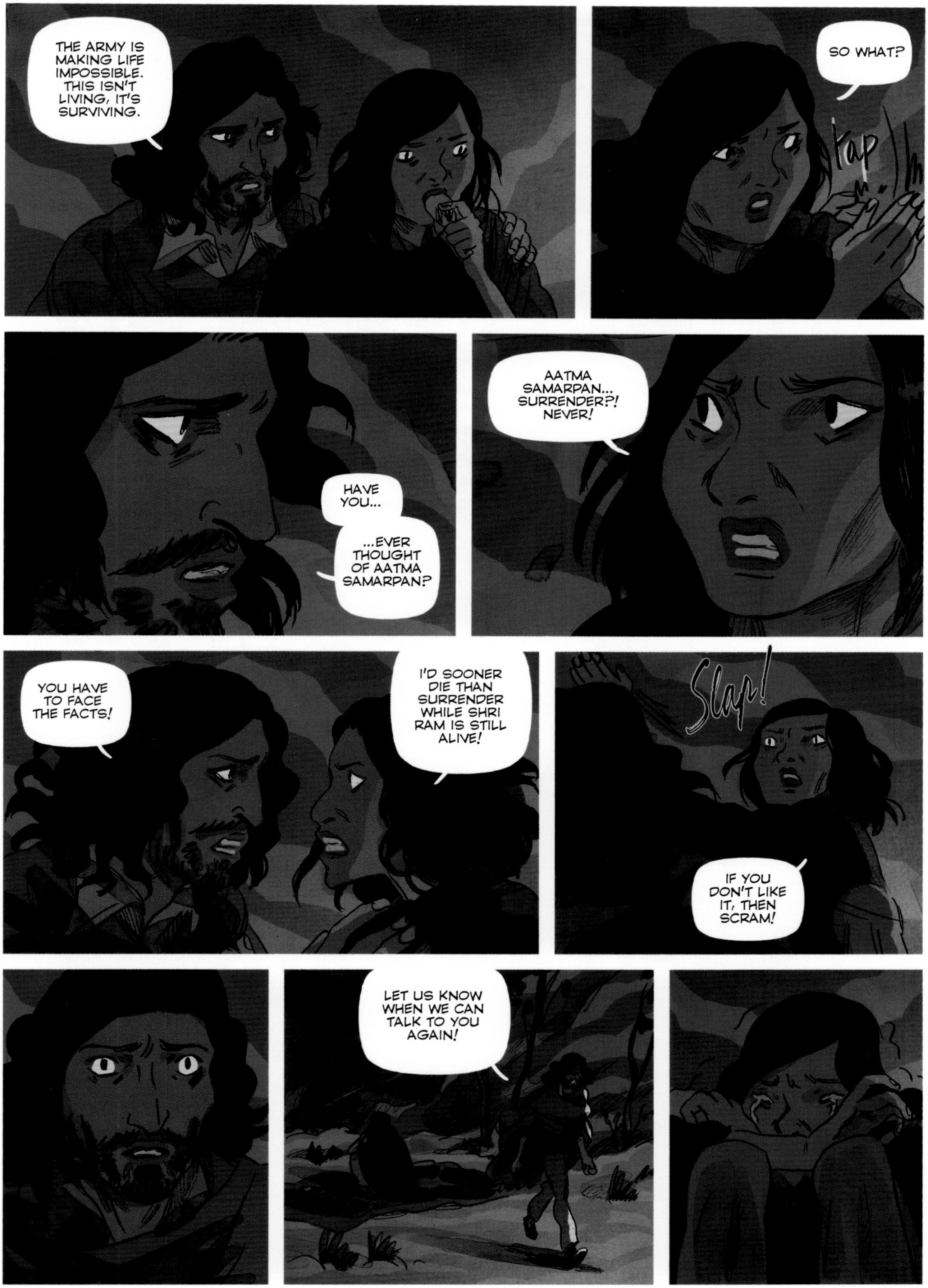

THE ARMY IS MAKING LIFE IMPOSSIBLE. THIS ISN'T LIVING, IT'S SURVIVING.
SO WHAT?
Yap
HAVE YOU...
...EVER THOUGHT OF AATMA SAMARPAN?
AATMA SAMARPAN... SURRENDER?! NEVER!
YOU HAVE TO FACE THE FACTS!
I'D SOONER DIE THAN SURRENDER WHILE SHRI RAM IS STILL ALIVE!
Slap!
IF YOU DON'T LIKE IT, THEN SCRAM!
LET US KNOW WHEN WE CAN TALK TO YOU AGAIN!

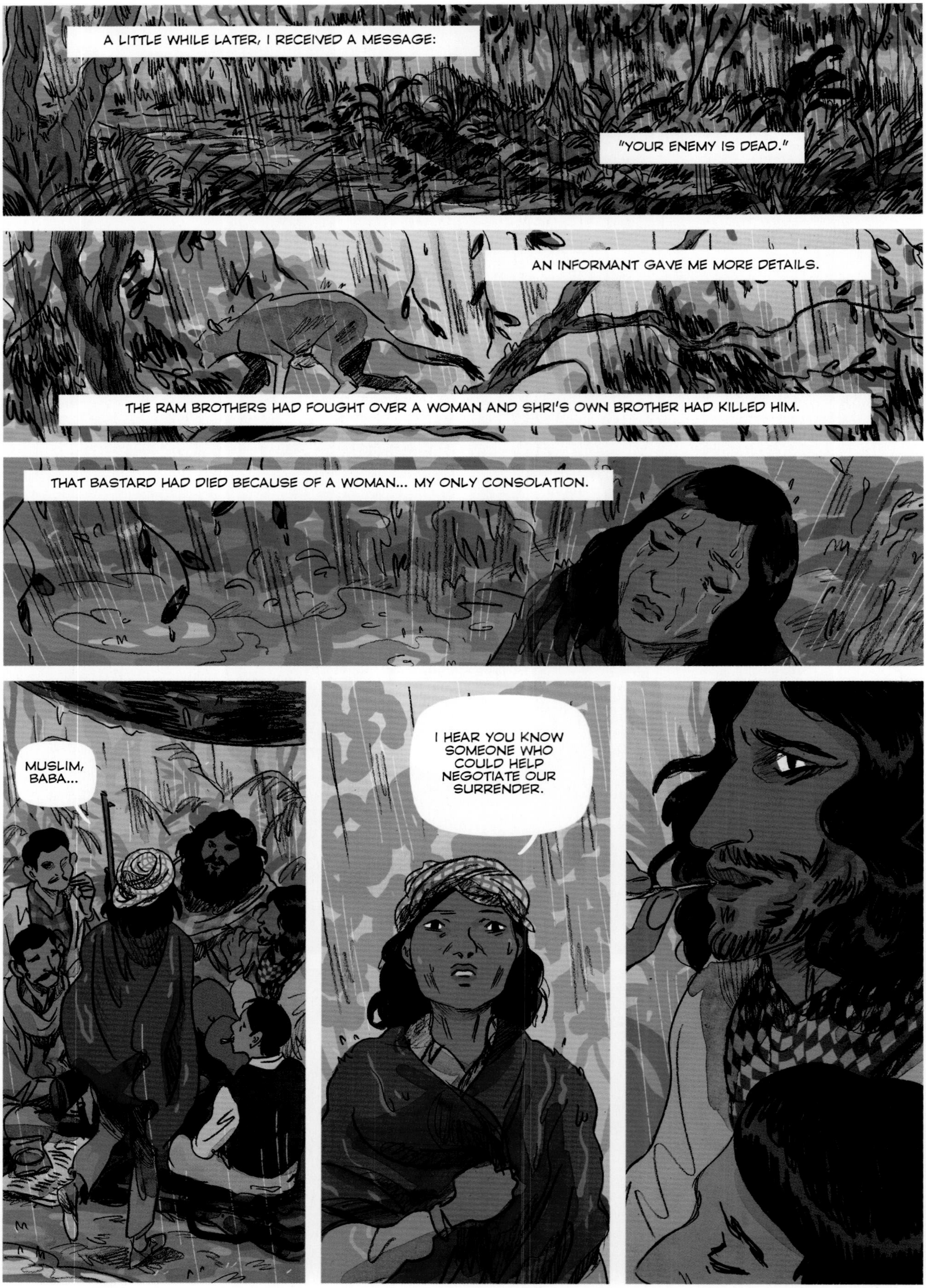
A LITTLE WHILE LATER, I RECEIVED A MESSAGE:
"YOUR ENEMY IS DEAD."
AN INFORMANT GAVE ME MORE DETAILS.
THE RAM BROTHERS HAD FOUGHT OVER A WOMAN AND SHRI'S OWN BROTHER HAD KILLED HIM.
THAT BASTARD HAD DIED BECAUSE OF A WOMAN... MY ONLY CONSOLATION.
MUSLIM, BABA...
I HEAR YOU KNOW SOMEONE WHO COULD HELP NEGOTIATE OUR SURRENDER.

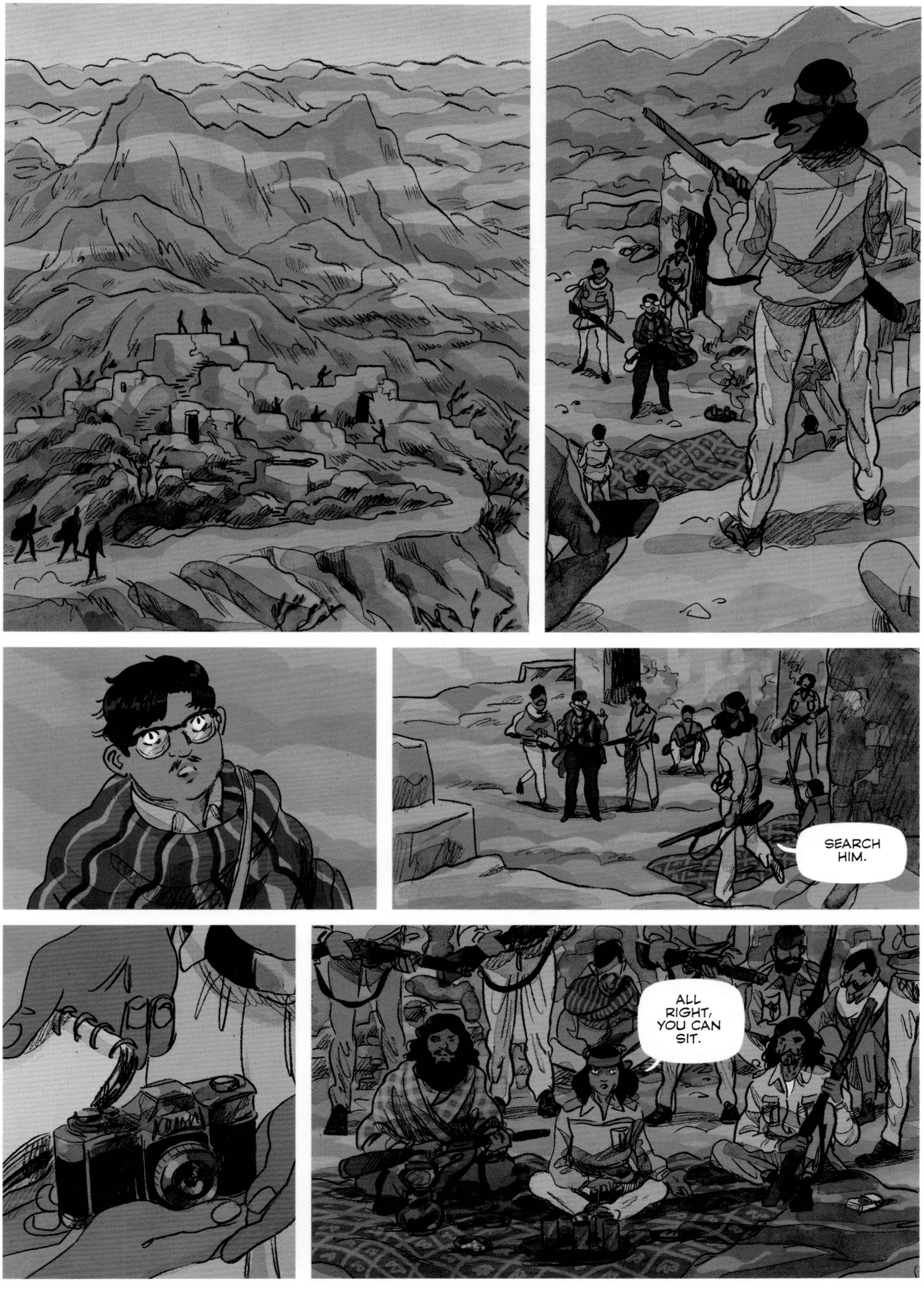
SEARCH HIM.
ALL RIGHT, YOU CAN SIT.

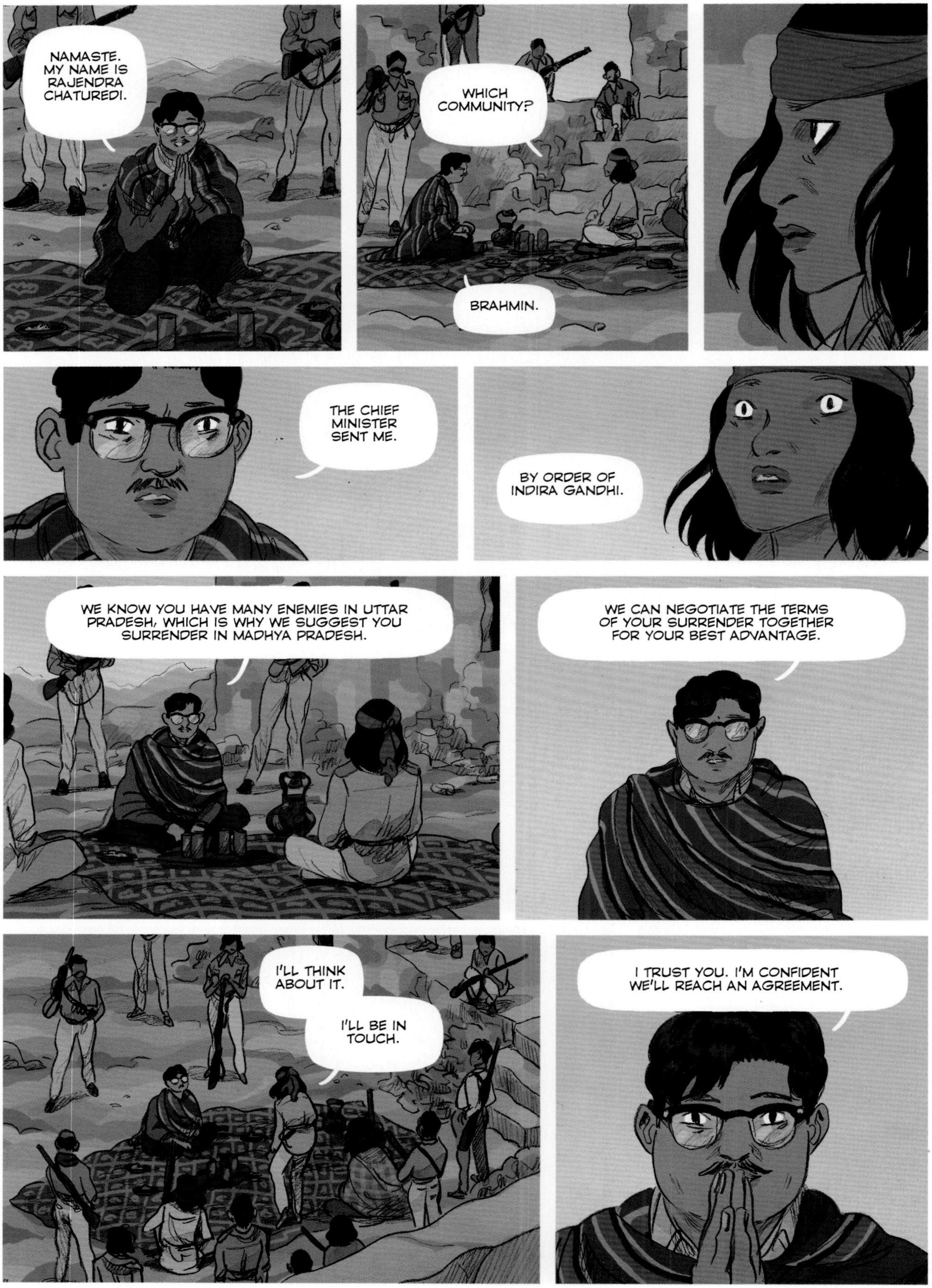
NAMASTE. MY NAME IS RAJENDRA CHATUREDI.
WHICH COMMUNITY?
BRAHMIN.
THE CHIEF MINISTER SENT ME.
BY ORDER OF INDIRA GANDHI.
WE KNOW YOU HAVE MANY ENEMIES IN UTTAR PRADESH, WHICH IS WHY WE SUGGEST YOU SURRENDER IN MADHYA PRADESH.
WE CAN NEGOTIATE THE TERMS OF YOUR SURRENDER TOGETHER FOR YOUR BEST ADVANTAGE.
I'LL THINK ABOUT IT.
I'LL BE IN TOUCH.
I TRUST YOU. I'M CONFIDENT WE'LL REACH AN AGREEMENT.

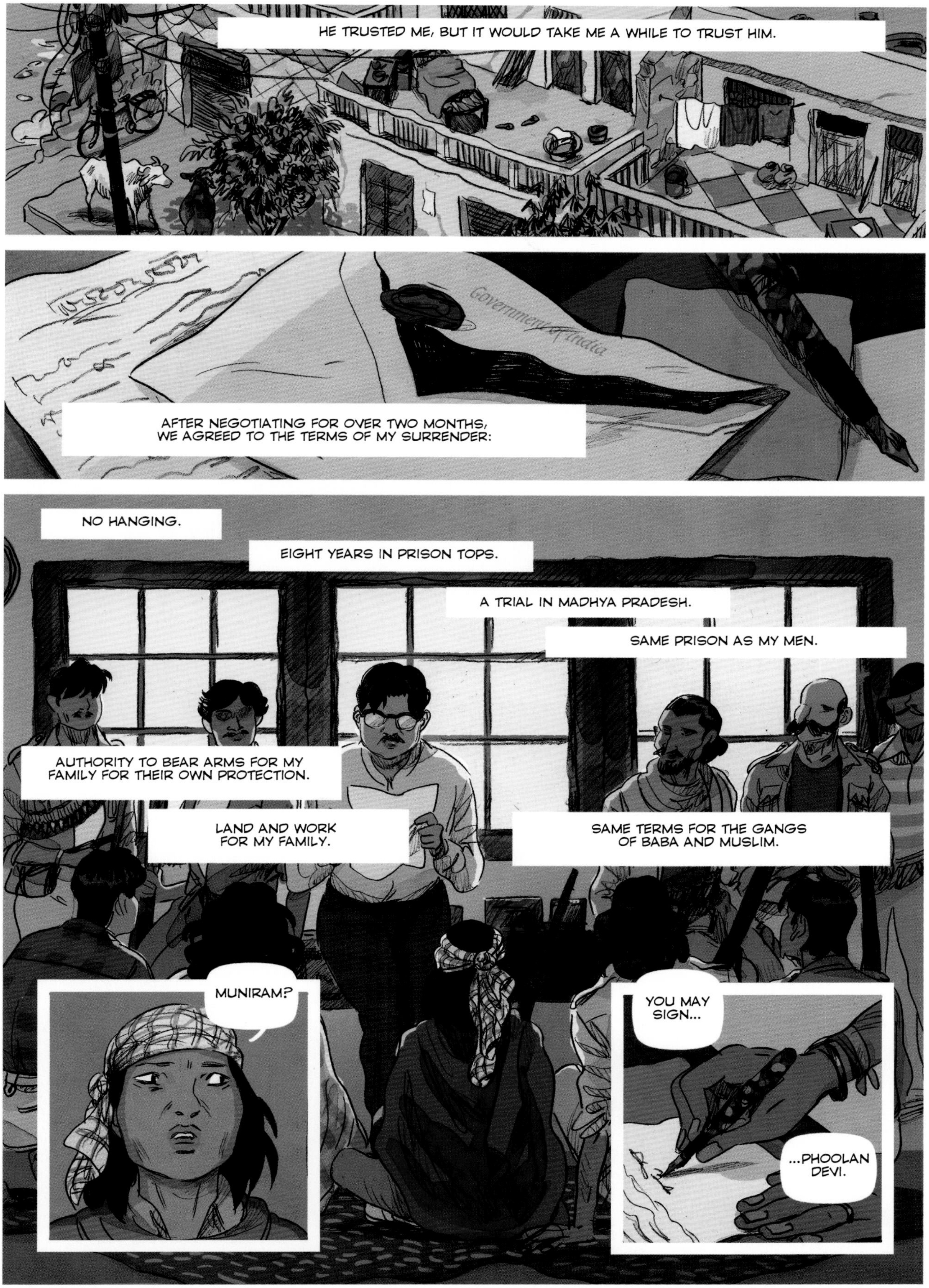
HE TRUSTED ME, BUT IT WOULD TAKE ME A WHILE TO TRUST HIM.
Government of India
AFTER NEGOTIATING FOR OVER TWO MONTHS, WE AGREED TO THE TERMS OF MY SURRENDER:
NO HANGING.
EIGHT YEARS IN PRISON TOPS.
A TRIAL IN MADHYA PRADESH.
SAME PRISON AS MY MEN.
AUTHORITY TO BEAR ARMS FOR MY FAMILY FOR THEIR OWN PROTECTION.
LAND AND WORK FOR MY FAMILY.
SAME TERMS FOR THE GANGS OF BABA AND MUSLIM.
MUNIRAM?
YOU MAY SIGN...
...PHOOLAN DEVI.

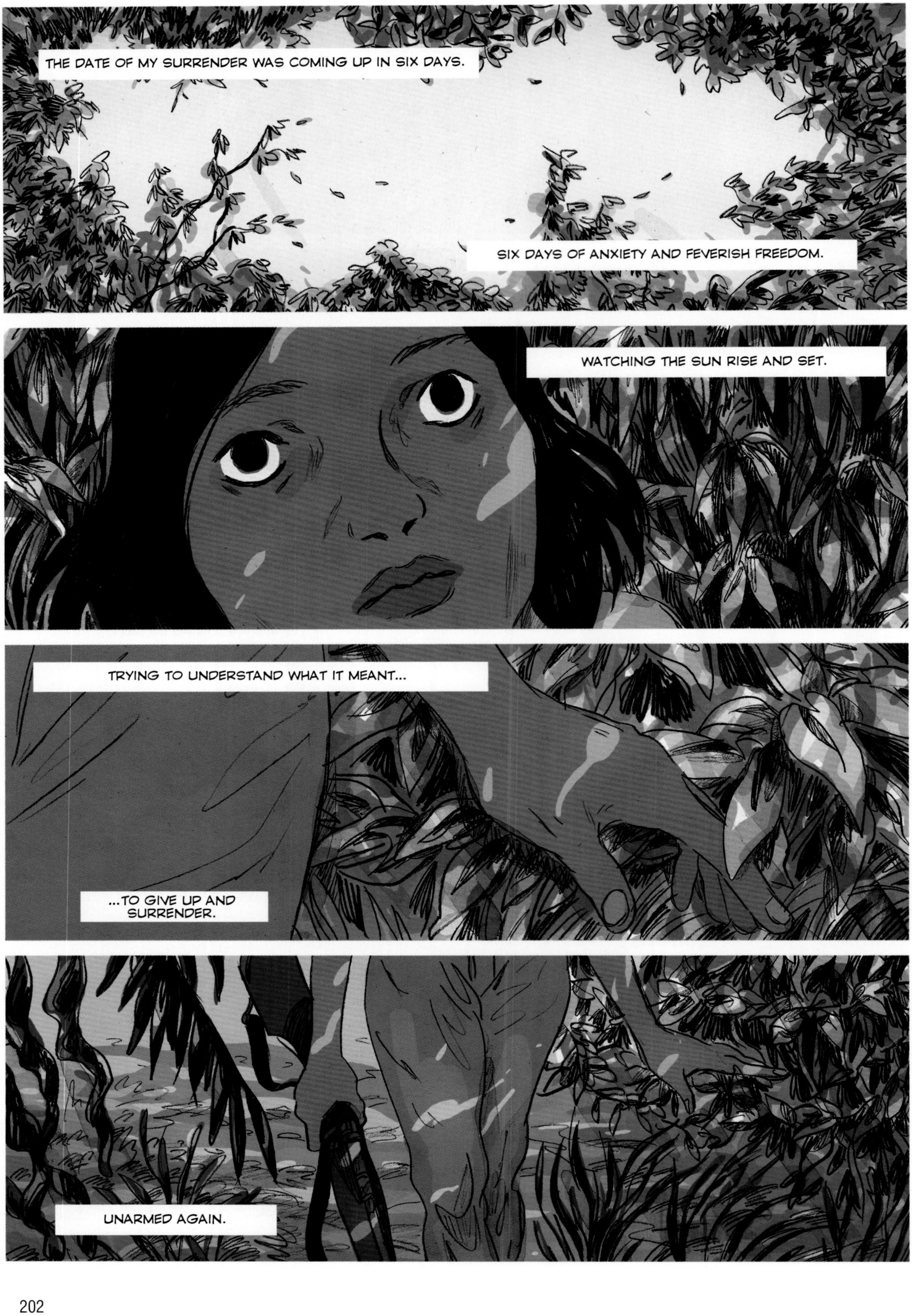
THE DATE OF MY SURRENDER WAS COMING UP IN SIX DAYS.
SIX DAYS OF ANXIETY AND FEVERISH FREEDOM.
WATCHING THE SUN RISE AND SET.
TRYING TO UNDERSTAND WHAT IT MEANT...
...TO GIVE UP AND SURRENDER.
UNARMED AGAIN.

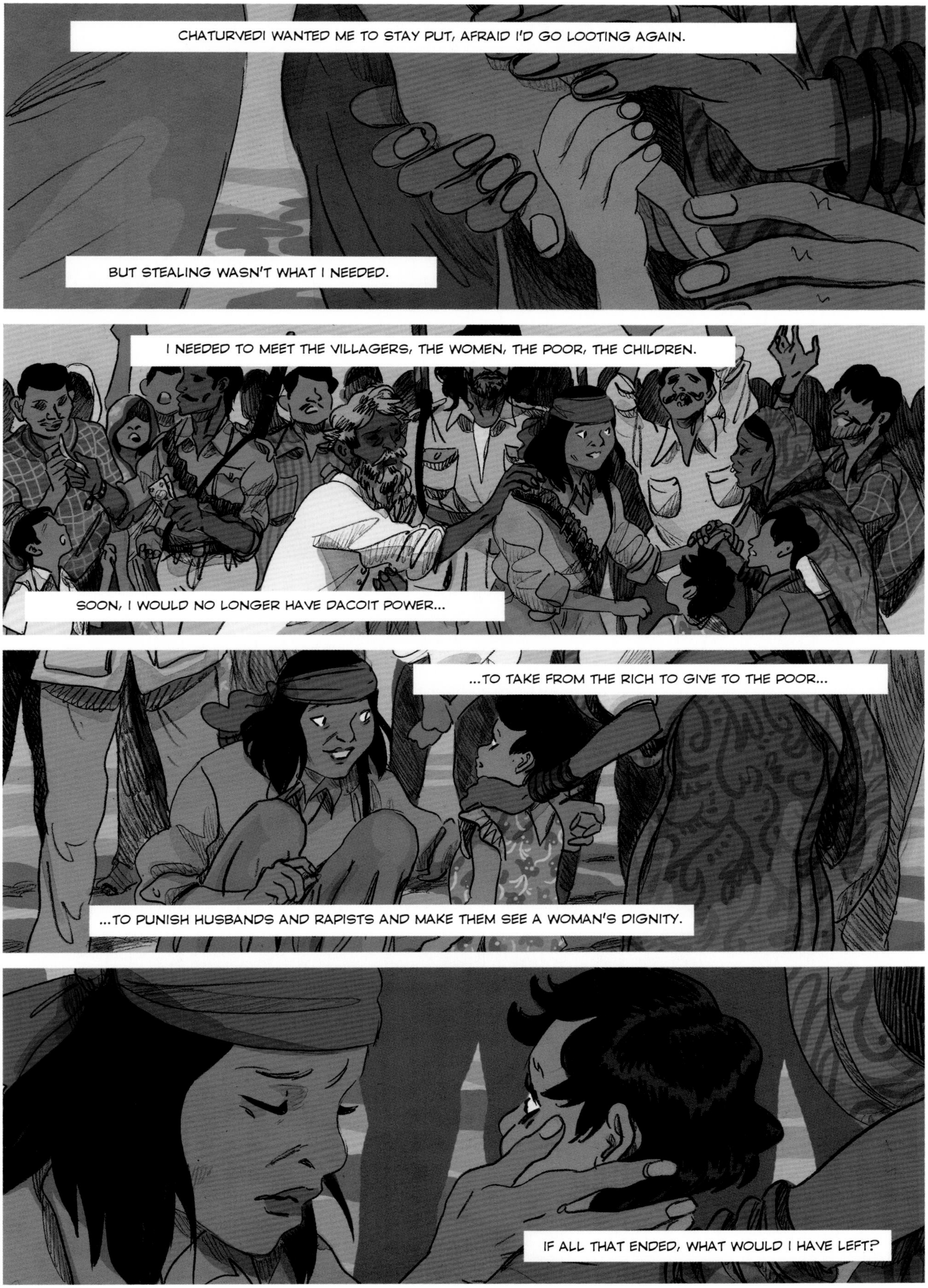
CHATURVEDI WANTED ME TO STAY PUT, AFRAID I'D GO LOOTING AGAIN.
BUT STEALING WASN'T WHAT I NEEDED.
I NEEDED TO MEET THE VILLAGERS, THE WOMEN, THE POOR, THE CHILDREN.
SOON, I WOULD NO LONGER HAVE DACOIT POWER...
...TO TAKE FROM THE RICH TO GIVE TO THE POOR...
...TO PUNISH HUSBANDS AND RAPISTS AND MAKE THEM SEE A WOMAN'S DIGNITY.
IF ALL THAT ENDED, WHAT WOULD I HAVE LEFT?

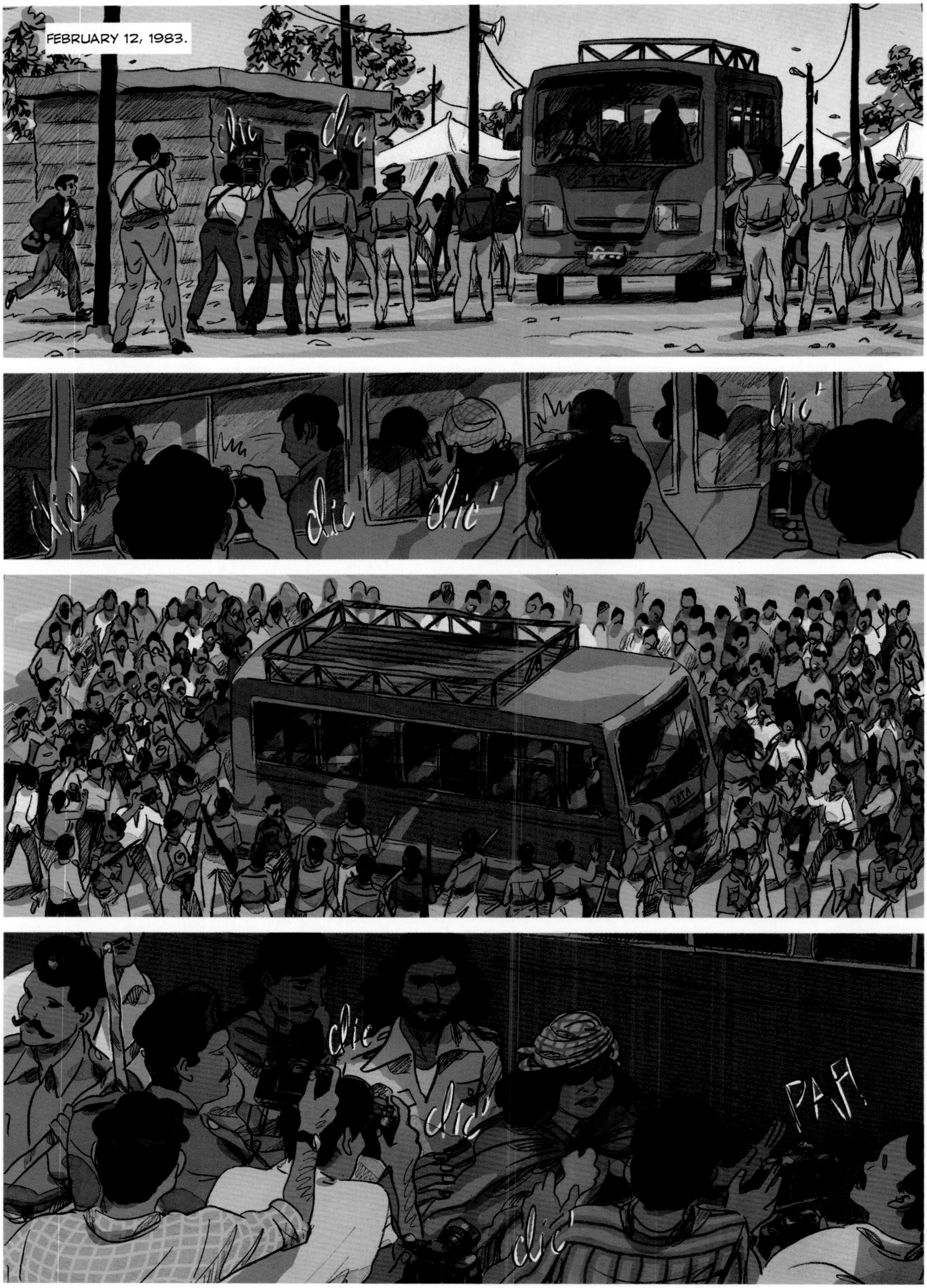
FEBRUARY 12, 1983.
clic
clic
clic
clic
clic
clic
clic
clic
PAH!
clic

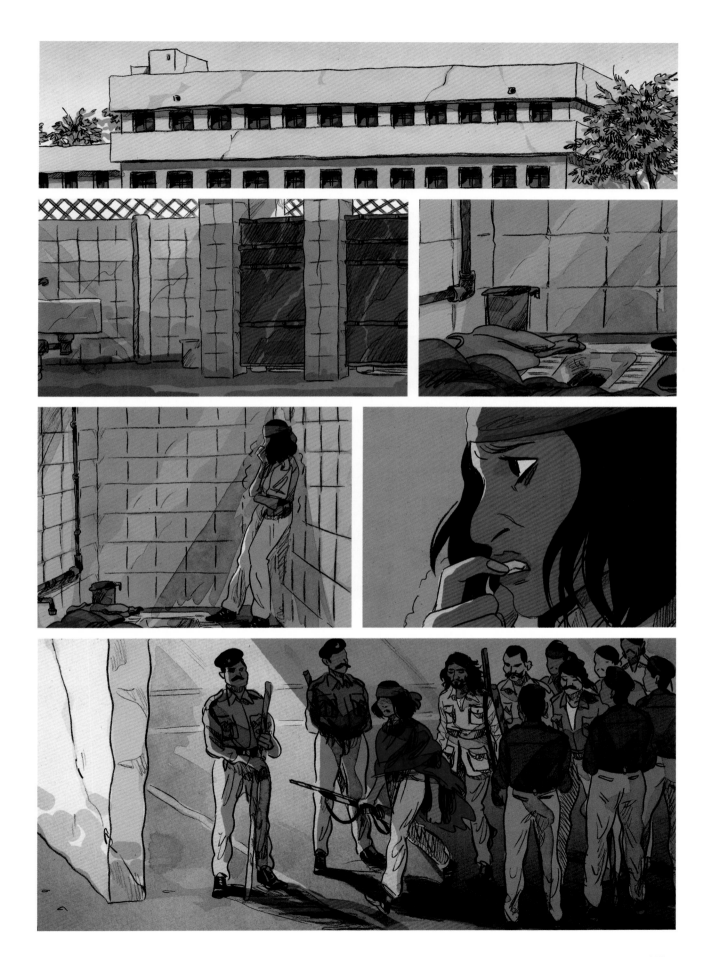

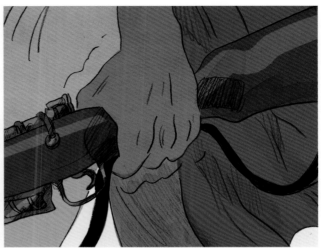

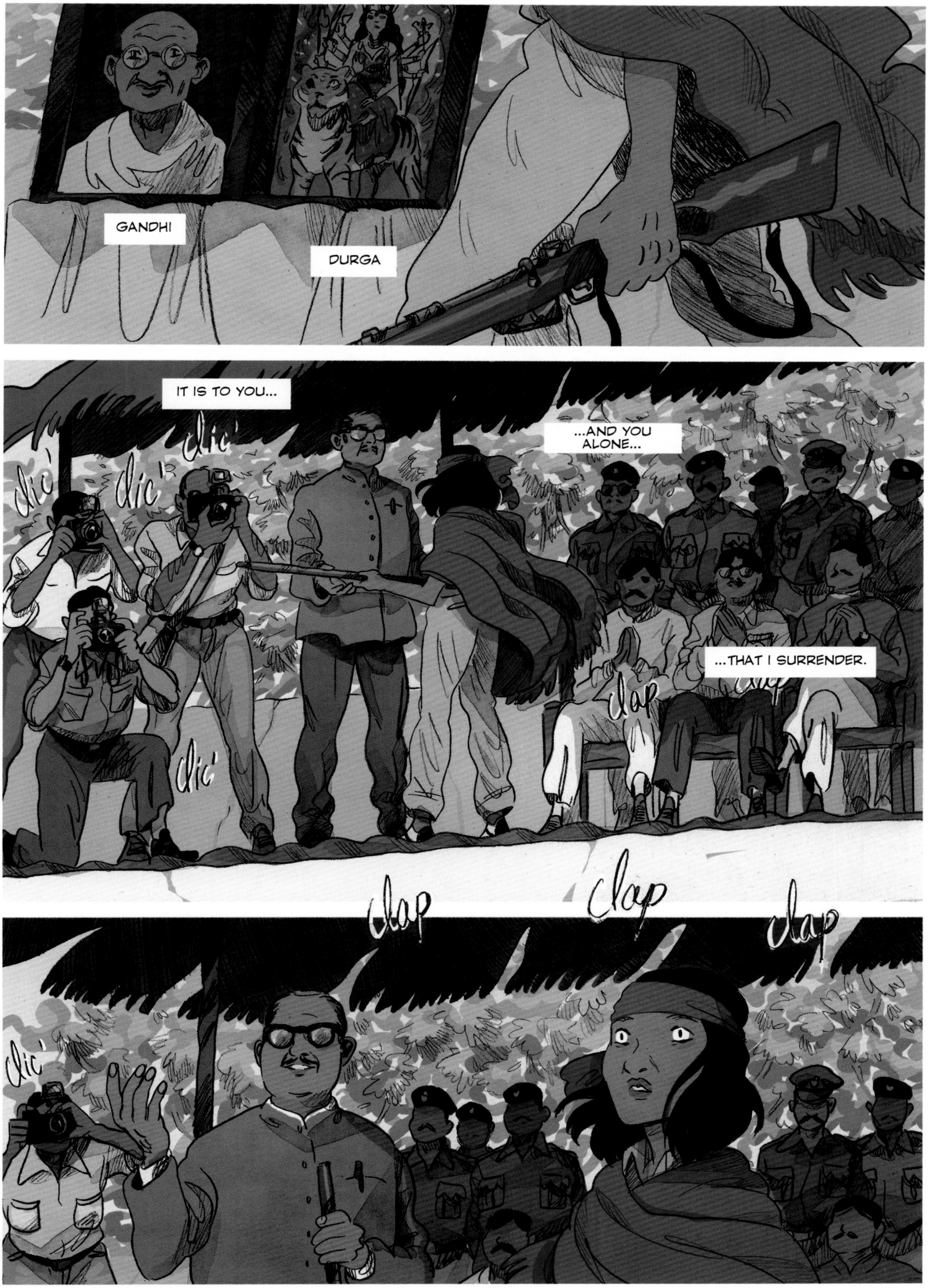
GANDHI
DURGA
IT IS TO YOU...
clic
clic
clic
...AND YOU ALONE...
...THAT I SURRENDER.
clap
clic
clap
clap
clap
clic

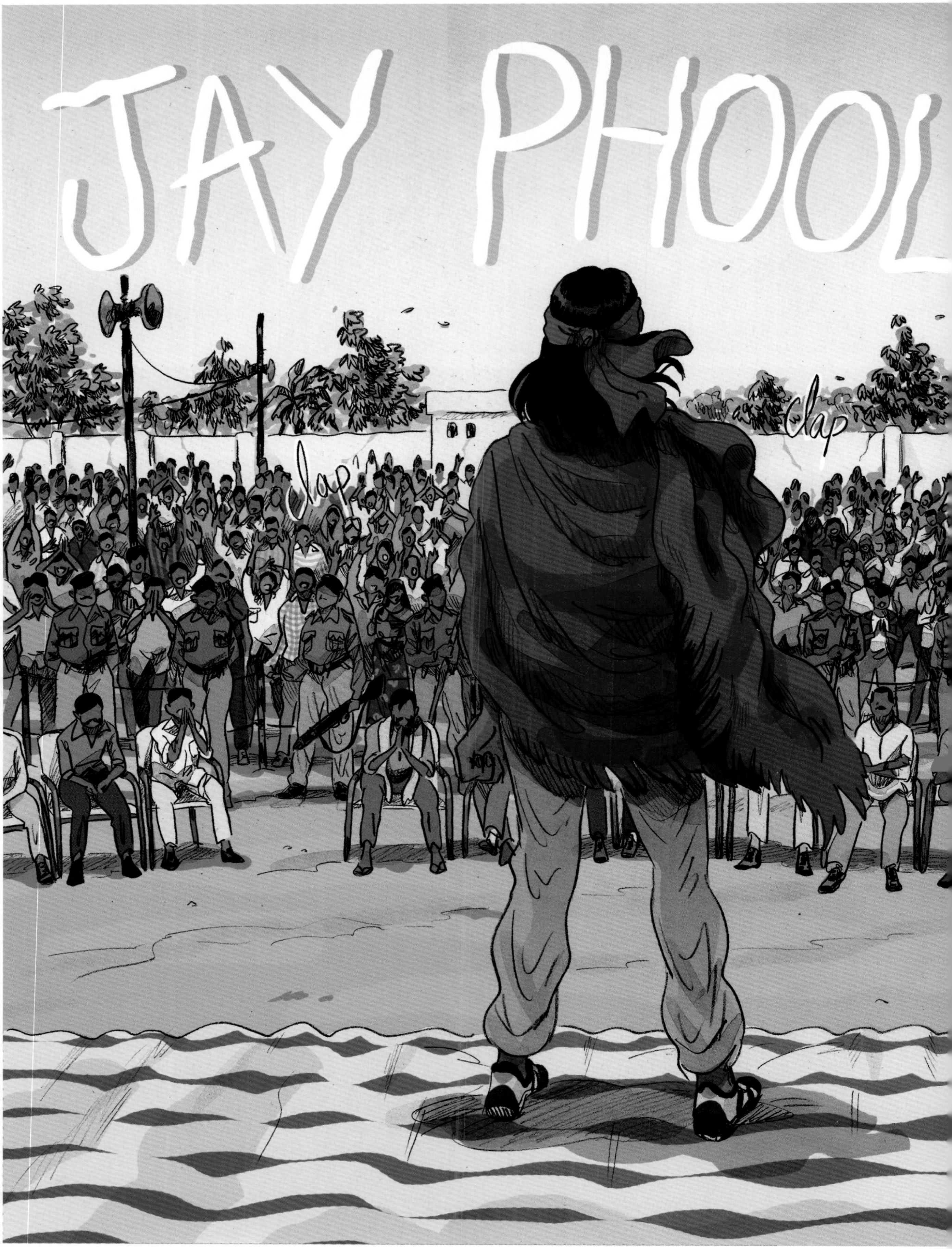
JAY PHOOL
clap
clap

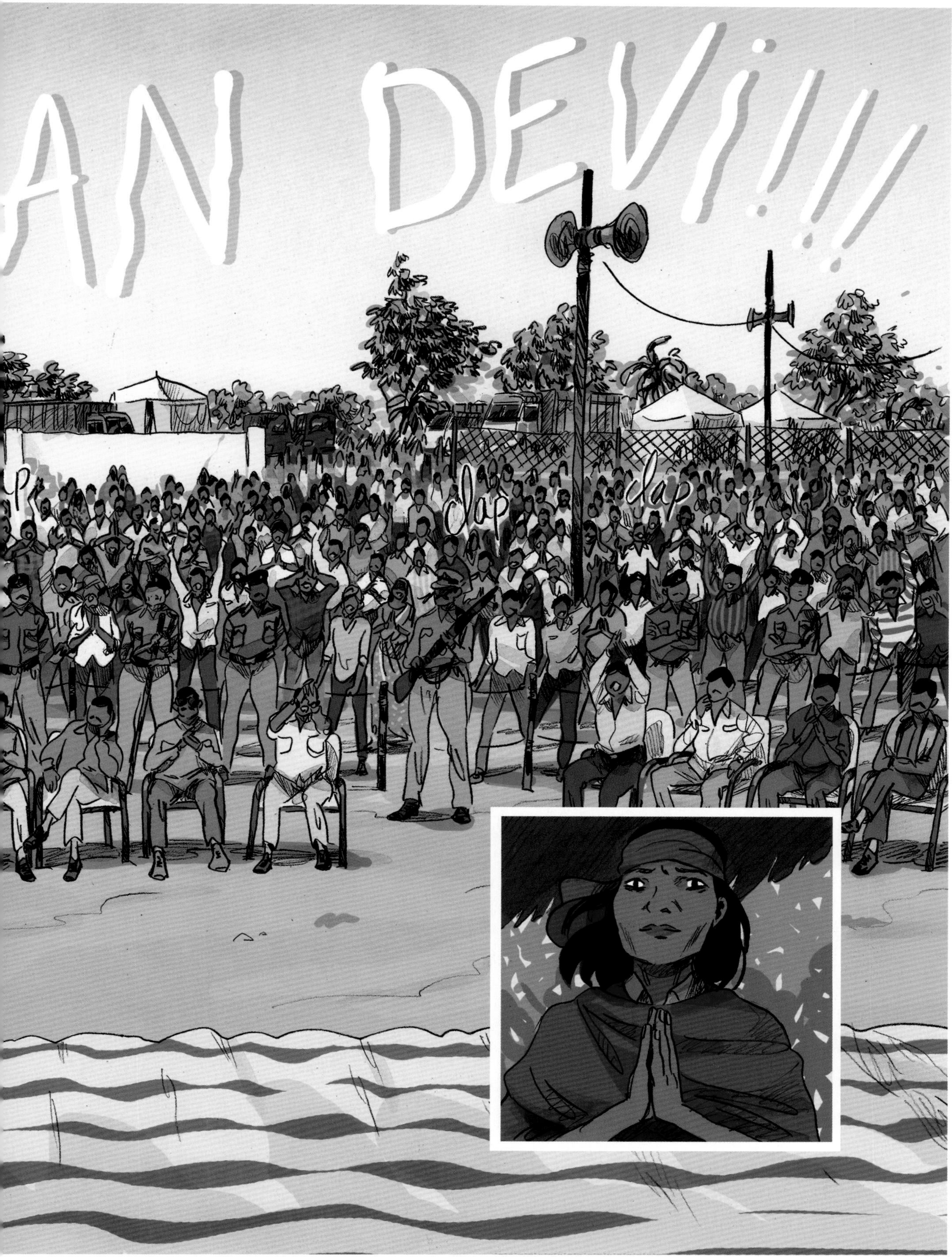
AN DEVI!!!
clap
clap
clap

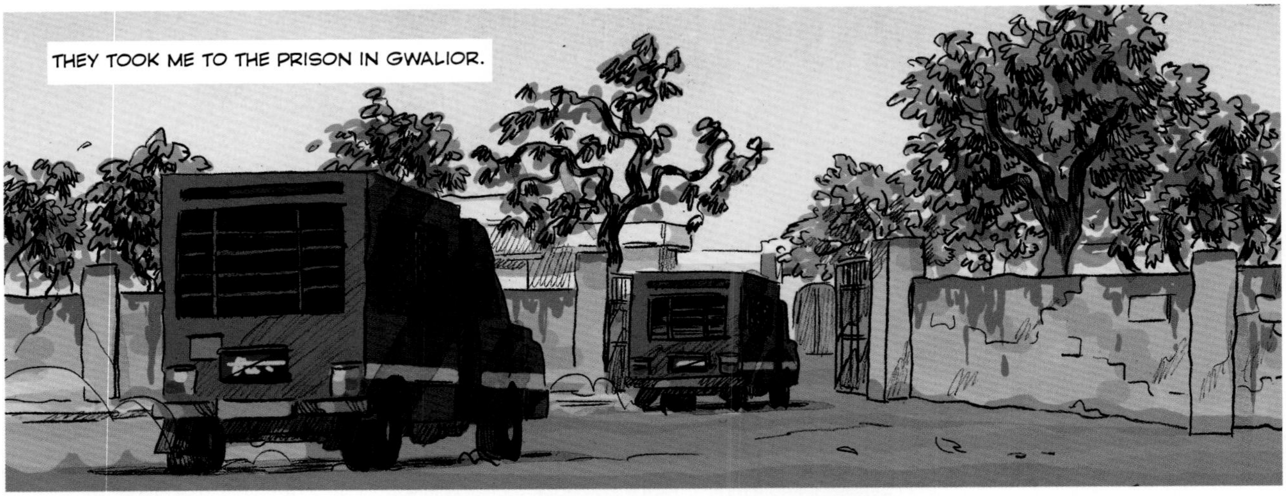
THEY TOOK ME TO THE PRISON IN GWALIOR.

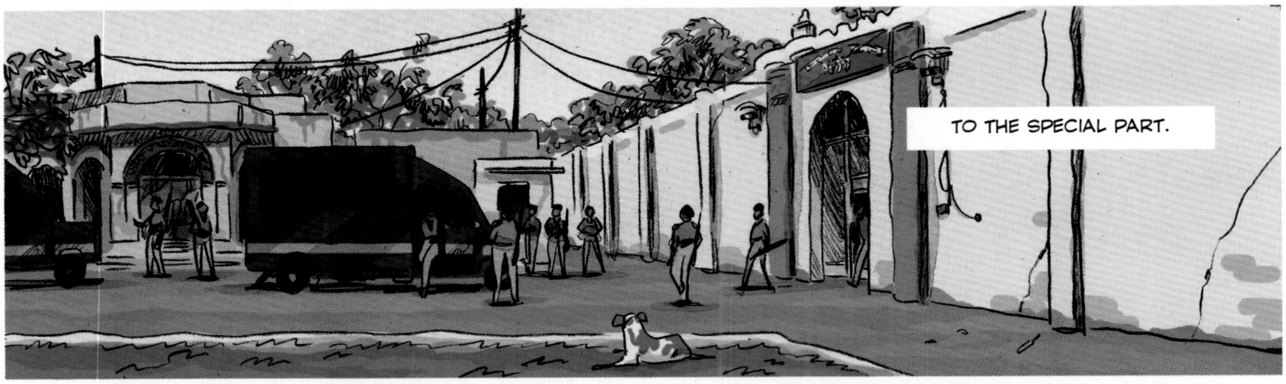
TO THE SPECIAL PART.

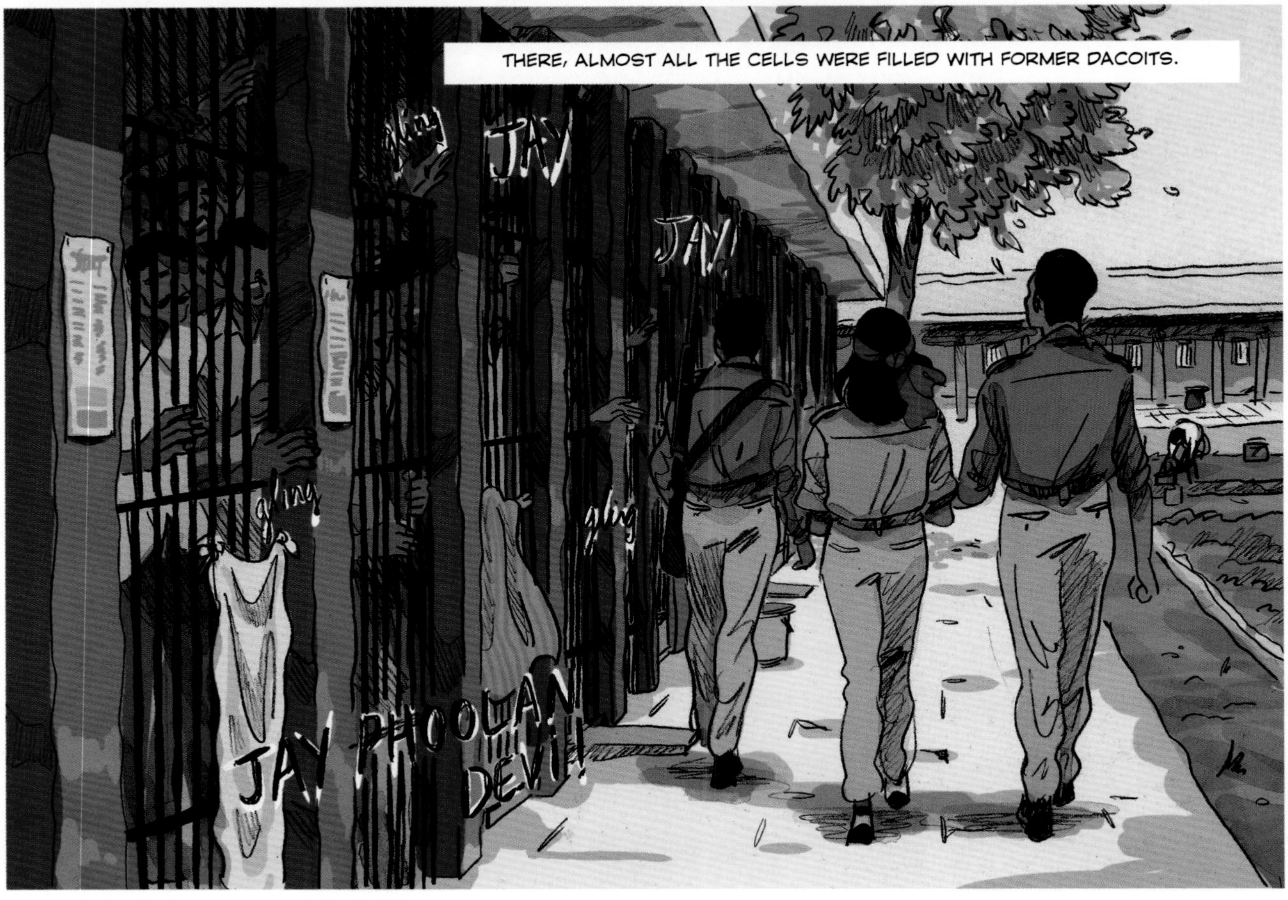
THERE, ALMOST ALL THE CELLS WERE FILLED WITH FORMER DACOITS.
JAY
JAY
JAY PHOOLAN DEVI!

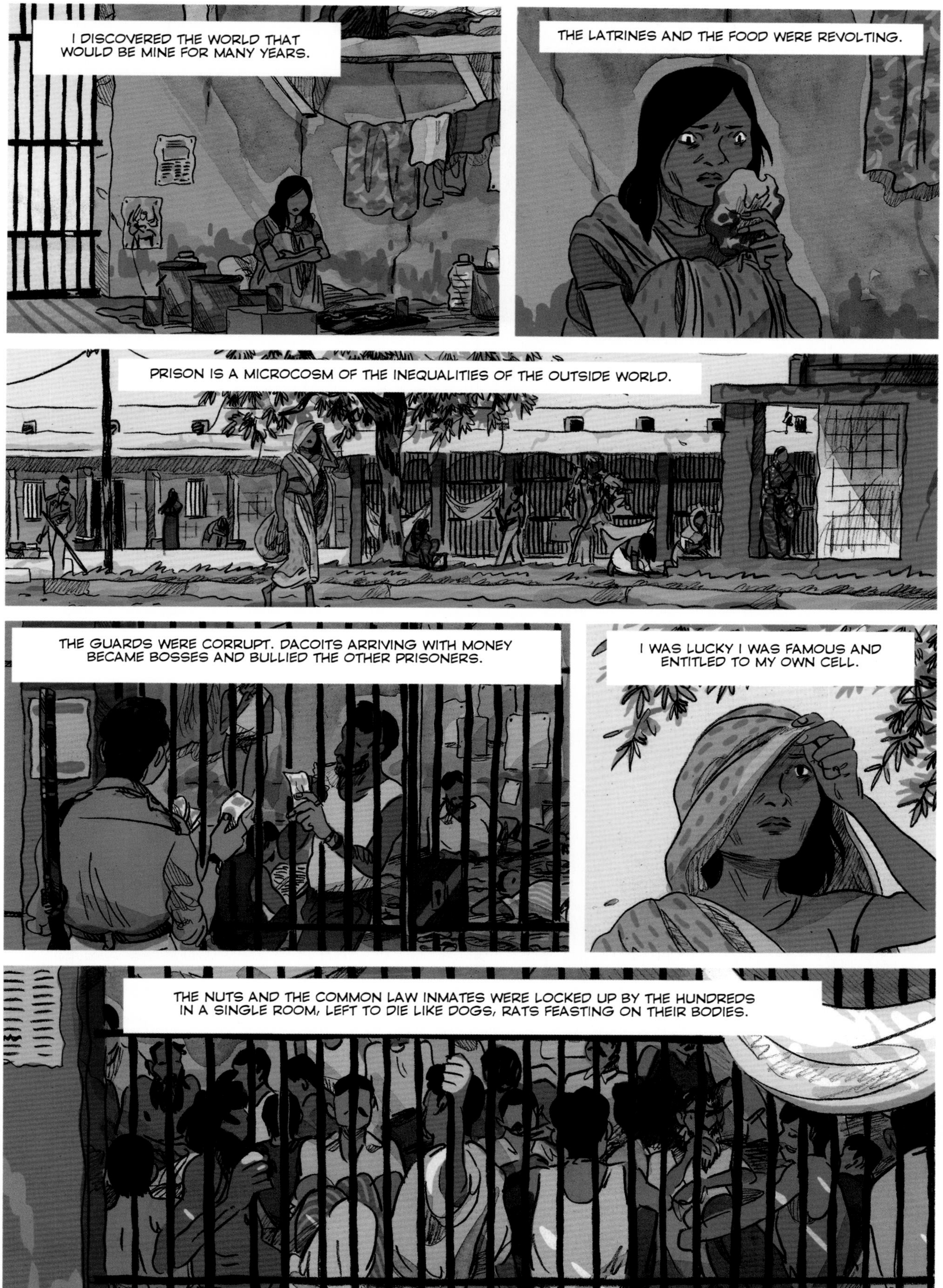
I DISCOVERED THE WORLD THAT WOULD BE MINE FOR MANY YEARS.
THE LATRINES AND THE FOOD WERE REVOLTING.
PRISON IS A MICROCOSM OF THE INEQUALITIES OF THE OUTSIDE WORLD.
THE GUARDS WERE CORRUPT. DACOITS ARRIVING WITH MONEY BECAME BOSSES AND BULLIED THE OTHER PRISONERS.
I WAS LUCKY I WAS FAMOUS AND ENTITLED TO MY OWN CELL.
THE NUTS AND THE COMMON LAW INMATES WERE LOCKED UP BY THE HUNDREDS IN A SINGLE ROOM, LEFT TO DIE LIKE DOGS, RATS FEASTING ON THEIR BODIES.

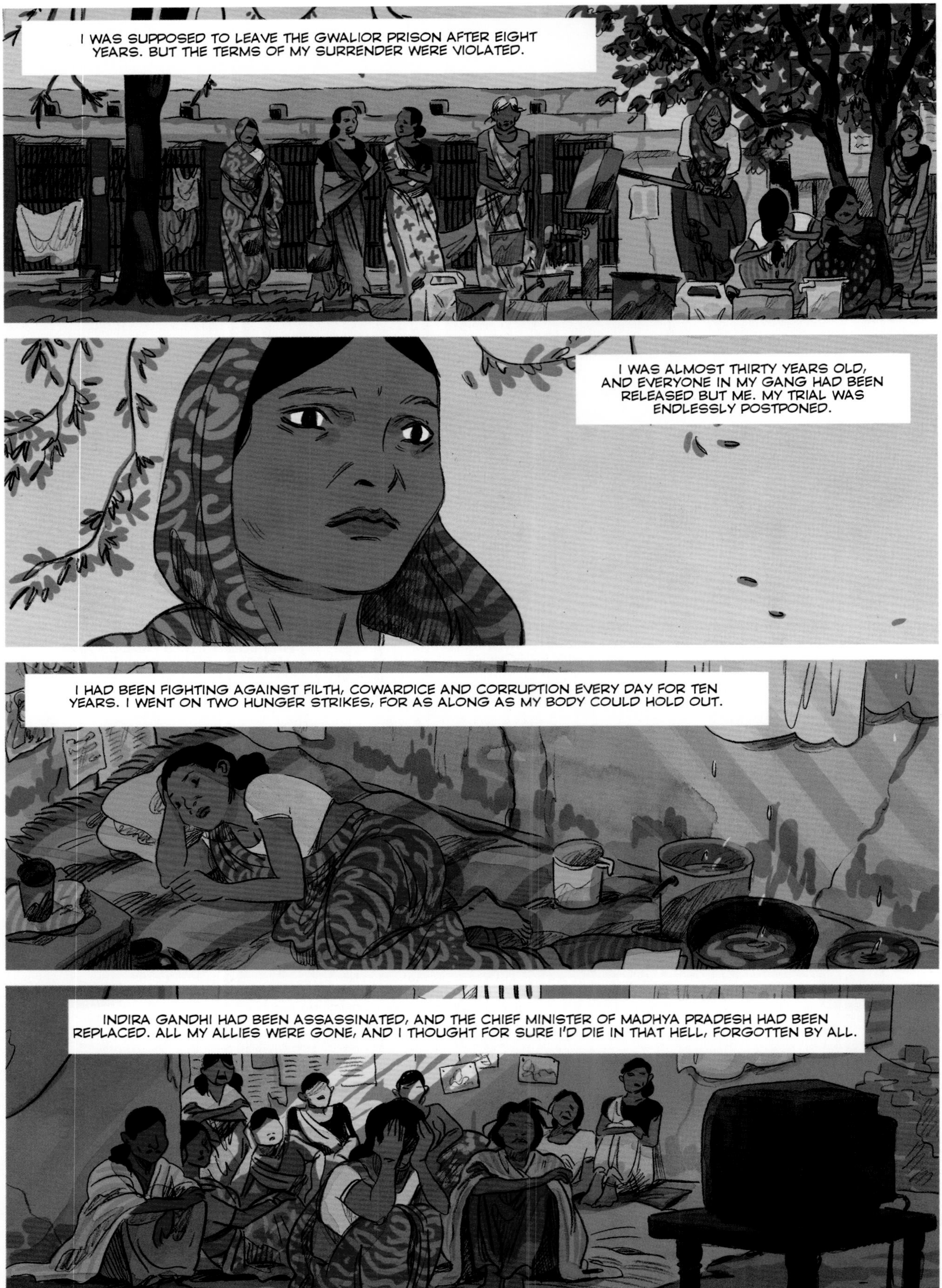
I WAS SUPPOSED TO LEAVE THE GWALIOR PRISON AFTER EIGHT YEARS. BUT THE TERMS OF MY SURRENDER WERE VIOLATED.
I WAS ALMOST THIRTY YEARS OLD, AND EVERYONE IN MY GANG HAD BEEN RELEASED BUT ME. MY TRIAL WAS ENDLESSLY POSTPONED.
I HAD BEEN FIGHTING AGAINST FILTH, COWARDICE AND CORRUPTION EVERY DAY FOR TEN YEARS. I WENT ON TWO HUNGER STRIKES, FOR AS ALONG AS MY BODY COULD HOLD OUT.
INDIRA GANDHI HAD BEEN ASSASSINATED, AND THE CHIEF MINISTER OF MADHYA PRADESH HAD BEEN REPLACED. ALL MY ALLIES WERE GONE, AND I THOUGHT FOR SURE I'D DIE IN THAT HELL, FORGOTTEN BY ALL.

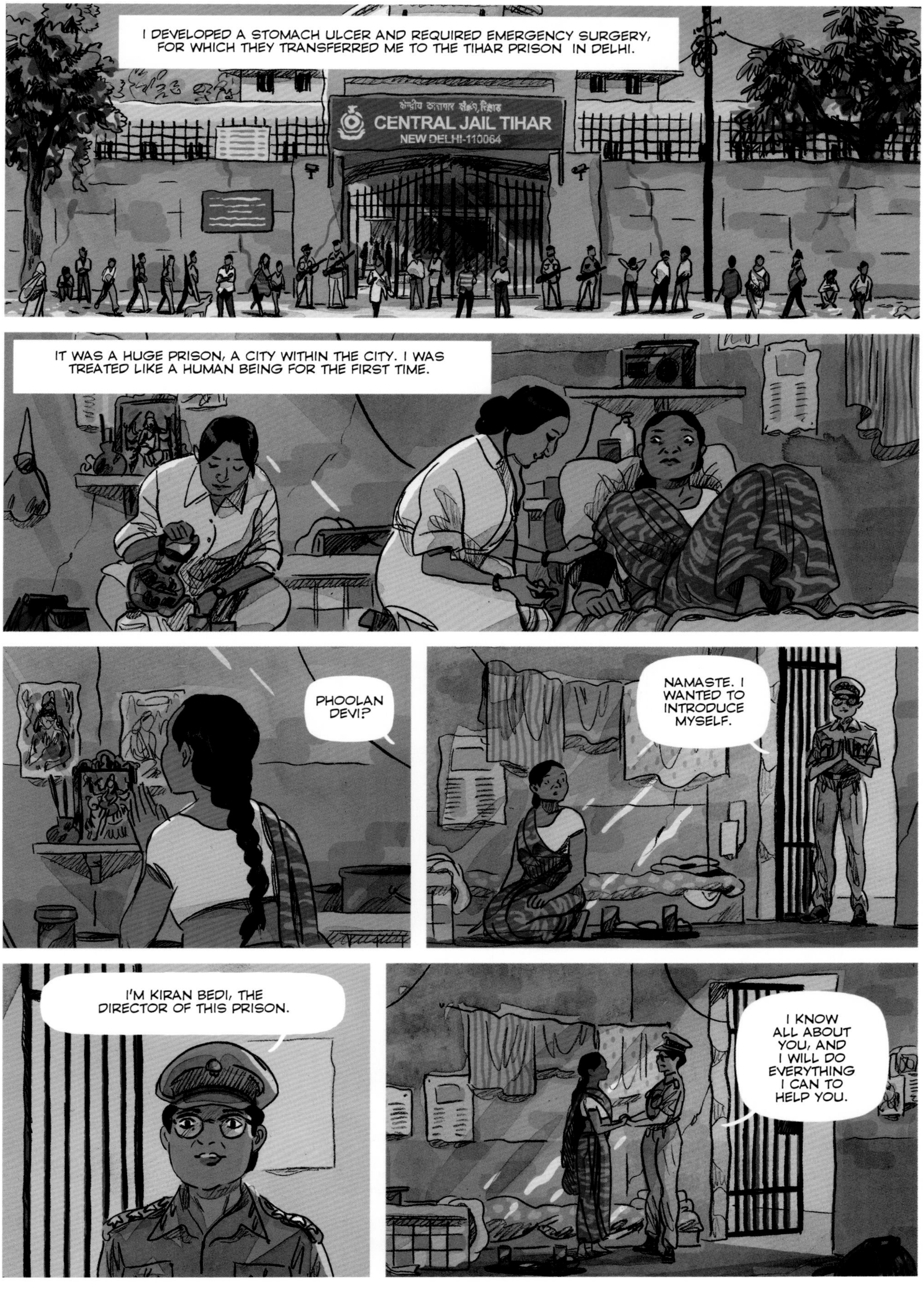

I DEVELOPED A STOMACH ULCER AND REQUIRED EMERGENCY SURGERY, FOR WHICH THEY TRANSFERRED ME TO THE TIHAR PRISON IN DELHI.
CENTRAL JAIL TIHAR
NEW DELHI-110064
IT WAS A HUGE PRISON, A CITY WITHIN THE CITY. I WAS TREATED LIKE A HUMAN BEING FOR THE FIRST TIME.
PHOOLAN DEVI?
NAMASTE. I WANTED TO INTRODUCE MYSELF.
I'M KIRAN BEDI, THE DIRECTOR OF THIS PRISON.
I KNOW ALL ABOUT YOU, AND I WILL DO EVERYTHING I CAN TO HELP YOU.

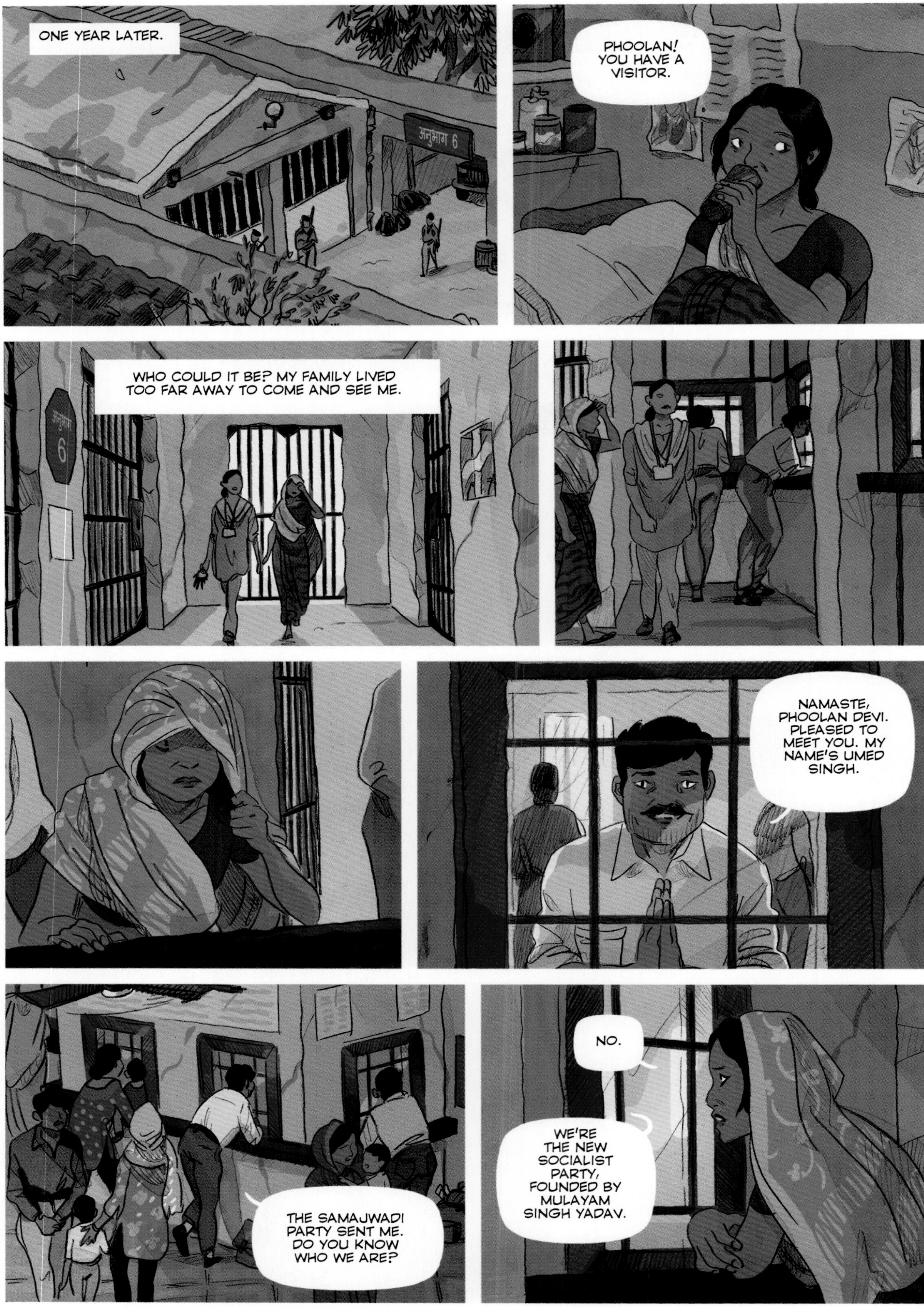
ONE YEAR LATER.
अनुभाग 6
PHOOLAN! YOU HAVE A VISITOR.
WHO COULD IT BE? MY FAMILY LIVED TOO FAR AWAY TO COME AND SEE ME.
अनुभाग 6
NAMASTE, PHOOLAN DEVI. PLEASED TO MEET YOU. MY NAME'S UMED SINGH.
THE SAMAJWADI PARTY SENT ME. DO YOU KNOW WHO WE ARE?
NO.
WE'RE THE NEW SOCIALIST PARTY, FOUNDED BY MULAYAM SINGH YADAV.

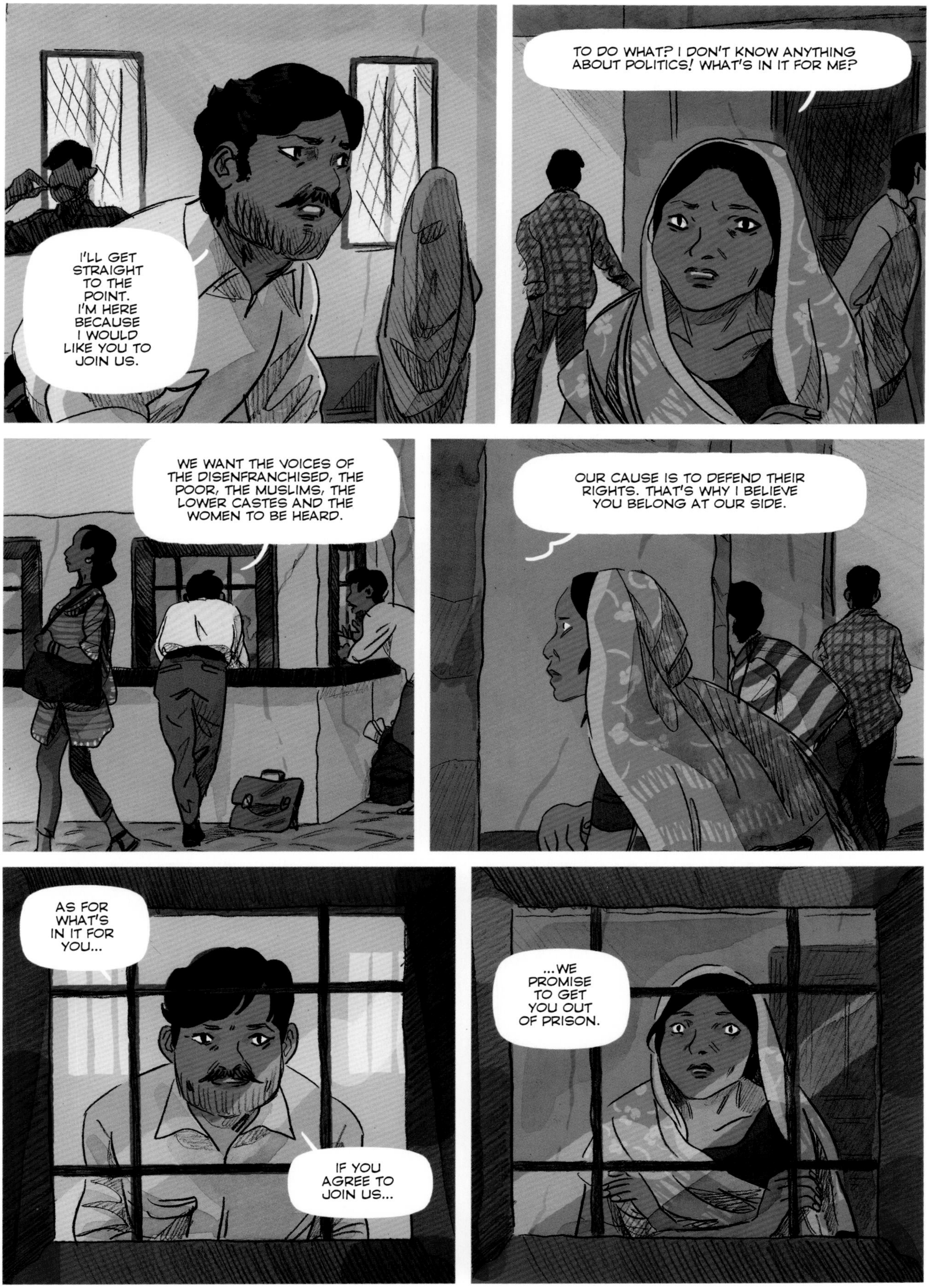
I'LL GET STRAIGHT TO THE POINT. I'M HERE BECAUSE I WOULD LIKE YOU TO JOIN US.
TO DO WHAT? I DON'T KNOW ANYTHING ABOUT POLITICS! WHAT'S IN IT FOR ME?
WE WANT THE VOICES OF THE DISENFRANCHISED, THE POOR, THE MUSLIMS, THE LOWER CASTES AND THE WOMEN TO BE HEARD.
OUR CAUSE IS TO DEFEND THEIR RIGHTS. THAT'S WHY I BELIEVE YOU BELONG AT OUR SIDE.
AS FOR WHAT'S IN IT FOR YOU...
IF YOU AGREE TO JOIN US...
...WE PROMISE TO GET YOU OUT OF PRISON.

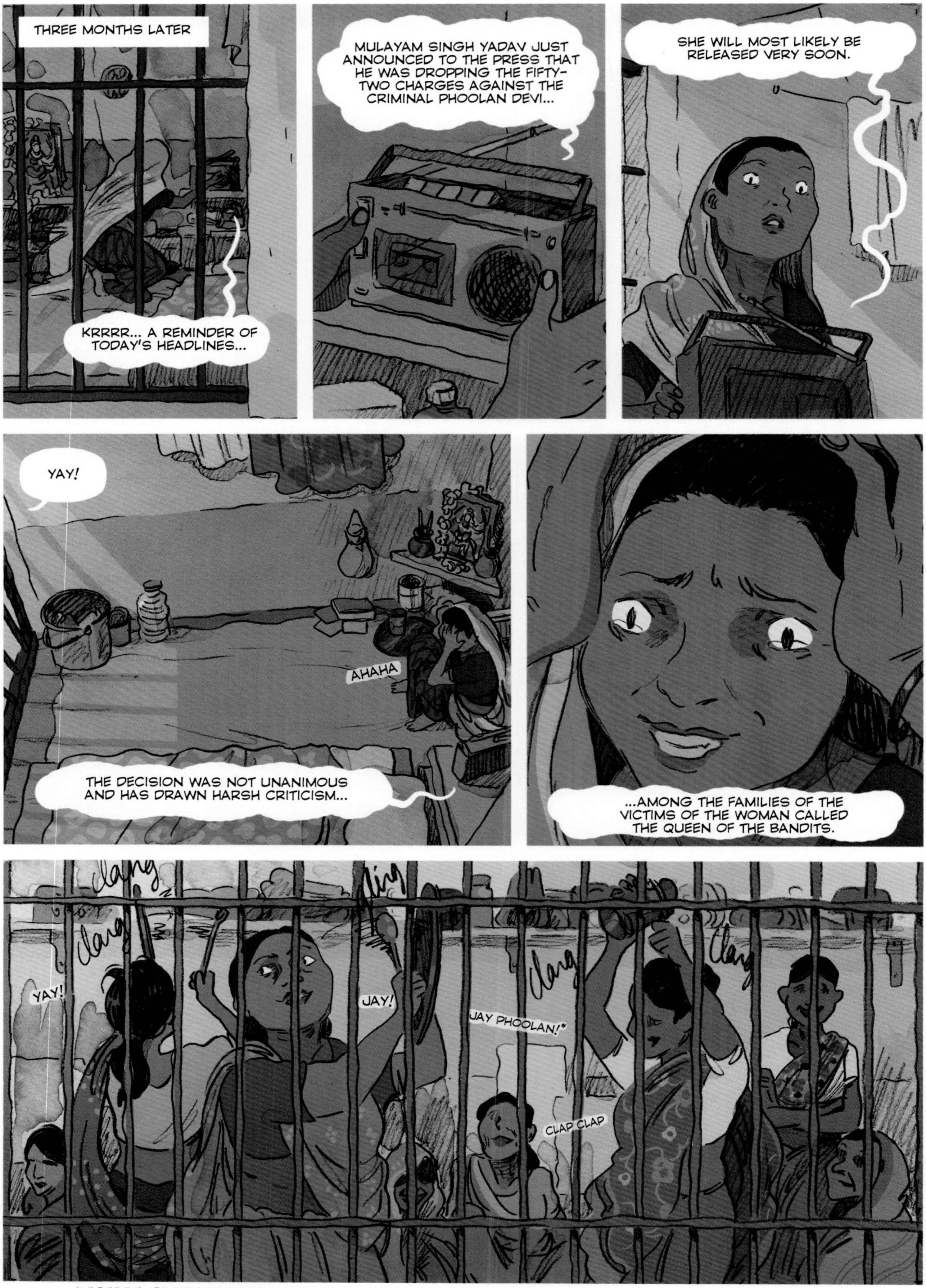
THREE MONTHS LATER
KRRRR... A REMINDER OF TODAY'S HEADLINES...
MULAYAM SINGH YADAV JUST ANNOUNCED TO THE PRESS THAT HE WAS DROPPING THE FIFTY-TWO CHARGES AGAINST THE CRIMINAL PHOOLAN DEVI...
SHE WILL MOST LIKELY BE RELEASED VERY SOON.
YAY!
AHAHA
THE DECISION WAS NOT UNANIMOUS AND HAS DRAWN HARSH CRITICISM...
...AMONG THE FAMILIES OF THE VICTIMS OF THE WOMAN CALLED THE QUEEN OF THE BANDITS.
clang
YAY!
JAY!
JAY PHOOLAN!*
CLAP CLAP

*VICTORY, GLORY TO PHOOLAN.

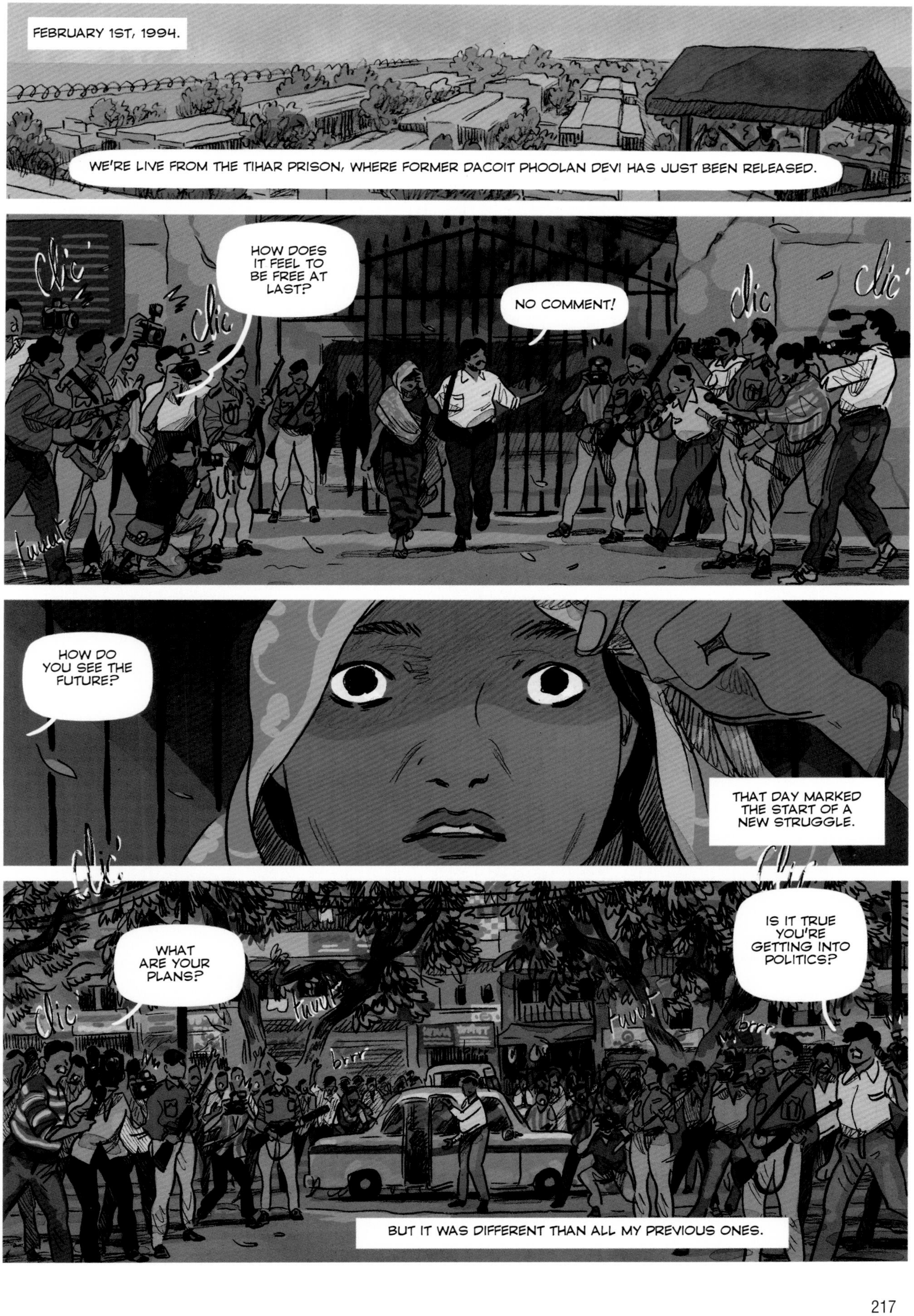
FEBRUARY 1ST, 1994.
WE'RE LIVE FROM THE TIHAR PRISON, WHERE FORMER DACOIT PHOOLAN DEVI HAS JUST BEEN RELEASED.
HOW DOES IT FEEL TO BE FREE AT LAST?
NO COMMENT!
clic
clic
clic
clic
tuuut
HOW DO YOU SEE THE FUTURE?
THAT DAY MARKED THE START OF A NEW STRUGGLE.
clic
clic
WHAT ARE YOUR PLANS?
IS IT TRUE YOU'RE GETTING INTO POLITICS?
clic
tuuut
tuuut
brrr
brrr
BUT IT WAS DIFFERENT THAN ALL MY PREVIOUS ONES.

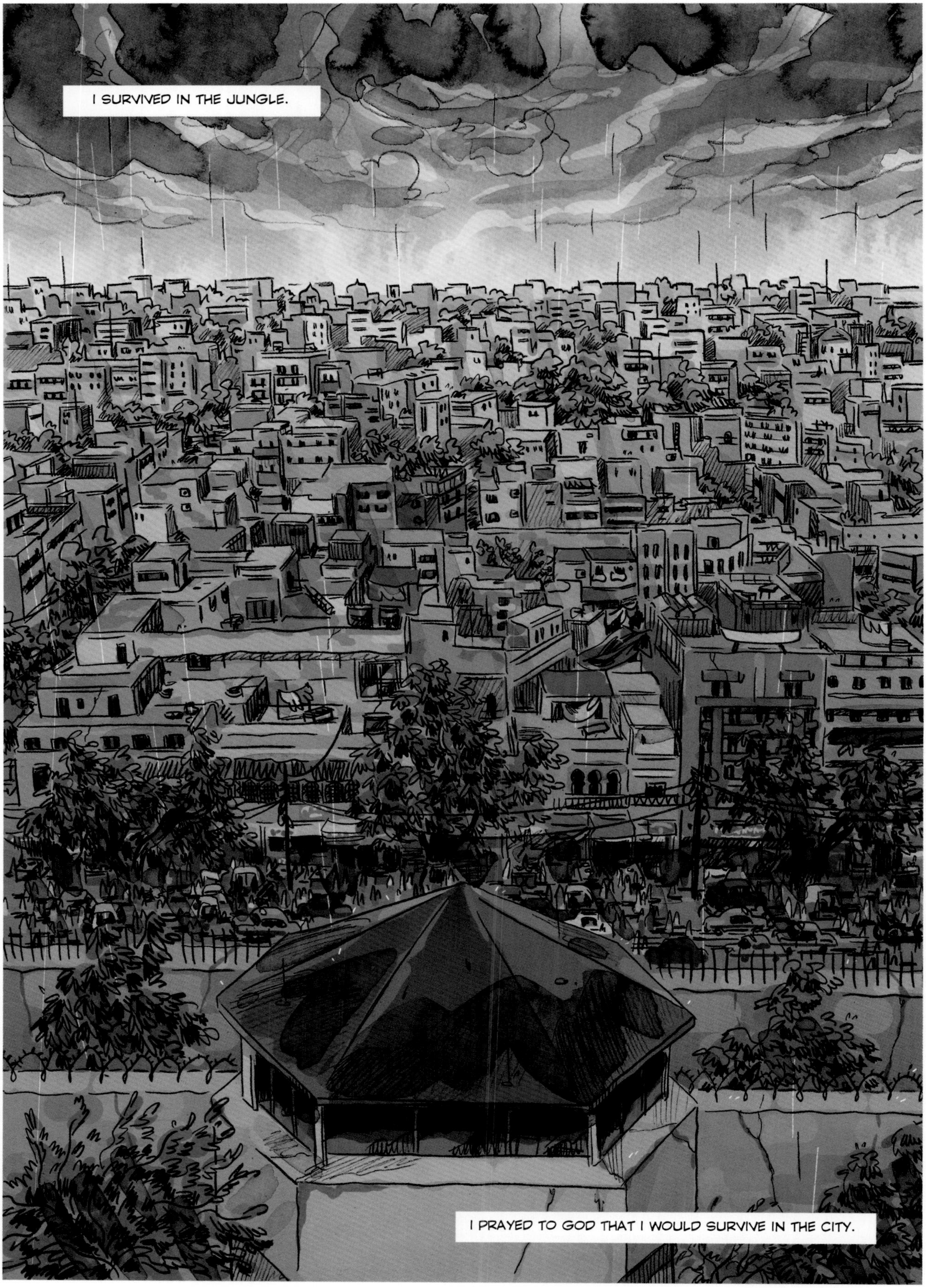
I SURVIVED IN THE JUNGLE.
I PRAYED TO GOD THAT I WOULD SURVIVE IN THE CITY.

IN MY VILLAGE, IT IS SAID THAT
WHEN KANS THE DEMON STRIKES
A LITTLE GIRL AT BIRTH AND KILLS HER,
THAT LITTLE GIRL FLOATS UP INTO THE HEAVENS
AND BECOMES THUNDER HERSELF.

DEMONS STRUCK ME DOWN,
SO I BECAME
THUNDER FOR THE OTHERS.

I DON'T SEE MYSELF AS A GOOD PERSON,
BUT I AM NOT A CRIMINAL, EITHER.

ALL I DID WAS DO TO MEN
WHAT THEY HAD DONE TO ME.

After being elected to Parliament in 1996 and again in 1999, Phoolan Devi, the voice of the oppressed, was assassinated in 2001 by a Thakur extremist, in retaliation for the Behmai massacre.

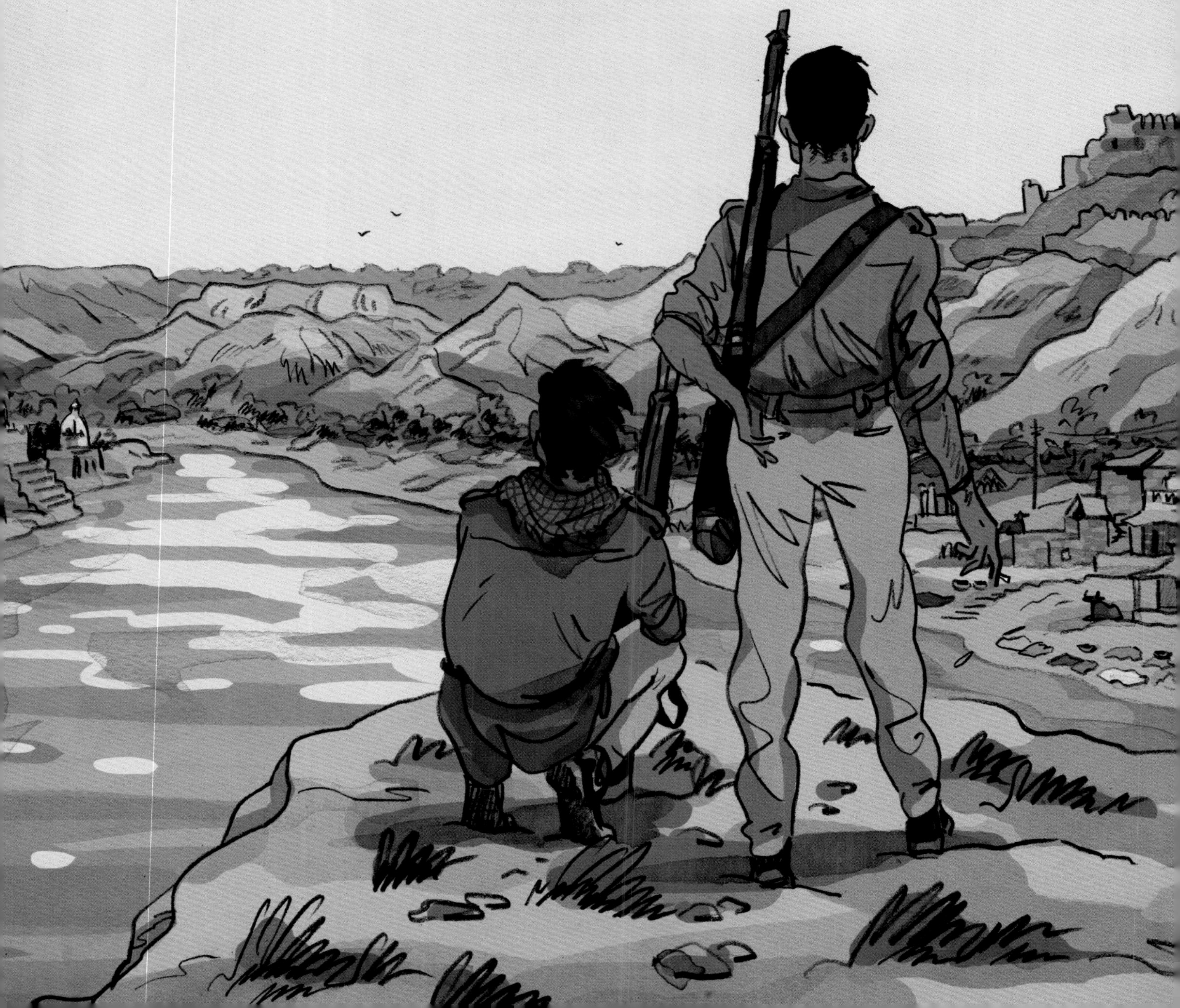

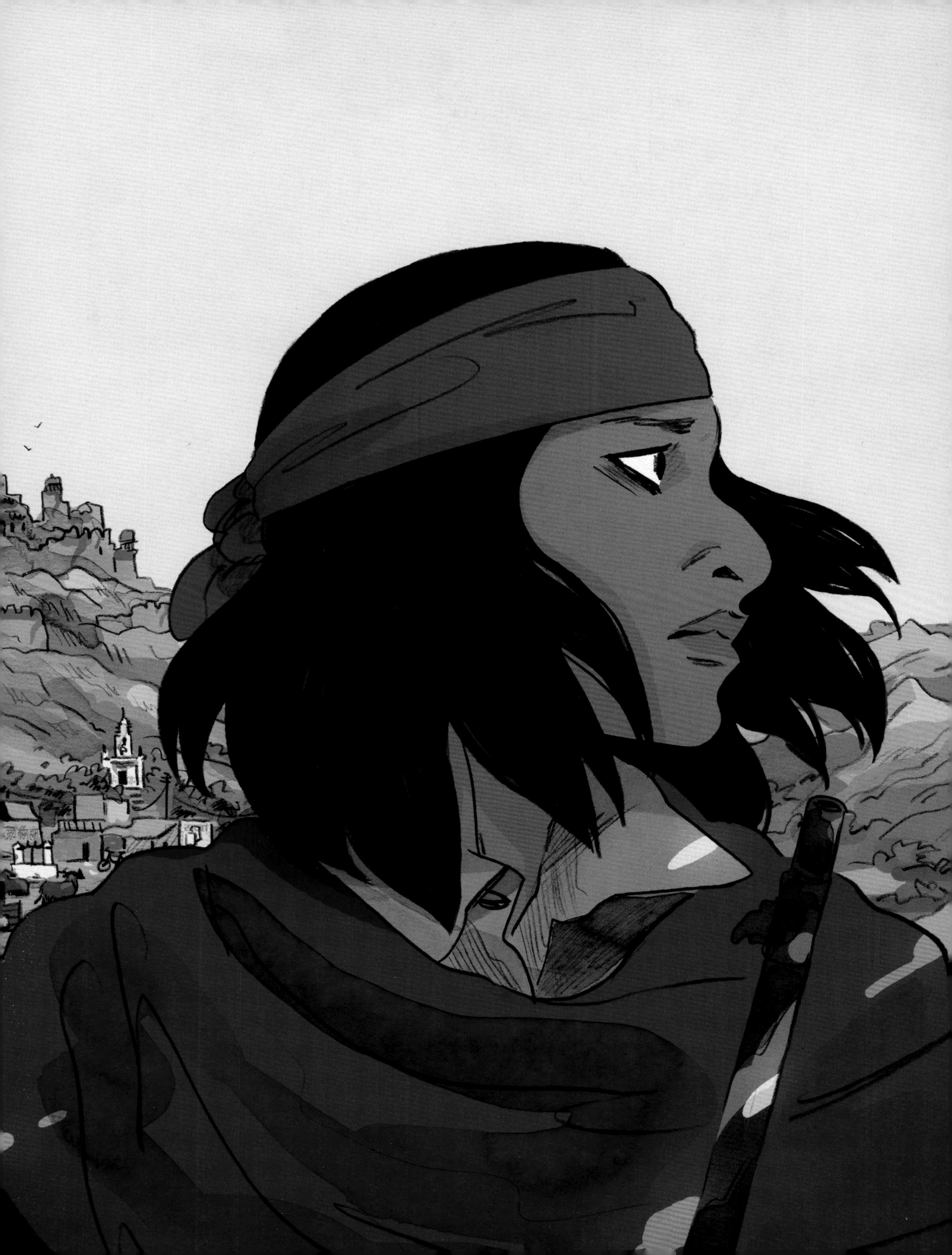

FURTHER READING

I, Phoolan Devi: The Autobiography of India's Bandit Queen by Phoolan Devi (Little Brown and Company, 1997). The book that inspired this graphic novel, to which author Claire Fauvel tried to remain faithful.

India's Bandit Queen by British-Indian writer and human rights activist Mala San (HarperCollins; Revised, Updated, Subsequent edition, 2001). It inspired the 1994 film *Bandit Queen* (see below).

The Bandit Queen of India: An Indian Woman's Amazing Journey From Peasant to International Legend, by Phoolan Devi, Marie-Therese Cuny, Paul Rambali (The Lyons Press; 1st edition, 2003)

"It took a Salman Rushdie to make the world discuss the Freedom of Expression... to discuss an individual's right to Justice, it takes a Phoolan Devi." -Arundhati Roy, Author of the International Best-Seller *The God of Small Things*

"She will remain one of the most talked-about people in the country." -The New York Times

"Phoolan Devi: A Dacoit, a Rape Survivor, a Politician, a Legend" Article by Maanvi in online Indian newspaper *The Quint* (reprinted 9-8-19).

Bandit Queen (1994), directed by Shekkhar Kapur, screenplay by Ranjit Kapoor, adapted from the book by Mala Sen and starring Seem Biswas as Phoolan Devi. A critically acclaimed film that premiered in Cannes and was nominated for an Oscar, it was adapted from the book by Mala Sen and contested for inaccuracy by Phoolan Devi, who tried to get it banned in India and even threatened to immolate herself before eventually dropping the complaint.

CLAIRE FAUVEL

After studying illustration at the prestigious Ecole Estienne in Paris, Claire Fauvel entered the famous Ecole Des Gobelins to study animation but adopted comics as a means of telling her own stories. This is her second graphic novel.

www.clairefauvel.ultra-book.com

A big thank you to:

Christine Cam and the entire
Casterman team,
Aelys Hasbun for sharing her
India experience with me,

My Christophe, invaluable
traveling companion and per-
sonal bodyguard in the heart of
the ravines of Uttar Pradesh,

and Kumar Vikas and Ramkali
Devi, who held the door to
Phoolan Devi's kingdom
wide open for us.

Claire F.

Also available from NBM Comics Biographies:
TAMBA, Child Soldier by Marion Achard & Yan Degruel
"My name is Tamba Cisso. When I was eight years old, I lived in the village with my father, my mother and my sister. I went to school and had learned to read. I knew there was war in my country, but I didn't know that children could wage it."

GHETTO BROTHER by Julian Voloj & Claudia Ahlering
"The gang truce back in the early seventies with Brother Benjy, with all the major street organizations, was powerful. It was the time to put down the weapons against each other and try to organize… It was deep. It was powerful… We were all in the same game."
-Afrika Bambaataa

Plus more than a dozen other bios of famous artists, musicians and scientists.

SEE MORE AT NBMPUB.COM

We have hundreds of graphic novels available.
Subscribe to our monthly newsletter
Request our catalog
NBM
160 Broadway, Suite 700, East Wing, New York, NY 10038

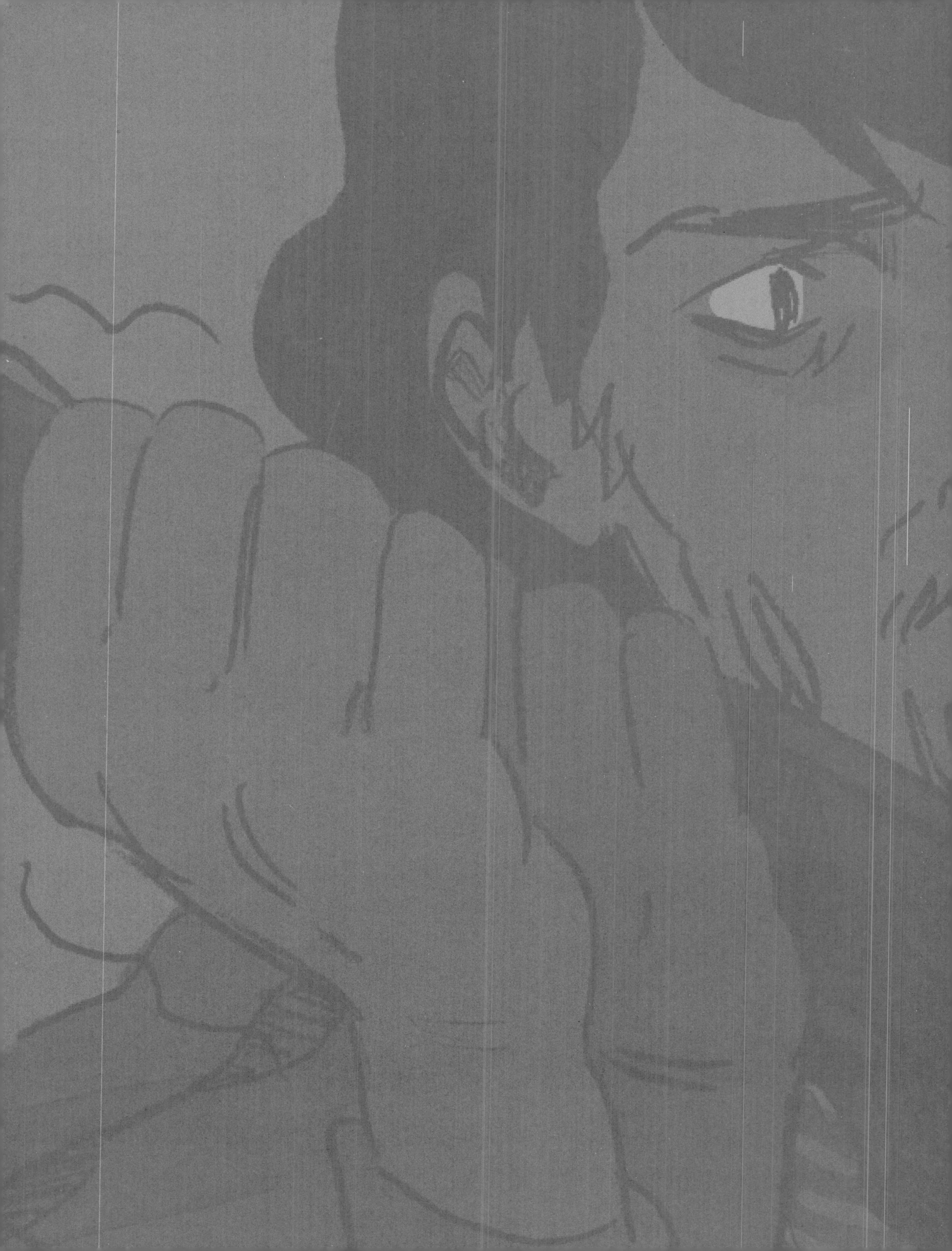